THE SCOTT AND LAURIE OKI SERIES
IN ASIAN AMERICAN STUDIES

THE SCOTT AND LAURIE OKI SERIES IN ASIAN AMERICAN STUDIES

From a Three-Cornered World: New and Selected Poems by James Masao Mitsui

Imprisoned Apart: The World War II Correspondence of an Issei Couple, by Louis Fiset

Storied Lives: Japanese American Students and World War II by Gary Okihiro

Phoenix Eyes and Other Stories, by Russell Charles Leong

Paper Bullets: A Fictional Autobiography, by Kip Fulbeck

Born in Seattle: The Campaign for Japanese American Redress, by Robert Sadamu Shimabukuro

Confinement and Ethnicity: An Overview of World War II Japanese American Relocation Sites, by Jeffery F. Burton, Mary M. Farrell, Florence B. Lord, and Richard W. Lord

Judgment without Trial: Japanese American Imprisonment during World War II, by Tetsuden Kashima

Shopping at Giant Foods: Chinese American Supermarkets in Northern California, by Alfred Yee

Altered Lives, Enduring Community: Japanese Americans Remember Their World War II Incarceration, by Stephen S. Fugita and Marilyn Fernandez

Eat Everything Before You Die: A Chinaman in the Counterculture, by Jeffery Paul Chan

Form and Transformation in Asian American Literature, edited by Zhou Xiaojing and Samina Najmi

FORM AND TRANSFORMATION

in Asian American Literature

Edited by

ZHOU XIAOJING AND SAMINA NAJMI

UNIVERSITY OF WASHINGTON PRESS
Seattle and London

This book is published with the assistance of a grant from the SCOTT AND LAURIE OKI ENDOWED FUND for the publication of Asian American Studies, established through the generosity of Scott and Laurie Oki.

Printed in the United States of America
Designed by Pamela Canell
12 11 10 09 08 07 06 05 5 4 3 2 1

University of Washington Press
PO Box 50096, Seattle, WA 98145
www.washington.edu/uwpress

Library of Congress Cataloging-in-Publication Data can be found at the back of this book.

The paper used in this publication is acid-free and 90 percent recycled from at least 50 percent pre-consumer waste. It meets the minimum requirements of American National Standard for Information Sciences—Permanence of Paper for Printed Library Materials, ANSI Z39.48–1984. ∞ ♲

The editors gratefully acknowledge permissions to reprint the following:
Chen, Tina Y, "Impersonation and Other Disappearing Acts in *Native Speaker* by Chang-rae Lee," an earlier version of "Recasting the Spy, Rewriting the Story: The Politics of Genre in *Native Speaker* by Chang-rae Lee," which appeared in *Modern Fiction Studies* 48.3 (2002), 637–50, 654–67. © Purdue Research Foundation. Reprinted with permission of The Johns Hopkins University Press.
Excerpts from Kimiko Hahn, "Cruising Barthes" and "The Hemisphere: Kuchuk Hanem" in *The Unbearable Heart*, reprinted with permission of the author.
Excerpts from Essex Hemphill, "Black Machismo," Cordon Negro," "The Tomb of Sorrow," "The Edge," and "Heavy Breathing" in *Ceremonies*, reprinted with permission of Penguin Group (USA) Inc.
Timothy Liu, "The Sized of It," "White Moths," and "Reading Whitman in a Toilet Stall" from *Burnt Offerings*. Copyright © 1995 by Timothy Liu. Reprinted with the permission of Copper Canyon Press.
Excerpts from John Yau, "Between the Forest and Its Trees," *Edificio Sayonara*, and *Forbidden Entries*, reprinted with permission of the author.

The editors are also grateful for the financial support from the University of the Pacific's James Irvine Diversity Foundation grant.

FOR OUR CHILDREN—

AS YOU LEARN TO SPAN THE CONTINENTS,

AND IN DOING SO, TRANSFORM THEM.

CONTENTS

FORM AND TRANSFORMATION IN ASIAN AMERICAN LITERATURE

INTRODUCTION

CRITICAL THEORIES AND METHODOLOGIES IN ASIAN AMERICAN LITERARY STUDIES

ZHOU XIAOJING

Since the late 1980s, Asian American studies has seen a significant shift away from the agendas and strategies of cultural nationalism and toward transnational perspectives and diasporic positionings.[1] This shift is mobilized by historical, conceptual, and institutional forces. Asian America has undergone profound demographic changes with the arrival of refugees from Southeast Asia and large numbers of professional immigrants from other Asian and Pacific regions, as a result of the aftermath of the Vietnam War, revisions in U.S. immigration laws, and changes in local and global economic and political structures. Scholars of Asian American studies have responded to these changes by calling for a new theoretical and critical framework—a paradigm shift not only necessitated by the changing demographics but also grounded in postcolonial, poststructuralist, "Third World" feminist, and queer theories. The mobilizing forces underlying this paradigm shift have also given rise to a greatly diversified range of literature from Asian America. Given the explosive diversity and rapid growth of Asian American literary productions, many scholars have begun to feel the urgency of developing new critical approaches.[2]

Susan Koshy, for instance, notes that Asian American literary theories and critical methodologies are lagging behind the demographic transformation of Asian America and the rapid expansion of Asian American literary productions. Koshy contends that "if the expansion of the field proceeds at this pace, without a more substantial theoretical investigation of the premises and assumptions underlying our constructions of commonality and difference, we run the risk of unwittingly annexing the newer literary productions within older paradigms" (317). Sau-ling C. Wong, in her

1995 essay "Denationalization Reconsidered: Asian American Cultural Criticism at a Theoretical Crossroads," has also pointed out that "dramatic changes" in Asian America "have been exerting mounting pressure on the field to reflect on its own operating assumptions and, if necessary, modify them" (1). The urgency in Koshy's argument and the caution in Wong's assertion reflect different perspectives within the current debates over the shift in Asian American studies.

These different perspectives have generated several important critical works.[3] Reconsidering and critically assessing cultural nationalist strategies, poststructuralist theories, and transnational perspectives, these works mark an important development in Asian American critical theories and methodologies. At the same time, their critical investigations raise questions about the cultural locations of Asian American literature—the locations of its formations and interventions—which are a focal point in emergent discourses on diaspora and transnationalism as well as in cultural nationalist rhetoric. Nevertheless, until recently, in much criticism the locations of Asian American literature were usually conceived in terms of geography, ethnicity, sociology, and national history. More often than not, critics have situated the formations of Asian American literary traditions within Asian and Asian American histories and cultures, in opposition to or separately from "mainstream" European American culture and literature. The relationship between Asian American literature and mainstream America has frequently been identified in terms of Asian American literature's resistance or subordination to mainstream America's domination. Constrained by binary positions, and confined to a thematically and sociologically oriented approach, critics tend to evaluate individual texts and authors according to a predominant formula, that is, according to whether the texts demonstrate complicity with or resistance to hegemonic ideologies of assimilation. This critical approach overlooks the ways in which Asian American authors have resisted, subverted, and reshaped hegemonic European American literary genres, as well as the ways in which such interventions demonstrate a much more dynamic and complex relationship between Asian American and traditional European American literature.

This volume provides compelling evidence of these dynamics, which belie the notion that Asian American writers are either independent from or guilty of complicity with dominant ideologies. We contend that dismissal of Asian American authors' incorporation and reinvention of dominant American literary genres as "assimilationist" not only ignores how writers have actively manipulated and reinvented literary conventions but also casts dominant ideologies and literary genres into fixed, totalizing, and invulnerable systems. As Elizabeth Grosz notes, "no system, method, or discourse can be as all-encompassing, singular, and monolithic as it represents itself" to be (62). Hence it is necessary to explore alternative critical approaches that will enable us to recognize the ways in which Asian American literature intervenes positively in the transformation of established canons and dominant conventional literary forms. This recognition is impossible to obtain within a purely binary scheme.

The agency of Asian American literature must be located in and realized through textual strategies, which include the formal structure of a text, whereby the articulation of conformity or resistance, and activities of preservation or transformation, are made possible. As Pierre Bourdieu emphasizes, "the structure of the work" is the "prerequisite for the fulfilling of its function, if it has one" (181). Formal and stylistic features are sites of struggles, for they are coded with ideologies and marked by subject positions. Discussing Gustave Flaubert's *Madame Bovary,* Bourdieu elaborates on the relationship between the social world and the formal structure of literature:

> If the work can reveal the deep structure of the social world and the mental worlds in which those structures were reflected, it is because the work of formalization gave the writer the opportunity to work on himself and thereby allowed him to objectify not only the positions in the field and their occupants that he opposed, but also, through the space that included him, his own position [207].

A particular literary form, then, is a mode of subject positioning, a means of articulating the writer's resistance or affiliations within the field of literature and in the social spaces. A recognition of the possibility of agency in modes of signification, such as literary genres and textual strategies, will break away from a binary division of the ideological and the aesthetic, thus allowing us to locate resistance productively in the formal aspects of Asian American literature, as well as in its thematic concerns and in its social, cultural, and historical contexts.

CULTURAL NATIONALIST DISCOURSE

Before it is possible to delineate the alternative modes of theoretical and critical approaches that this anthology explores, it will be necessary to examine the problematic premises and assumptions underlying some major critical works, and the current critiques of them. Some of these premises and assumptions—those involving the social conditions and cultural locations for the formation of Asian American literature—first emerged in the cultural nationalist rhetoric of the editors of an early Asian American literary anthology, *Aiiieeeee!* (1974). The various editors—Frank Chin, Jeffery Paul Chan, Lawson Fusao Inada, and Shawn Wong—attempt to establish "an Asian American literary tradition based on the Asian American literature in history" ("*Aiiieeeee!* Revisited" xxv). They locate the formation of this tradition in Asian American history and experience and in Asian Americans' racially and culturally distinct attributes. Protesting institutionalized racism, and critiquing Asian Americans' internalized racism—"contempt for self, fellow yellow, and yellow history"—the *Aiiieeeee!* editors seek to construct an Asian American literary tradition grounded in "the history and source of the yellow literary tradition and sensibility" (Chin et al., "*Aiiieeeee!* Revisited" xxv–xxvi, xxv). For the editors, the source of Asian Americans' racially distinct history and culture, defined on their own terms, can be traced to "the heroic tradition" of Chinese and Japanese classical literatures as represented by *Romance of the Three Kingdoms* and *Tale of the Loyal 47 Ronin* (*Chushingura*), which, according to the editors, mold Asian American sensibility and writings (xxxvi).

In the context of the 1970s, this formulation of the "sources" that determined the characteristics of Asian American literature was an empowering political gesture that resisted the hegemony of European American culture and literature.[4] Like their masculine rhetoric, the editors' insistence on the connection between Asian American literature and classical Chinese and Japanese literary and cultural traditions articulated a problematic counterdiscourse in response to the gendered racial stereotypes of Asians and Asian Americans that had been produced by mainstream American culture and literature. With development in critical perspectives, especially in feminist and queer theories since the 1980s, Asian American scholars are increasingly critical of the *Aiiieeeee!* editors' "nationalist" identity construction and their reinscription of hegemonic ideologies of gender and sexuality. Despite this development, however, some major premises and assumptions underlying the editors' formulation of Asian American literature have been overlooked and continue to be reproduced in Asian American literary criticism.

In postulating a direct transmission between "yellow" sensibility and

Asian American literature, the *Aiiieeeee!* editors assumed an unproblematic cause-and-effect relationship between ethnicity and literature. This expressive critical method, along with its assumptions of original, stable cultural traditions as the true sources of Asian American literature, suggests an ethnic essence that Asian American literature is presumed to express or reveal. It seemed to be this construction of an essentialist identity as the locus of agency that led the editors to condemn such "Chinese American Christian writers" as Yung Wing, Pardee Lowe, and Jade Snow Wong (Chin et al., "*Aiiieeeee!* Revisited" xx) and specifically led Frank Chin to denounce Maxine Hong Kingston's, Amy Tan's, and David Henry Hwang's representations of Chinese myths and culture as "inauthentic" ("Come All Ye Asian American Writers of the Real and the Fake" 8). Although the *Aiiieeeee!* editors' concept of ethnic cultures in terms of discrete origins has been contested and dismissed, their formulation of an Asian American literary tradition that develops separately from, or in opposition to, mainstream America, and their insistence on the primacy of a social, historical context for understanding Asian American literature, continued to constitute the premises for a thematically oriented, expressive mode of Asian American literary criticism in the 1980s.[5]

Take, for example, Elaine H. Kim's groundbreaking 1982 study, *Asian American Literature: An Introduction to the Writings and Their Social Context.* Kim discusses the major themes in a substantial body of Asian American literature, with a focus on works by Chinese Americans, Japanese Americans, Korean Americans, and, to a lesser extent, Filipino Americans, in relation to these themes' social contexts, including Asian and Asian American stereotypes present in mainstream literature and popular culture. Since her book was the first full-length study of Asian American literature, her focus and critical methodology were determined to a large extent by the cultural and historical conditions in which Asian American literary texts are produced and read. As Kim asserts, she chose to "emphasize how the literature elucidates the social history of Asians in the United States" because when the sociohistorical and cultural contexts of Asian American literature are unfamiliar to readers, "the literature is likely to be misunderstood and unappreciated." Given the fact of the predominant racial stereotypes of Asians and Asian Americans in American popular culture, Kim finds it necessary to provide readers with the cultural and sociohistorical contexts for Asian American writers' "self-expression" (xv).

Kim's book provides a valuable analysis of major themes in Asian American literature and their social contexts. Nevertheless, it does not offer an alternative methodology that would enable a break from the *Aiiieeeee!* editors' binary critical mode. Rather, its premises reflect the predominant paradigm of its time. In Kim's study, as in the *Aiiieeeee!* anthology, Asian American literature's assimilation to or protests against mainstream America constitute the major framework of the relationship between the two. The characteristics of Asian American literature are seen as merely reflections of or reactions to the social conditions imposed on Asian Americans; alternative possibilities for Asian American writers to intervene in dominant ideologies, and to transform American literary traditions and genres, are not thoroughly considered. Hence Kim, while paying attention to the "increasingly diverse perspectives" that reflect dramatic demographic changes in Asian America, nonetheless asserts that the new forms and uses of languages in Asian American literature are expressions of Asian American writers' "unique sensibilities" (Kim, *Asian American Literature* 214). As Koshy points out, "The focus of Kim's analysis, as [of] Chin's, is on positioning a literature that is expressive of the Asian American experience understood as sociologically distinct, separate from the mainstream, and shaped by settlement in the United States and [by] the effects of American racism" (326). Koshy's 1996 critique of Kim's 1982 critical methodology reflects Asian American scholars' growing awareness that the expressive model, and thematically oriented sociological methodology within a cultural nationalist framework, are inadequate for the analysis of current developments in Asian American literature.[6]

CULTURAL NATIONALISM VERSUS EXILIC POSITIONING

Since the late 1980s, the impetus of demographic changes and theoretical development has given rise to paradigm shifts in Asian American studies. Some leading scholars of Asian American studies, while relocating Asian American history and experience within global contexts of imperialism, colonialism, transnational capitalism, and diaspora, have begun to theorize new models of Asian American identity reconstruction and to call for investigations into the complexity and diversity of Asian America. In an influential 1991 essay, Lisa Lowe advocates, among other things, a redefinition of Asian American subjectivity, in terms of diversity and transnational mobility, as a strategic positionality that can open up possibilities of "crucial alliances with other groups—ethnicity-based, class-based, gender-based, and sexuality-based—in the ongoing work of transforming hegemony" ("Heterogeneity, Hybridity, Multiplicity" 39–40). Likewise, Elaine Kim calls for a reconceptualization of Asian American identities, with emphasis on transnational border crossings and on the diverse complexity within Asian America. In her presidential address at the 1993 annual conference of the Association of Asian American Studies, Kim observed that the earlier anti-assimilationist strategy for constructing an Asian American identity as a set of "cultural nationalist defenses . . . [was] fixed, closed, and narrowly defined, dividing 'Asian American' from 'Asian' as sharply as possible, privileging race over gender and class, accepting compulsory heterosexuality as 'natural'" ("Beyond Railroads and Internment," cited in Okihiro et al., eds., *Privileging Positions* 12). But, said Kim, "the lines between Asian and Asian American, so crucial to identity formations in the past, are increasingly blurred: transportation to and communication with Asia is no longer daunting, resulting in new crossovers and intersections and different kinds of material and cultural distances today" (14). Thus Kim emphasized that "Asian American identities are fluid and migratory" (14), and she urged "a casting off of the old jargon and schema" in order to pay necessary attention to "complexities, layers, paradoxes, [and] contradictions" within and among Asian American communities (16).

These reconceptualizations of Asian American identity raise provocative questions about the functions and effects of diversity, or rather "difference," including the difference of transnational subjectivity, in "transforming hegemony," to borrow Lowe's phrase again. What are the possibilities for differences within Asian America to become more than a form of resistance to assimilation? In what way and to what extent can difference become transformative agency? It seems that for both Lowe and Kim, the broadened categories of Asian American identity are in themselves a form of transformation, particularly the transformation of a previously unified, homogeneous cultural nationalist identity politics. Yet, in this sense, it is more a matter of transformation within Asian America than of transformation in the hegemony of mainstream America.

In a similar vein, but with different emphases, the notion of Asian American "diversity, multiplicity, and heterogeneity," used as a strategic positioning in challenging the narrowness of a cultural nationalist identity politics and critical mode, underlies two Asian American critical anthologies, *Reading the Literatures of Asian America* (1992), edited by Shirley Geok-lin Lim and Amy Ling, and *An Interethnic Companion to Asian American Literature* (1997), edited by King-Kok Cheung. Lim and Ling state in their introduction that, rather than suggesting "an unproblematic, homogeneous ethnic identity," the collected essays, with their "diversity and range of subjects, critical stances, styles, concerns, and theoretical grids[,] compellingly demonstrate the heterogeneous, multiple, divergent, polyphonic, multivocal character of Asian American cultural discourse" (9). A major new strategy for redefining Asian America and its literatures is to read a distinct ethnic Asian American literature as a literature of exile and diaspora rather than as a variety of immigrant narratives.

This model of constructing literary traditions, on the basis of ethnicity and an Asian national history, raises further questions. These questions concern where to locate the formation of Asian American literature, and where to situate its resistance and relations to the U.S. nation-state, to hegemonic ideologies, and to mainstream American literary traditions. And these questions are directly related to the central concerns of the present anthology: the conditions for the formation of Asian American literary traditions and genres, and for possibilities of intervention through various strategies of writing. What are the implications of a "fluid and migratory" Asian American identity for Asian American literature? Can this category of identity automatically constitute resistance? In what way might diversity, difference, and multiplicity become the basis of more effective means than cultural nationalist strategies for resisting hegemonic ideologies, or even for "transforming hegemony"? These questions and related issues resurface and become more poignant in Cheung's *An Interethnic Companion*.

Like the Lim and Ling volume, Cheung's anthology foregrounds the diversity of Asian America, but with more focused attention to literary traditions defined according to ethnicity within Asian America. It also reflects the paradigm shift in repositioning Asian American identities. In her introduction to the anthology, Cheung gives a substantial review, from various perspectives, of the ongoing debates in Asian American literary studies. Many of the issues raised in these debates converge on the consequences of constructing Asian American identities in terms of a cultural nationalist stance versus an exilic positioning.

Critics such as Sau-ling Wong and Shirley Lim engage in dialogic discussions about the implications for these seemingly opposite and mutually exclusive positions. Wong, for example, insists on "a nation" as a "political location" for Asian Americans' struggle to transform racially structured power relations ("Denationalization Reconsidered" 19). While acknowledging the various advantages of a diasporic perspective in enabling a more inclusive cultural base for the diversity of Asian America, Wong asserts that "a denationalized Asian American cultural criticism may exacerbate liberal pluralism's already oppressive tendency to 'disembody,' leaving America's racialized power structure intact" (18–19). Lim, differing with Wong, argues for an exilic paradigm as an alternative to the cultural nationalist strategy. Lim contends that complicity with the dominant ideologies of the United States underlies the "assimilationary position" of some popular Asian American writings, including Maxine Hong Kingston's *The Woman Warrior,* Gish Jen's *Typical American,* and Bharati Mukherjee's *Jasmine* ("Immigration and Diaspora" 299, 301–4). Thus Lim seeks, in transnational, diasporic writings, possibilities for resisting hegemonic ideologies of assimilation as an alternative strategy to the cultural nationalist model. Diasporic subjectivity and exilic literary texts, however, are not necessarily formed in opposition to or in separation from dominant ideologies of the United States, as Lim's discussion of the Filipino American writer Bienvenido Santos's work reveals ("Immigration and Diaspora" 307). Both Wong's and Lim's essays indicate the inadequacy of any single paradigm or binary framework for the study of Asian American literature.[7]

BEYOND THE BINARY

Since the critical premise for this anthology was conceived and the assembling of the essays started, critics have begun to explore alternative approaches that break away from binary constructions of Asian American identity and literature. While these new approaches help confirm our critical premise, they also demonstrate the impetus for this anthology: the need to further explore and build on currently developed theories and methodologies, and to apply them to a wider range of literature from Asian America.

Jinqi Ling, for instance, in *Narrating Nationalisms,* calls into question the replacement of one paradigm with another. Although Ling recognizes the necessity for rethinking the cultural nationalist critical model, he is suspicious of the effectiveness of claiming identity difference as a discrete, dehistoricized category (4–5). Rather than reading texts as direct reflections of experiences, Ling examines Asian American literary discourse from 1957 to 1980 "as a contested and multiply negotiated process of transformation" (9). In broadening the conditions and locations for agency in Asian American literature, and in complicating the relationships between ideology and literary form, Ling's study helps advance critical methodology beyond the model that assumes a simple dichotomized relationship between Asian American literature and mainstream America.

David Leiwei Li's study *Imagining the Nation* also breaks away from the model of dichotomy in its judicious analysis of contemporary Asian American literature. It "affirms the inventive and interventional power of 'Asian America(n),' not as a thing in itself but as an insistent dialogue among dominant, ethnic, and diasporic communities" (17). The construction and reshaping of the nation-state of the United States is a focal point in Li's examination of Asian American writers' inventions and interventions. Considering the United States "as an Asian American geopolitical space so that Asian Americans can secure the rights and obligations of citizenship in the nation-state," Li asserts concerns over the current "paradigm shift," which "seriously questions 'race' and 'nation' as essential components of the Asian American construct" (185, 186). Li critiques the political disengagement of poststructuralist notions of identity "difference" and the counterproductive effects of "the concept of the diaspora," which renders "Asia-Pacific" and "Asian American" "mutually exclusive" (194–97).

Further illustrating the interlocking relationship of Asian American literature with mainstream America, E. San Juan, Jr., in his study *The Philippine Temptation,* locates the formations of Filipino American literary traditions in a complex neocolonial relationship between the Philippines and the United States. While rejecting a wholesale exilic paradigm that would erase the difference of class and historical specificity, San Juan demonstrates that reading Filipino American literature only within the framework of "American nationalism" and ideologies of assimilation would deprive Filipino American writers of the agency of resistance and intervention (121–28).

Viet Thanh Nguyen calls critical attention to another reductive aspect of a predominant binary framework for reading Asian American literature. In *Race and Resistance,* Nguyen contends that the paradigm for reading Asian American literature in terms of either "resistance" or "accommodation" allows "polarizing options that do not sufficiently demonstrate the *flexible strategies* often chosen by authors and characters to navigate their political and ethical situations" (4; emphasis in original). Nguyen notes further that criticism as such, limited by "an ideological rigidity," has resulted in grave misreading of literary texts (5). Expanding on Jinqi Ling's critical view and methodology, Nguyen examines Asian American writers' representations of the body as a "troubled" site/sight in the American body politic.

David Palumbo-Liu's study *Asian/American* offers an even more enabling methodology for radically breaking away from binary paradigms. Most relevant to the central concerns of the present anthology is the fact that Palumbo-Liu's critical methodology situates Asia and America in a mutually constitutive and transformative relationship. He argues that "discursive articulation is produced," like Asian America itself, from complex interactions of historical forces. Hence, "to understand the subject positions of 'white' as absolutely apart from those of 'Asian' in the discursive interplay of nation formation is to play into the very alibi that serves to fortify racism. Similarly, to deny the effect of Asians on 'America' is to render 'America' invulnerable and Asians without agency; neither is true historically" (7–8). It is precisely in this kind of mutually constitutive, reciprocally transformative relationship between Asian America and mainstream America that the essays in this anthology aim to locate the formations of Asian American literary traditions and genres, as well as individual writers' strategies and styles.

POSSIBILITIES OF AGENCY

The studies of Palumbo-Liu, Nguyen, San Juan, Li, and Ling, among others, point to the fact that Asian American agency resides in negotiation with, not separation from, dominant ideologies and literary traditions—a fact that underlies the theoretical assumptions and critical methodologies of this anthology. These studies suggest that in order to recognize the possibilities of Asian American authors' agency in transforming hegemony, it is necessary to understand that dominant American literary discourses are neither homogeneous nor bounded by a discrete culture. Therefore, the limitations of binary paradigms lie not only in their reduction of the historical specificity and complexity of Asian American experiences and literature but also in their assumption that a hegemonic ideology is itself homogeneous, consisting of closed belief systems.

Stuart Hall's remarks about discursive conceptualization of ideology "in terms of the articulation of elements" can help us escape the dichotomy of ideological positionings. Reiterating Voloshinov's views, Hall writes that

> the ideological sign is always multi-accentual, and Janus-faced—that is, it can be discursively rearticulated to construct new meanings, connect with different social practices, and position social subjects differently. . . . As different currents constantly struggle within the same ideological field, what

> must be studied is the way in which they contest, often around the same idea or concept [9].

This view of ideology—and of the subsequent possibilities for rearticulation, for repositioning subjects, and for contestations around the same idea or concept—destabilizes ideologies and their reproduction, thus opening up more possibilities for intervention. Furthermore, Hall's emphasis on the idea that "what must be studied is the way in which [different ideological currents] contest, often around the same idea or concept" calls critical attention to modes of signification—the writers' textual strategies through which ideological positionings are articulated and agency is activated.

Hall's argument suggests, then, that privileging the sociohistorical determinism of the author's subjectivity over the writing subject's positionings through literary forms—genres, styles, languages, and so on—will seriously limit the possibility of resistant and transformative agency. Locating Asian American literature in a binarized identity politics is a politically confining, if not entirely disabling, methodology. Judith Butler has pointed out the epistemological and methodological problems of binary identity construction:

> As part of the epistemological inheritance of contemporary political discourses of identity, this binary opposition is a strategic move within a given set of signifying practices, one that establishes the "I" in and through this opposition and which reifies that opposition as a necessity, concealing the discursive apparatus by which the binary itself is constituted. The shift from an *epistemological* account of identity to one which locates the problematic within the practices of *signification* permits an analysis that takes the epistemological mode itself as one possible and contingent signifying practice. Further, the question of *agency* is reformulated as a question of how signification and resignification work [184].

Butler's observation on locating agency in "how signification and resignification work" resonates with Hall's emphasis on the ways in which competing ideologies are articulated and rearticulated differently. Both authors' attention to modes of signification foregrounds the formal aspects of literature as an integral part of ideology, and both Hall and Butler point to what Bourdieu calls "the question of the internal logic of cultural objects, their structure as *languages*," which must be addressed in literary studies, for "the structure of the work" is the "prerequisite for the fulfilling of its function, if it has one" (181; emphasis in original). These theoretical perspectives offer a methodological alternative to a binary paradigm and the impasse it creates in Asian American literary studies.

GENRES

This anthology concentrates on Asian American writers' appropriations and transformations of what have been considered exclusively European American literary genres. Recently a few critics have begun to examine genres in Asian American literature, with attention to the multiple possibilities and complex functions of the novel of formation. For instance, in her discussion of Carlos Bulosan's 1943 novel *America Is in the Heart,* Lisa Lowe discusses the ways in which this text departs from the prevailing generic characteristics of the bildungsroman, a genre that has a "special" canonical status because of its narrative function of constituting "an idealized 'national' form of subjectivity" (*Immigrant Acts* 98). Rather than developing "the narrating subject's identification with a uniform American nation," Lowe notes, *America Is in the Heart* foregrounds "the subject's critical estrangement from and dissymmetrical relationship to American culturalist, economic, and nationalist formations" (47–48). Thus Bulosan's narrative not only undermines the ideological function of the bildungsroman in constituting national subjects, it also transforms the generic characteristics of the novel of formation.

Expanding on Lowe's views of the bildungsroman, Patricia P. Chu, in *Assimilating Asians,* interrogates the national ideological function of the bildungsroman and the possibilities of generic revision. Chu asserts that Lowe's formulation of the novel of formation "lays bare a function that was always present but generally undiscussed: *assimilating subjects*" (12). Like Lowe, Chu calls critical attention to the ideological functions of the genre and the possibilities for the writer to resist cultural hegemony by way of negotiating with a particular genre. Chu notes that the difference between "the Asian American subject's relation to the social order" and that of "the genre's original European subjects" results in departures from the original model of the genre (12). The fact that difference in the writing subject's social status can result in generic changes raises questions about the efficacy of the bildungsroman's national ideological function of "assimilating subjects." Both Chu's and Lowe's discussions of the genre make significant contributions to the study of Asian American literature. But their emphasis on the European origin of the novel of formation in terms of a national ideological function seems to attribute to the genre too narrow a range of possibilities.

Critics have pointed out that, even within the European tradition of the bildungsroman, the kind of "normalizing" teleology that Lowe describes is seldom fulfilled. In his study of the French bildungsroman, for example, Franco Moretti observes that youth, rather than striving to conform to social norms, finds its meaning in breaking them (75). Far from regarding the bildungsroman as a most canonical genre, Marianne Hirsch contends that the novel of formation in the twentieth century is the most salient genre for the literature of social outsiders, especially women and minority groups ("The Novel of Formation as Genre").[8] More radically, feminist critics and scholars of color have challenged any definition of the bildungsroman that confines it to a fixed time and a single culture. In so doing, these critics and scholars have also illustrated the genre's reinvention across national, cultural, and racial boundaries.[9]

This anthology—instead of focusing on one particular genre or examining a literary mode within binary relations of the state versus the individual, or complicity versus resistance—seeks to dislodge genres from seemingly fixed cultural boundaries and hierarchies of race and gender. Mikhail Bakhtin argues that the "special significance" of genres lies in the fact that they "accumulate forms of seeing and interpreting particular aspects of the world" (5). Thus genres are open to change in formalizing particular experiences, concepts, and ideologies. As such, genres, then, as Claudio Guillén observes, offer writers "a very special sort of assistance in the fact that the fitting of matter to form has *already* taken place. To offer this assistance is the function of genre." Moreover, Guillén emphasizes that "a pre-existent form can never be simply 'taken over' by the writer or transferred to a new work. The task of form-making must be undertaken all over again" (111). Whereas Bakhtin's remarks suggest the instability of literary genres that are shaped by particular values, ideologies, subject positions, and concepts of time and space, Guillén's assertion highlights the challenges that writers face in negotiating with generic conventions for various purposes.

Bakhtin's and Guillén's different views on the formations, functions, and transformations of genres help clarify our contention in this volume that it is often reductive, if not impossible, to construct a straightforward cause-and-effect relationship between the ethnic background of the writing subject and the distinctive thematic and formal features of a literary text. Asian American literature cannot be theorized in an a priori fashion through appeals to an inherent relationship between ethnicity and a specific linguistic or narrative strategy. It can be addressed only through investigation of the interactive effects and conflicts among multiple structures of determination within specific historical, social, and cultural contexts. This critical perspective breaks away from the expressive and binary models of constructing a literary tradition in terms of a discrete cultural origin or a singular, oppositional subject position. It is crucial for Asian American literary studies to investigate the various historical, cultural, and discursive elements that determine individual writers' poetics and enable certain modes of signification. Rather than striving to explain individual writers' oeuvres in terms of the authors' unique sensibilities or establish Asian American literary traditions by assuming direct correlations between race/ethnicity and theme/style, the essays in this collection explore the impacts of historical forces and various cultural and literary traditions on Asian American writers, as well as the writers' appropriations of, negotiations with, and transformations of established literary genres and traditions.

This anthology, shifting away from a thematically oriented approach, focuses attention on the possibilities of intervention in Asian American writers' subversive and creative interactions with dominant cultural discourses through negotiations with and transformations of literary conventions. In so doing, this collection also engages with the ongoing critical debates initiated by the *Aiiieeeee!* editors and invigorated and developed by feminist and other Asian American scholars. Against the backdrop of current debates over paradigm shifts in Asian American studies, the essays in this anthology probe hotly debated issues as well as understudied topics in Asian American literature, including the relations between Asian American and other minority American writings. The works discussed in these pages range from the earliest to contemporary writings; the genres examined include fiction, essay, poetry, autobiography, and short story. Rather than attempting to demonstrate plurality, diversity, and heterogeneity in terms of Asian American identity and literature, this collection seeks to further our understanding not only of the ideological functions of literary genres but also of the possibilities for agency in generic appropriations and transformations.

SYNOPSES OF THE ESSAYS

Because the scope of our inquiry in this volume ranges from the earliest to contemporary writers, we begin with Dominika Ferens's "Winnifred Eaton/Onoto Watanna: Establishing Ethnographic Authority," which investigates the intersections of ethnography and popular fiction. Ferens situates the form and content of Eaton/Watanna's ethnographic novels and their popularity in the contexts of Western racial ideology, the military and political ascendancy of Japan, and the economic gains to be had in marketing a pleasurable, exoticized Japanese culture at the turn of the twentieth century. At the same time, Ferens locates Eaton's oeuvre and "success" within the tradition of modern ethnography, whose assumptions of "authority" and "authenticity" conflate race and culture. Further complicating the production of Eaton's ethnographic writings, as Ferens examines them, are Orientalist readings that insist on a correlation between the "childlike simplicity" and "peculiar charm" of Eaton's "untutored style," and the "authenticity" of her books about Japanese culture. Ferens notes that Eaton, in writing her ethnographic fiction, appropriated and transformed "other people's Japanese 'fieldwork,'" seizing upon male authors' presumed "power to represent" the Other. Ferens's reading of Winnifred Eaton calls critical attention to the epistemological and political implications of assuming a direct connection between race/gender/ethnicity and literary genres.

Issues of race and ethnicity take on a different dimension in David Shih's "The Seduction of Origins: Sui Sin Far and the Race for Tradition." Shih's essay questions the making of an Asian American literary tradition that installs Edith Eaton/Sui Sin Far as the foremother of Chinese American letters on the basis of her identity as "Chinese American," which erases her Eurasian background and overlooks the author's subversion of essentialized identities. Shih contends that the construction of "a Chinese American literary genealogy based upon the achievements of recognizable literary 'ancestors'" is made possible "only by an ahistorical and uncritical eye toward race and nation." Even though this practice results from "a historically determined need for race to exist in a stable sense," Shih notes, its underlying assumptions regarding the formation of the canon need to be interrogated. For the resulting reification of race "as the basis of a connection between Sui Sin Far and contemporary Chinese American writers" suggests a problematic similarity to T. S. Eliot's "tradition"—which, according to Terry Eagleton, Eliot sometimes called the "European mind." Conducting a rigorous textual analysis of Eaton/Sui Sin Far's exploration of complex, ambivalent identities of race and gender, both in her writing and in her use of visual images, Shih argues that Sui Sin Far's 1909 "Leaves from the Mental Portfolio of an Eurasian" challenges "the uncritical insertion of race" into our discourse about the canon of Asian American writers, whose heterogeneous "disruptive and subversive energies" can be smothered by the homogenizing category of racial identity.

Floyd Cheung's essay, "Political Resistance, Cultural Appropriation, and the Performance of Manhood in Yung Wing's *My Life in China and America*," examines the subversive effects of generic appropriation from a different critical perspective. Cheung questions the consequences of constructing an Asian American literary tradition that privileges particular texts at the expense of others. He takes the *Aiiieeeee!* editors and Asian American feminist critics alike to task for their exclusionary agendas. He argues that the former group privileges a certain hypermasculinity in Asian American texts, and the latter valorizes intimate and diasporic narratives, but works such as Yung Wing's are devalued by both groups because they operate in ways that are "largely invisible to presentist perspectives." Resituating Yung's text in its historical context and in contemporary "discourses of hegemonic and subordinated masculinities," including canonical European American and African American autobiographies, Cheung argues that Yung's "appropriation of conventional language, forms, and values" in his autobiography is a "strategy of resistant appropriation."

Rather than addressing possibilities of resistance, Christopher Douglas's essay, "Reading Ethnography: The Cold War Social Science of Jade Snow Wong's *Fifth Chinese Daughter* and *Brown* v. *Board of Education*," deals with the limits of Asian American writers' agency with respect to resistance, the limits themselves being outcomes of generic conventions, subject positions, and political and sociohistorical forces. Douglas investigates the persistence of ethnographic readings of the works of such contemporary Chinese American authors as Maxine Hong Kingston and Amy Tan, tracing this tendency back to the mainstream reception of Wong's *Fifth Chinese Daughter* in the 1950s, the Cold War era, when the racial ideology embedded in U.S. citizenship was in crisis. Situating Wong's work and its reception in the context of the paradigm shift under way in social science, from biological "race" to ethnic culture, Douglas interrogates the role of ethnography in naturalizing "culture," restructuring "race," and representing racialized minorities' citizenship status. His investigation undermines the image of the United States as an international beacon of democracy, liberty, and racial harmony. At the same time, he deconstructs the constitutive role of the ethnographic gaze in shaping ethnocentric readings of Chinese American texts as "windows" onto the real world of Chinese America. Douglas argues that modern ethnography, which is characterized by claims for "transparency of representation and immediacy of experience," has helped cast such Chinese American literary texts as Jade Snow Wong's autobiography and Tan's and Kingston's fiction in the same mode of realism, thus placing on them the burden of "authentically" representing ethnicity. By exposing the historical, political, and ideological forces that shape the way Asian American texts are read and marketed, Douglas's essay confronts us with the politics and ethics of pedagogy in the teaching of Asian American literature.

Rajini Srikanth, in her essay "Abraham Verghese Doctors Autobiography in His Own Country," extends the investigation into the relation between ethnography and autobiography by exploring an Indian American writer's narrative strategy, which distances the author from his racial and ethnic identity while locating him geographically and symbolically in the heartland of the American nation-space. Srikanth notes that Verghese's memoir, *My Own Country: A Doctor's Story of a Town and Its People in the Age of AIDS,* gained a wide audience in mainstream America in part because of a crucial "interplay between individual and community" in Verghese's profession as a doctor and in his position as an Indian American. The book's wide appeal, Srikanth argues, comes from its interstitial position among many categories of work, including immigrant writing, medical ethics, AIDS writing, and autobiography. Analyzing Verghese's shifting subject positions in terms of his narrators, Srikanth notes that Verghese "doctors" the genre of autobiography in departing from the centrality of the European American autobiographical narrator and directing the reader's attention to community, to his "othered" AIDS patients, and to ethical questions in the age of AIDS, even as he appropriates the generic convention of recording the narrator's transformation in the course of his life. Relating Verghese's book to several models of American autobiography, such as the autobiographies of Benjamin Franklin and Frederick Douglass and Native American autobiographical essays, Srikanth contends that Verghese rewrites "American notions of the proper relationship between the individual and the collective." The interplay between individual and community in Verghese's memoir is particularly complex in the trajectory of Verghese's self-transformation from doctor with a green card, working in a small town in Tennessee, to celebrated hero fighting AIDS on the front lines, and from diasporic and immigrant, eager to assimilate into mainstream America, to model citizen whose memoir "has taught us how to live," as a university director of liberal education puts it. Is the story of Dr. Verghese's success a typical story of assimilation, or is it a form of intervention? Is his image as model citizen merely a version of the "model minority"? Srikanth's essay raises provocative questions without offering easy answers.

Teri Shaffer Yamada's essay, "Cambodian American Autobiography: Testimonial Discourse," further explores the functions of autobiography and issues of "authenticity" in yet another historical context. With a focus on Chanrithy Him's *When Broken Glass Floats: Growing Up under the Khmer Rouge* and Loung Ung's *First They Killed My Father: A Daughter of Cambodia Remembers,* Yamada investigates the characteristics of Cambodian American autobiography, situating the popularity of this genre in the historical context of the atrocities in recent Cambodian history and their impact on Cambodian refugees' lives. Yamada notes that Cambodian autobiographies differ from mainstream American autobiographies of immigrants' narratives that celebrate individualism, and from contemporary autobiographical writings by other Asian Americans, among them Vietnamese American autobiographies, which have seen a shift in emphasis from experience in Vietnam to acculturation in America. Moreover, Cambodian American autobiographies, like other minority discourses, do not readily or completely embrace the postmodern notions of multiplicity and indeterminacy that raise questions about representation, truth, and authenticity. In fact, Yamada points out, truthful representation and authenticity of the self are crucial in Cambodian American autobiographies, which aim to bear witness to the horrors of the "killing fields" and to demand social justice. In addition, the truthfulness and authenticity of these autobiographies are important conditions for a process of redress and healing among Cambodian Americans who were forced by the Khmer Rouge regime to give false confessions and were traumatized by the killing and torture they witnessed. The personal history of the Cambodian American autobiographical "I" is intertwined with a national history and with international interventions. Yamada emphasizes the fact that the genre of autobiography provides Cambodian Americans with a textual space for individual as well as collective voices, and the latter in turn transform a genre that has been considered the epitome of Western individualism.

This intricate relationship between self and the collective is central to my own essay, "Two Hat Softeners 'in the Trade Confession': John Yau and Kimiko Hahn." The essay contends that when criticism of Asian American poetry is embedded in a polarizing identity politics, it reduces both the complexity and the possibilities for intervention of Asian American poetics. Departing from a critical model that takes the poet's ethnicity as its primary frame of reference, the essay examines the poetics of John Yau and Kimiko Hahn in relation to their racialized and gendered subject positions, and in terms of their resistance to and appropriations of a mainstream lyric tradition—the "confessional" poem. The essay argues that although both poets reject the authoritative, transcendental, privileged "lyric I," the confessional mode enables them to explore the boundaries between private and public space and to investigate the relationships between personal and collective identities. Through intertextual appropriation and revision, as well as generic transgression, Yau and Hahn destabilize subject positions as well as raced and gendered identities, giving voice to the repressed and silenced "Other" while transforming lyric conventions.

Richard Serrano, revealing additional limitations of the binary and ethnocentric critical models, directs the reader's attention to yet another important aspect of Asian American literature: the interlocking of race, gender, and sexuality. Serrano's essay, "Beyond the Length of an Average Penis: Reading across Traditions in the Poetry of Timothy Liu," locates Liu's poetry at the intersection of several literary traditions, including the traditions of lesbian and gay poets of color, the Euro-American traditions of Walt Whitman and William Carlos Williams, and the classical tradition of Chinese poetry. Serrano examines how Timothy Liu engages in a dialogue with the African American poet Essex Hemphill, "by performing an ironic rereading of the canonical, nineteenth-century poet and gay icon Walt Whitman" in a twentieth-century context. Serrano's analysis of Liu's openly gay poems critiques the "gay American obsession with the most superficial manifestations of masculinity," an obsession entangled with a racial ideology that constructs the Caucasian male body as the norm. Rather than situating Liu and Hemphill comfortably in the poetic tradition that begins with Whitman, Serrano reads them "against the hyperadequacy and loquacious omnipresence of Whitman and the sort of masculinity celebrated in *Leaves of Grass*."

Samina Najmi, from a feminist perspective, brings new complications to the intertwining of race, gender, and sexuality, interrogating the ways in which the transformation of literary genres is shaped by differences of race, gender, sexuality, and nationality. In her essay, "Decolonizing the Bildungsroman: Narratives of War and Womanhood in Nora Okja Keller's *Comfort Woman*," Najmi situates her analysis of Keller's novel in a new tradition of "female coming-of-age stories told against the backdrop of a violent political history of invasion and colonization," arguing that the novel fuses two traditionally male genres—the bildungsroman and the war narrative—"simultaneously gendering and 'Asianizing' them." She takes issue with feminist critics who assume a universal female experience based only on white women's bildungsromane. At the same time, she argues that Asian American women's bildungsromane written in the 1990s differ from those of other women of color, and from those of an older generation of Asian American women writers, by synthesizing this genre with the war narrative. And, as is the case with bildungsromane, Asian American women's war narratives also differ from those written by white women. "If white women's war literature 'runs the gamut from patriotic propaganda to pacifist protest,'" Najmi writes, citing Jane Marcus, "Asian American women's writings resist these polarities in a unique synthesis of the two, which informs both the form and the content of their works." Focusing on *Comfort Woman,* Najmi's analysis extends feminist investigations into the relationship between gender and genre to also include race as a catalyst of generic transformation.

Rocío G. Davis's essay, "Short Story Cycle and Hawai'i Bildungsroman: Writing Self, Place, and Family in Lois-Ann Yamanaka's *Wild Meat and the Bully Burgers,*" adds to Najmi's discussion of Asian Americans' transformation of the bildungsroman, arguing that literary genres, like identities of race and culture, are hybrid and constantly reinvented. Davis explores the ways in which Yamanaka's work "expands the range of the short story cycle" even as it subverts the conventions of a traditional American literary form in order to invent new modes of inscribing distinct Hawaiian[10] local realities and the perspectives of working-class Japanese Americans in Hawai'i. Situating Yamanaka's work in the tradition of Asian American short story cycles, and attending to its unique Hawaiian elements, Davis shows how Yamanaka appropriates and transforms the hybrid, transcultural genre of the short story cycle and the European model of the bildungsroman. Two traditional Hawaiian themes, *aloha 'aina* (love of the land) and *'ohana* (family), and the father's talk-story play significant roles in the development of the Japanese American child narrator/protagonist, whose individual growth is bound up with family, community, and the land. Davis compares Yamanaka's invention of a hybrid literary form to Asian Americans' rearticulation of ethnic identities, showing that literary genres and ethnic identities are historically, culturally, and locally determined constructs rather than reflections of essential categories.

Tina Chen's essay, "Recasting the Spy, Rewriting the Story: The Politics of Genre in *Native Speaker* by Chang-rae Lee," explores the ways in which Asian American subject formation can entail the revision of generic conventions in literature. Noting *Native Speaker*'s affinity with and departure from more traditional "spy stories," Chen contends that Chang-Rae Lee deliberately reworks the genre of the spy novel, "altering it to accommodate the exigencies of a spy whose racially determined invisibility signals not license but a debilitating erasure of self and power." Rather than presenting the protagonist Henry Park's silence and invisibility as an essentially ethnic "cultural legacy," Chen attributes such characteristics both to Korean Americans' assigned racial position in U.S. society and to Henry's prescribed performance as a spy. Chen contends that Henry, as an Asian American spy, figures as a response to characters like Charlie Chan, Mr. Moto, and Fu Manchu—all of whom exemplify stereotypes of Asians created by whites, and two of which are, to a certain degree, sustained by Asian Americans' acquiescence to the "model minority" myth. Chen also examines *Native Speaker*'s connection to "the thematization of racial invisibility offered by the African American literary tradition" and "minority and women writers' ongoing literary revisions of the generic conventions of spy and detective fiction." She emphasizes *Native Speaker*'s special contribution to generic revisions by comparing it with David Henry Hwang's *M. Butterfly* and Leonard Chang's *Over the Shoulder: A Novel of Intrigue.*

Pallavi Rastogi's essay, "Telling Twice-Told Tales All Over Again: Literary and Historical Subversion in Bharati Mukherjee's *The Holder of the World,*" brings the anthology full circle, to issues raised in Ferens's essay and further explored in others. While engaging with opposing critical views on Mukherjee, Rastogi offers an alternative perspective, one that disrupts reductive polarities in the reading of this complex author. She contends that *The Holder of the World* marks a shift in the assimilationist stance advocated in Mukherjee's other novels, such as *Jasmine, The Tiger's Daughter,* and *Wife,* and instead articulates a cosmopolitan dialectic of intercultural contact through which mainstream American society is changed by its immigrant population as much as it seeks to mold these immigrants in its own Eurocentric image. This thematic shift, Rastogi maintains, is enacted by Mukherjee's hybridization and disruption of the literary canon, particularly by her subversive rewriting of Nathaniel Hawthorne's *The Scarlet Letter.* Thus, Rastogi argues, the novel, in seeking a ubiquitous hybridity, splits the idea of American citizenship from whiteness, suggesting that no one, not even white Puritan Americans, has a holistic claim to American identity. Rastogi's analysis forcefully demonstrates the possibilities for interventional agency in Asian American writers' subversive, transformative appropriations and reinventions of literary genres.

The essays in this collection seek to reframe questions of identity and Asian American literature as first posed by the *Aiiieeeee!* editors, explored by pioneer scholars, and currently debated among Asian American literary critics. Rather than proposing to replace one critical paradigm with another, we both draw upon and critique various critical perspectives. The groundbreaking work done by leading Asian American scholars enables us to explore alternative methodologies and to mine a wider range of interventional possibilities embedded in Asian American literature. Scholarship in Asian American studies, and in the studies of race, gender, and sexuality, has profoundly advanced the way we understand categories of identity, which are naturalized through discourses and narratives and through what Butler calls "sustained social performances" (180). In other words, modes of identity articulation should be regarded, not as expressive of racial or cultural essence, but rather as "performative" in Butler's sense of entailing "a dramatic and contingent construction of meaning" (177). By extension, examination of Asian American literature as naturalized and transparent expressions of Asian Americans' discrete cultures, racially unique sensibilities, or dichotomized subject positions may be more than merely reductive of the complexity of literary productions and articulations. It may also unwittingly help reinforce the epistemological ground for racial, gender, and cultural hierarchies built on naturalized essential attributes. Thus it is necessary to interrogate not only social and historical contexts but also formal strategies for identity construction, wherein resides the possibility of subversion.

This anthology explores multiple possibilities for enacting the specific task that David Palumbo-Liu proposes for minority discourse: "to ascertain the interpenetration of minor and dominant cultures," and to see the resulting "reconfiguration" as "a site of a politicized aesthetics" ("Universalism" 202). This "interpenetration" is embedded in Asian American writers' appropriations and reinventions of generic conventions, operations that have the effect of transforming dominant cultures from within these cultures' modes of articulation, through a politicized aesthetics. It is precisely here—in this mutually constitutive process and transformative engagement—that this anthology seeks to foreground the agency of Asian American literature.

BIBLIOGRAPHY

Bakhtin, Mikhail M. *The Dialogic Imagination: Four Essays.* 1981. Ed. Michael Holquist. Trans. Caryl Emerson and Michael Holquist. Austin: University of Texas Press, 1990.

Bourdieu, Pierre. *The Field of Cultural Production: Essays on Art and Literature.* New York: Columbia University Press, 1993.

Butler, Judith. *Gender Trouble: Feminism and the Subversion of Identity.* 1990. New York: Routledge, 1999.

Cheung, King-Kok. *Articulate Silences: Hisaye Yamamoto, Maxine Hong Kingston, Joy Kogawa.* Ithaca: Cornell University Press, 1993.

———. "Of Men and Men: Reconstructing Chinese American Masculinity." *Other Sisterhoods: Literary Theory and U.S. Women of Color.* Ed. Sandra Kumamoto Stanley. Urbana: University of Illinois Press, 1998. 173–99.

———, ed. "Re-viewing Asian American Literary Studies." Introduction. *An Interethnic Companion to Asian American Literature.* New York: Cambridge University Press, 1997. 1–36.

Chin, Frank. "Come All Ye Asian American Writers of the Real and the Fake." *The Big Aiiieeeee! An Anthology of Chinese American and Japanese American Fiction.* Ed. Jeffery Paul Chan et al. New York: Meridian, 1991. 1–92.

———, et al. Preface. *Aiiieeeee! An Anthology of Asian-American Writers.* Ed. Frank Chin et al. New York: Meridian, 1974. xi–xxii.

———. "*Aiiieeeee!* Revisited." Preface. *Aiiieeeee! An Anthology of Asian American Writers.* 1974. Ed. Frank Chin et al. New York: Mentor, 1991. xxiii–xli.

Chu, Patricia P. *Assimilating Asians: Gendered Strategies of Authorship in Asian America.* Durham: Duke University Press, 2000.

Eng, David L., and Alice Y. Hom, eds. *Q & A: Queer in Asian America.* Philadelphia: Temple University Press, 1998.

Feng, Pin-Chia. *The Female Bildungsroman by Toni Morrison and Maxine Hong Kingston.* New York: Peter Lang, 1997.

Grosz, Elizabeth. "Derrida's Politics of Sexual Difference." *Space, Time, and Perversion: Essays on the Politics of Bodies.* New York: Routledge, 1995. 59–80.

Guillén, Claudio. *Literature as System: Essays toward the Theory of Literary History.* Princeton: Princeton University Press, 1971.

Hall, Stuart. *The Hard Road to Renewal: Thatcherism and the Crisis of the Left.* London: Verso, 1988.

Hirsch, Marianne. "The Novel of Formation as Genre: Between Great Expectations and Lost Illusions." *Genre* 12 (1979): 293–311.

Kim, Elaine H. *Asian American Literature: An Introduction to the Writings and Their Social Context.* Philadelphia: Temple University Press, 1982.

———. "Beyond Railroads and Internment: Comments on the Past, Present, and Future of Asian American Studies." *Privileging Positions: The Sites of Asian American Studies.* Ed. Gary Y. Okihiro et al. Pullman: Washington State University Press, 1995. 11–19.

Koshy, Susan. "The Fiction of Asian American Literature." *Yale Journal of Criticism* 9.2 (1996): 315–46.

Labovitz, Esther. *The Myth of the Heroine: The Female Bildungsroman in the Twentieth Century*. New York: Peter Lang, 1988.

Lee, Rachel C. *The Americas of Asian American Literature: Gendered Fictions of Nation and Transnations*. Princeton: Princeton University Press, 1999.

Li, David Leiwei. *Imagining the Nation: Asian American Literature and Cultural Consent*. Stanford: Stanford University Press, 1998.

Lim, Shirley Geok-lin. "Immigration and Diaspora." *An Interethnic Companion to Asian American Literature*. Ed. King-Kok Cheung. New York: Cambridge University Press, 1997. 289–311.

———, and Amy Ling, eds. Introduction. *Reading the Literatures of Asian America*. Philadelphia: Temple University Press, 1992. 1–9.

Lima, Maria Helena. "Decolonizing Genre: Jamaica Kincaid and the Bildungsroman." *Genre* 26.4 (1993): 431–59.

Ling, Amy. *Between Worlds: Women Writers of Chinese Ancestry*. New York: Pergamon, 1990.

Ling, Jinqi. *Narrating Nationalisms: Ideology and Form in Asian American Literature*. New York: Oxford University Press, 1998.

Lowe, Lisa. "Heterogeneity, Hybridity, Multiplicity: Marking Asian American Differences." *Diaspora* 1.1 (1991): 22–44.

———. *Immigrant Acts: On Asian American Cultural Politics*. Durham: Duke University Press, 1996.

Ma, Sheng-mei. *Immigrant Subjectivities in Asian American and Asian Diaspora Literatures*. Albany: State University of New York Press, 1998.

Marcus, Jane. "Corpus/Corps/Corpse: Writing the Body in/at War." *Arms and the Woman*. Ed. Helen Cooper et al. Chapel Hill: University of North Carolina Press, 1989. 124–67.

Moretti, Franco. *The Way of the World: The Bildungsroman in European Culture*. Trans. Albert Sbragia. London: Verso, 1987.

Nguyen, Viet Thanh. *Race and Resistance: Literature and Politics in Asian America*. New York: Oxford University Press, 2002.

Palumbo-Liu, David. *Asian/American: Historical Crossings of a Racial Frontier*. Stanford: Stanford University Press, 1999.

———. "Universalism and Minority Cultures." *Differences: A Journal of Feminist Cultural Studies* 7.1 (1995): 188–208.

San Juan, E., Jr. *The Philippine Temptation: Dialectics of Philippines–U.S. Literary Relations*. Philadelphia: Temple University Press, 1996.

Wong, Sau-ling Cynthia. "Denationalization Reconsidered: Asian American Cultural Criticism at a Theoretical Crossroads." *Amerasia Journal* 21.1&2 (1995): 1–27.

———. *Reading Asian American Literature: From Necessity to Extravagance*. Princeton: Princeton University Press, 1993.

———, and Stephen H. Sumida, eds. *The Resource Guide to Asian American Literature.* New York: Modern Language Association, 2001.

Wong, Sunn Shelley. "Sizing Up Asian American Poetry." *The Resource Guide to Asian American Literature.* Ed. Sau-ling Cynthia Wong and Stephen H. Sumida. New York: Modern Language Association, 2001. 285–308.

NOTES

I am grateful to Samina Najmi for her invaluable advice, insights, and proofreading in the process of my writing this introduction. I wish also to thank David Palumbo-Liu and the anonymous readers of the University of Washington Press for their astute comments and constructive suggestions.

1. See, for instance, Lisa Lowe's seminal essay "Heterogeneity, Hybridity, Multiplicity." For a summary of the agendas and ideologies of cultural nationalism, and of the material and conceptual forces that have generated this "paradigm shift" (Sau-ling Wong's phrase) in Asian American studies, see Wong's essay "Denationalization Reconsidered."

2. For a recent resource guide to Asian American literature, see Wong and Sumida.

3. See, for instance, David Eng and Alice Hom, eds., *Q & A*; Rachel C. Lee, *The Americas of Asian American Literature*; and Sheng-mei Ma, *Immigrant Subjectivities,* among other works.

4. See King-Kok Cheung, "Of Men and Men."

5. It would be reductive to say that until recently all major groundbreaking Asian American literary critical works have been simply "separatist" or "expressive and thematically oriented." See, for instance, Amy Ling, *Between Worlds*; King-Kok Cheung, *Articulate Silences*; and Sau-ling Cynthia Wong, *Reading Asian American Literature.* Both Ling and Cheung employ a thematic approach, with attention to gendered experience and to narrative and rhetorical strategies. Rather than focus on a unifying theme, Wong explores four shared motifs in Asian American literature, across gender, class, generational, and sociohistorical contexts. These motifs, like the themes of "in-between worlds" and modes of "silence" that Ling and Cheung, respectively, explore, are considered to be distinct features of Asian American experience and literature. Wong states that "the best way" for Asian Americans to "'claim America' . . . may well be to *differentiate* Asian American symbolic configurations from those considered 'mainstream American'" (14). My discussion of several characteristics of a major Asian American literary critical mode is by no means intended to dismiss the significant contributions of these groundbreaking works, or to replace their approaches altogether. Rather, my analysis, as shown in my discussion of Elaine Kim's *Asian American Literature,* aims to explore the limits of a predominant critical mode as well as the possibilities for alternative methodologies.

6. In the same essay, Koshy also critiques Shirley Geok-lin Lim's critical methodology for Asian American literature.

7. Sunn Shelley Wong, in her essay, "Sizing Up Asian American Poetry," offers an eloquent and provocative critique of the binarism underlying the predominant approaches to Asian American poetry. Although her focus is on poetry, her criticism is also applicable to a prevailing mode of literary studies that reduces Asian American literary texts to polarizing categories.

8. See Hirsch, "The Novel of Formation as Genre."

9. See, for instance, Esther Labovitz, *The Myth of the Heroine*; Pin-Chia Feng, *The Female Bildungsroman*; and Maria Helena Lima, "Decolonizing Genre."

10. See n. 1 of Davis's essay for her explanation of the terms "Hawai'i" and "Hawaiian."

WINNIFRED EATON / ONOTO WATANNA

ESTABLISHING ETHNOGRAPHIC AUTHORITY

DOMINIKA FERENS

> This novel is written, we are told, by a young Anglo-Japanese girl whose opportunities for observing her countrywomen have been exceptional. . . . It has thus an interest apart from its literary merit. . . . One expects an amount of ethnological truth which is difficult to get from the descriptions, however convincing, of the outsider, and this expectation is certainly not disappointed. — Review of Onoto Watanna's *A Japanese Nightingale* (*New York Times Book Review*)

> Authenticity cannot be determined simply by retailing the objective material attributes of the artifact. It has to do not only with genuineness and the reliability of face value, but with the interpretation of genuineness and our desire for it. — BRIAN SPOONER ("Weavers and Dealers: The Authenticity of an Oriental Carpet")

"I can speak about the subject with authority because I have been there" is the conventional claim nineteenth-century orientalist travelers made to assert discursive authority. Having "been there" remains the ethnographer's most powerful claim to representing Other people and places (Clifford 22; Behdad 100). When in 1982 Florinda Donner, author of the ethnographic novel *Shabono*,[1] failed to produce evidence of having "been there" (in the Venezuelan jungle), the novel came close to being discredited not only as a scientific document—which it never purported to be—but also, through insinuations of plagiarism, as a work of fiction. Speaking from "there" (Venezuela), the anthropologist who denounced Donner in *American Anthropologist* (DeHolmes 667) listed Donner's borrowings from existing ethnographic materials but left the most damning evidence for last: Donner simply hadn't been there. Pratt's insightful placement of the novel in the contested ground between scientific practice and fiction has won for *Shabono* a place on reading lists for academic anthropology courses (Pratt 29). Apparently, the thicker the aura of ambiguity that surrounds the novel, the more copies it will sell.

Discussions about epistemology and authenticity, like those surrounding Donner's work, would have sunk Winnifred Eaton as a writer in her lifetime. Though some reviewers had their doubts about Onoto Watanna's being genuinely Japanese, most assumed she either was Japanese or had experienced Japan at first hand. Those who did not make these assumptions, such as the *Independent* reviewer who pointed out glaring historical, geographical, and cultural inaccuracies in Eaton's *The Daughters of Nijo* (1904), were outnumbered by those who did. Fortunately for Eaton, the doubters had neither time nor opportunity to investigate her past. That her father was English was public knowledge, but she kept the fact that her mother was Chinese veiled at all times, allowing the curious public an occasional glimpse in authorized and largely fictional biographical notes. Meanwhile, the publishers—Rand McNally, Harper's, Dodd, and Doubleday—stood firmly by their investment.

One way to understand the ease with which Eaton established herself as an authority on things Japanese is to rethink the meaning we assign to the term "authenticity." As the anthropologist Brian Spooner points out (200), authenticity has as much to do with the objective attributes of an artifact as with our "interpretation of genuineness and our desire for it." To redefine authenticity, Spooner uses the intriguing case of Oriental carpets in Western culture. Since the time, several hundred years ago, when such carpets began arriving in the West as a rare commodity, their quality, availability, and provenance have radically changed—without these changes having affecting their price range and symbolic value. The authenticity of imported carpets, Spooner argues, is constructed on the basis of incidental lore that each dealer in a chain of dealers acquires together with the wares. Connoisseurs have always been aware that they "scarcely control the sources of the information," yet they settle for unverifiable lore because of the desire to maintain the value of Oriental carpets as status symbols in Western culture (Spooner 198–200).

A similar mechanism, we could argue, operated on the novels of Onoto Watanna, seen as commodities. Her public persona was as much a figment of her imagination as it was a product of white mainstream readers' desire for the exotic, for a new yet intelligible aesthetic, and for an insight into Japan's leap from the "feudal" era directly into modernity. At the price of a dollar or two, the American reader could purchase a little piece of Japan in a decorative silk binding—a romance that doubled as a lesson in Japanese customs, morals, and manners. Like Oriental carpets, Onoto Watanna's novels arrived in the marketplace "divorced from their social context" (Spooner 199). The publishing industry, which had an investment in the authenticity of the novels, sought to reconstruct that context for the reader in the form of biographical notes on Onoto Watanna and photographs of the author. References to the making of the stories—"trade lore," to use Spooner's words—helped to authenticate Onoto Watanna's wares and maintain her ethnographic authority. Her youth and gender made Eaton a perfect synecdoche for the New Japan; her biracial status, in turn, seemed to predestine her for the role of cultural mediator and interpreter. The Japanese persona became inseparable from the commodities Eaton produced. It not only authorized her to produce ethnographic texts but also became a commodity in itself, subject to the rigors and constraints of the marketplace.

As a literary celebrity, Eaton was the subject of countless biographical articles, interviews, and reviews. All these she scrupulously collected and pasted into scrapbooks. In one of the scrapbooks covering the earliest part of her career, from about 1897 to 1900, fragments of printed stories and typescripts are interspersed with biographical notes and reviews. Scrawled next to the reviews are the names of cities in which they appeared. To read these place names—Boston, Brooklyn, Chicago, Detroit, Houston, Indianapolis, Los Angeles, New Orleans, New York, Omaha, Philadelphia, St. Louis—is to acknowledge that Eaton's work was marketed and read across the continent before she turned twenty-five. Yet these clippings were only a foretaste of the publicity Eaton would experience after 1900. Every city and small town between New York and San Francisco seemed eager to acknowledge Onoto Watanna—however briefly—in print. No less eagerly, Eaton pasted the reviews onto the map of her conquest. To explain her phenomenal success, I shall attempt to answer the following questions: How did Eaton understand her own strategy of self-authorization? What made passing a thinkable career move for her in the late 1800s? What popular assumptions about race and culture enabled Eaton to become an authority on things Japanese? And, finally, what issues do her writings raise about contemporary academic standards of literary authenticity?

Since her position as an ethnographic authority depended on sustaining the fiction of her Japanese descent, Eaton did not indulge in much public introspection or attempt to theorize her work. There are, however, stories in which she obliquely approaches the problem of wresting authority from those privileged by gender, race, and class. One in particular, "Eyes That Saw Not" (1902), is useful in understanding Eaton's social positioning and offers a rare insight into her understanding of authorship. Since the text published in *Harper's Monthly* is signed jointly by Onoto Watanna and Bertrand W. Babcock (the author's first husband), the reader is drawn into a game of detecting shifts in style and narrative point of view so as to attribute the authorship of certain ideas or passages to one or the other of the writers. The undecidability makes for an unusual reading dynamic and reflects back on the thematic content.

In this story, the recently orphaned protagonist, Elizabeth, becomes at the age of fifteen a ward of "Graytown's leading family," the Swinnertons. She and young John Swinnerton fall in love, with the family's approval. John leaves home for college and then embarks on a journalistic career, which is disrupted after three years, when he loses his sight in unexplained circumstances. When John comes home, he keeps up his spirits by making ambitious plans to become a fiction writer and thus capitalize on his experience as a reporter. John's mother volunteers Elizabeth as his assistant, a job the younger homebound woman takes up with utter devotion. She reads aloud from John's notebooks; he narrates the stories behind the notes and then formally dictates the stories, and she writes them down. Yet as John attempts to transform the raw stuff of experience into "literature," his penchant for purple prose proves fatal. Publishers reject one manuscript after another. Elizabeth, whose literary talent has never had a chance to develop, takes matters into her own hands. Partly for her lover's sake, and partly to give vent to her unfulfilled ambition, she begins rewriting John's stories and sending them out in his name. John Swinnerton soon becomes, in his own words, "an author whom the world recognizes," and, having thus proved his manhood, he asks Elizabeth to marry him. Elizabeth's deception comes to light when John's blindness is cured. Being a man who "despised dishonesty," he spurns her. But after rereading his own prose and realizing it is inferior to hers, he recants.

"Eyes That Saw Not" raises a number of fundamental questions: What is a story? Who owns it? How does a story relate to field notes? Can a good storyteller do without participant observation? What if social conventions prevent the storyteller from doing her own fieldwork? These questions, the text implies, are related to the unequal treatment of young men and women in Middle America. Allusions to John's freewheeling lifestyle—nights spent in a New York morgue, hair-raising adventures in San Francisco's Tenderloin district, even assignments to visit women's clubs, "with orders from the city editor 'to write up a funny story about them' "—contrast with the absence of any information on Elizabeth's life in the same period, presumably because there is nothing to tell (Eaton, "Eyes That Saw Not" 31). Mrs. Swinnerton, whose life consists of waiting outside closed doors with breakfast trays and straining to hear what is happening inside, is a good model of what Elizabeth may expect to become. On one level, then, the text reinscribes the ideology that valorizes men's activities "out there," while it devalues the domestic. On another level, though, the domestic is recentered by the love plot: since the entire drama takes place in the home, John's prior adventures seem pale and juvenile in comparison. It is Elizabeth's transformation of John's accounts of his adventures that provides the drama and the tension in "Eyes That Saw Not."

Thus Elizabeth, who has no story, must wrest authority from John, who has many stories, though he tells them in the manner of an "ecclesiastic who enters the pulpit in cleric robes, but lacks the message of the living word" (Eaton, "Eyes That Saw Not" 32). In principle, John owns the stories because he has "been there." He justifies his decision to become a writer by arguing, "I have had three years of living where life most abounds. I have plenty of incident and plenty of color" (31). The fieldwork he has done among the urban poor, among the criminal underclass, and even among New York's club women is the capital he banks on. Elizabeth, by contrast, has untapped literary talent and a prospective mother-in-law who, on hearing of her blind son's plans to "write," exclaims enthusiastically, "And Elizabeth and I will be your secretaries!" (31). The Swinnertons' conviction that Elizabeth will remain their son's subordinate is so strong that when she decides to take up the pen, she does so covertly, late at night, scribbling "with a quick nervous pencil . . . on an old pad of John's" (33), and then she transfers the credit for her work to John. By day, "hour after hour she took his dictation. She thought of those prisoners condemned to work forever at machines that merely registered their efforts—a round of endless labor with nothing but a dial face to show what might have been accomplished"; by night, she guiltily appropriates John's stories, and, on seeing them printed under his name, wonders guiltily whether they are "not as much John's as hers" (33).

In contrast to her fictional character, Eaton did not hesitate to sign her name to the finished product when she appropriated ethnographic material from travel narratives and fiction on Japan. The most direct parallel between her own appropriations and Elizabeth's is the fact that neither woman, because of her gender and class, had the resources or freedom of movement necessary to "be there"—in other words, to see for herself the places and people that mainstream readers paid to read about. A variety of institutionalized restrictions, such as social taboos, gender-segregated spaces, and women's financial dependence on men, turned certain places into almost exclusively male preserves, and this exclusivity, in turn, raised the prestige of these places or endowed them with the aura of adventure. Even if Elizabeth had been able to afford leaving the shelter of the Swinnerton mansion, romping around the Bowery would have compromised her respectability. Similarly, Japan remained the travel destination of America's wealthiest citizens and of a handful of middle-class professionals: academics, journalists, teachers, and medical missionaries. The very inaccessibility of places like the squalid Bowery and glamorous Japan created a market demand for their literary representations. To write marketable stories, Elizabeth and her author had to get story material through alternate channels.

A "story," as the Babcocks demonstrate, has multiple layers and locations. The story is John's immediate construction of what he observes. The story also resides in the jottings that Elizabeth reads back to John, and in the newspaper articles John wrote. The story is furthermore in John's lively narrative of his "personal experience," prompted by his notes and shared with Elizabeth, which he then transforms through dictation back into the "time-chipped phrases of the daily newspaper" (Eaton, "Eyes That Saw Not" 32). From Elizabeth's point of view, what matters is "'the story of the story' as told by the reporter," whom she sees as an active participant in the events he is reporting (32). The farther one goes into the narrative, the more blurred becomes the line between copy and original. Right after John has regained his sight,

> he arose and stumbled around the room, more helpless than when he was totally blind. He began feverishly gathering the scrap-books in which the printed stories cut out from the magazines were pasted. Then he groped his way across the room to a chest of drawers. He drew out the original manuscripts—'the copies' she had called them. These, at least, were his own [38].

Ultimately, John accepts Elizabeth's interpretation of what a story is. Her storytelling talent is understood to legitimate her appropriation of John's material. What makes "Eyes That Saw Not" particularly interesting for my discussion of the role of ethnography in Eaton's writing is the way in which the two coauthors attempted to subordinate "fieldwork" to "literature" and split these activities between two subjects. The story rationalizes Eaton's literary practice, which involved appropriating and transforming other people's Japanese "fieldwork." The fact that in "Eyes That Saw Not" a home-bound woman empowers herself by wresting authority from a freewheeling man suggests that Eaton saw her own representations of Japanese subjects in similar terms. It was from male literary figures like William Elliot Griffis, Sir Edwin Arnold, John Luther Long, and Lafcadio Hearn, and not from the represented Japanese subjects, that she saw herself taking the power to represent.[2]

"Eyes That Saw Not" also gives us an important insight into Eaton's epistemology. Although the Babcocks suggest that there are many ways of telling a story, they imply on the epistemological level that each narration still reflects the same objective truth. John's narrative of a particular experience projects for Elizabeth an image of that experience that is as true as if she had witnessed it herself. The possibility that Elizabeth might have a different perspective on John's Others (corpses, working-class women, club women), or that the *living* Others, at least, might see themselves differently, is absent from the text. Elizabeth's sole concern is to make the story "sufficiently attractive" (33) to be publishable. When she rewrites John's words, the truth of the experience supposedly remains intact—only the telling is better. "Being there" is not essential when it comes to writing about the Other.

Eaton could not have afforded to "be there" before she won recognition as a writer. But it is not certain that she would have gone out into the "field" in search of Japanese material had she been in a position to do so. Even after her Japanese novels made her famous and her children grew up, she did not visit Japan. We do know that her independent life began with a voyage to the Caribbean—a firsthand experience that might have provided ample ethnographic material, had she been looking for it. Eaton's 1915 fictionalized account of her 1895 sojourn in Jamaica begins like the classic island ethnographies of Louis de Bougainville, Raymond Firth, and Bronislaw Malinowski, with a reconstruction of the arrival scene dominated by the speaker's initial reaction to her racial Others:

> A crowd seemed to be swarming on the wharves, awaiting our boat. As we came nearer, I was amazed to find that this crowd was made up almost entirely of negroes. We have very few negroes in Canada, and I had only seen one in all my life. I remember an older sister had shown him to me

> in church—he was pure black—and told me he was the 'Bogy man,' and that he'd probably come around to see me that night. . . . It was, therefore, with a genuine thrill of excitement and fear that I looked down upon that vast sea of upturned black and brown faces. Never will I forget that first impression of Jamaica. Everywhere I looked were negroes—men, women and children, some half naked, some with bright handkerchiefs knotted about their heads, some gaudily attired, some dressed in immaculate white duck, just like the people on the boat [Eaton, *Me: A Book of Remembrance* 19–20].

Many anthropologists have recently suggested that there can never be an unmediated encounter with the Other. As Greg Dening notes, "the other is rarely met in a present divorced from all the meetings that have gone before" (464). Eaton's narrator's "first encounter" seems to have been thoroughly overdetermined. Her position on board ship, high above the "sea of upturned black and brown faces," above the nakedness and gaudiness, becomes reified in the course of her stay as the prejudices brought from home are reinforced by the frank professions of racism she hears from white Jamaicans. Before her fear of the vast, undifferentiated blackness has time to wear off, the young journalist flees the island, physically sickened by the marriage proposal and kiss of a black member of Parliament. Her initial reaction to blackness foreshadows this turn of events, each encounter with black Jamaicans being loaded with fear and revulsion, so that the rushed departure appears as justifiable as it is inevitable.

On reaching the United States, the narrator uses the "Bogy man" story to win the sympathy of a wealthy Southerner, but when she embarks on her literary career, she does not reach for the Jamaican experience. Instead, she immerses herself in a fantasy world she calls "my mother's land" (Eaton, *Me* 178). The story of Eaton's real voyage and cross-cultural encounter would have to wait almost twenty years to be told. Presumably, when Eaton started writing fiction, the story of a white woman's encounter with blackness in Jamaica and her rejection of a wealthy black suitor would have appeared to lack literary potential. But an account of a white woman's voyage to Japan and her tragic love affair with a Japanese nobleman was another matter. A book with just such a plot, titled *Miss Numè of Japan: A Japanese-American Romance,* did launch Eaton as a novelist in 1899. And the claim on which she built her career was this: I can speak about Japanese culture with authority because I am the daughter of a Japanese woman.

The question to ask at this point seems to be, Why Japanese? Why not

Chinese? To better understand the label Eaton rebelled against, we may look to a text by the mainstream author Jean Webster, Eaton's contemporary and good friend. "It's awfully queer not to know what one is—sort of exciting and romantic," says Judy, the orphan-narrator of Webster's *Daddy Long-Legs* (1912):

> There are such a lot of possibilities. Maybe I'm not American; lots of people aren't. I may be straight descended from the ancient Romans, or I may be a Viking's daughter, or I may be the child of a Russian exile and belong by rights in a Siberian prison, or maybe I'm a gypsy. . . . There's one thing I'm perfectly sure of. I'm not a Chinaman [Webster 64].

What Judy is anxious about is her class identity: an unknown benefactor has lifted her out of poverty and given her an elite education. Yet she finds consolation in the knowledge that she is white: in the racial hierarchy of the day, the Chinese and other people of color constituted a buffer between her and rock bottom. Her choice of the gendered word "Chinaman" is more than a slip of the tongue. It suggests that, because of the unbalanced male-to-female ratio among Chinese immigrants to North America, Chineseness was associated with masculinity of a particular kind. If being a Viking, or a Russian, or a gypsy could be thought romantic and at least potentially American, "Chinese" signified the reverse: un-American, unromantic, unheroic, undesirable, effeminate, and low-class.

Winnifred Eaton, I would suggest, constructed her "Japanese" persona in reaction both to the "Chinaman" stereotype and to Chineseness as represented by her sister Edith Eaton. In missionary circles, Edith had tapped in to an alternative discourse of Chineseness, and through those circles she had claimed a limited authority to study and represent the Chinese in print. Edith's Chinese pen name, Sui Sin Far, and her self-representation as a writer of Chinese descent, reinforced that authority. Missionaries resisted scientific theories that conflated race and culture, arguing instead for the shared humanity of the races and the possibility of replacing pernicious, backward cultural practices with Christian values and norms of conduct. However, the "positive" meaning of Chineseness offered by the missionaries came at a high price. When Edith Eaton selectively embraced that ideology, she also committed herself to an unpopular social cause—that of Chinese immigrants—and in so doing had to curb the desire for commercial success as a writer.

To Winnifred Eaton, the material and psychological cost of claiming

Chinese descent must have seemed prohibitive.[3] But, for a variety of reasons, passing for Japanese was a logical career move for her at the turn of the century. As Amy Ling points out, Eaton had "a keen marketing instinct and sense of timing" (310). Neither fifteen years earlier nor fifteen years later would it have made as much political or economic sense to embrace a Japanese identity. In the 1870s and 1880s, Japan was still an insignificant player in the international arena. Its name connoted little of the glamour that it would acquire in subsequent years. However, in the year preceding Winnifred Eaton's arrival in the United States, the Sino-Japanese war, which had long been making headlines in the Western press, ended with Japan's victory and unofficial annexation of Korea. China's defeat and the deprecation of things Chinese, then, was directly correlated in the North American media with the valorization of Japan and Japonica. Yet the fascination with Japan would prove short-lived: first the Californians and then most other Americans began to perceive Japan's military prowess as menacing. Thus the turn of the century was a perfect moment to become a Japanese novelist.

The aesthetic current known as *Japonisme* reached a high point in America in the 1890s. European and American art dealers worked aggressively to educate mainstream Americans in the new aesthetic and to promote the artifacts that entered the United States in ever-increasing quantities. Japan itself capitalized on the favorable climate by sending lavish exhibits of art and architecture to American world's fairs (Meech and Weisberg 31–34; Harris 24–54). In literature, Japanese influences resonated as strongly as in art. Eaton read the orientalist writings of Pierre Loti, Lafcadio Hearn, and Sir Edwin Arnold as a young woman in Canada, and she could scarcely have ignored their ubiquitous presence in Chicago and New York.[4] For the young apprentice writer, then, there already existed a thirty-year-old tradition she could step into. It was an orientalist tradition strongly dominated by the male traveler's perspective on the Other. To insert herself into that tradition, Winnifred Eaton found it necessary to take on the role of the exotic Other.

Whether Eaton made this move after grave deliberation or on a wild impulse, she could not have chosen better. At the personal level, her strategy for passing constituted what Teresa Kay Williams describes as a shift "from one 'minority' status to the 'more acceptable minority' status—in order to raise [one's] prestige and advance [one's] chances for a qualitatively improved life" (62). Eaton's ambiguous phenotype would thus no longer be a risk factor—which it had been in her passing for white. By passing for Japanese, Eaton shifted her status from undesirable to desirable immigrant at a time when West Coast lobbyists were stepping up the pressure on

Congress to contain Chinese immigration. In 1902, the year the Geary Act was renewed and Chinese exclusion secured, we read: "Miss Watanna's striking success in this country ought to encourage other Japanese novelists to learn English and come to this country" (*Buffalo Commercial* 24 Sept. 1902).

Professionally, being half-Japanese catapulted Eaton onto another plane, where her work was no longer held up to Western literary standards. Her naïveté and lack of literary technique, which would have disadvantaged her as a white writer, suddenly became part of what reviewers recognized as the "peculiar charm" of her untutored style. For some, the "childlike simplicity" of the texts (*Chicago Tribune* 6 Jan. 1904) guaranteed their authenticity, thanks to an assumption that reflects mainstream conceptions of race and evolutionary progress. It was also true that the reading public, fascinated by Japan's phenomenal success in the international arena, clamored for ethnographic knowledge that would explain the Japanese.

At the economic level, passing for Japanese afforded Eaton a degree of exceptionality that she would not have had as a white woman. When she began seeking employment in the Midwest, passing for white had removed the disadvantage of race in the job market, but her sex and class status had also limited her opportunities, confining them to the lowest-paying, most tedious clerical positions. By becoming Onoto Watanna, however, Eaton enacted mainstream orientalist fantasies. Her gender, instead of being a disadvantage, as it would have been in other walks of life, became a major selling point in the publishing marketplace. Next to a story manuscript in her scrapbook, Eaton scrawled a comment that sheds light on her early relations with magazine editors: "I wrote this story inside of an hour one morning, took it to the editor of the American Home Journal, waited while he read it, and it was accepted on the spot—cheque being handed me at once—quick work—and profitable! However, the story is trite—poor."

Passing for Japanese was not a single act but a process of sustaining and adjusting the public persona. Like the Oriental carpets Spooner uses in his discussion of authenticity, Eaton's "Japanese" stories, articles, and novels needed to be accompanied by the appropriate "trade lore." But whereas carpet weavers have no control over "trade lore" (it is the dealers and connoisseurs who spin the narrative of each carpet's provenance, age, and aesthetic attributes), in the case of Onoto Watanna it was the "weaver" herself who provided most of the information about the public persona. What is more significant, readers had direct input into the making of Onoto Watanna: in order to evaluate her assets and fine-tune her persona, she had to see herself reflected in the public eye and thus became an avid collector of reviews of her own work. On the basis of these reviews, it is possible to reconstruct the discourses that invested Eaton with ethnographic authority.

The general consensus among those who enjoyed the work of Onoto Watanna was that its charm "does not lie in the plot but in the telling, in the strange method of expression, in the delightful descriptions of Japanese habits of life and thought, and in the somewhat mysterious success with which the author gives the reader the Japanese point of view" (*Seattle Times* 10 July 1904). An Australian reviewer would go so far as to say that Onoto Watanna's work "gives a deeper insight into Japanese life than exhaustive tomes of erudite scholars" (*Sydney Herald* 30 July 1904). In the same year, an American commentator claiming familiarity with the field would assure readers, "Onoto Watanna is, after the late Lafcadio Hearn, the best foreign delineator of Japanese life. She possesses a thorough knowledge of the people and country" (*Baltimore Sun* 21 Dec. 1904). What all these statements seem to express is a desire for authentic *inside* knowledge about Japan—a desire to which Eaton responded astutely.

Since Eaton's authority did not originate in her actual knowledge or seniority "in the field," it seems appropriate to ask what made her a credible and sought-after source of information on Japan in the eyes of her readers. Aside from Eaton's good timing and her rare ability to anticipate readers' expectations, there must have been several other reasons. Three of them strike me as particularly significant.

The first of these is that nineteenth-century scientific theories of race had succeeded in conflating race and culture in the popular imagination, and so the Japanese half of Onoto Watanna's heredity was understood to carry an essential Japaneseness—a form of cultural knowledge, not just the visible markers of race. At the turn of the century, Franz Boas had barely begun his lifelong project of cleaving the concept of "culture" from that of "race." Cultural patterns were understood to be at least partly hereditary. Little wonder, then, that in the popular imagination "blood" conferred ethnographic authority on a writer in much the same way that documented presence in the "field" does today. The discourse of biological determinism was so pervasive in her day that Eaton, who had an avid interest in race theory, probably deceived herself as much as anyone else. This is how she presented her position through her fictional counterpart Nora in *Me*:

> I told him of the stories I was writing about my mother's land, and he said:
> "But you've never been there, child."

"I know," I said, "but, then, I have an instinctive feeling about that country. A blind man can find his way over paths that he intuitively feels. And so with me. I feel as if I knew everything about that land, and when I sit down to write—why, things just come pouring to me, and I can write anything then."

I could feel his slow smile, and then he said: "I believe you can" [176].

Although Eaton, like her character Nora, concealed the hours of library research that must have gone into the making of her stories, she was not being entirely disingenuous. In the many interviews Eaton gave, and in biographical notes in the popular press for which she supplied the "facts" of her life, she never claimed to have lived in Japan after early childhood. That she was raised in the West as an Englishman's daughter was public knowledge. Yet, odd as it may seem, for Eaton's early readers her "being Japanese" was a more important credential than her having "been there."

The second additional reason for Eaton's credibility was that, while Westerners had been exposed to Japanese artifacts, few of her readers had any sense of Japanese literary conventions; the charm and naïveté of Eaton's writing were therefore recognized as expressive of the Japanese aesthetic. Readers scrambled for pop-anthropological explanations of the "primitive," invoked the discourse of the "eternal feminine," and were generally willing to give Eaton the benefit of the doubt. "Needless to say," wrote one baffled critic, "this type is new, the ethical quality is foreign, and the artistic form a thing by itself. There is beauty and a spirit of fine breeding in this curious love story, as well as in the pictures which are Japanese in detail and delicacy of line" (*Critic* Aug. 1904). The winds of modernism, fanned by Eaton's contemporaries Yone Noguchi[5] and Sadakichi Hartmann,[6] among others, wreaked pleasurable havoc in the aesthetic sensibilities of mainstream audiences. Hartmann, a writer of haiku, symbolist poetry, and drama, thus defined the new trends in literature:

> We do not want representations of facts, but of appearances, or merely the blurred suggestion of appearances. The swift reflections and subtle quivering light do not permit exact copyism. . . . Peculiarities of style like these may easily deteriorate into trickery and mannerisms, but even then they are preferable to pure mimicry. . . . The art connoisseur of today wants to see subjects bathed in light and air, and wants an actual atmosphere to be interposed between his eyes and the representation of figures, flowers, fields, trees, etc. [Hartmann 151–52].

Eaton excelled at creating appearances and atmosphere. Nevertheless, although mimicry was her basic literary strategy, she mimicked not "life" but existing textual representations of Japan, and she imbued them with the mystique of an "authentic" Japanese sensibility. As one enthusiast attests, "her language is the flower talk of the flower land. It is musical, and when one reads her book he seems to be enveloped in an atmosphere sweet with the mellow, fruity, lulling odor of opium. And like the smoker of the drug, he must have more" (*American Illustrator* May 1903).

Literary critics and ordinary readers alike succumbed to *Japonisme*. Henry James was an admirer of Pierre Loti, while William Dean Howells found Eaton's *A Japanese Nightingale* (1901) "irresistible." Given Howells's insistence on writing from experience, his wholehearted endorsement of Onoto Watanna is nicely ironic. He commends her on her "very choice English" and expounds on the

> indescribable freshness in the art of this pretty novelette . . . which is like no other art except in the simplicity which is native to the best art everywhere. . . . It has its little defects, but its directness, and sincerity, and its felicity through the sparing touch make me unwilling to note them. In fact I have forgotten them [875].

Howells and most of his contemporaries responded to a repertoire of icons—chrysanthemum, bamboo, spray of almond blossoms, geisha, samisen—popularized through countless travelogues. By naming any one of these not yet hackneyed icons, Eaton could conjure up associations "redolent" of the spirit of old Japan.

But I would suggest that what readers sought in Eaton's work was not just her Japaneseness and the ability to suffuse her narratives with a poetic atmosphere. The ethnographic narratives that underlie many of her plots—stories of "first encounters" and the "salvage" of exotic cultures threatened by progress—were an important source of interest and pleasure for her readers and constituted the third additional reason why she was considered credible. Ethnography emerged as a subdiscipline of anthropology toward the end of the nineteenth century, precisely as a method for studying exotic cultures at the moment of their first encounter with modernity, or before the native lifeways were irrevocably tainted and displaced by Western ones. Japan, though understood to have an advanced rather than a "primitive" culture, was an unusual case in point, having long isolated itself from contacts with the Western world. Not only was the memory of the recent "first encounter" in 1855 very strong; remote islands and out-of-the-way settlements continued to provide Western travelers with opportunities to experience the thrill of transition from "New Japan" to "Old Japan," and Eaton was quick to see the usefulness of this ethnographic paradigm for her fiction. One critic admired her novel *The Wooing of Wistaria* for the "delicate touch" of its rendition of "Japanese life in the days before the entering of the wedge of civilization" (*Globe Democrat* 5 Oct. 1902). *The Daughters of Nijo* garnered praise for its treatment of "the period of transition, [a] by no means gradual and natural evolution, when Japan elected to cast off her ancient civilization, and hastily adopt, with magazine rifles and torpedo boats, the often incongruous habits of the West" ([Winnipeg] *Telegram* 14 May 1904). Those who craved ethnographic knowledge and relished the drama of "salvage ethnography" treated the romantic conventions of Onoto Watanna's prose as transparent and unproblematic; as one critic argued, "romance permits a view of the conflict . . . between the old and the new social customs, and shows Japan in its evolutionary stage of becoming a member of the family of nations" (*Washington Star* 7 May 1904).

Certainly not all were taken in by the Japanese persona. A doubting voice from the West Coast comments, "This little lady who is pleased to write under a Japanese name and who has done some very pretty stories of Nippon, has yielded, it is to be feared, to that bane of all authors, popularity, and now she is simply retilling the field that brought her first success" (*San Francisco Call* 30 Oct. 1904). The doubters were many, and the further into Eaton's career, the more skeptical the reviewers (though apparently not the general readers, for her novels continued to sell well into the 1910s). Even among the doubters, though, there was a general willingness to suspend disbelief for the sake of immersion in the exotic, authentic or not. For instance, a Londoner who suspected that *The Daughters of Nijo* might be "the work of a shrewd artificer who knows the market for local color" nevertheless found value in the book, "for the tale is excellent and we should scarcely enjoy it the less for knowing that the theme and treatment were merely pseudo-indigenous. It brings Japan a little nearer to us . . . and in itself it has the stimulating freshness of unfamiliar ways" ([London] *Pall Mall Gazette* 21 May 1904).

Winnifred Eaton asserted her authority to write insofar as others—her publishers, her readers, and her husband-manager—enabled her to pass. Once she stepped into the popular fiction marketplace, however, she was subject to what Clifford describes as "the action of multiple subjectivities and political constraints beyond the control of the author" (25); in response to these forces, she reached for the available strategies of authority. That her sister Edith Eaton was relatively more resistant to mainstream orientalist discourses was due in part to the fact that the Chinese identity that marginalized her as a writer also removed her from the field of market forces. Winnifred Eaton's writings, troubling and contradictory, nonetheless provide a rare insight into the interplay of reinscription and contestation. Understanding what made for her success is no less important than understanding what kept Edith Eaton from achieving it in the same historical moment.

BIBLIOGRAPHY

Anonymous (Eaton, Edith/Sui Sin Far). "The Persecution and Oppression of Me." *Independent* 71.3273 (1911): 421–24.

Behdad, Ali. *Belated Travelers: Orientalism in the Age of Colonial Dissolution*. Durham: Duke University Press, 1994.

Clifford, James. *The Predicament of Culture: Twentieth-Century Ethnography, Literature, and Art*. Cambridge: Harvard University Press, 1988.

DeHolmes, Rebecca B. "Is Shabono a Scandal or Superb Social Science?" *American Anthropologist* 85 (1983): 664–67.

Dening, Greg. "The Theatricality of Observing and Being Observed: Eighteenth-Century Europe 'Discovers' the Century Pacific." *Implicit Understandings of Observing, Reporting, and Reflecting on Other Peoples in the Early Modern Era*. Ed. Stuart B. Schwartz. Cambridge: Cambridge University Press, 1944. 451–83.

Donner, Florinda. *Shabono*. New York: Delacorte Press, 1982.

Eaton, Winnifred/Onoto Watanna. *The Daughters of Nijo*. New York: Macmillan, 1904.

———. "The Half Caste." *Conkey's Home Journal* Nov. 1898. Winnifred Eaton Reeve Fonds, Special Collections, University of Calgary Library.

———. *Me: A Book of Remembrance*. New York: Century, 1915.

———. *Miss Numè of Japan: A Japanese-American Romance*. Chicago: Rand McNally, 1899.

———. *The Wooing of Wistaria*. New York: Harper, 1902.

———, with Bertrand W. Babcock. "Eyes That Saw Not." *Harper's Monthly* June 1902: 30–38.

Ferens, Dominika. *Edith & Winnifred Eaton: Chinatown Missions and Japanese Romances*. Urbana: University of Illinois Press, 2002.

Harris, Neil. "All the World a Melting-Pot: Japan at American Fairs, 1876–1904." *Mutual Images: Essays in American-Japanese Relations*. Ed. Akira Iriye. Cambridge: Harvard University Press, 1975. 24–54.

Hartmann, Sadakichi. *Sadakichi Hartmann: Critical Modernist: Collected Art Writings*. Berkeley: University of California Press, 1991.

Howells, William Dean. "A Psychological Counter-Current in Recent Fiction." *North American Review* 173.541 (1901): 872–88.
Ling, Amy. "Creating One's Self: The Eaton Sisters." *Reading the Literatures of Asian America*. Ed. Shirley Lim and Amy Ling. Philadelphia: Temple University Press. 305–18.
Meech, Julia, and Gabriel P. Weisberg. *Japonisme Comes to America: The Japanese Impact on the Graphic Arts, 1876–1925*. New York: Abrams, 1990.
Noguchi, Yone. *Selected English Writings of Yone Noguchi: An East-West Literary Assimilation*. Ed. Yoshinobu Hakutani. London: Associated University Press, 1992.
Pratt, Mary Louise. "Fieldwork in Common Places." *Writing Culture: The Politics and Poetics of Ethnography*. Ed. James Clifford and George E. Marcus. Berkeley: University of California Press, 1986. 27–50.
"Sadakichi Hartmann." *American Poets 1880–1945. Dictionary of Literary Biography* 54. Detroit: Gale Research, 1987. 154–63.
Spooner, Brian. "Weavers and Dealers: The Authenticity of an Oriental Carpet." *The Social Life of Things: Commodities in Cultural Perspective*. Cambridge: Cambridge University Press, 1986. 195–235.
Webster, Jean. *Daddy Long-Legs*. 1912. New York: Bantam, 1982.
Williams, Teresa Kay. "Race-ing and Being Raced: The Critical Interrogation of 'Passing.'" *Amerasia Journal* 23.1 (1997): 61–65.

NOTES

A longer version of this paper is included in my book *Edith and Winnifred Eaton: Chinatown Missions and Japanese Romances*. The book reviews I refer to in this essay come from the Winnifred Eaton Reeve Fonds, Special Collections, University of Calgary Library. My generalizations are based on a sample of over a hundred reviews, covering most of Eaton's career, but with a concentration around 1903–04, the peak of her popularity. Because the reviews were accessible only in the form of clippings that Eaton pasted into a scrapbook, no page numbers are available.

1. *Shabono* is a gripping, self-reflective novel of extended cross-cultural interaction. The narrator is a young female anthropologist studying Indian healing practices in Venezuela. An elderly tribeswoman asks the narrator to follow her to her *shabono* (village) in the jungle. A year-long ritual of initiation into the Yanomama culture follows. The narrator loses her notebooks and ethnographic equipment; unable to write up her experience as a scholarly text, she decides to narrate it as a novel.

2. Eaton's novels *Miss Numè of Japan: A Japanese-American Romance* and *Tama* clearly contain borrowings from all these authors.

3. See Edith Eaton's anonymously published article "The Oppression and Persecution of Me" (1911) for a sampling of the day-to-day abuses a person who claimed Chinese descent could expect to face.

4. Eaton's father, Edward Eaton, studied art in Paris and was already involved in the Far Eastern trade in the 1860s. In an early article titled "The Half-Caste," Eaton writes about the plight of children born to biracial couples in Japan and the West, but she ends with these words: "Perhaps the children of Lafcadio Hearn, the American writer, and those of Sir Edwin Arnold, the English writer, whose mothers are Japanese women, will prove exceptions, as they will doubtless have the protection and love of these great men."

5. Yone Noguchi, born in Japan in 1875, emigrated to the United States at the age of eighteen. He studied poetry under Joaquin Miller and had his first five poems accepted by *The Lark*, a small San Francisco literary magazine. Alternately derided and highly praised, Noguchi went on to become a widely published critic and propagator of the Japanese aesthetic in art and literature (Noguchi 13–54).

6. The Japanese-German writer Sadakichi Hartmann (1850–1904), born in Japan but brought up in Germany, turned the Japanese half of his racial heritage into an asset when writing art criticism. His *A History of American Art* (1902) and *Japanese Art* (1904) were well received, and in the 1910s Hartmann was still producing magazine articles on Japanese poetry, fiction, and drama. See Hartmann, *Sadakichi Hartmann: Critical Modernist*; "Sadakichi Hartmann" 154–63.

THE SEDUCTION OF ORIGINS

SUI SIN FAR AND THE RACE FOR TRADITION

DAVID SHIH

> What might skin have to do with autobiographical writing and autobiographical writing with skin? Certainly discursive capillaries circulate one's "flesh and blood" through the textual body of self-writing, wrapped up as it is in the anatomy of origins and genealogies. Filiations are forged back through forerunners, sometimes forward toward offspring.
>
> —SIDONIE SMITH ("Identity's Body")

On the acknowledgments page of her only book, *Mrs. Spring Fragrance* (1912), Sui Sin Far thanks the editors of some two dozen periodicals "who were kind enough to care for my children when I sent them out into the world, for permitting the dear ones to return to me to be grouped together within this volume" (vii). Edith Maude Eaton, who wrote under the pseudonym Sui Sin Far for most of her literary career, was never married and never bore any children. She considered her stories to be her progeny, and when they "returned" two years before her death—handsomely dressed and bound by A. C. McClurg of Chicago—she must have felt the pride of a mother at the center of a family circle. Over the past decade, Asian American literary criticism has seen fit to extend this metaphor by installing her as the grand maternal figure of *all* Asian American letters. Elizabeth Ammons, for instance, has Sui Sin Far "anticipating her spiritual great granddaughter Maxine Hong Kingston" (106). Annette White-Parks calls her the "foremother to the women writers of Chinese ancestry . . . to whom such contemporary writers as Maxine Hong Kingston and Amy Tan look for roots" (6). Indeed, even other writers of fiction have acknowledged her primacy in the field: the narrator of Fae Ng's novel *Bone* (1993) teaches at the fictitious "Edith Eaton school" on the outskirts of San Francisco's Chinatown. What is it about

Sui Sin Far that inspires such uniform homage? It is fair to say that such positive regard responds in part to her ostensibly unambiguous politics and good timing: Sui Sin Far is widely held to be the first Asian American writer of fiction to portray her subjects in a realistic and sympathetic fashion.[1] White-Parks, for one, is convinced "beyond doubt that the tradition of writers in North America of Asian descent began with Sui Sin Far; more specifically, that she is the founder of the Chinese North American woman writer's tradition" (6).[2] And, in *Assimilating Asians,* Patricia Chu adds that "it is striking how well Eaton, an isolated foremother of the yet to be written Asian American literature, anticipates later writers' concerns" (100). It is as if Sui Sin Far herself had birthed the tradition of Asian American letters, leading many in the field to claim her as a fundamental representative ancestor.

This essay treats a relatively late addition to her oeuvre, the piece for which she arguably is best known, the 1909 autobiographical essay "Leaves from the Mental Portfolio of an Eurasian."[3] "Leaves" in many ways validates the position of priority assigned to her by her scholars: Sui Sin Far did indeed see herself as a pioneer, but not of a transcendent literary tradition. In this essay I argue that her installation as a foremother to current Asian American writers, and to the field as a whole, requires her interpellation as a discrete *racial* and *national* subject—a Chinese American—to the neglect of alternate subject positions developed in her autobiography, positions that deliberately work to destabilize race as a dangerous trope of difference. Although Sui Sin Far featured Chinese Americans in her fiction, and despite her change of name, she resisted identifying herself exclusively along racial or national lines. Her conviction developed out of her experiences with a dominant society that stubbornly persisted in seeing her race as a "natural" or biological component of her identity and as a barrier to equal participation as a national subject. Responding to this preoccupation with her body, Sui Sin Far supplemented her written text with a portrait photograph of herself—a visual text that should be considered as crucial to her self-presentation as her words. Modern reprintings of "Leaves" fail to include the portrait, an oversight attributable, perhaps, to the logocentrism of traditional autobiographical studies. Far from consolidating her reputation as a racial subject—and, as we will see, a national subject—as was a common duty of photography at the turn of the century, her photograph works in tandem with her words to promote an autonomous self free from racial or national determination. Together, both texts challenge the biological rationale of race as a meaningful category by exposing race as a social effect. Read as it originally appeared in the *Independent,* "Leaves" constructs an autobiographical self that necessarily contradicts any uncritical acceptance of Sui Sin Far as a stable "Chinese American" or "Asian American" subject.[4] As we will see, the message behind her autobiographical act raises important questions about the viability and even the need for such a thing as an Asian American literary tradition.

As the title of "Leaves" proclaims, Sui Sin Far was "an Eurasian," the daughter of Grace Trefusis, a Chinese Canadian, and Edward Eaton, a British Canadian. Her birth name, Edith Maude Eaton, eventually gave way to Sui Sin Far, an adopted name that she used in everyday life as well as in her writing.[5] An English transliteration from the Cantonese, Sui Sin Far means "water lily" or "narcissus" (literally "water fragrant flower").[6] Because of her decision to champion the cause of the Chinese in America, a commitment made most visible by her change of name, her biracial heritage stands as no bar sinister to her acceptance today as an "authentic" Asian American. Sui Sin Far led a migratory life that took her from England to England's colonial outposts and across the interior of the United States. Born in Macclesfield, England, in 1865, she left with her family for North America. The family stopped briefly in New York before settling in Montreal. As an adult, Sui Sin Far crisscrossed the continent usually in search of work, making stops in the American Midwest, Jamaica, San Francisco, Los Angeles, Seattle, and Boston before going back to Montreal. The fact that she spent most of her life in Canada (and only fifteen or so years in the United States) clearly problematizes any attempt to claim her solely as an "Asian American," a point to which I will return later in the essay. Certainly most of her important work was written in the United States, and she felt most at home with the Chinese on the West Coast. Yet the pull back to her family in Montreal was always great, and that is where she died in 1914. As she came to understand and articulate, however, racial and national labels meant little to the determination of her authentic self—a conviction that went largely unshared by her editors and reviewers.

Sui Sin Far enjoyed an extended relationship with the magazine *Land of Sunshine*, the preeminent Los Angeles monthly at the fin de siècle, whose editor laid claim to "discovering" her. In his preference of local flavor over literary "merit," Charles F. Lummis shared the tastes of his fellow editors of regional magazines. He found that the stories of Sui Sin Far, "while they lack somewhat of literary finish . . . the instinct of the story is in them all; and while literary graces do count, and are entitled to count, the chief part of a story is—the story" (336). His words augured later reviews, which continued to subordinate her skill as a writer to her authenticity as a cultural insider. The *New York Times* reported, "Miss Eaton has struck a new note in American fiction. She has not struck it very surely, or with surpassing skill. But it has taken courage to strike it at all, and, to some extent, she atones for lack of artistic skill with the unusual knowledge she undoubtedly has of her theme" ("A New Note in Fiction" 405). Compared to her contemporaries Frank Norris and Jack London—writers who largely depended on racist stereotypes for their characterizations of the Chinese—Sui Sin Far managed to translate her access to Chinese immigrant communities into a novel literary perspective.[7] Her Chinese stories were unprecedented in their appearance of authenticity. Lummis praised her characters for having "an insight and sympathy which are probably unique. To others the alien Celestial is at best mere 'literary material'; in these stories he (or she) is a human being" (336). It is clear that the credibility of these characters owed particularly to the *race* of their author: Sui Sin Far was an authentic writer of Chinese stories, not because she circulated among the Chinese—enough writers of sensationalist material did that—but because she herself *was* one of them.[8] Lummis effectively reinvents Sui Sin Far's nationality and racial heritage when he boldly states, "For all her father, she is evidently her mother's daughter—a Chinawoman transplanted and graduated" (336). Reviewers found her work important because it reflected the sensibility of a racial, that is to say, a Chinese, essence.

Modern estimations of Sui Sin Far have continued to promote her authenticity as a racial subject over and above her talent as a literary artist. As an early Chinese American writer, Sui Sin Far "found herself alone in an essentially formless field," explains S. E. Solberg, and had "she been physically stronger and had a more sophisticated literary apprenticeship, she might have been able to create that new form" ("Sui Sin Far" 32–33). In the end, according to Solberg, Sui Sin Far "was not a great writer; she has only one book (a collection of her stories) to her credit, but her attempts deserve recognition" ("Sui Sin Far" 27). Likewise, Amy Ling admits that "though she may not be a writer for all ages, she was certainly an extraordinary person in her own time. As a champion of Chinese rights and women's rights and a writer who focused her attention on depicting the daily lives of Chinese in America, she was a pioneer" ("Edith Eaton" 297). Once again we are asked to judge Sui Sin Far not on the basis of stylistic innovation but on her literary priority as the "First Chinese-American Fictionist" (Solberg, "Sui Sin Far" 27). By conceding that the work of Sui Sin Far does not meet the traditional aesthetic requirements for canonization while insisting that it remains worthy of consideration, Solberg and Ling lay the groundwork for the construction of an alternate literary tradition with altogether different criteria for inclusion. The privileging of genres whose production requires formal apprenticeship, or, at the very least, extended stretches of leisure time, fails to question the partisanship of cultural forces that itself works to establish literary canons and the types of writing (novels, epic poetry, and so forth) constituting them. Rather than pursue the critique of Western canon formation through the writing of Sui Sin Far, however, critics have imagined the possibilities of new traditions and the processes required for their construction. Elizabeth Ammons and Annette White-Parks, for example, have endeavored to install Sui Sin Far as the foundation of a Chinese American literary tradition. Few can deny that over the last decade the figure of Sui Sin Far has undergone a remarkable and important metamorphosis. Why and by what means has a Eurasian short-story writer been transformed into the mother of Chinese American letters?

It may be obvious that my title alludes to Barbara Christian's influential article "The Race for Theory," which questions the move of many influential African American literary critics toward poststructuralist theory in the 1980s. In this essay, I am more concerned about a separate critical practice that also borrows from dominant models and is as intimately involved with the idea of race. What I call the "race for tradition" is the more or less consensual endorsement of a Chinese American literary genealogy based upon the achievements of recognizable literary "ancestors," a practice made possible only by an ahistorical and uncritical eye toward race and nation. The race for tradition coincides with the institutionalization of Asian American literature in the academy, a process that requires Asian American literature to demonstrate, among other things, that its development follows a natural course of progression from its origin to the present. In the recent and continued success of such writers as Amy Tan and Maxine Hong Kingston one may see the inspiration behind a search for literary "roots," even if no direct link exists to the so-called literary ancestors.[9] As a result, race is reified as the basis of a connection between Sui Sin Far and contemporary Chinese American writers, just as T. S. Eliot's "tradition" (what Terry Eagleton notes Eliot sometimes called the "European mind") worked to link the efforts of English poets past and present (Eliot 38–39; Eagleton 40). We can see the materialization of this attitude in Asian American literature course syllabuses, whose organization of materials often serves to naturalize the progression of themes and tropes explored in Sui Sin Far's fiction. Racial identity, in this arena of canon formation, supersedes other possible influences—non–Asian American writing, cultural trends, aesthetic conventions—especially when understood in the context of literary genealogy. Far from establishing her as a suitable literary ancestor, however, Sui Sin Far's half-Chinese heritage necessarily problematizes any facile effort to define her as a racial and national subject. In other words, how we have come to know Sui Sin Far reflects an evident, if not conscious, disregard of her autobiographical self on the part of her scholars.

The effacement of Sui Sin Far's Eurasian (not to mention Canadian) identity by such conspicuous semantic operations as use of the term "Chinese North American" signals a fast and loose interpretation of history, but an interpretation whose ends, however problematic, are not necessarily illaudable.[10] Nevertheless, the present need for Sui Sin Far to be classified as a "Chinese American" (or as one of its cognates) is a historically determined need for race to exist in a stable sense. In other words, the quality that has come to distinguish Sui Sin Far most meaningfully from her contemporaries who also wrote about the Chinese in America is, finally, her race—an especially problematic maneuver in light of recent scholarship on her later writing.[11] In the 1980s, the academy witnessed a signal process of canon building when Henry Louis Gates, Jr., determined that H. E. Wilson, the author of the 1859 sentimental novel *Our Nig,* was not a white man, as had been previously suggested, but Harriet Wilson, a free black woman. "Harriet Wilson became most probably the first Afro-American to publish a novel in the United States," Gates then asserted (cited in Gates xiii). That Wilson was black made all the difference.[12] Any ethnic literary tradition founded on the merits of a single author—even a tradition that appears to oppose dominant interests—participates in a hegemonic process of academic professionalization that privileges canonization as the eminent measure of the worth of that and any other ethnic literature. An unfortunate effect of such a process is the transparent promotion of race as a natural and primary signifier of difference.[13] It is not my purpose to argue that race is a historically based "illusion" that will disappear once people realize it has no biological rationale, but to show how certain critical responses to race and racism can be appropriated by the hegemonic order and stripped of their political value. Sui Sin Far's self-stated claim to be "an Eurasian," for instance, a subject position that she recognized as potentially subversive, has been neglected in the present, in the service of tradition building. "Leaves," as the autobiography of such a contradictory subject, disrupts the taxonomy of the canonization process that would have Sui Sin Far as a representative "Chinese American." Rather, through photography and written text, "Leaves" calls attention to the specific historical circumstances that can and do shape racial formation, namely those nineteenth-century labor interests that "produced" the Chinaman as an economic foe of white labor and the Chinese woman as a detriment to white decency. It is, finally, Sui Sin Far's recognition, in "Leaves," of this alienable quality of race and racism that places this work among her most important contributions.

It is useful periodically to remind ourselves—as Alexander Saxton (*The Indispensable Enemy*), Michael Omi and Howard Winant (*Racial Formation in the United States*), and Henry Louis Gates, Jr., have done—that "race" is a sociohistorical formation whose meaningfulness as a form of categorization emerges out of specific historical conditions. Race is best understood as "an unstable and 'decentered' complex of social meanings constantly being transformed by political struggle" (Omi and Winant 55). As such, it is a constitutive part of our society that is not a "problem" to be overcome so much as it is a process that can be understood and explicated. The origins of racism are not in the body—though racism could not exist without the body, racism's master signifier—but rather in social contact that has allowed a dominant group to ascribe certain negative associations and characteristics to other groups. Saying that race has its origins in the ideological and not in the biological, however, should discount neither its presence nor the importance of its very real and damaging effects. To be sure, one may persuasively argue that it was racism that led to Sui Sin Far's lifelong frailty and premature death. "I have no organic disease," she admits, "but in the light of the present I know that the cross of the Eurasian bore too heavily upon my childish shoulders" (L 127). The "cross" of race was not essential to her being, she recognized, but was a burden *imposed* upon her by the dominant society of her time, as it had been imposed upon Jesus Christ himself by the dominant society of his own. Sui Sin Far remains one of the most evocative figures in Asian American literary studies because she lived and wrote during a remarkable time in Asian American history—the period of incipient and elevating hostility toward the Chinese immigrant that culminated in explicit exclusionary acts based solely on race.

Although there were virtually no Chinese in Montreal by the time Edith Eaton arrived there in 1873, the anti-Chinese movement had been a reality on the Pacific Coast of the United States and Canada for over twenty years. Official and unofficial anti-Chinese sentiment arose in the United States around 1849, soon after the Chinese arrived in California in large numbers.[14] Significant Chinese immigration into British Columbia began nine years later, with anti-Chinese sentiment and legislation also developing there soon afterward. Both immigrations responded to the discovery of gold in the "New" World and stifling economic conditions in the "Old" and were exacerbated in no small part by Western imperial and colonial interventions. Workingmen, politicians, and the sensationalist press, not surprisingly, constituted the majority of the anti-Chinese forces, while the merchant and landowning class primarily made up the pro-Chinese contingent. The threat of unchecked Chinese immigration moved labor interests in California and British Columbia to lobby their state and provincial governments for restrictive measures. These regional measures eventually inspired national exclusionary legislation. In May 1882, California finally convinced President Chester Arthur to sign a revised version of the Chinese Exclusion Act, which made Chinese immigration illegal for the next ten years. The Geary Act of 1892 extended exclusion for another ten years before President Theodore Roosevelt finally made exclusion "permanent" in 1902. The historian Roger Daniels cannily notes that the "burden of much anti-Chinese propaganda can be reduced to a short phrase: 'the Chinese worked cheap and smelled bad'" (52). That economic circumstances caused the initial reaction against the Chinese has been well documented.[15] Out of these circumstances rose objections to immigrants—alleging their foul odor, their diseased touch, their proclivity for thievery and prostitution—that inhered in immigrants as essential to their being.

One can say that it was the pervasiveness of these stereotypes that launched Sui Sin Far's career as a writer. Before adopting her pseudonym, Edith Eaton wrote under her given name as a journalist for the *Montreal Star.* In an 1896 letter ("A Plea for the Chinaman") addressed to the editor of that paper, she advocates the revocation of an 1885 head tax of fifty dollars on Chinese immigrants entering Canada, as well as the dismissal of a proposal to increase the tax to five hundred dollars. The letter calls attention to ignorant, misinformed images of Chinese immigrants, myths that Eaton debunks with common sense and personal testimony. Her most incisive observation focuses on how visual difference is elemental in the production of race. "I believe the chief reason for the prejudice against the Chinese," she writes, "is that they are not considered good looking by white men. . . . That the Chinese do not please our artistic taste is really at the root of all the evil there, and from it [spring] the other objections to the Chinese" (Ling and White-Parks, eds., *Mrs. Spring Fragrance and Other Writings* 197). Eaton's use of the possessive adjective "our" ("our artistic taste") connotes her identification with the dominant white society, but she is already beginning to understand how the body as a visual text is an unfaithful signifier of the "essential" self. Accordingly, it is also in this letter that Eaton introduces her maxim "Individuality is more than nationality" (196). Both observations would take on more significance during her career as Sui Sin Far, achieving their most sustained, powerful, and sophisticated articulation thirteen years later, in "Leaves." Over the course of those years she found outlets for her creative energies in the form of short fiction, though her presentation of these stories ran counter to her developing theories on race.

The many stories Sui Sin Far placed in the popular magazines of the time—*Land of Sunshine, Century, Hampton's, Good Housekeeping*—are accompanied by sketches and designs depicting important scenes or images from the narratives. A number of the stories open with a graphic that either incorporates the title in its design or offsets the start of the written text. In either case, readers encounter a visual element that prepares them in a certain way for the narrative to follow. "A Chinese Boy-Girl" (1904), published in *Century*, even includes the byline of its illustrator, Walter Jack Duncan.[16] The opening graphic features a Chinese youth in "traditional" Chinese attire standing before a bamboo fence (fig. 2.1).[17] *Land of Sunshine* prefaced Sui Sin Far's stories with a few different stock graphics—a bamboo hut, a Chinese youth in ceremonial dress, Chinese women engaged in artistic activities—often using the same graphic for more than one story. The decision to include these illustrations clearly did not issue from the author; *Land of Sunshine* seemingly made their inclusion a standard editorial procedure. These illustrations operate as hermeneutic markers; that is, even before reading the written text, one comes to expect a narrative with "Oriental" characteristics. As a result, the story's characters acquire a distinct "racialized" aspect. By this I mean that the reader expects, or is at least not surprised by, the characters' "exotic" actions—they speak irregular English, commit suicide, and so on—behavior that is socially determined, though such images encourage the reader to believe that they are inherent in "race."

Since its first appearance in the *Independent*, "Leaves" has been reprinted in a number of anthologies and collections. *Chinese America: History and Perspectives*, the journal of the Chinese Historical Society of America, reprinted the essay in its entirety in 1987. The essay appeared in 1991 in *The Big Aiiieeeee!* (ed. Chan et al.) and, in 1995, in *Mrs. Spring Fragrance and Other Writings* (ed. Ling and White-Parks). Its most widespread exposure came from its inclusion in the *Heath Anthology of American Literature* (ed. Lauter, 1990, with editorial contributions by Amy Ling).[18] As originally published, "Leaves" featured a prominent, half-page embellishment atop the first page: a formal portrait photograph of the author, enclosed in an elliptical graphic frame and captioned "Sui Sin Far" (fig. 2.2).[19] This photograph is not reproduced in any of the anthologies that reprinted "Leaves."[20] It is

FIG. 2.1 Illustration by Walter Jack Duncan that accompanied Sui Sin Far's "A Chinese Boy-Girl," *Century*, 1904

unclear whether the decision to include the portrait was that of the editor, William Hayes Ward, or of Sui Sin Far herself.[21] Either way, its inclusion—unlike that of the drawings accompanying Sui Sin Far's stories—could not have occurred without the author's knowledge and participation. To what extent, then, does the addition of the photograph change the autobiographical act? If we are to go by the analyses of extant scholarship, the answer is: not much.[22] Only Nicole Tonkovich appreciates the photograph as an integral part of the essay, and then as a resistant text—a representation of a subject whose cultural codes refuse to cohere with those of the imagistic narrative to follow (253).[23] If, however, Sui Sin Far did indeed intend to proffer her photograph as a consistent and cooperative component of her autobiographical self, what might be its purpose?

The obvious answer is, for the purpose of simple referentiality—to put a face to the story, as it were, and thus defuse the reader's natural suspicion of the autobiographer's art. Insofar as the reader might be skeptical about the veracity of the autobiographical narrative, the photograph "proves" that the writer does, at least, *exist*. But, more important, the photograph ushers the reader into the processes of the autobiographical act. That is, the photograph not only proves to the reader that the author is a real person, it also simultaneously reveals the author's cognizance of the reader—and not just of the reader's materiality but of the reader's condition as a social subject within an established system of signification. The photograph, then, adds another dimension to what Philippe Lejeune has called the "autobiographical pact," which, like Elizabeth Bruss's speech-act model of autobiography, defines the autobiography as "a historically variable *contractual effect*,"

FIG. 2.2 A formal portrait photograph of Sui Sin Far that accompanied the *Independent*'s publication of "Leaves from the Mental Portfolio of an Eurasian," 1909

since it is "a mode of reading as much as it is a type of writing" (Lejeune 30). The reader, in other words, in entering into this contract, stipulates the autobiographer's conformity to standard conventions of narrative and referentiality. To adopt Lejeune's definition, then, we must make a conceptual leap in order to accept that "Leaves" is indeed the product of a person named "Sui Sin Far" at the same time that we understand her "self" to be an effect of language. To accept both propositions is not to contradict ourselves; rather, it is to consider the possibility that autobiography has survived as a discrete genre because of a social need to accept its referentiality. In making the distinction between the autobiographer (understood as an actual person) and the autobiographer's "self" (understood as an effect of language), I agree with Linda H. Rugg, who observes that the "need for a continued assertion of autobiography's referential power is perhaps most obvious in studies of women's and minority autobiography, which deal with the culturally defined bodies of their autobiographical subjects" (10). This understanding is especially critical in reading the autobiography of Sui Sin Far, whose awareness of her body as a social construct is something that can be communicated only by the dialectical relation of her visual and written texts.

The portrait of Sui Sin Far captures the *pose de la femme civilisée,* a three-quarter view of the subject. In this case, we see a dark-haired woman, not quite at middle age, wearing what appears to be a white blouse that covers her neck and arms. A serious expression on her face returns the gaze of the viewer—perhaps the only unusual aspect of the middle-class portrait, whose conventions dictated that the subject not look directly at the camera. Although the name that ostensibly refers to the woman is recognizably Chinese, the woman is not. Neither the woman's face nor her clothing signifies beyond doubt that she is Chinese or Eurasian, though the formal aspect of her visage announces that she may belong to a social class not far removed from that of the reader. Her image is, at first glance, not especially remarkable. Yet the prominence of two other textual signs, "Eurasian" and "Sui Sin Far," force a critical reevaluation of the woman in the portrait: is she really Eurasian, and what makes her so? In her 1895 newspaper article "Half-Chinese Children,"[24] Edith Eaton, speaking of Eurasian children, remarks that "a person who has been informed of the child's parentage, notices at once a peculiar cast about the face. This cast is over the face of every child who has a drop of Chinese blood in its veins. *It is indescribable—but it is there*" (*Mrs. Spring Fragrance and Other Writings* 188; my emphasis). "This cast," that of race, is clearly a social effect, appearing only after one has been informed of its existence. Though "indescribable," it is nonetheless "there" and no less real in its implications. The opening paragraph of "Leaves" describes the author's nurse disclosing to another white woman that the young Sui Sin Far's mother is Chinese. This woman, Sui Sin Far recalls, "turns me around and scans me curiously from head to foot" (L 125). An old man informed of the same fact responds similarly: "He adjusts his eyeglasses and surveys me critically. 'Ah, indeed!' he exclaims, 'Who would have thought it at first glance. Yet now I see the difference between her and other children. What a peculiar coloring! Her mother's eyes and hair and her father's features, I presume. Very interesting little creature!'" (L 126). If the reader returns to the portrait from the written text, he or she must note a change in its significance. Not only does it depict the author of the text that follows, it is now also a separate history itself, open to the interpretation of the viewer. The narrative tempts one to look at the face, not holistically but with a view to its component features: the eyes, the nose, the hair, the coloring. By gazing at the separate features, readers implicate themselves as operating within a system of racial signification, not unlike the nurse's friend and the old man. It is the "fragmented materiality of bodies," Sidonie Smith reminds us, that "helps sustain the illusion of indisputable continuity between biology and culturally constructed identities, the illusion of stable categorizations" (268). But what if the body resists easy categorization? Certain scholars have posited that "race" has become such a naturalized category in our society that an encounter with "someone whom we cannot conveniently racially categorize—someone who is, for example, racially 'mixed' . . . becomes a source of discomfort and momentarily a crisis of racial meaning" (Omi and Winant 59). It is the office of the portrait of Sui Sin Far to bring the individual reader to this discomfiting crisis of meaning.

At this moment of crisis, the observer recognizes that he or she bears the onus of racial signification. As the locus of ambiguous ethnic signs, the Eurasian forces the otherwise transparent process of "reading" race to the fore of consciousness. The possibility always exists, of course, that the observer will pause only long enough to reinscribe race onto the Eurasian ("Ah, indeed!"), and the moment of crisis is irrevocably lost. But the critical observer—he or she who has willingly entered into the autobiographical pact—protracts the moment for the duration of the autobiographical act. It is for this implied reader that Sui Sin Far works to expose the gap between what her portrait "truly" represents and what it might come to signify in a racially hierarchized state: she must articulate how *who she is* contradicts received notions of what is "Chinese." Not surprisingly, what the Chinese do signify to the dominant society is almost uniformly negative in her experience. She admits that when she was a young girl she was no different from white children when it came to regarding the Chinese. In New York, when she comes face to face with the first Chinese other than her mother, she "recoil[s] with a sense of shock" upon spying two "uncouth specimens of their race, drest in working blouses and pantaloons with queues hanging down their backs" (L 126). Only when she and her brother are set upon by a group of children who mock them with cries of "Chinky, Chinky, Chinaman, yellow-face, pig-tail, rat-eater" does she begin to recognize the fallacious correspondence between appearance and behavior (L 126). As a child, she can only respond by asserting an elementary kind of cultural pride: "I'd rather be Chinese than anything else in the world" (L 126). The cues that come to signify race are largely visual: working blouses and pantaloons, queues or pigtails, yellow faces. These lead to the charge of "rat-eater," an association that may have its origins in the ideological or the historical, but not in the biological as the children imply here. The white children derive, however illogically, the behavior of rat eating from having yellow skin and a pigtail. There is little that changes in this regard when

Sui Sin Far and her family move from New York to Montreal. There, she says, the older French and English Canadians "pause and gaze upon us, very much in the same way that I have seen people gaze upon strange animals in a menagerie" (L 127). These people follow this dehumanizing gaze with questions about what it means to be "Chinese": Sui Sin Far remembers that they ask "what we eat and drink, how we go to sleep, if my mother understands what my father says to her, if we sit on chairs or squat on the floors, etc., etc., etc." (L 127). Sui Sin Far, having always had the gaze precipitate a dehumanizing racist response in these and other experiences, and now speaking through the photograph and the written text, cautions her implied reader not to perpetuate such a faulty line of reasoning.

In a society that insists upon attaching meaning to phenotypic signs, one recourse of the racial subject is to compensate by manipulating such signs in order to pass as belonging to another race. Although Sui Sin Far herself never accepted passing as a viable strategy for equal social participation, her siblings made no point of hiding their intent to reject or efface their Chinese ancestry. The "acquaintance" mentioned in "Leaves" who advises her to stop "walking" with Chinamen, out of propriety, is likely her older brother Edward Charles (White-Parks 156). She also speaks of a "half Chinese, half white girl" who lives in fear of being discovered as a Eurasian instead of "one of Spanish or Mexican origin," and who "plaster[s] [her face] with a thick white coat of paint and her eyelids and eyebrows are blackened so that the shape of her eyes and whole expression of her face is changed" (L 131). Scholars identify this woman as Sui Sin Far's sister May (Birchall 19; Ling, "Creating One's Self" 311; White-Parks 37, 156). Later, when Sui Sin Far notes the contemporary phenomenon of Chinese Eurasians passing as Japanese Eurasians, she references another sister, Winnifred, even though she does not mention her by name. By this time she has already seen Winnifred, writing under the pen name of Onoto Watanna, consolidate her reputation as a best-selling Japanese writer by including photographs—including one of herself in a kimono—in her novels *Miss Numè of Japan: A Japanese-American Romance* (1899) and *The Wooing of Wistaria* (1902). Sui Sin Far's appreciation of the colonizing effects of racism allows her to be more forgiving of her siblings than of the dominant society. "The unfortunate Chinese Eurasians!" she laments. "Are not those who compel them to thus cringe more to be blamed than they?" (L 131). "Leaves" even alludes to a "Eurasian," most likely Sui Sin Far herself, who is asked by her fiancé to pretend that she is Japanese once they are married (L 132). The woman refuses and ends the engagement. As an adult, Sui Sin Far realized that her siblings' attempts at passing and her own adolescent assertions of cultural superiority were ultimately ineffective reactions against what amounted to a racist semiotic system. Abetted by visual cues, both reactions reaffirmed the primacy of race and nation in the definition of the self. Any challenge to such an entrenched semiotic system would have to involve a more sophisticated deconstruction of "race" and its phenotypic markers.

By 1909, Sui Sin Far had deliberately divorced her mature self from any one national or racial category. "After all I have no nationality and am not anxious to claim any," she repeats. "Individuality is more than nationality" (L 132).[25] This statement—the defining statement of her oeuvre—cautions against the use of artificial categories of race and nation to objectify the individual. Even the Chinese she meets are culpable, though in a less oppressive manner: they accept her "Chinese hair, color of eyes and complexion," and her love of "rice and tea" as suitable criteria to "settle the matter" of race for them (L 131). But even then she is careful not to align herself with them. "My mother's race is as prejudiced as my father's," she charges. "*Only when the whole world becomes as one family will human beings be able to see clearly and hear distinctly.* I believe that some day a great part of the world will be Eurasian. I cheer myself with the thought that I am but a pioneer. A pioneer should glory in suffering" (L 129; my emphasis). Here, the subject position of the Eurasian allows Sui Sin Far to claim an identity familiar to multiracial persons: as being "beyond" race because she defies easy racial categorization.[26] In the present, people are unable to "see clearly and hear distinctly" because their senses—as possible pathways to enlightenment—are occluded by the artificial meanings produced by visual cues: the almond eye, the pigtail, and so on. The blanched face and blackened eye only underscore and perpetuate the primacy of visual difference as a master signifier. Sui Sin Far prophesies that in time a radical shift in the racial makeup of the dominant society will liberate the senses. Only then will racism cease to exist, because racial difference itself will ostensibly be bred out of existence. In the meantime, she implies, we must train ourselves to avoid seeing race as the sine qua non of identity.

Toward this end, Sui Sin Far synthesizes the authorizing discourses of autobiography and photography. Although classification as autobiography has never shielded a text from suspicion of fictionalization, it remains true that the genre in all its myriad forms—memoir, confession, and the like—has been and still is the genre most closely associated with authenticity. By the beginning of the twentieth century, authenticity and the "human element" had become even greater imperatives within biographical letters, displacing the distant hagiographic style of nineteenth-century biographies of "great men." According to Scott E. Casper, "twentieth-century critics dismissed biographies written for didactic, political, or moral purposes as 'impure.' Instead they championed ones that revealed the subject's 'innermost self'" (319). Casper notes that biography took a psychological turn at this cultural moment, a development owing in part to the influence of Freud's psychoanalytic theories, so that "ordinary" people became interested in their own selves, the unconscious currents running through them, and the benefit of writing about them (326). It was around this time that autobiography, which had been considered a kind of biography through the nineteenth century, grew out of such personal investigations to become an ontologically separate form. In June 1909, five months after the publication of "Leaves," William Dean Howells offered his impressions on the state of autobiography (795), whose yet indeterminate aesthetic was rather remarkably represented in material form by a two-volume autobiography by F. B. Sanborn—one volume treating his public life, the other his personal life. Howells was clear, however, that future American autobiographical writing should resemble the latter of the two volumes, and he called for a more intimate correspondence between the real and the represented, especially from that part of society not traditionally associated with the genre: "We shall ourselves go no farther than to express the wish that more women would write their own lives, and be entirely frank about them" (797). As we have seen, in its focus on "real" feeling, particularly its concern with how the psychological damage wrought by racism can be physically debilitating, "Leaves" was a product of this liminal moment of autobiographical writing in America.

Given the dissonance that Sui Sin Far reports having experienced in her relationships with others, most of whom saw in her only what they wanted to see—a white woman, a Chinese prostitute, a Japanese bride—it is not surprising that photography should have entered the autobiographical act as an additional means of control over self-image. Indeed, we are encouraged to view Sui Sin Far's portrait as a representation of the sovereign subject, the self unmediated by artificial meanings, just as "pure" autobiography eschewed the moral or political tropes of nineteenth-century biography. Photographs, according to Rugg, "can (have been, are, will) be taken as 'natural' signs, the result of a wholly mechanical and objective process, in which the human holding the camera plays an incidental role in recording 'truth'" (5).[27] This conviction was even stronger at the turn of the century. The great task of the nineteenth-century portrait photographer was to reveal the subject's inner or moral "character" on his or her exterior appearance (Trachtenberg 27–29). If the subject were pure or sincere in intention, then his or her face would register that state (just as the body would betray a criminal or pathological element). Because her image proffers no obvious signifiers of racial difference, Sui Sin Far left it to the viewer to identify them: unlike the publishers of her short stories, she refused to determine the reading of her written text by overdetermining the visual. She deliberately resisted the temptation to "trade" on her "nationality," the advice of those who, as she remembers, "tell me that if I wish to succeed in literature in America I should dress in Chinese costume, carry a fan in my hand, [and] wear a pair of scarlet beaded slippers" (L 132). Her adoption of a pioneering identity without racial or national borders coincided with a movement of "internationalism" brought about by the invention of photography, whose message did not require translation, as did the written or spoken word, and so suggested a universal system of language (Rugg 134). Her portrait, as Sui Sin Far represented in her most pure and enlightened state, completes the autobiographical self *and* indexes the relative enlightenment of her peers. Will race continue to be a divisive and destructive category? Can individuality be more than nationality? The portrait intends to demystify race—and thus defuse its exploitative potential—by demonstrating at first hand that race is a production of the dominant gaze, the paradigmatic impaired sense.

It is easy to say now that Sui Sin Far did not fully appreciate how her self-presentation signified white bourgeois mores more than it did the condition of the Chinese immigrant working class.[28] She was an adherent of the tenets of bourgeois humanism, and her conception of the individual self was an idea invigorated by the mid-nineteenth-century practice of photography as a referential art. As a medium of representation, photography especially revealed the distance between her situation and that of the Chinese immigrant. As Shawn M. Smith has noted, by the turn of the century photography was playing an important role in linking racial essence to national identity. "Within eugenics itself," says Smith, "photographs were used to illustrate the biological roots of social structures" (162). Thus Sui Sin Far's photograph aligns her, regardless of her intentions, with those who chose to sit for a portrait rather than with the Chinese (opium addicts, female "slaves") whose likenesses were objectified by the pseudosociological photography of the time and those whose images were catalogued for official documentary purposes (with immigration papers, marriage certificates, and so on).[29] Just as photography developed as a mode of self-expression, so too did it become an instrument of the state, a means of classification and control. Given the lack of agency these immigrants (or slaves, criminals, and others) had over the presentation of their images, photography not only heightened the difference between them and the bourgeois individual but also made that difference appear "natural" and self-evident. The portrait of Sui Sin Far, if originally conceived as a visual text that would, in conjunction with the written one, disrupt the play of signifiers, likely served to lessen any sense of difference felt by the Republican readership of the *Independent.*[30] The meaning produced by her dress and posture worked to bring her social status into line with that of her readership: the "individual" looked suspiciously like a white middle-class woman.[31] Her advocacy of the Chinese in America derived from her position *between* the Chinese immigrant working class and white middle-class society, a role that enabled readers of the *Independent, Century, Good Housekeeping,* and other journals to imagine a Chinese presence through her but without having to confront radical difference themselves.[32] As a result, Sui Sin Far came across less as a pioneer in any radical sense than as the sort that had descended from nineteenth-century ideals of democratic reform, allowing her readers to resolve their respective "crises" of meaning by locating her within a familiar tradition of feminine discourse.

From the subject position of the Eurasian, Sui Sin Far estimated "race" to be an obsolete effect that eventually would be bred out of existence, but one that could be overcome in the present through a concerted effort by the dominant society and the racial subject. Rather than catalyzing a revolution in thought, however, her portrait illustrates that race is a discourse that can be discarded only insofar as the racial subject is able to pass as white. For all the political potential of the message "Individuality is more than nationality," it is one not easily adopted by others of Chinese ancestry. Though Sui Sin Far meant to liberate the subject from racial and national identification, only she as a British Eurasian could do so. Perhaps the most widely voiced objection to the Chinese, from the nineteenth century through the present, and one that often has precipitated violence against them, has been their supposed indifference to American political institutions (no matter that state and national legislation systematically excluded them from participation in the legal system, and from the rights to naturalization, suffrage, property, and testimony in court against whites). Their perceived allegiance to China contributed to their reputation as a people inassimilable to American society. After 1882, only Chinese diplomats, students, and merchants could enter the country legally. For all other Chinese, race was married to nationality by law:

if they lived in the United States and did not belong to one of the three aforementioned classes, they *had to be* American citizens. The only ways for Chinese to gain entry into the country were to prove native citizenship or claim a citizen as a parent (the latter circumstance makes one a citizen regardless of one's country of birth). Sui Sin Far's ease in crossing national borders—from Canada to Jamaica, and from Canada to the United States and back again—speaks to the privilege she enjoyed as a half-white, educated woman. She had "no nationality" and was "not anxious to claim any," but thousands of Chinese "paper sons" endured interrogation and risked deportation in hopes of claiming an American citizenship denied them by law.[33] For these men and women (women, too, could be "paper sons"), the path to enfranchisement necessarily went through the adoption of a national identity.

In her later writing, Sui Sin Far furthers the troubling notion that acculturation through dress and habit is a positive step toward the social harmony she envisioned in "Leaves." Nine months before her death, in 1914, the article "Chinese Workmen in America" (1913) describes the state of her thoughts on the relation between race and nation:

> I noticed in one of the Sunday schools I visited in San Francisco that half of the little girls were dressed like American children, while the other half wore the dress of the Chinese woman, which is almost as old in style as the setting sun. I was told that in some cases, the ancient dress was obliged to be worn as a punishment, the modern permitted as a reward. . . . In the eastern states the Chinese public school children wear only the American dress [57–58].

Sui Sin Far's radical prophecy, in "Leaves," of an inevitable Eurasian society softens into a patient anticipation of melting-pot assimilation. The shift that Sui Sin Far now envisions is primarily ideological, not biological: "There are hundreds of Chinese children in America. Most of them are born here, and as their environment is more American than Chinese, *it is safe to say that the next generation will see many Americans whose ancestors were Chinese*" (57; my emphasis).[34] Not only does the assimilation she describes erase the histories of discrimination and violence specific to the Chinese, it also is predicated on the continued exclusion of Chinese immigrants, whose presence necessarily alters the cultural homogeneity of San Francisco or Boston.

How far critical interpretation strays from authorial intention has never been as interesting as why the interpretation is what it is. I hardly need repeat that the legacy of Sui Sin Far is a valuable one. As early as 1974 the editors of *Aiiieeeee!* (Chin et al.) identified Sui Sin Far as one of three Chinese American writers not writing from a white racist tradition. As such, she anticipated the works of such writers as John Okada and Louis Chu, who have appreciably lost some of the cultural prestige won for them by the *Aiiieeeee!* group in the 1970s.[35] (Sui Sin Far precedes all other creative writers—including Okada and Chu—in the later volume edited by Chan et al., *The Big Aiiieeeee!*) The revival of interest over the past decade in Sui Sin Far's work is also related to the popularity of more recent works by such women as Maxine Hong Kingston and Amy Tan. This alternate tradition emphasizes the significant social contributions of Chinese American women, whose presence is effaced by every mention of a Chinese American "bachelor society." In light of this project, the emergence of Sui Sin Far as the spiritual foremother to Kingston and Tan seems entirely logical because it is only upon her work that a *tradition* of Chinese American literature can be built. But the terrain of tradition is a contested one, to say the least. Does the prose of Sui Sin Far lead up to that of, say, Louis Chu—altogether bypassing that of Jade Snow Wong—or does it not reference him at all and instead leap forward to greet that of late-twentieth-century women writers? Either way, what seems not to be in dispute is that Sui Sin Far stands at the fore of multiple versions of the Chinese American literary "tradition." These traditions, whether born of cultural nationalist or feminist politics, tend to obscure or vitiate Sui Sin Far's achievement in "Leaves." A critical reading of Sui Sin Far enables us not to assemble an alternate canon from the ground up, but rather to consider how ethnic texts emerge out of particular historical circumstances and not out of one or another mythic tradition.

Literary traditions are related to cultural traditions by their invented nature. When scholars claim Sui Sin Far as a "spiritual foremother" to later writers, their message should be taken to assert less the existence of an essential racial connection than the consistency of a hegemonic order capable of producing "Leaves from the Mental Portfolio of an Eurasian" or *The Woman Warrior*. In the case of Sui Sin Far, the tastes of literary culture at the fin de siècle demanded regionalia and exotica at the expense of artistic "merit." Dominika Ferens credits the literary careers of Sui Sin Far and Onoto Watanna partly to an established and healthy tradition of missionary and amateur ethnographic writing about China and Japan (21). And while Kingston's *The Woman Warrior* is largely regarded as the epitome of Asian American artistry, it too arose out of and benefited from a confluence of emerging and ascendant movements and sensibilities in the 1970s: postmodernism, ethnic studies, feminism, and others. In the absence of any acknowledged influence between Sui Sin Far and Kingston or Tan, it may be more appropriate to say that the literary tastes of the 1990s, shaped by the material realities resulting from post-1965 immigration, are descended from the tastes of the 1890s, which reflected the changes brought on by the great waves of southern and eastern European immigrants and the nation's emergence as a world power. Richard Brodhead has argued that the late-nineteenth-century rise of regional and "local color" fiction in American literature reflected an elite acknowledgment of the changes that ethnic immigration posed for cultural and national homogeneity (137). In a similar vein, David Palumbo-Liu explains that "one way to understand the recent interest in diversity is to see it as a mode of managing a crisis of race, ethnicity, gender, and labor in the First World and its relations with the Third as late capitalism has fostered the uneven flow of capital, products, materials, and labor across more porous borders" (6). The question of how these fin de siècle crises of diversity are managed by their respective cultural institutions—publishing houses, universities, and the like—may be the most salient link between the works of such writers as Sui Sin Far and Maxine Hong Kingston. (Is it any surprise that autobiography was and still is the dominant discourse through which the Asian enters the national consciousness?) Though it is more romantic to imagine a genealogical line of literary succession, it is important to remember that the line is simply that: an imaginary construct whose purpose is to legitimate the place of an alternate tradition—here, Asian American literature—within or alongside the dominant Western canon.

As the recognized progenitor of the Chinese American—and, by extension, Asian American—literary tradition, Sui Sin Far is the logical starting point for a critique of contemporary canon formation. Many scholars have already pointed out the pitfalls of an uncritical multiculturalism that merely juxtaposes a "minor" canon to the "major" canon without first challenging the process of canon formation itself (West, "Minority Discourse" and *Keeping Faith*; Lowe, "Canon, Institutionalization, Identity" and *Immigrant Acts*). Perhaps, in an effort to legitimate Asian American literature during a time of the greatest mainstream interest in it, we have fallen back on tradition building as the most direct path to such a goal. For this purpose, Sui Sin Far is a seductive cultural icon. The flattening effect of liberal multiculturalism as university policy, however, can smother disruptive and subversive energies (those released by group-specific discrimination) under the ostensibly democratic aegis of "diversity." As critical multiculturalists, we must remain aware of our own participation in this particular hegemony and remember that even

> so-called noninstrumental approaches [to literature] are themselves always already implicated in the raging battle in one's society and culture. The fundamental question is not how one's canon can transcend this battle but rather how old or new canons, enlarged or conflicting canons, guide particular historical interpretations of this battle and enable individual and collective action within it [West, *Keeping Faith* 43].

"Leaves," at its most useful and radical, challenges the uncritical insertion of race into our discourse, a reification that must, to some degree, attend the canonization process. For if we imagine canonization as the process by which a dominant authority agrees to accept nontraditional works, on condition that they conform to a normative aesthetic, then we might visualize its material analogue in those uniform(ed) rows of Chinese American schoolchildren who will not see another Chinese freely enter the country for another thirty years.

BIBLIOGRAPHY

Ammons, Elizabeth. *Conflicting Stories: American Women Writers at the Turn into the Twentieth Century.* New York: Oxford University Press, 1992.

Bergland, Betty. "Rereading Photographs and Narratives in Ethnic Autobiography: Memory and Subjectivity in Mary Antin's *The Promised Land.*" *Memory, Narrative, and Identity: New Essays in Ethnic American Studies.* Ed. Amritjit Singh, Joseph T. Skerrett, Jr., and Robert E. Hogan. Boston: Northeastern University Press, 1994. 45–88.

Birchall, Diana. *Onoto Watanna: The Story of Winnifred Eaton.* Urbana: University of Illinois Press, 2001.

Brodhead, Richard H. *Cultures of Letters: Scenes of Reading and Writing in Nineteenth-Century America.* Chicago: University of Chicago Press, 1993.

Bruss, Elizabeth W. *Autobiographical Acts: The Changing Situation of a Literary Genre.* Baltimore: Johns Hopkins University Press, 1976.

Casper, Scott E. *Constructing American Lives: Biography and Culture in Nineteenth Century America.* Chapel Hill: University of North Carolina Press, 1999.

Chan, Jeffery Paul, et al., eds. *The Big Aiiieeeee! An Anthology of Chinese American and Japanese American Literature.* New York: Meridian, 1991.

Chin, Frank, et al., eds. *Aiiieeeee! An Anthology of Asian American Writers.* 1974. New York: Mentor, 1991.

Christian, Barbara. "The Race for Theory." *Cultural Critique* 6 (1987): 51–63.
Chu, Louis. *Eat a Bowl of Tea*. 1961. Secaucus: Lyle Stuart, 1979.
Chu, Patricia P. *Assimilating Asians: Gendered Strategies of Authorship in Asian America*. Durham: Duke University Press, 2000.
Daniels, Roger. *Asian America: Chinese and Japanese in the United States since 1850*. Seattle: University of Washington Press, 1988.
Dougherty, Robin. "The Scholar and the Novel: A Case of Literary Detection." *Boston Globe* 23 June 2002: E4.
Doyle, James. "Sui Sin Far and Onoto Watanna: Two Early Chinese-Canadian Authors." *Canadian Literature* 140 (1994): 50–58.
Eagleton, Terry. *Literary Theory: An Introduction*. Minneapolis: University of Minnesota Press, 1983.
Eliot, T. S. "Tradition and the Individual Talent." *Selected Prose of T. S. Eliot*. Ed. Frank Kermode. New York: Harcourt Brace, 1975: 37–44.
Ferens, Dominika. *Edith & Winnifred Eaton: Chinatown Missions and Japanese Romances*. Urbana: University of Illinois Press, 2002.
Gates, Henry Louis, Jr. Introduction. *Our Nig; or, Sketches from the Life of a Free Black*. By Harriet E. Wilson. New York: Vintage, 1983.
Hartnell, Ella S. "Some Little Heathens." *Land of Sunshine* 5 (1896): 153–57.
Howells, William D. "Editor's Easy Chair." *Harper's Monthly* 119.713 (1909): 795–98.
Kim, Elaine H. Preface. *Charlie Chan Is Dead: An Anthology of Contemporary Asian American Fiction*. Ed. Jessica Hagedorn. New York: Penguin, 1993: vii–xiv.
Lauter, Paul, ed. *The Heath Anthology of American Literature*. Vol. 2. Lexington: Heath, 1990.
Lejeune, Philippe. *On Autobiography*. Ed. Paul John Eakin. Trans. Katherine Leary. Minneapolis: University of Minnesota Press, 1989.
Lim, Shirley G. "The Tradition of Chinese American Women's Life Stories: Thematics of Race and Gender in Jade Snow Wong's *Fifth Chinese Daughter* and Maxine Hong Kingston's *The Woman Warrior*." *American Women's Autobiography: Fea(s)ts of Memory*. Ed. Margo Culley. Madison: University of Wisconsin Press, 1992. 252–67.
Ling, Amy. *Between Worlds: Women Writers of Chinese Ancestry*. New York: Pergamon, 1990.
———. "Creating One's Self: The Eaton Sisters." *Reading the Literatures of Asian America*. Ed. Shirley Geok-lin Lim and Amy Ling. Philadelphia: Temple University Press, 1992. 305–18.
———. "Edith Eaton: Pioneer Chinamerican Writer and Feminist." *American Literary Realism* 16 (1983): 287–98.
Lowe, Lisa. "Canon, Institutionalization, Identity: Contradictions for Asian American Studies." *The Ethnic Canon: Histories, Institutions, and Interventions*. Ed. David Palumbo-Liu. Minneapolis: University of Minnesota Press, 1995. 48–68.
———. *Immigrant Acts: On Asian American Cultural Politics*. Durham: Duke University Press, 1996.

Lummis, Charles F. "In Western Letters." *Land of Sunshine* 13.5 (1900): 332–36.
McCunn, Ruthanne L. *Chinese American Portraits: Personal Histories, 1828–1988*. San Francisco: Chronicle Books, 1988.
Mott, Frank L. *A History of American Magazines, 1741–1930*. 5 vols. Cambridge: Harvard University Press, 1958.
Nee, Victor G., and Brett de Bary Nee. *Longtime Californ': A Documentary Study of an American Chinatown*. New York: Pantheon, 1973.
"A New Note in Fiction." *New York Times* 7 July 1912: 405.
Ng, Fae M. *Bone*. New York: Hyperion, 1993.
Omi, Michael, and Howard Winant. *Racial Formation in the United States from the 1960s to the 1990s*. 2nd ed. New York: Routledge, 1994.
Palumbo-Liu, David. Introduction. *The Ethnic Canon: Histories, Institutions, and Interventions*. Ed. David Palumbo-Liu. Minneapolis: University of Minnesota Press, 1995. 1–27.
"Recent Makers of Chautauqua Literature." *The Chautauquan* 43.5 (1906): 421–47.
Ropp, Steven M. "Do Multiracial Subjects Really Challenge Race? Mixed-Race Asians in the United States and the Caribbean." *Amerasia Journal* 23.1 (1997): 1–16.
Rugg, Linda H. *Picturing Ourselves: Photography and Autobiography*. Chicago: University of Chicago Press, 1997.
Ruland, Richard. "Art and a Better America." Review of *The Heath Anthology of American Literature*. *American Literary History* 3.2 (1991): 357–59.
Saxton, Alexander. *The Indispensable Enemy: Labor and the Anti-Chinese Movement in California*. Berkeley: University of California Press, 1971.
Shih, David. "'Against Being Aggressively Chinese': The Autobiographical Writings of Sui Sin Far." Theorizing Culture and Political Strategies panel. Association for Asian American Studies Conference. Cathedral Hill Hotel, San Francisco. 8 May 2003.
Smith, Shawn M. *American Archives: Gender, Race, and Class in Visual Culture*. Princeton: Princeton University Press, 1999.
Smith, Sidonie. "Identity's Body." *Autobiography and Postmodernism*. Ed. Kathleen Ashley, Leigh Gilmore, and Gerald Peters. Amherst: University of Massachusetts Press, 1994. 266–92.
Solberg, S. E. "Sui Sin Far/Edith Eaton: First Chinese-American Fictionist." *MELUS* 8.1 (1981): 27–39.
———. "Sui, the Storyteller: Sui Sin Far (Edith Eaton), 1867–1914." *Turning Shadows into Light: Art and Culture of the Northwest's Early Asian/Pacific Community*. Ed. Mayumi Tsutakawa and Alan Chong Lau. Seattle: Young Pine Press, 1982. 85–90.
Sui Sin Far. "A Chinese Boy-Girl." *Century* Apr. 1904: 828–31.
———. "The Chinese in America: Intimate Study of Chinese Life in America, Told in a Series of Short Sketches—An Interpretation of Chinese Life and Character." *Westerner* 10 (1909): 24–26.

———. "Chinese Workmen in America." *Independent* 3 July 1913: 56–58.

———. "The Gamblers." *Fly Leaf* 1 (1896): 14–18.

———. "Leaves from the Mental Portfolio of an Eurasian." *Chinese America: History and Perspectives* 1 (1987): 169–83.

———. "Leaves from the Mental Portfolio of an Eurasian." *Independent* 21 Jan. 1909: 125–32.

———. *Mrs. Spring Fragrance.* Chicago: A. C. McClurg, 1912.

———. *Mrs. Spring Fragrance and Other Writings.* 1912. Ed. Amy Ling and Annette White-Parks. Urbana: University of Illinois Press, 1995.

———. "The Sugar Cane Baby." *Good Housekeeping* May 1910: 570–72.

Tonkovich, Nicole. "Genealogy, Genre, Gender: Sui Sin Far's 'Leaves from the Mental Portfolio of an Eurasian.'" *Beyond the Binary: Reconstructing Cultural Identity in a Multicultural Context.* Ed. Timothy B. Powell. New Brunswick: Rutgers University Press, 1999. 236–60.

Trachtenberg, Alan. *Reading American Photographs: Images as History, Mathew Brady to Walker Evans.* New York: Hill and Wang, 1989.

West, Cornel. *Keeping Faith.* New York: Routledge, 1993.

———. "Minority Discourse and the Pitfalls of Canon Formation." *Yale Journal of Criticism* 1.1 (1987): 193–201.

White-Parks, Annette. *Sui Sin Far/Edith Maude Eaton: A Literary Biography.* Urbana: University of Illinois Press, 1995.

Wong, Sau-ling C. *Reading Asian American Literature: From Necessity to Extravagance.* Princeton: Princeton University Press, 1993.

Wu, William F. *The Yellow Peril: Chinese Americans in American Fiction, 1850–1940.* Hamden: Archon, 1982.

Yin, Xiao-Huang. "Between the East and West: Sui Sin Far—the First Chinese-American Woman Writer." *Arizona Quarterly* 47.4 (1991): 49–84.

NOTES

1. Her short story "The Gamblers" (1896) in the journal *Fly Leaf* is generally considered to be the first work of fiction published in the United States by a person of Chinese ancestry.

2. Others have reached the same conclusion. The *Aiiieeeee!* editors acknowledge Sui Sin Far as "one of the first to speak for an Asian American sensibility that was neither Asian nor white American" (Chin et al. 3). The title of S. E. Solberg's 1981 article ("Sui Sin Far/Edith Eaton: First Chinese-American Fictionist") is the most concise expression of this deduction. The same goes for Xiao-Huang Yin's "Between the East and West: Sui Sin Far—the First Chinese-American Woman Writer." Amy Ling concludes that in "a sympathetic and realistic way, Eaton was the first to explore this field [of writing about the Chinese in America]" ("Edith Eaton" 297). And James

Doyle regards her as "the first professional writer of Chinese ancestry in North America" (50).

3. Henceforth all page-number citations of this work, in the body of this essay and in the notes, will be preceded by L. This work will be otherwise referred to as "Leaves."

4. It is not my intention to conflate these two terms, especially given the influence that "earlier" Asian American groups, such as Chinese Americans and Japanese Americans, have had in determining the image of the "Asian American" in the dominant imagination. Rather, I am responding to earlier estimations of Sui Sin Far, which, in their effort to define an "Asian American" literary tradition, have extrapolated "Asian American" identity from "Chinese American," itself extrapolated from Sui Sin Far's preferred term of "Eurasian" (White-Parks 6).

5. The author notes being called "Little Miss Sui" as a child by her nurse, though this may be an obvious case of embellishment (L 125). She is quoted as saying that she used "both an English and a Chinese name" in real life (Yin 81). Hereafter, speaking within the context of "Leaves," I will refer to the author as Sui Sin Far and not as Edith Eaton.

6. The spelling of her name underwent minor phonetic changes throughout her career—from Sui Seen Far to Sui Sin Fah—but had fixed on Sui Sin Far by the time of her autobiography.

7. See Wu for an extensive study of the characterization and use of the Chinese in American fiction.

8. The extent to which "race" determines what does and does not constitute ethnic literature—that is, can a person who is white represent the experiences of those who are not?—continues to be an important and controversial topic of discussion within the field. One might regard the tacit understanding that only works written by persons of Asian descent be considered "Asian American" as a provisional intervention responding to such racialist works as those of Sax Rohmer (Fu Manchu) and Earl Derr Biggers (Charlie Chan). The urgency of this understanding will fade when more writers of color are allowed greater access to publishing. The popularity of such recent works as Robert Olen Butler's *A Good Scent from a Strange Mountain* (1992), David Guterson's *Snow Falling on Cedars* (1994), and Arthur S. Golden's *Memoirs of a Geisha* (1997) will undoubtedly keep the debate open and lively within the academy.

9. When asked about a Chinese American autobiographical tradition, Kingston says: "I am not sure that I got help from a former generation of Chinese-American writers except for Jade Snow Wong: actually her book was the only available one" (quoted in Lim 256).

10. Sau-ling C. Wong sees the common practice of subsuming Asian Canadian literature beneath the rubric of Asian American literature as a "matter of temporary, strategic alliance-forging" (16) that must, at least for now, remain in effect.

11. The pitfalls associated with understanding race as a viable narrative through

which to read disparate texts are, I hope, readily perceived. Still, we should consider that Sui Sin Far's association with the Chinese and with Chinese culture has been called recently into question. Dominika Ferens (21) reveals that much of Sui Sin Far's knowledge of Chinese culture came from her reading of Reverend Justus Doolittle's *Social Life of the Chinese.* Likewise, I have suggested ("'Against Being Aggressively Chinese'") that Sui Sin Far, in a later autobiographical essay, distanced herself from the Chinese in America on the basis of her biracial identity and social class.

12. Gates learned of Wilson's race from the death certificate of her son, George, which lists her as a black woman. "Ironically," Gates says, "George's death certificate helped to rescue his mother from literary oblivion" (Gates xiii). Twenty years later, in 2002, Gates again made history when he announced that he had purchased the only known copy of the first novel written by a black slave—also a woman—Hannah Crafts's *The Bondwoman's Narrative* (reported in Dougherty, "The Scholar and the Novel" E4).

13. Though nothing like the debate over race and theory among Joyce A. Joyce, Henry Louis Gates, Jr., and Houston Baker has occurred within Asian American literary studies, one can see how an obdurate insistence upon "tradition" might inspire similar essentialisms.

14. By 1852, anti-Chinese sentiment had inspired resolutions passed by white miners complaining of unfair competition; it also led to gubernatorial directives addressing checks on Asiatic immigration (Daniels 33–36).

15. See Saxton, "The Indispensable Enemy," for an analysis of the effect of Chinese immigration on California labor practices.

16. "The Sugar Cane Baby" (1910), in *Good Housekeeping,* also includes an illustrator credit (Cushman Parker). The opening graphic is of an Asian baby's face surrounded by butterflies.

17. The most lavishly presented of her stories, "A Chinese Boy-Girl" also included a near-full-page drawing by Duncan (rendered as a halftone engraving by J. W. Evans) and a concluding graphic depicting three Chinese babies playing with a dragon.

18. The *Heath Anthology* was significant for its inclusion of previously "marginalized" or "minority" authors. Critics of the project complained that it reduced "aesthetic value" to a negligible criterion in evaluating creative expression. See Ruland, "Art and a Better America," for an overview of the anthology's inception and reception.

19. This was not the only photograph of the author to appear in a publication during her lifetime. A photograph of a similarly posed—though much younger—Sui Sin Far (then Sui Sin Fah) accompanied *Land of Sunshine* editor Charles F. Lummis's "In Western Letters" column, which introduced the magazine's readers to its contributors. Similarly, the *Chautauquan,* in 1906, included another portrait photograph ("Recent Makers of Chautauqua Literature" 443). These photographs are an element of the editors' texts, however, not of Sui Sin Far's.

20. Betty Bergland's essay "Rereading Photographs and Narratives in Ethnic

Autobiography" identifies the same type of omission from recent reprintings of Mary Antin's 1912 "ethnic" autobiography, *The Promised Land.*

21. Frank L. Mott notes that after Ward assumed the editorship of the *Independent,* in 1896, he began to change the journal to include "articles on current problems by competent men and women, some fiction, and a little illustration," and that this "latter feature increased, especially after 1902" (377).

22. In *Between Worlds,* Amy Ling provides two photographs of Sui Sin Far, though not the one that accompanies "Leaves." S. E. Solberg ("Sui Sin Far" 27) mentions two published photographs of Sui Sin Far, including fig. 2.2 above, and observes how easy it would have been for her to pass as white. In a separate essay ("Sui, the Storyteller" 85) he includes the original photograph along with excerpts from the essay. Xiao-Huang Yin includes the same photograph as Ling and adds a footnote echoing Solberg's assertion: "Both her photo and her own testimony seem to indicate that her appearance is much more 'Occidental' than 'Oriental'" (81). Ruthanne L. McCunn does the same (83). Annette White-Parks observes, "A photo covers half of the first page, the face behind the name 'Sui Sin Far' looking intense and somber," adding that the narrator speaks "with a straightforward sobriety that matches the eyes in the photograph" (154–55). Solberg and Yin touch on the relation of visual cues to "race," but their intention is to underscore the point that Sui Sin Far bravely chose not to pass as a white woman. Most interest in the photographs seems to arise from their capacity to supplement the *biographical,* not autobiographical, act.

23. Tonkovich reads the essay itself as a figurative photo album whose individual scenes evoke the quality of snapshots in their presentation and description. She argues that this aspect of "Leaves" destabilizes the public's confidence in photography—particularly that of children—as a reliable measure of genetic "purity" (244).

24. Though no byline appeared with the article, Annette White-Parks traces the piece to Edith Eaton; see Ling and White-Parks (170) for her criteria.

25. At this point there is a decided conflation of the concepts of race and nationality in Sui Sin Far's writing. First, in the inaugural article of a series titled "The Chinese in America" (1909), published after "Leaves," and then later, in "Chinese Workmen in America" (1913), she uses the term "Chinese-Americans" to denote those "Chinese who come to live in this land, to make their homes in America, if only for a while" ("Chinese Workmen in America" 56).

26. Steven M. Ropp notes the contemporaneity of this idea of an idealized multiraciality, which "denies" race by taking the form of "'pretty soon, everyone will be mixed,' or 'race doesn't matter'" (4).

27. Rugg notes that such men as Roland Barthes and Paul de Man, infinitely skeptical about the referentiality of language, "seem to become remarkably gullible when it comes to photographs," believing them to be actual representations of a past reality (11).

28. This should not imply that Sui Sin Far was not attuned to her situation as a lower-middle-class working woman. As a part-time journalist and writer, she found

it difficult to earn a living wage, a situation that effectively precluded her aspirations to complete a novel. In addition to supporting herself, she regularly sent checks back to her family in Montreal. The regular remittances she received from magazines were an important supplement to her income.

29. See Hartnell's "Some Little Heathens" for an example of this kind of photography. The article appeared in *Land of Sunshine*, a journal that, as we have seen, published a number of Sui Sin Far's stories.

30. Originally conceived as a Congregationalist journal, the *Independent* had endorsed progressive political movements from its inception, from abolition (and its denouncement of the fugitive slave law) to women's suffrage.

31. My reading of the bourgeois quality of the photograph differs from that of Tonkovich, who sees the "disjunction between image and text echo[ing] the episodic and non-linear structure of 'Leaves' and the portfolio form generally" (252).

32. In *Edith & Winnifred Eaton: Chinatown Missions and Japanese Romances*, Dominika Ferens convincingly argues that Sui Sin Far adopted an ethnographic approach in her fiction about the Chinese in America, particularly as concerns the stories in *Mrs. Spring Fragrance*.

33. Those Chinese known as "paper sons" were admitted into the country fraudulently, through claims of kinship with Chinese American citizens who had declared having a number of sons in China. These Chinese American citizens sold these "slots" to strangers in China, who then claimed the sellers, usually older men, as their fathers. See Nee and Nee for a detailed explanation of the "paper son" process.

34. More so than "Leaves," this article, also published in the *Independent*, clearly espoused the journal's politics. Despite a move away from partisan editorship, the *Independent* was, at this time, "wholly committed to the policy of 'expansion' and 'taking up the white man's burden'" (Mott 377).

35. In her preface to the recent fiction anthology *Charlie Chan Is Dead*, Elaine Kim refers to the Asian American prose tradition superseded by that of the volume's contributors as one of "dead yellow men" (ix–x).

POLITICAL RESISTANCE, CULTURAL APPROPRIATION, AND THE PERFORMANCE OF MANHOOD IN YUNG WING'S *MY LIFE IN CHINA AND AMERICA*

FLOYD CHEUNG

Since the inception of Asian American studies, in the late 1960s, the criterion of political resistance has served as a litmus test for the value of a literary text. Recently, some scholars have challenged this tendency. For example, Viet Thanh Nguyen argues that "resistance and accommodation are actually limited, polarizing options that do not sufficiently demonstrate the *flexible strategies* often chosen by authors and characters to navigate their political and ethical situations" (4; emphasis in original), and Esther Mikyung Ghymn laments, "How dull literature would be if it were used to serve only political causes!" (14). Nevertheless, many voices still look to "literature as a vehicle for change."[1] Building on this tradition of valuing resistance, albeit with awareness of its limitations, editors Rajini Srikanth and Esther Y. Iwanaga titled their anthology of Asian American literature, published in 2001, *Bold Words.*

Among critical perspectives, however, differing political priorities have resulted in different ways of identifying boldness, of defining resistance, and thus of evaluating texts. For instance, the editors of *Aiiieeeee!* (Chin et al., 1974) and *The Big Aiiieeeee!* (Chan et al., 1991) prioritize resistance against the racist "white stereotype" of the emasculated Asian American man as an important sign of a text's value (14). In contrast, such critics as King-Kok Cheung, Elaine Kim, and Amy Ling argue that resistance against sexism must accompany resistance against racist stereotypes; scholars of Asian American literature are intimately familiar with the debate between these priorities.[2] Consequently, instead of reviewing these two critical camps' differences, this essay examines their common interests and exclusions, using the works of Sui Sin Far and Yung Wing as points of reference. After examining these critics' political and axiological biases, this essay resituates Yung's work in its contemporary context, reading its appropriation of conventional language, forms, and values not as a sign of capitulation to dominant, oppressive forces but rather as a strategy of ambivalent accommodation in the service of an idiosyncratically defined resistance.

Like scholars of other ethnic American literatures, Asian American literary critics have turned to autobiographical writing as an especially rich resource for the investigation of individual resistance.[3] While the *Aiiieeeee!* editors and their critics usually approve of Sui Sin Far's autobiographical writings, including "Leaves from the Mental Portfolio of an Eurasian" (1909), they consistently find little of value in Yung Wing's autobiography, *My Life in China and America,* published in the same year. From their perspective, Sui Sin Far's writing evidences political resistance, whereas Yung's does not. Sui Sin Far's work, most often read as a personal history of her experience of racism and sexism in the United States and Canada, has garnered much praise and critical attention. In contrast, Yung's autobiography is usually read as a work in the success-story genre and has received dismissive remarks and little attention from literary critics.[4]

It is worth noting that both critical perspectives object to Yung's performance of Asian American manhood. Equating manhood with resistance, the *Aiiieeeee!* editors consider Yung's appropriation of allegedly "white" language, forms, and cultural assumptions to be a sign of his nonresistance and hence of his emasculation. Amy Ling, equating manhood with success, cites the same appropriative tendencies in order to suggest that Yung gains both success and manliness at the cost of political resistance. From these two influential perspectives, then, Yung's text fails the litmus test of political resistance, its author faulted by one camp for not being masculine enough and by the other for being too masculine.

The issue of appropriation is the crux of these negative evaluations of Yung's politics and manhood. For the *Aiiieeeee!* editors, as for Ling, Yung's appropriation of the language, forms, and values that these scholars associate with mainstream Euro-American tastes signals disloyal assimilation and opportunistic acquiescence. However, the feminist theorists Joan Radner and Susan Lanser have defined appropriation as a set of "coding strategies" that adapt "forms or materials normally associated with [Euro-American] male culture" to resistant purposes (415). Along these lines, the *Aiiieeeee!* editors themselves profess that "all behavior is strategy and tactics" (*Big Aiiieeeee!* xv), and Amy Ling admits that the master's tools can be used to dismantle the master's house ("I'm Here" 155). From this perspective, Yung's text can be interpreted as a strategic and masterful adaptation of American conventions of autobiography and manliness. Specifically, *My Life in China and America* draws on discursive traditions established by autobiographers like Benjamin Franklin, Frederick Douglass, and Booker T. Washington, and it appropriates the rhetoric of individual and national manliness popularized by Theodore Roosevelt to perform a problematic yet bold personal and political resistance.

Assumptions held by the *Aiiieeeee!* editors in the early 1970s, when they set out on "the great work of rediscover[ing]" Asian American literature, prevented them from recognizing Yung's strategy of resistant appropriation (*Aiiieeeee!* xxiv). Influenced by the Black Power movement, the *Aiiieeeee!* editors valued an openly confrontational style that Frank Chin termed "backtalk" in a 1972 essay by that title, in which he announces, "We have not been black. We have not caused trouble. We have not been men" ("Backtalk" 556). Citing Yung's autobiography as a primary example, the *Aiiieeeee!* editors surmised that the political comportment of most Chinese American writers fell short of "the vision Malcolm X and other blacks had for their 'minority'" (*Aiiieeeee!* xix). To rectify this shortcoming, the original *Aiiieeeee!* editors themselves adopted an overtly resistant stance and celebrated Asian American writers who had done the same. In this spirit, they later anthologized Sui Sin Far's autobiography and two of her short stories, which, as they put it, resist the stereotype of "the intelligent and sexually repugnant sissy Chinese man" (*The Big Aiiieeeee!* 111). The stories feature a Euro-American woman who leaves her Euro-American husband and eventually marries a Chinese man, Liu Kanghi. Far from being a "sissy" or emasculated, Liu Kanghi is described in terms of normative manhood. His wife declares that "he is always a man. . . . I can lean upon and trust in him. I feel him behind me, protecting and caring for me" (Sui Sin Far, "The Story of One White Woman Who Married a Chinese" 233).[5] In addition to being a good husband, Liu Kanghi participates in the manly arena of Chinese politics as a member of the "Reform Club" (Sui Sin Far, "Her Chinese Husband" 135).[6] Such overt resistance against stereotypical Chinese emasculation held much value for the *Aiiieeeee!* editors, since it not only signaled resistance against Euro-American racism but also affirmed Asian American agency.

The *Aiiieeeee!* editors, interested in measuring the "amount and kind of noise of resistance generated" by Asian American writers (*Aiiieeeee!* 9), were impressed by Sui Sin Far's loud and clear defense of Asian American manhood, but they were deaf to Yung's comparatively subtle yet still resistant efforts. They could hear only Yung's "beautiful, correct, and well-punctuated English sentences," which, according to them, betrayed his acceptance of "white supremacy" (23). Like Malcolm X, who was annoyed by "ultra-proper-talking Negroes" (*The Autobiography of Malcolm X* 284), the *Aiiieeeee!* editors, in their distrust of Yung's use of language, registered their discomfort with appropriating the master's tools, for fear of picking up the master's racism as well. For these back-talking editors, the choice to write standard English was tantamount to allying with the enemy. Consequently, they interpreted Yung's linguistic appropriation as evidence of his traitorous internalization of Euro-American racism. Furthermore, they argued, since racism prevented him from gaining equality and power, Yung unwittingly accepted "self-contempt and self-destruction" along with "successful assimilation" (*Aiiieeeee!* 12). In terms of the *Aiiieeeee!* editors' favorite metaphor, he emasculated himself by embracing standard English: "Without a language of his own, he no longer is a man" (*Aiiieeeee!* 37).

Amy Ling agrees that Yung Wing compromises his political resistance by appropriating hegemonic language and values, but in her analysis, he is too much a man. Working in a tradition of feminist scholarship that arose in the 1970s and gained prominence in the 1980s, Ling, with others, has critiqued the styles of manhood supported by such critics as the *Aiiieeeee!* editors and by such writers as Yung. For scholars like Cheung, Kim, and Ling, the *Aiiieeeee!* editors' advocacy of a manhood predicated on the subordination of women, and Yung's appropriation of a manhood based in part on stereotypical male success, undermine these men's attempts at political resistance.

In part, by critiquing these men's texts, Ling cleared space for her project of "unearthing and reclaiming . . . forgotten women writers" ("I'm Here" 151). Her 1990 book *Between Worlds: Women Writers of Chinese Ancestry*, which contributes invaluably to this important work of recovery, was so successful that Ling declared an Asian American literary "renaissance in which women are playing a prominent, if not dominant part" ("'Emerging Canons' of Asian American Literature and Art" 192). The *Aiiieeeee!* editors bitterly confirm Ling's assessment, complaining that the popularity of such writers as Maxine Hong Kingston and Amy Tan derives from their pandering to mainstream expectations for portrayals of Asian American women oppressed by male-dominated Asian cultures. These mainstream expectations, the *Aiiieeeee!* editors argue, unfairly overlook writings by Asian American men. Ling contends, however, that "the women's books are more authentic, more numerous, quite simply—better," as a result of Asian American women's "double silencing" in terms of race- and gender-based oppression (*Between Worlds* xxi; "'Emerging Canons'" 192). In a chapter of *Between Worlds* titled "Writing as Rebellion," Ling explains:

> In the case of Chinese women, whose repression has been protracted and extreme, the reaction from one who has managed to break free will be strong and vocal. Such a woman is imbued with so intense a sense of her own identity and the validity of her personal experience and perspective that despite, or perhaps more accurately because of, opposition, her perspective must come forth and be expressed [16].

Following this logic, one might conclude that most Asian American men have not experienced repression sufficiently odious for them to react with comparable intensity. Asian American women, in contrast, have suffered both racism and sexism. Therefore, within the axiology of "writing as rebellion," women's success, won in the face of double oppression, is more valuable than almost any success won by a less oppressed man.[7]

Using Sui Sin Far's and Yung Wing's autobiographies as examples, Ling, in her essay "Reading Her/stories against His/stories in Early Chinese American Literature," clarifies the distinction between these two kinds of success. In Ling's estimation, Sui Sin Far's autobiography enjoys greater success than Yung's because Sui Sin Far's work records a more introspective, personal struggle against oppression than does Yung's. Sui Sin Far, instead of listing her public accomplishments, writes an "intimate piece" and "focuses on the development of her own Chinese identity and pride, forged in the furnaces of pain and humiliation" (Ling, "Reading Her/stories" 79). Yung—to his discredit, according to Ling—"is expansive and detailed" regarding his public honors but relatively silent about his personal life and his encounters with racism (75). Ling's valorization of the private over the public accords with the feminist project of recovering the oftentimes hidden, silenced, and neglected lives of women. In a male-dominated world that generally values the public over the private, and activity over introspection, such recovery is necessary; but the distinction between public and private is not always clear, and discussing what might be categorized as public is not necessarily less valuable than treating private topics. Yet Ling categorically maintains that "in the genre of autobiography, greater awareness of the interior self and greater revelation of this interiority result undoubtedly in more interesting and better autobiographies" (85).

In addition to denigrating Yung's relative silence regarding his "interior self," Ling accuses Yung of failing the litmus test of political resistance. While

Ling admires Sui Sin Far's account of her personal experiences with racism and sexism, she notes that "nothing" in Yung's autobiography "gives the slightest indication of [his] awareness of or concern about how others perceived" him (83–84). According to Ling's analysis of Yung, he avoids treating oppression because it is not a "safe" subject, and because revealing dissatisfaction would detract from his success story (75).[8]

Indeed, Yung in his autobiography does remain largely silent regarding his efforts against racism, such as his work as a diplomat arguing against the ill treatment of Chinese laborers. As China's deputy minister to the United States between 1878 and 1881, Yung Wing passionately defended Chinese rights. In 1880, for instance, Yung complained to Secretary of State William Evarts that the United States was not honoring its commitment to the Burlingame Treaty of 1868, which outlined rules of mutual respect for American immigrants in China and for Chinese immigrants in the United States. With polite yet bold clarity, Yung protested:

> Tens of thousands of thousands of my countrymen are by law deprived of shelter and prohibited from earning a livelihood and are in hourly expectation of being driven from their homes to starve in the streets. Under such circumstances I could not acquit myself of my duty if I did not protest earnestly, but most respectfully, against the wrong in which they have been subjected [letter to William Evarts].

In spite of such efforts, Yung and his diplomatic cohort failed to stop anti-Chinese legislation. By 1882, the first ten-year Chinese exclusion act had been passed, and by 1904 Congress had made Chinese exclusion permanent. As Ling correctly observes, Yung does not comment directly on these injustices or on his role in fighting against them. His failures of open and official confrontation, however, help explain Yung's turn to a different strategy of resistance. In fact, because diplomatic argument at the national level proved ineffective, Yung chose to make his case in a more individualistic way.

After years of frustration, Yung surmised that Euro-Americans held disrespectful attitudes toward Chinese and Chinese Americans largely because China as a nation did not command respect. Losing the Opium Wars of 1839–42 and 1856–60 against Britain and losing the Sino-Japanese War of 1894–95 severely damaged China's international stature. In contrast, Japanese and Japanese Americans were afforded a greater degree of respect because Japan had impressed the world with military victories over China in 1895 and Russia in 1905. Partly in deference to Japan's military power,

Theodore Roosevelt pressured the San Francisco Board of Education in 1905 to admit Japanese American students to the city's public schools, whereas, despite a court challenge in 1903 (*Wong Him* v. *Callahan*, 119 F. 381), Chinese American students had to attend the "Oriental School" (Chan, *Asian Americans* 59). Thus, Yung observed, the relative strength of an Asian or Asian American individual's country of real or perceived origin was correlated with how much respect that individual could expect in the United States.

In addition, Yung realized that he could not depend on official channels, either in China or in the United States, to meet his goals. Having enjoyed only limited success in his plan to reform China through legal and administrative means, Yung turned to underground activism, eventually working with the Hundred Day Reformers, Sun Yat-sen, and Homer Lea.[9] Having failed to protect the rights of Chinese Americans in the United States by writing letters to the government, Yung turned to writing an autobiography meant to change the minds of the American reading public. This two-pronged strategy is not unlike that practiced by Yung's contemporary Booker T. Washington, who lived a life of behind-the-scenes activism while also fashioning a publicly acceptable and influential persona (Harlan xvii-xix). Like Washington in his 1901 *Up from Slavery*, Yung in his autobiography judiciously avoids discussing his less official albeit politically resistant work in order to maintain a character worthy of his target audience's respect. Also like Washington, Yung employs strategic accommodation not only in his choice of topics but also in his use of standard English and his appropriation of the traditional American success narrative. In sum, both authors make sacrifices and draw from an American autobiographical tradition, but not merely to capitulate to dominant expectations for their own individual benefit; rather, they are effectively pursuing one mode of political action in print while acting in more obviously politically resistant ways in other contexts.

With Washington's model as a precedent, Yung's *My Life in China and America* appropriates success-story conventions established by Franklin and Douglass to articulate political resistance through autobiographical narrative. Borrowing Roosevelt's logical equation between the character of individual men and that of their nations—"As it is with the individual, so it is with the nation" (13:321)—Yung argues not only for his own manhood but also for the dignity of all Chinese. Perhaps Yung's strategic silences and success-story framework distract Ling. Perhaps his standard English deafens the *Aiiieeeee!* editors. Contrary to their evaluations, however, Yung's autobiography does reveal awareness and concern about racism, but his method is largely invisible to presentist perspectives. In order to recognize his appropriative strategy as complexly resistant rather than simply complicit, it is necessary to place Yung's work in its historical context, with special attention to the discourses of hegemonic and subordinated masculinities that were active during the period.

In the past few decades, scholars have considerably increased our understanding of American manhood as a constantly reimagined construction.[10] Only recently, however, have critics begun to explain how a seemingly unmarked American manhood has been historically naturalized as *Euro*-American manhood.[11] Furthermore, as Joan Wallach Scott has explained, ideologies of *racial* superiority sometimes draw rhetorical power from the language of *male* superiority (45–48). In this process, whereby racism and sexism work together, normative discourses of American manhood confer rights and positive qualities specifically on Euro-American men at the expense of non–Euro-American men, often by figuring the latter as effeminate or emasculated. Thus, at the turn of the twentieth century, Theodore Roosevelt was able to argue for U.S. imperialism vis-à-vis the Philippines, Puerto Rico, and Cuba on the grounds that Euro-Americans were of a "stronger and more manful race" than the local inhabitants of these territories (13:328). Manliness, here, assumes the capacity for self-government and self-defense, which were "essential virtues" of Euro-Americans and supposed deficiencies of non–Euro-Americans (13:446).

Of all the non–Euro-Americans that Roosevelt raised as foils, Chinese and Chinese Americans were his favorites. According to one historian, Roosevelt "so thoroughly deplored their racial character that he used the term 'Chinese' as an epithet of opprobrium" (Dyer 140). During a speech that Roosevelt delivered in 1899, he contrasted the United States with China, finding the latter "heedless of the higher life, the life of aspiration, of toil and risk" (13:322); moreover, he claimed that China "does not possess the power to fight" (20:522). Simply put, China lacked "manly and adventurous qualities" (13:322). But Roosevelt's analogy worked in both directions. In this speech, he not only complimented his audience for being citizens of a strong American nation but also harangued the individual men of Chicago's Hamilton Club to act manly by supporting his imperial designs and hence upholding the manliness of the United States. The character of a nation was associated with individual citizens, but individual character also reflected on national identity.

Yung Wing's *My Life in China and America* draws on this logic to refute

Roosevelt's assessment of China and the Chinese.[12] If, as Roosevelt maintained, the individual represented the nation, then Yung could use his life story to counter misperceptions regarding China. Essentially, the autobiography presents Yung as an exemplar of a national character that contests dominant stereotypes, thereby undermining the warrants for anti-Chinese legislation. For himself and for his country, Yung recounts his success story to dispute Roosevelt's claim that Chinese are "heedless of . . . the life of aspiration . . . toil and risk," and Yung relates anecdotes of physical combat to demonstrate his "power to fight." Yet Yung, as a Chinese American, faced special challenges in his quest to prove his manhood. He had to assert himself to avoid being considered a docile Chinaman, but he could not assert himself so strongly that he would be feared as a member of the yellow peril.

Given the constraining discourses of Chinese American manhood during his era, how can Yung represent himself with integrity? He smartly and intricately appropriates versions of manhood already accepted by and popular with his intended audience in the United States. From Franklin, Yung gains a model of the self-made man and old-fashioned virtue; and from Douglass, he gains a model of physical resistance.[13] To reach an early-twentieth-century audience, however, Yung inflects these models with Roosevelt's rhetoric of manliness. Thus Yung transforms Franklin's honest toil into manly work, and he qualifies Douglass's famous insubordination with Roosevelt's manly dictum to be "vigorous in mind and body" (13:32). This combination of models allows Yung to recuperate two senses of manhood. Being mentally capable recuperates manhood in terms of Yung's ability to govern himself, and being physically capable recuperates manhood in terms of his ability to defend himself. With regard to dominant stereotypes, a vigorous mind answers those who would call Yung an unthinking, murderous member of the yellow peril, and a vigorous body shields him from being labeled as an effeminate, docile Chinaman. Through this balanced strategy of appropriation, Yung represents himself as successful, manly, and ultimately resistant.

As Judy Hilkey attests in *Character Is Capital,* the success-story genre enjoyed tremendous popularity from 1870 until 1910 (1). Although Franklin wrote his autobiography in the eighteenth century, his success story still resonated for readers at the turn of the twentieth century. In an 1888 review, William Dean Howells asserted that Franklin was "more modern [and] more American than any of his contemporaries," and the popular 1891 success manual *The Way to Win* advocated the "need to go back to the gospel of old-fashioned honesty, industry and frugality, which Franklin so admirably set forth" (Dale 442). So compelling was Franklin as a model of success that his autobiography was reprinted more than a dozen times between 1870 and 1910.

Yung draws on Franklin's remarkable cultural capital by paralleling and emphasizing, in his own life story, his model's "self-made man" success narrative, public spirit, and work ethic. Franklin's autobiography, understood in basic terms, tells the tale of one man's rise. As Franklin puts it, he writes after "having emerg'd from the Poverty and Obscurity in which I was born and bred, to a State of Affluence and some Degree of Reputation in the World" (1). He then recounts his rise from assistant tallow chandler to printer to statesman. Yung, echoing this narrative of ascent, relates his own occupational history, starting with his humble beginnings as a candy hawker and rice gleaner to business successes as a tea packer and munitions importer. Eventually, Yung relates some of his experiences as an educator and diplomat. In the beginning of the autobiography, though, in order to establish the low starting point of his rags-to-riches climb, Yung recounts his father's untimely death and his family's poverty. At the age of twelve, he rose "at three o'clock every morning, and . . . did not come home until six o'clock in the evening"; after having spent his day selling candy in nearby villages, his "daily earnings netted twenty-five cents" (8–9). He ascends from this point, as he puts it, using the Franklinesque cliché of his day, "by dint of hard work and self-denial" (41). A simple but stately portrait of himself used as the book's frontispiece (fig. 3.1), and, on the title page, a brief résumé listing some of his honors and titles, attest to his successful climb from rags to riches. Thus Yung, to assert his own authority, references Franklin's route to successful manliness.

Clearly, however, Yung also reminds his readers that he is not totally different from other Chinese immigrants. Indeed, like Franklin, he knows how to make the most of an opportunity, but, like most other Chinese in mid-nineteenth-century China, he once lived in poor economic conditions. Pluck sets him apart, but so does luck: he "happened" to have a family friend associated with the nearby English-language school, and his teacher decided to return with a group of Chinese boys to New England (*My Life in China and America* 2). At once, then, Yung is both representative and exceptional. This is a tension found in many American autobiographies, but it is especially problematic in Yung's case, since, as Sylvia Yanagisako has observed, practitioners of Asian American studies usually prefer to celebrate representative working-class resisters, not exceptional, upwardly-mobile figures like Yung Wing.

FIG. 3.1 A portrait of Yung Wing from his autobiography *My Life in China and America*, 1909

Franklin and Yung, perhaps anticipating charges of self-aggrandizement, both represent themselves as always aspiring to act in their own interests but also in their countrymen's. Yung, like Franklin, details not only his pursuit of a comfortable living for himself but also his lifelong engagement with public service. In fact, each justifies the personal accumulation of capital as a necessary step on the way to his ultimate goal. While Franklin writes that he "consider'd Industry as a Means of obtaining Wealth and Distinction" and the resultant leisure time and reputation as ways to "enlarge my Power of doing Good" (64, 101), Yung concludes that "any substantial hope of promoting any scheme of educational or political reform for the general welfare of China" requires him to turn his "thoughts to the idea of making a big fortune as my first duty, and as the first element in the successful carrying out of other plans for the future" (*My Life in China and America* 123). Throughout his life, Yung believed that educational and political reforms inspired by Western models could strengthen China's government, but he also believed that he could not convince officials to take his ideas seriously without first building personal credentials. His success in business, as represented in his autobiography, eventually brought him to the attention of Tsang Kwoh Fan, an influential viceroy. Like Franklin, who represents himself as surprised by the "spontaneous Testimonies of the public's good Opinion . . . by me entirely unsolicited" (101), Yung, with equal modesty, remarks upon hearing of Tsang's desire to speak with him: "What could such a distinguished man want of me? Had he got wind of . . . my late enterprise to the district of Taiping for the green tea?" (137). Indeed, according to Yung, his reputation, developed in part through this business enterprise, led to his opportunity to "do good," as Franklin would put it.

After securing the support of the viceroy, Yung guided scores of Chinese students across the Pacific to study in the United States. Under the auspices of the Chinese Educational Mission, these students lived and learned in Hartford, Connecticut, and nearby cities from 1872 to 1881. Yung aimed to reform what he perceived as China's limitations by educating a cadre of leaders like himself, who could carry on military, political, and scientific reforms within the structure of Chinese government. For a variety of reasons, including dissent within the Chinese government and anti-Chinese sentiment in the United States, Yung's plan never ran its full course, but some argue that the mission's students did have an important impact on China during the early twentieth century.[14] One former student wrote in 1939 that he and his comrades had learned from their experience a "manly bearing," which ultimately served their country well (S. Yung 240). Thomas LaFargue's biographies of Yung's students reveal that while a few remained in the United States, most took positions in China's military and government. These students, like the gatling guns and factory equipment Yung obtained for China as a munitions importer, were supposed to fortify his country's manhood, as defined by Roosevelt. Yung's own manliness, evidenced by his accounts of struggle and success, made his public aspirations possible.

In addition to echoing the culturally sanctioned narrative of Franklin's trajectory from humble beginnings to self-made success to public service, Yung also mimics Franklin's penchant for performance.[15] Franklin, for example, represents himself as transporting supplies for his press "thro' the Streets on a Wheelbarrow" (54). Here, Franklin puts a version of himself onstage for all to view. In particular, he attempts to make visible for his audience the intangible quality of his industriousness. Similarly, Yung figures himself as a foreman willing to throw himself into labor to make his manliness visible. To do so, however, Yung inflects his Franklinesque performances with strong allusions to Roosevelt's "hit the line hard" rhetoric (13:407). Referencing Roosevelt's advice that a real man "enters into the contest and bears his part as a man should, undeterred by . . . the sweat" (13:28), Yung recounts his experience as a tea packer in the following terms:

> The river . . . was quite shallow and a way had to be dug to float the boats down. In one or two instances the boatmen were very reluctant to jump into the water to do the work of deepening the river, and on one occasion I had to jump in, with the water up to my waist, in order to set them an example. When they caught the idea and saw me in the water, every man followed my example and vied with each other in clearing a way for the boats, for they saw I meant business and there was no fooling about it either [*My Life in China and America* 134].

What would have been a show of honest industry in the late eighteenth century is represented in Yung's period as a demonstration of manly leadership. Franklin, despite being the owner of a printing press, parades his willingness to sweat. Similarly, Yung, although no one would expect him, as the foreman, to get wet, jumps into the river, and he reinforces this move for the reader with the Rooseveltian phrase "no fooling about it either." Just as turn-of-the-century success manuals draw on Franklin's old-fashioned ideals for their own purposes, so does Yung echo Franklin's self-promotional strategies with Roosevelt's rhetoric in order to put his racially qualified manhood in a better light.

Although Yung gains substantial authority from referencing Franklin's structure and ethics, this appropriation attests to his manliness mainly in terms of mental strength and leadership ability. At the turn of the century, as Theodore Roosevelt repeatedly reminded his audience, men had to be "vigorous in mind *and body*" (13:32; emphasis added). Furthermore, during this period Joseph Hull's illustration for Bret Harte's *The Heathen Chinee* (1870) was undermining public perceptions of Chinese American bodily vigor (fig. 3.2). In this widely printed poem, a fight breaks out between two cheating card players, Bill Nye and Ah Sin. Hull's illustration shows Nye, a taller, stockier, Euro-American man, kicking his slighter Chinese opponent in the stomach or groin. Ah Sin appears utterly defenseless and unbalanced; his arms, which could have been weapons, are instead flailed back and as useless as his flowing queue. For further contrast, Nye sports black boots, whereas Ah Sin wears daintier footgear. A bow tied at the end of Ah Sin's queue completes the effeminizing picture. If we agree with Gail Bederman's observation that "turn-of-the-century manhood constructed bodily strength and social authority as identical" (8), then this image of Chinese American weakness allows for no social authority. Although Harte did not intend to advocate anti-Chinese sentiment, most Euro-American readers applauded Nye's violence (Kim, *Asian American Literature* 14–15). Yung found it necessay to respond to this insulting characterization of Chinese American physical manliness and social authority, but he had to do so with care.

Frederick Douglass had to assert his manhood with care as well. Though conditions faced by African Americans differed vastly from those faced by Asian Americans, the two autobiographers' restrained displays of physical manliness are comparable.[16] In his 1845 *Narrative of the Life of Frederick Douglass,* he employs the following chiasmus to preface his famous fight: "You have seen how a man was made a slave; you shall see how a slave was made a man" (107). Expanded, revised, and republished under the titles *My Bondage and My Freedom,* in 1855, and *The Life and Times of Frederick Douglass,* in 1881, Douglass's narrative always features his manly physical resistance to Edward Covey, a slave breaker. The 1881 edition highlights this scene with an illustration, and such turn-of-the-century critics as Booker T. Washington (*Frederick Douglass* 40–41) emphasize the importance of this fight. As David Leverenz has observed, Douglass himself paid special attention to this scene, carefully revising it to present his manhood as marked by both "dominance" and "dignified self-control" (108). Yung's relation of a fight between himself and an impolite Scotsman benefits from the model provided by Douglass's assertive yet qualified narration. Although physical assertion is valued as manly for men of all races, a non–Euro-American man's unrestrained performance of violence might have been understood as dangerously uncivilized. Douglass must stand his ground with Covey but not represent himself as a brute; as for Yung, he must counter perceptions of himself as emasculated but avoid associating himself with the stereotype of the yellow peril.

Douglass justifies his physical resistance to Covey in two ways. He makes it clear that Covey abuses him, since the slave breaker draws not only first blood but also an unreasonable amount of blood, even for a society that tolerates the beating of slaves. Furthermore, Douglass emphasizes that he exhausts nonviolent means of rectifying the situation before he is forced to defend himself against Covey's relentless physical abuse. The critical scene that leads to Douglass's transition from the state of slavery to the state of manhood opens with him literally reduced to his lowest point and suffering excessive punishment: "While down in this sad condition, and perfectly helpless, the merciless Negro-breaker took up the hickory slab . . . and, with the edge of it, he dealt me a heavy blow upon my head . . . and caused the blood to run freely" (*The Life and Times of Frederick Douglass* 145). Throughout this beating, Douglass does not resist with force; instead, he appeals with words to his master, Covey's supervisor. The master fails, however, to cen-

FIG. 3.2 Joseph Hull's illustration for Bret Harte's *The Heathen Chinee*, 1870

sure Covey. Thus, when Covey next attempts to tie and beat Douglass, the latter appears only right and manly to respond. Douglass represents the ensuing battle as one between men rather than as one between representatives of different races, "as if [they] stood as equals before the law. The very color of the man was forgotten" (158). Yet Douglass carefully notes his restraint, even as he draws blood:

> Every blow of his was parried, though I dealt no blows in return. As I was strictly on the *defensive*, preventing him from injuring me, rather than trying to injure him. I flung him on the ground several times when he meant to have hurled me there. I held him so firmly by the throat that his blood followed my nails. He held me, and I held him [158; emphasis in original].

With an emphasis on defensiveness accented by short, evenly balanced phrases, the tone of this critical passage reinforces the experience of a temperate man who finds that intolerable conditions require assertive but controlled resistance.

Yung, in addition to echoing Douglass's resistance to Covey, adapts Roosevelt's logic of manly fistfighting for his own purposes. Roosevelt advises that men should be "able to hold our own in rough conflict with our fellows, able to suffer punishment without flinching, and, at need, to repay it in kind with full interest" (13:32). While Roosevelt was interested in crafting a model of turn-of-the-century American manhood that balanced imperial violence and domestic governance, bodily vigor and mental vigor, Yung borrows Roosevelt's logic to improve his own image and that of his countrymen.[17] In essence, Yung uses Roosevelt's logic of balanced manhood to distance his character from the extremes of stereotypical passivity and irrational violence.

In Yung's autobiography, the occasion for this balanced performance involves a fight between himself and a "stalwart six-footer of a Scotchman" who ties "a bunch of cotton balls to [his] queue" (70). Referencing both Douglass's and Roosevelt's philosophies of confrontation, Yung first exercises restraint and uses words to demand removal of the cotton balls; but the Scotsman, rather than comply and apologize, throws a punch. Yung is careful to note that he can suffer punishment without flinching as he describes how the Scotsman "thrust his fist against my mouth, without drawing any blood, however" (70). Yung then repays with interest, but he is careful to deliver an equal and fair blow in order to distance himself from association with the devious stereotype of the yellow peril: "I struck him back in the *identical* place where he punched me, but my blow was a *stinger*. . . . It drew blood in great profusion from lip and nose" (70–71; emphasis added). Since the punches are identically placed, the language emphasizes not Yung's tactics but his opponent's weakness. Douglass's reflections on his own fight present a similar comparison: "He [Covey] had not, in all the scuffle, drawn a single drop of blood from me. I had drawn blood from him" (*The Life and Times of Frederick Douglass* 160). Both Yung and Douglass thus present their readers with the blood evidence necessary to judge each autobiographer's manliness favorably, but, since both are men of color guarding against the potential charge of unthinking brutality, they immediately remind their readers that their actions were justified and temperate. Douglass explains, "My aim had not been to injure him, but to prevent his injuring me" (*The Life and Times of Frederick Douglass* 160). After Yung delivers his stinging blow, he and the Scotsman are separated; a crowd member asks Yung if he wants to fight, and Yung responds, "No, I was only defending myself. Your friend insulted me and added injury to insult. I took him for a gentleman, but he has proved himself a blackguard" (71). Yung then comments on this response: "With this *stinging* remark, which was heard all over the room, I retired" (71; emphasis added). Here, the repetition of *sting*—his "stinger" of a punch, his "stinging remark"—accents his dual ability to resist both physically and verbally. Moreover, throughout this relation Yung maintains a balanced yet assertive tone, writing with parallel constructions. With controlled language, Yung reinforces his self-control in this fight.

In this way, Yung begins to solve a peculiarly Chinese American problem. To avoid effeminization, he fights, but to avoid association with the stereotype of the yellow peril, he invokes reason and acts with restraint. Yung echoes Douglass's great fight, which made a slave a man, but he also draws on Roosevelt's ideal of vigorous mind and body. Thus Yung asserts a double defense of his manhood, both on the level of language and on that of rough conflict.

Yet this is not just an isolated, individual victory. Admittedly, the very fact that Yung could write and publish a book in English distinguishes him from most other Chinese American men of the period, since most were manual laborers without access to formal education or publishing venues, even though the literary historian Xiao-huang Yin has recovered a few short pieces published by manual laborers—in California newspapers, for instance (16–35). On the whole, the class and educational differences between Yung and most other Chinese immigrants were vast. Yung studied English before leaving China; he did not perform manual labor in America (though he labored in China); he lived in New England; and when he reentered the country in 1902, he avoided the usual immigration screening process by traveling first-class and carrying a letter from his college classmate's associate, a judge in Honolulu, to another judge, in San Francisco, vouching for Yung (*Diary* 9 May 1902, 6 June 1902). But, regardless of his class or connections, Yung was subjected to—and resisted—the same gendered stereotypes that all Chinese men living in the United States experienced.

In *My Life in China and America,* Yung uses Roosevelt's logic and rhetoric to stage a defense not only of his own manhood but also of the manhood of his nation of birth. Yung's personal achievements, in his leading a higher life of toil and risk, represent the possibility that others from his country of origin could also succeed in the right conditions. While class, in later life, may have separated Yung from most other Chinese Americans, his autobiography establishes that he grew up in a state of poverty. But his poverty was leavened with unusual conditions: the opportunity for an English-language education and the chance acquaintance of progressive-minded Euro-American mentors. Truly, in the spirit of Benjamin Franklin and Frederick Douglass, Yung represents himself as someone who bears adversity and seizes opportunity; but ultimately, Yung argues that all Chinese (men, at least) could succeed as he had if presented with different circumstances, namely, a more Westernized government in China and a more respectful atmosphere in America. His carefully represented encounter with the Scotsman serves not only to assert his own "power to fight" but also to preface the following statement, which overflows with a defiant, communal pride and presages the national conditions necessary for success: "The time will soon come . . . when the people of China will be so educated and enlightened as to know what their rights are, public and private, and to have the moral courage to assert and defend them whenever they are invaded" (73).

Yung Wing's autobiography counters Roosevelt's estimation of the Chinese, but it also answers the criticisms of the *Aiiieeeee!* editors, and of scholars like Amy Ling. Read within its proper historical and intertextual contexts, *My Life in China and America* passes the litmus test of political resistance, since it defends Chinese American manhood and treats a politically engaged Chinese American's struggle against racism. Yung's idiosyncratic mode of political resistance differs, however, from the modes preferred by his critics. The *Aiiieeeee!* editors advocate an openly confrontational, non–standard English rhetoric, whereas Ling prefers a similarly confrontational yet introspective stance, but Yung perceived a situation in which his purpose would be better served by his practicing subtler forms of confrontation and appropriating conventional modes of American autobiography and manhood.

Of course, one can disagree with Yung's literary choices and models, but they should not be comprehended as "fake" or less "authentic," as in the view of Frank Chin ("This Is Not an Autobiography" 109–10) or Amy Ling (*Between Worlds* xxi). Rather, no matter how noble the literary or cultural historian's political concerns may be, he or she has a responsibility to evaluate authors and their works within their own contexts. Even if a text appears to fail a particular litmus test of political resistance, such a conclusion cannot be offered as judgment of the text's or its author's authenticity in any universal or categorical way. As Gayatri Chakravorty Spivak once said in a conversation with Sneja Gunew, notions of authenticity are always constructed and never essential (61). Hence, contingencies of authenticity accompany what Barbara Herrnstein Smith has famously called "contingencies of value." The *Aiiieeeee!* editors and Ling strategically define notions of the "real" and the "authentic" in accordance with their own contingent values. Despite the important political and scholarly work they have done, their contingencies sometimes ossify into standards that filter and limit the field. At first glance, texts like *My Life in China and America* do not appear to meet current standards or serve current political goals, and so they are largely excluded from scholarly studies, anthologies, and course syllabi. As the important work of developing the materials and methods of Asian American literary studies continues, however, its practitioners ought to reflect on their assumptions, not to abandon political concerns altogether but rather to question how and why certain criteria of evaluation achieve legitimacy.

BIBLIOGRAPHY

Andrews, William L., ed. *The Oxford Frederick Douglass Reader.* New York: Oxford University Press, 1996.

Bederman, Gail. *Manliness and Civilization: A Cultural History of Gender and Race in the United States, 1880–1917.* Chicago: University of Chicago Press, 1995.

Butler, Judith. *Gender Trouble: Feminism and the Subversion of Identity.* New York: Routledge, 1990.

Caldwell, Dan. "The Negroization of the Chinese Stereotype in California." *Southern California Quarterly* 53 (1971): 123–32.

Chan, Jeffery Paul, et al., eds. *The Big Aiiieeeee! An Anthology of Chinese American and Japanese American Literature.* New York: Meridian, 1991.

Chan, Sucheng. *Asian Americans: An Interpretive History.* Boston: Twayne, 1991.

Cheung, King-Kok. "The Woman Warrior versus the Chinaman Pacific: Must a Chinese American Critic Choose between Feminism and Heroism?" *Conflicts in Feminism.* Ed. Marianne Hirsch and Evelyn Fox Keller. New York: Routledge, 1990. 234–51.

Chin, Frank. "Back-talk." *News of the American Place Theatre* 3 (1972): 2. Rpt. *Counterpoint: Perspectives on Asian America.* Ed. Emma Gee. Los Angeles: Asian American Studies Center of UCLA, 1976. 556–57.

———. "Come All Ye Asian American Writers of the Real and the Fake." *The Big Aiiieeeee! An Anthology of Chinese American and Japanese American Fiction.* Ed. Jeffery Paul Chan et al. New York: Meridian, 1991. 1–92.

———. "This Is Not an Autobiography." *Genre* 18 (1985): 109–30.

———, et al., eds. *Aiiieeeee! An Anthology of Asian American Writers.* 1974. New York: Mentor, 1991.

Copjec, Joan. *Read My Desire: Lacan against the Historicists.* Cambridge: MIT Press, 1994.

Dale, John T. *The Way to Win, Showing How to Succeed in Life.* Chicago: Hammond, 1891.

Douglass, Frederick. *The Life and Times of Frederick Douglass.* 1881. New York: Pathway, 1941.

———. *Narrative of the Life of Frederick Douglass, an American Slave, Written by Himself.* 1845. New York: Penguin, 1982.

Dyer, Thomas G. *Theodore Roosevelt and the Idea of Race.* Baton Rouge: Louisiana State University Press, 1980.

Franklin, Benjamin. *Autobiography.* Ed. J. A. Leo Lemay and P. M. Zall. New York: Norton, 1986. 1–146.

Ghymn, Esther Mikyung. *The Shapes and Styles of Asian American Prose Fiction.* New York: Peter Lang, 1992.

Harlan, Louis R. Introduction. *Up from Slavery.* By Booker T. Washington. New York: Penguin, 1986. vii–xlviii.

Harte, Bret. *The Heathen Chinee.* Chicago: Western News, 1870.

Hilkey, Judy. *Character Is Capital: Success Manuals and Manhood in Gilded Age America.* Chapel Hill: University of North Carolina Press, 1997.

Holte, James Craig. *The Ethnic I: A Sourcebook for Ethnic-American Autobiography.* Westport: Greenwood, 1988.

Howells, William Dean. "Editor's Study." *Benjamin Franklin's Autobiography.* Ed. J. A. Leo Lemay and P. M. Zall. New York: Norton, 1986. 276.

Kaplan, Amy. "Black and Blue on San Juan Hill." *Cultures of United States Imperialism.* Ed. Amy Kaplan and Donald E. Pease. Durham: Duke University Press, 1993. 219–36.

Kim, Elaine H. *Asian American Literature: An Introduction to the Writings and Their Social Context.* Philadelphia: Temple University Press, 1982.

———. "'Such Opposite Creatures': Men and Women in Asian American Literature." *Michigan Quarterly Review* 29 (1990): 68–93.

Kimmel, Michael. *Manhood in America: A Cultural History.* New York: Free Press, 1996.

LaFargue, Thomas E. *China's First Hundred.* Pullman: State College of Washington, 1942.

Leverenz, David. *Manhood and the American Renaissance.* Ithaca: Cornell University Press, 1989.

Ling, Amy. *Between Worlds: Women Writers of Chinese Ancestry.* New York: Pergamon, 1990.

———. "'Emerging Canons' of Asian American Literature and Art." *Asian Americans: Comparative and Global Perspectives.* Ed. Shirley Hune et al. Pullman: Washington State University Press, 1991. 191–97.

———. "I'm Here: An Asian American Woman's Response." *New Literary History* 19 (1987): 151–60.

———. "Maxine Hong Kingston and the Dialogic Dilemma of Asian American Writers." *Ideas of Home: Literature of Asian Migration.* Ed. Geoffrey Kain. East Lansing: Michigan State University Press, 1997. 141–56.

———. "Reading Her/stories against His/stories in Early Chinese American Literature." *American Realism and the Canon.* Ed. Tom Quirk and Gary Scharnhorst. Newark: University of Delaware Press, 1994. 69–86.

———. "Yan Phou Lee on the Asian American Frontier." *Re/collecting Early Asian America: Essays in Cultural History*. Ed. Josephine Lee, Imogene L. Lim, and Yuko Matsukawa. Philadelphia: Temple University Press, 2002. 273–87.

Malcolm X. *The Autobiography of Malcolm X*. New York: Grove, 1965.

McCullough, Kate. "'Such was Liu Kanghi—a man': Sui Sin Far and the Production of Chinese American Masculinity." Ethnic Masculinities Forum. Modern Language Association convention. Sheraton Centre, Toronto. 29 Dec. 1997. Unpaginated.

Moy, James. *Marginal Sights: The Staging of the Chinese in America*. Iowa City: University of Iowa Press, 1993.

Nguyen, Viet Thanh. *Race and Resistance: Literature and Politics in Asian America*. Oxford: Oxford University Press, 2002.

Payne, James Robert, ed. *Multicultural Autobiography: American Lives*. Knoxville: University of Tennessee Press, 1992.

Radner, Joan N., and Susan S. Lanser. "The Feminist Voice: Strategies of Coding in Folklore and Literature." *Journal of American Folklore* 100 (1987): 412–25.

Roosevelt, Theodore. *The Works of Theodore Roosevelt*. 20 vols. New York: Scribner, 1926.

Rotundo, E. Anthony. *American Manhood: Transformations in Masculinity from the Revolution to the Modern Era*. New York: Basic Books, 1993.

Scott, Joan Wallach. *Gender and the Politics of History*. New York: Columbia University Press, 1988.

Smith, Barbara Herrnstein. "Contingencies of Value." *Critical Inquiry* 10 (1983): 1–35.

Smith, Sidonie. "Performativity, Autobiographical Practice, Resistance." *a/b: Auto/Biography Studies* 10 (1995): 17–33.

Spivak, Gayatri Chakravorty. "Questions of Multiculturalism." *The Post-Colonial Critic: Interviews, Strategies, Dialogues*. Ed. Sarah Harasym. New York: Routledge, 1990. 59–66.

Srikanth, Rajini, and Esther Y. Iwanaga, eds. *Bold Words: A Century of Asian American Writing*. New Brunswick: Rutgers University Press, 2001.

Stecopoulos, Harry, and Michael Uebel, eds. *Race and the Subject of Masculinities*. Durham: Duke University Press, 1997.

Sui Sin Far. "Her Chinese Husband." *The Big Aiiieeeee! An Anthology of Chinese American and Japanese American Fiction*. Ed. Jeffery Paul Chan et al. New York: Meridian, 1991. 133–38.

———. "Leaves from the Mental Portfolio of an Eurasian." *The Big Aiiieeeee! An Anthology of Chinese American and Japanese American Fiction*. Ed. Jeffery Paul Chan et al. New York: Meridian, 1991. 111–23.

———. "The Story of One White Woman Who Married a Chinese." *The Big Aiiieeeee! An Anthology of Chinese American and Japanese American Fiction*. Ed. Jeffery Paul Chan et al. New York: Meridian, 1991. 123–33.

Takaki, Ronald. *Iron Cages: Race and Culture in Nineteenth-Century America*. New York: Oxford University Press, 1990.

Testi, Arnaldo. "The Gender of Reform Politics: Theodore Roosevelt and the Culture of Masculinity." *Journal of American History* 81 (1995): 1509–33.

Wan, Peter Pei-de. "Yung Wing, 1828–1912: A Critical Portrait." Diss. Harvard University, 1997.

Washington, Booker T. *Frederick Douglass*. 1907. New York: Greenwood, 1969.

———. *Up from Slavery*. 1901. New York: Penguin, 1986.

Will, Barbara. "The Nervous Origins of the American Western." *American Literature* 70 (1998): 293–316.

Wong Him v. *Callahan*, 119 F. 381 (1902). Circuit Court of California. 5 Dec. 1902.

Wong, K. Scott. "Cultural Defenders and Brokers: Chinese Responses to the Anti-Chinese Movement." *Claiming America: Constructing Chinese American Identities during the Exclusion Era*. Ed. K. Scott Wong and Sucheng Chan. Philadelphia: Temple University Press, 1998. 3–40.

———. "The Transformation of Culture: Three Chinese Views of America." *American Quarterly* 48 (1996): 201–32.

Worthy, Edmund H. "Yung Wing in America." *Pacific Historical Review* 34.3 (1965): 265–87.

Yanagisako, Sylvia. "Transforming Orientalism: Gender, Nationality, and Class in Asian American Studies." *Naturalizing Power: Essays in Feminist Cultural Analysis*. Ed. Sylvia Yanagisako and Carol Delaney. London: Routledge, 1995. 275–98.

Yarborough, Richard. "Race, Violence, and Manhood: The Masculine Ideal in Frederick Douglass's 'The Heroic Slave.'" *Frederick Douglass: New Literary and Historical Essays*. Ed. Eric J. Sundquist. Cambridge: Cambridge University Press, 1990. 166–88.

Yin, Xiao-huang. *Chinese American Literature since the 1850s*. Urbana: University of Illinois Press, 2000.

Yung, Shang Him. "The Chinese Educational Mission and Its Influence." *T'ien Hsia Monthly* 9 (1939): 225–56.

Yung Wing. *Diary of Yung Wing*. 1902. Manuscript. Connecticut State Library Archives, Hartford.

———. Letter to William Evarts. 9 March 1880. Notes from the Chinese Legation to the Department of State. National Archives, Record Group 98.

———. *My Life in China and America*. New York: Holt, 1909.

NOTES

Versions of ideas explored in this essay were first presented at the 1998 meeting of the Northeast Modern Language Association in a panel titled "Imagining American Manhood" and organized by Elizabeth Abele. My thanks to Maria S. Castellanos, Sheri Cheung, Matthew DeVoll, Rebecca Mark, David Palumbo-Liu, Felipe

Smith, Maaja Stewart, Zhou Xiaojing, and the anonymous readers of the University of Washington Press for their comments. Thanks also to Chow S. Cheung and Sharon Domier for their help with Chinese-language sources. Stefanie Grindle provided both research assistance and valuable feedback.

1. Vassar College's 1998 conference on Asian American literature was titled "Visions and Voices: Literature as a Vehicle for Change."

2. Representative articles engaged in this debate include Cheung's "The Woman Warrior versus The Chinaman Pacific: Must a Chinese American Critic Choose between Feminism and Heroism?"; Kim's "'Such Opposite Creatures': Men and Women in Asian American Literature"; Ling's "Maxine Hong Kingston and the Dialogic Dilemma of Asian American Writers"; and Chin's "Come All Ye Asian American Writers of the Real and the Fake."

3. Holte discusses the importance of autobiography for scholars of ethnic American literatures in his introduction to *The Ethnic I*. Essays in Payne's *Multicultural Autobiography* and in *MELUS*'s winter 1997 issue, on ethnic autobiography, attest to the genre's continuing significance.

4. Although they do not explain why, Srikanth and Iwanaga follow suit, including Sui Sin Far in their anthology but excluding Yung Wing. The exception to this trend is K. Scott Wong; see his "The Transformation of Culture" and "Cultural Defenders and Brokers."

5. McCullough argues that these stories by Sui Sin Far participate in a "conversation" with the "stereotypes in circulation around Chinese masculinity."

6. Rotundo notes in his history of American manhood, "Politics . . . was seen, even by its detractors, as a masculine pursuit" (170).

7. Of course, this additive notion of oppression has since been questioned by Angela Davis, Yen Le Espiritu, and Chandra Mohanty, among others.

8. Ling's posthumously published essay "Yan Phou Lee on the Asian American Frontier" qualifies her earlier position by stating that resistant performances may reside among "silences, . . . irony and indirection" (276).

9. For a critical assessment of Yung's reformist activities, see Wan.

10. Butler, for instance, explains, "There is no gender identity behind the expressions of gender; that identity is performatively constituted by the very 'expressions' that are said to be its results" (24); further, she argues, "gender is an identity tenuously constituted in time, instituted in an exterior space through a *stylized repetition of acts*" (140; emphasis in original). Copjec, basing her conclusions on Lacanian psychoanalysis, states, "All pretensions of masculinity are . . . sheer imposture; just as every display of femininity is sheer masquerade" (234).

11. For examples of recent scholarly work on race and masculinity, see Kaplan's "Black and Blue on San Juan Hill," and articles in Stecopoulos and Uebel's *Race and the Subject of Masculinities*.

12. As a diplomat and concerned Chinese American, Yung was no doubt aware

of Roosevelt's positions on China and the Chinese. Furthermore, Yung's diary provides evidence that he read often and widely, and that he even had a subscription to the periodical *Outlook,* in which Roosevelt frequently published his speeches and other essays; see Yung's *Diary,* 24 Nov. 1902.

13. For an extended treatment of the "self-made man," see Kimmel 13–78. Kimmel suggests that Franklin is "the first American prototype of the Self-Made Man" (20). See Hilkey 131–41 for a discussion of the popularity of Franklinesque "old-fashioned" virtue during this period. Yarborough discusses Douglass's use of physical violence as a means of establishing manhood.

14. For an explanation of the reasons behind the recall of the mission, see Worthy.

15. For a fuller treatment of Franklin and performance, see Sidonie Smith, "Performativity, Autobiographical Practice, Resistance." Another instance of Yung's performativity can be observed in his dress. Numerous entries in his diary account for money spent at his tailor's shop in Boston for suits, such as the one in which he is pictured in the autobiography's frontispiece. In China, however, Yung wore Chinese-style robes to perform an authoritative version of himself there.

16. For a discussion of the relationship between Euro-American notions of African Americans and Euro-American notions of Chinese Americans, see Caldwell, "The Negroization of the Chinese Stereotype in California," and Takaki, *Iron Cages* 215–22.

17. See Testi, "The Gender of Reform Politics," and Will, "The Nervous Origins of the American Western," for excellent analyses of Roosevelt's motives, especially with regard to his desire to balance the intellectualism necessary for government with the physical strength necessary for defense and imperialism.

READING ETHNOGRAPHY

THE COLD WAR SOCIAL SCIENCE OF JADE SNOW WONG'S *FIFTH CHINESE DAUGHTER* AND *BROWN V. BOARD OF EDUCATION*

CHRISTOPHER DOUGLAS

By the mid-1990s, a curious writerly protest had emerged from Asian American literature's most popular writer, Amy Tan. "I am not an expert on China," Tan declared in the Fall 1996 issue of *The Threepenny Review*:

> Contrary to what is assumed by some students, reporters, and community organizations wishing to bestow honors on me, I am not an expert on China, Chinese culture, mah jong, the psychology of mothers and daughters, generation gaps, immigration, illegal aliens, assimilation, acculturation, racial tension, Tiananmen Square, the Most Favored Nation trade agreements, human rights, Pacific Rim economics, the purported one million missing baby girls of China, the future of Hong Kong after 1997, or, I am sorry to say, Chinese cooking [28].

Later excerpted in *Harper's,* Tan's article lamented the way her fiction is read in terms of the ethnographic knowledge it supposedly provides about Chinese America, and, by apparent extension, Chinese society. "I am alarmed," she wrote, "when reviewers and educators assume that my very personal, specific, and fictional stories are meant to be representative down to the nth detail not just of Chinese Americans but, sometimes, of all Asian culture" (28). Tan told of receiving a permission request to reprint an excerpt from *The Joy Luck Club* in a multicultural anthology; in the proposed excerpt, related Tan,

> a Chinese woman invites her non-Chinese boyfriend to her parents' house for dinner. The boyfriend brings a bottle of wine as a gift and commits a number of social gaffes at the dinner table. Students were supposed to read this excerpt, then answer the following question: "If you are invited to a Chinese family's house for dinner, should you bring a bottle of wine?" [28]

In other examples, a literature professor had informed her that he taught her books in his class while criticizing passages depicting China as "backward or unattractive" or describing "spitting, filth, poverty, or superstitions," and a male student in line at a book signing had asked her loudly, "Don't you think you have a responsibility to write about Chinese men as positive role models?"

Though these readerly reactions seem hopelessly naïve, Tan's faux surprise at being read ethnographically—at being taken as an authoritative chronicler of real American lives of Chinese descent—is just as shocking. Tan, protesting too much, may have read Sau-ling Wong's 1995 indictment of her work in "'Sugar Sisterhood': Situating the Amy Tan Phenomenon." Wong, reading white American reviewers' comments on Tan's novels, found that Tan was lauded for the presence of cultural details as well as myth in her fiction, and that Tan's fiction was understood to share with "quasi-ethnographic Orientalist discourse on China and the Chinese" the qualities of "temporal distancing" and "authenticity marking" (184). Wong suggested, against Tan's denial of ethnic expertise, that Tan was "in effect inviting trust in her as a knowledgeable cultural insider and a competent guide familiar with the rules of the genre in question: quasi ethnography about the Orient" (188). Though Wong took note of the counter-Orientalist possibilities in Tan's work, she argued forcefully against letting Tan off the hook for the way she is read: "*Joy Luck Club* is not a misunderstood, co-opted ethnic text that has been unfortunately obscured by a culturalist haze and awaits recuperation through class- or gender-based readings. To suggest so risks explaining away the persistence of Orientalism as a matter of the individual reader's ignorance, inattention, or misguidedness" (194).

While Sau-ling Wong was certainly right to point out Tan's collaboration in structuring the ethnographic reception of her novels, the problem Wong names is not peculiar to Tan, but one that haunts Chinese American fiction, and Asian American literature more generally. Ethnography continues to structure Asian American literature in its public reception, even in the academy, which, Sau-ling Wong notes at the end of her article, constructs a different Asian American canon from that constructed by the publishing industry. My argument in this essay is that the reception and production of *fth Chinese Daughter* thus structures an ethnographic reading in two tions. The first direction partakes of the kind of ethnography already blished by Chinese American autobiography and travel writing. It pro-s a white American audience with knowledge of the Chinese American munity, and, by a problematic extension, grows to include a knowledge her Asian ethnicities in different Asian countries. The logic of this exten- is articulated in a passage of the introduction to the second edition, re Wong recalls a visit from a Vietnam-bound soldier:

> have been rewarded beyond expectations. I recall a handsome young para-rooper in full military dress who appeared at my San Francisco studio on his way to Vietnam. He came to thank me for writing the book, which he had read in a Texas military base, for he would better understand the Asians where he was going [vii].

ng betrays no impulse to urge the paratrooper to distinguish among Asian ples, or between Asians in Asia and Americans of Asian descent. For young soldier, Wong's Cantonese-speaking Chinatown will stand for a in the most general sense. But the second direction of ethnographic ding is as interesting as the first. Wong's book, in translated form, will vide Asian peoples with a sociology of America. *Fifth Chinese Daughter* s translated by the U.S. State Department into several Asian languages, luding, according to Wong, those of "Japan, Hong Kong, Malaya, Thail-l, Burma, East India, and Pakistan" (vii). In 1953, the year the Korean War ded—and, not coincidentally, one year before the Supreme Court struck wn the separate-but-equal distinction that was the foundation of segre-tion in the United States—Wong tells us that

> the State Department sent me on a four-months' grant to speak to a wide variety of audiences, from celebrated artists in Kyoto to restless Indians in Delhi, from students in ceramic classes in Manila to hard-working Chinese immigrants in Rangoon. I was sent because those Asian audiences who had read translations of *Fifth Chinese Daughter* did not believe a female born to poor Chinese immigrants could gain a toehold among prejudiced Americans [viii].

'ong's narrative of making good in America thus functions for her Asian idiences as a window onto contemporaneous economic, social, and cul-ıral realities in the United States.

Chinese American fiction are still laboring under c were established half a century ago, at the interstices social sciences. This way of reading Tan's work can publication of Jade Snow Wong's *Fifth Chinese Dau* autobiography responded to, and accepted the terms paradigm shift from biological "race" to ethnic "cul becoming increasingly influential at midcentury. Won was interpreted as an intervention into a concurrent c citizenship.[1] Indeed, it was the autobiography's ambiv American citizenship that made it suitable as a kind raphy, with the U.S. State Department translating *Fifth* several Asian languages and funding Wong's four-n through Asia. During the Korean War, with the entre War "domino theory" in that region, and during a do status of African American citizenship, in the form of hearing the case of *Brown* v. *Board of Education*, Ame needed buttressing in Asian countries by a propaganda p States as an international beacon of democracy, libert racial harmony. Jade Snow Wong's ethnography helped a

Fifth Chinese Daughter arrived on the American lite by expectations that it would provide ethnic knowledge in America, since it was an example of the established prose genre of autobiography. In her original author's r tion, Wong openly acknowledges the book's role in pro to a white American readership, declaring her intentior "a careful record of an American Chinese girl's first t (xiii). *Fifth Chinese Daughter* is a tale of growing up in a town, and of negotiating between Chinese custom and t rounding mainstream American culture. Told chronologi speaks of the conflict between "Jade Snow"—as she calls person—and her father, and it depicts along the way detail ways and cultural practices. But in her introduction to edition, published in 1989, Wong goes beyond claiming "record" of her experience of these things: *Fifth Chinese* vides Americans with knowledge of the Chinese in Ameri provides Asia with knowledge about America. Her book, created "more than the hoped-for understanding of Chine Beyond America (even including Chinese), *Fifth Chinese Da* insight into life in America" (vii).

In so framing Asia's reception of the book by "a female born to poor Chinese immigrants" living among "prejudiced Americans," Wong invokes the racial classifications historically crucial to American citizenship law. The State Department organized Wong's tour in response to a conceptual crisis in this racialized citizenship law. Its juridical dimension had been slowly working its way through the courts of the nation, and in 1954 it took the form of the desegregation decision by the United States Supreme Court in *Brown* v. *Board of Education*. At the end of the 1940s, and in the early 1950s, the National Association for the Advancement of Colored People (NAACP) began a series of cases that attacked the separate-but-equal distinction that lay at the root of segregation. In three decisions announced in June 1950—*Sweatt* v. *Painter, McLaurin* v. *Oklahoma State Regents,* and *Henderson* v. *United States*—the Supreme Court began to undermine the legal basis for the separate-but-equal distinction. But between the publication of Wong's 1950 work and her tour in 1953, other cases on segregation in public educational institutions were working their way through the courts, and they would end in the *Brown* decision. During this time, the U.S. government intervened on behalf of the NAACP (see Kluger 253). This intervention included a submission by Secretary of State Dean Acheson, who wrote in December 1952 that

> the continuation of racial discrimination in the United States remains a source of constant embarrassment to this government in the day-to-day conduct of its foreign relations; and it jeopardizes the effective maintenance of our moral leadership of the free and democratic nations of the world [quoted in Dudziak 111–12].

The internal American crisis in racialized citizenship—what parts of the U.S. Constitution and its amendments applied to African-descended inhabitants, and did *Plessy* v. *Ferguson*'s separation of American subjectivities into black and white violate those sections?—had external implications for U.S. foreign policy, the head of the State Department declared, only months before the same department sent Jade Snow Wong on a tour to reinforce American "moral leadership" in Asia.

Indeed, the Truman administration recognized the international implications for American foreign policy of segregation in the United States. Asian, African, and Latin American attention to race discrimination in the United States posed a profound obstacle to the portrayal of the United States as an upholder of democratic liberty in opposition to Communist tyranny (Dudziak, "Desegregation as Cold War Imperative"). With Communism advancing—particularly in China and Korea and, later, in Vietnam—Asia, which seemed to be up for grabs in the Cold War, was of particular concern (Klein, "Family Ties and Political Obligation"). The State Department responded to this concern in part with its sponsorship of speaking tours by members of American minorities, as when Jade Snow Wong was sent to Asia and Louis Armstrong was sent to Africa (Eschen, "Who's the Real Ambassador?"; Dudziak 99–100). Meanwhile, State Department officials like Acheson also participated in amicus curiae (third-party) briefs in various segregation cases before the Supreme Court. The Justice Department, too, in its own amicus curiae briefs during this time, stressed the foreign policy considerations of segregation, quoting Acheson at length (Dudziak 105–11). As Dudziak suggests (82, 110), international hostility (save in South Africa) toward American segregation was cast in terms of citizenship, as was the Justice Department's amicus curiae in *Brown*. The State Department recognized the foreign policy importance of the internal American debate on citizenship: on May 17, 1954, within an hour of the reading of the *Brown* decision, the Voice of America broadcast the news to the world, in thirty-four languages (Kluger 701; Dudziak 113).

The State Department understood *Fifth Chinese Daughter* and *Brown v. Board of Education* as texts that could be put to strategic use in the Cold War. And, crucially, they were viewed by the State Department as useful interventions precisely because they registered—and were made possible by—a fundamental transformation in the social sciences in the early twentieth century, signaled by anthropology's paradigm shift from race to ethnicity. In the context of a collapsing colonial world, in which subaltern peoples were militating against European rulers abroad (for example, in Indochina, North Africa, and South Asia) and at home (for example, in African American demands for the integration of the armed forces after World War II, and against Jim Crow), the State Department thought that *Fifth Chinese Daughter* was suitable for the purpose of reinforcing "moral leadership" in Asia because it was not a radical manifesto on Wong's struggle to become American. What was valuable was its ambivalent, ethnic response to the institution of racialized citizenship, and in this sense, the genre of ethnography Wong used was suited exactly to an ambivalent claim to citizenship. On the one hand, Wong's book lays claim to the mythologies of the nation, and so in part to its concept of citizenship. As a discourse of realism, ethnography permits the fundamental inscription of the minority subject into the national fabric. On the other hand, ethnography permits the reinstallation of citizenship as the domain of whiteness insofar as it redefines citizenship from the domain of racial whiteness to that of cultural whiteness; in Wong's case, the Chinese "other" in America is underlined as a possibly "model minority," but one with irreducible qualities that make the Chinese American community ever different from white norms of U.S. citizenry.

While most major commentators on *Fifth Chinese Daughter* necessarily speak about Wong's project of cultural mediation between America and China,[2] none has addressed the way this mediation was produced by Wong's introduction to the social sciences. Social science discourse not only conceptually enables this text's mediation, it also, by substantially determining its ethnographic content, allows Jade Snow Wong to see herself, as if for the first time. In her first semester at San Francisco Junior College, in 1938, she found, among courses including Latin and chemistry, that "sociology was the most stimulating," a new discipline that "completely revolutionized her thinking, shattering her Wong-constructed conception of the order of things" (125). The specific idea that falls "suddenly upon Jade Snow's astounded ears" is the idea of culture: the notion that, whereas in early "American" culture parents demanded obedience from children, "we" now see children as "individuals." Though the "norm" of "American" culture is individualism, Wong is paradoxically moved to see her own family's practices as evidence of culture: while her family was "living in San Francisco in the year 1938," it still observed familial rules produced in "the Chinese world of thirty years ago," with the possible result that these forces might be making her "a woman in old China" instead of "a woman in a new America" (125).[3]

It is this "devastating discovery" (125–26), announced by her sociology class, that shortly thereafter leads directly to Wong's own American "declaration of independence" from her family's strict Chinese rules. She delivers this speech to her family "in a manner that would have done credit to her sociology instructor" (128), thus adopting both the discourse and the posture of her newfound social science. It is this discipline that affords her a cognitive structure that places her "Chinese" family beside the "American" culture, aspects of which she aspires to: American sociology brings into sharp focus, for the first time, herself as "Chinese" instead of any number of different values, practices, and relations. This discipline so moves her that she "changed her major to the social studies" at the end of her freshman year (132). In a foreshadowing of the ethnographic reading dynamics that would govern the reception of multiethnic American literature for decades to come, the humanities corroborates her sociological discovery of culture when, in an English class devoted to the exploration of "individual expression," she learns "that her grades were consistently higher when she wrote about

Chinatown and the people she had known all her life" (132). From this moment on, a new figure of subjectivity animates *Fifth Chinese Daughter*: Wong begins to describe herself as a spectator of the community to which she has belonged. Now a "critical spectator" rather than a "participant" at a local wedding (143), Jade Snow takes some of her college classmates on a tour of her father's clothing factory and comments, in an interesting ocular metaphor, that "although everyone seemed more or less at home, the parents as well as guests, Jade Snow suddenly felt estranged, for while she was translating conversation between instructor and parents, she was observing the scene with two pairs of eyes—Fifth Daughter's and those of a college junior" (165). We need to understand this powerful estrangement as a social science effect akin to her writing in the third person—allowing us to see her culturalist explanation for writing her autobiography in the third person as itself performative of cultural difference. This feeling becomes acute when she completes her degree in economics and sociology; "after two years away from them and from Chinatown, she now felt more like a spectator than a participant in her own community" (199).

My argument here is not that the ocular power of sociology serves as a pair of false, ethnocentric "white" glasses for Wong—that they blur the image, so that she doesn't see the "real" Chinatown. Nor am I arguing that this real Chinatown is becoming obscured because Wong has gained greater understanding, recapitulating the nineteenth-century white proto-anthropologist Henry Rowe Schoolcraft's anxiety that autoethnographic self-comprehension had muddied his Iroquois informant David Cusick's pure information, his intellectually unmediated access to his essential cultural identity (Michaelson 46–48). The problem is that she sees herself in terms of an ethnic typology for the first time.

To be sure, Jade Snow Wong was not the first "ethnic" writer to situate herself within social scientific discourse in order to address a white reading public. *Fifth Chinese Daughter,* arriving on the scene in 1950, can perhaps best be understood in terms of the domestic American ethnography that preceded it. During the 1930s, sociological inquiry and documentary were part of what Alfred Kazin identifies as a dominant descriptive nonfiction, and they were responses to the twin crises of the Depression and the "progressive disintegration of the European order" into fascism (363). As Michael Staub describes the generic mood of the period,

> documentary and ethnography . . . became the Depression era's characteristic genres for representing a widespread societal preoccupation with

> the plight of the disempowered. The 1930s were a time when not only writers sponsored by the Works Progress Administration, but also scores of other ethnographers, documentarians, and journalists[,] sought to preserve oral memories they perceived as rapidly vanishing [425].

One of Staub's primary examples of 1930s ethnography is John Neihardt's *Black Elk Speaks,* which was transcribed, composed, and published in 1931. Although Staub sees Neihardt's narrative strategy as one that thematizes the inescapable distortions of *writing* the "recollection and representation of Indian speech" (452)—thus anticipating some of the meta-ethnographic issues raised by postmodern ethnography[4]—he acknowledges this text's place in current debates about the power, authenticity, and fictionalized nature of modern ethnography.

Zora Neale Hurston's work in the 1920s and 1930s can also be understood as producing ethnography akin to *Black Elk Speaks,* although with Hurston, as with Wong, the ethnography is produced by a cultural insider (as opposed to a white ethnographer, such as Neihardt, doing fieldwork). As Hurston incorporated African American folklore into her fiction in the middle and late 1920s, she was concurrently collecting and publishing this folklore (Hemenway 84); in 1931, for instance, she published a one-hundred-page article titled "Hoodoo in America" in the *Journal of American Folklore,* "the first scholarly treatment of hoodoo by a black American folklorist" (Hemenway 77). Her interest in the folklore of her Eatonville, Florida, home gained a disciplinary edge when she studied anthropology under Franz Boas at Barnard College in the late 1920s. As was also true for Wong, Hurston's writing ethnography out of her lived culture required a subtle dissociation:

> From the earliest rocking of my cradle, I had known about the capers Brer Rabbit is apt to cut and what the Squinch Owl says from the house top. But it was fitting me like a tight chemise. I couldn't see it for wearing it. It was only when I was off in college, away from my native surroundings, that I could see myself like somebody else and stand off and look at my garment. Then I had to have the spy-glass of Anthropology to look through at that [*Mules and Men* 3].

Like Wong, Hurston adopts an ocular metaphor to speak of the powerful estranging effect offered by social science discourse in the period between the wars. During this time, Richard Wright also came under the power of the scientific potential of sociology. In Chicago, in 1929, Wright pursued his self-education by reading Stein, Crane, and Dostoevsky but recalled the importance of sociology above these "new realms of feeling":

> But the most important discoveries came when I veered from fiction proper into the field of psychology and sociology. I ran through volumes that bore upon the causes of my conduct and the conduct of my family. I studied tables of figures relating population density to insanity, relating housing to disease, relating school and recreational opportunities to crime, relating various forms of neurotic behavior to environment, relating racial insecurities to the conflicts between whites and blacks [*Black Boy* 327].

Although Hurston and Wright sought to use anthropology and sociology to create very different pictures—southern black folklife for Hurston and nationwide black oppression for Wright, with each accusing the other of merely ventriloquizing stereotypes about African Americans in their works[5]—both proceeded from the assumption that an authentic portrait of African American life was the desired end.

In the Chinese American tradition, Jade Snow Wong's autobiography was not the first English-language work that could be considered to fall within the genre of ethnography. Sui Sin Far (Edith Maude Eaton) had published stories and sketches about the Chinese in North America at the beginning of the century, and one thinks as well of Helena Kuo's 1942 autobiography *I've Come a Long Way* as a predecessor to Wong's autobiography, but perhaps a more popular example is Pardee Lowe's *Father and Glorious Descendant,* which took as its focus the culture and lives of Chinese America. Lowe's book is an autobiographical sociology of the customs, manners, and goings-on of Lowe's Chinese American community, often told with reference to Lowe's slightly rebellious father, whose attraction to the "modern" and "barbarian" ways of America is a quality shared by his son. Because of the book's emphasis on cross-cultural musings, the reader is often informed of details that would be prominent in an autobiography only by way of a father's reaction to news from his son— which is precisely Lowe's way of informing the reader about his meeting and courting of his white American bride, whose name we never learn. Lowe recounts that after finishing degrees at Stanford and Harvard, he accepted an offer from a Stanford professor "to join him in conducting a sociological investigation of San Francisco's Chinatown" (228). When he later accedes to his stepmother's request to observe Chinese custom upon his return to his father's house with his new wife, he does so because, as he puts it, "this was as good a way as any of gathering sociological material" (235). In these and other ways, Lowe frames his tale in terms of the discourse of sociology, which he had grown to admire, as Richard Wright had done in the same period.

Black Elk, Hurston, Wright, Lowe, and Wong embraced the associated disciplines of ethnography, anthropology, and sociology and their claim to authoritative representation of group identities.[6] The ascendant sociology when Wong was in college was the work of University of Chicago sociologist Robert Park. Park had adopted Boas's assumption of racial equality and his empirical research methods (for example, gathering data by interviewing urban and ethnic subjects), and when Park's and Ernest W. Burgess's *Introduction to the Science of Sociology* was published, in 1921, it became "the dominant text in the field for the next twenty years" and "disseminated Park's conception of sociology" (Ross 359), enabling, both theoretically and methodologically, Gunnar Myrdal's *An American Dilemma* some twenty years later. It was probably Park and Burgess's textbook that Wong used in her freshman and subsequent years, just as it was the key textbook that confronted her contemporary Ralph Ellison at the Tuskegee Institute in 1935 or 1936.

"The heart of the text" by Park and Burgess, Ross notes, "was a group of chapters on competition, conflict, accommodation, and assimilation" (359). Park grappled for years with what would become a central problem in this vision of Americanization: Could racialized minorities marked by skin-color difference be assimilated? As Ross analyzes Park's career, "the one area of social life Park had not been able to subdue to his vision of liberal history was race relations. . . . Until the mid-1920s Park remained uncertain about racial assimilation" (438). Park's new research interest in American-Japanese relations helped settle the question, however: "Listening to a young Japanese American woman, he felt that he was listening to 'an American woman in a Japanese disguise'" (438). By the late 1920s, Park began to argue for the potential of racial assimilation, a marginal position that he extended to African Americans, and that became academically influential in the 1930s and 1940s. Park's vision of biological racial equality, with his new assertion of the possibility for racialized minorities to be culturally assimilated, was not an idle concern during those years; in the spring of 1942, as Wong, having transferred to Mills College, accepted her degree in sociology, the head of the Western Defense Command was recommending the internment of Japanese Americans and providing overtly biological reasoning for this measure, declaring that Japanese Americans had an "undiluted" "racial strain" that connected them to Japan and rendered them incapable of forming ties of loyalty to the United States (Irons 146).

Park's work was the theoretical foundation of the NAACP's challenge to segregation, resting as it did on Franz Boas's decades-long questioning of the empirical basis for supposed biological inequalities of race. By the advent of the Cold War, Boas's new, liberal theory of ethnicity had largely replaced earlier conceptions of biological race in anthropology and sociology. The NAACP accepted Boas's concept of racial equality but, strategically, not his anthropological concept of slow cultural historical change, opting instead for Park's more culturally flexible model of social evolution, which involved the four stages of competition, conflict, accommodation, and assimilation (Baker 179). This strategic combination became compelling in the Cold War context, as "the Supreme Court eventually embraced the 'new' scientific claims about racial equality, ending Jim Crow segregation in public schools in 1954" with *Brown* (Baker 100). Robert Lee makes the case that the Asian American as "model minority" was a similar Cold War possibility in the context of this larger paradigm shift: "The representation of Asian Americans as a racial minority whose apparently successful ethnic assimilation was a result of stoic patience, political obedience, and self-improvement was a critically important narrative of ethnic liberalism that simultaneously promoted racial equality and sought to contain demands for social transformation" (Lee 145). Lee understands this new representation to have been made possible by "an emergent discourse of race in which cultural difference replaced biological difference as the new determinant of social outcomes" (145). These changes were already in the works in Jade Snow Wong's day: as she was embracing sociology in 1938, Gunnar Myrdal was beginning his study (1938–40), whose outcome would be the 1944 publication of *An American Dilemma,* a very public document that dismissed theories of race in favor of a view of the cyclical effects of poverty and the possibility of assimilation. Overtly racial social science had helped buttress notions of exclusionary citizenship in the *Dred Scott* and *Plessy* cases (Baker 15, 28), although there were moments when this social science was seen to conflict with commensensical definitions of race, as in the important Asian American citizenship case of *United States* v. *Bhagat Thind* (Lee 142–44); but mid-twentieth-century social science appeared to open up possibilities for citizenship, or so it seemed to Myrdal, and to the NAACP after him.

An identical move constitutes *Fifth Chinese Daughter*'s radical edge. Wong, sensing the potential of her chosen discipline, incorporates its techniques of description, spectatorship, typology, and the interpretation of individual, familial, or group practices with reference to an essentialized cultural ideal, thus opening up the possibility of ethnic assimilation to a culture that was still ideologically committed to the notion of racial difference (as the *Korematsu* cases showed in the same year that saw publication of *An American Dilemma*). Wong rejects, for instance, her father's "Your skin is yellow. Your features are forever Chinese" (130), with its implied commitment to biological race, and opts instead for the assimilable ethnicity of the model minority. She casts a common child-parent struggle in terms of essential cultural difference, and, in her most obvious debt to Robert Park's four-stage model of assimilation, enlists the figure of the generation gap (125) to help make possible the idea of ethnic assimilation in her text. In these ways, social science discourse not only methodologically enables her realistic, ethnographic portrayal of Chinese America to white America, it also formulates the content of that portrayal as a newly ethnicized community whose children are gradually losing what is now understood to be a Chinese "cultural" distinctiveness and embracing American practices and values.

Jade Snow Wong's speech to Asian audiences during her State Department–sponsored trip similarly deploys this rhetoric of cultural difference and displays the unsettled problems that accompany it. Her speech pits the "old-world Chinese standards" in which she was raised, which include the "standard of Chinese womanhood" and the "doctrines of Confucius," against the "American new-world values" that she learned at school and in the culture at large, and which include the "American principles of freedom and independence" as well as the lessons of "individuality, self-expression, and analytical thought" (*No Chinese Stranger* 94–95). For Wong, these two sets of essentialized values represent "conflicts" that must be resolved. But, problematically, this cultural conflict is necessarily imagined in the racial terms that the United States had not abandoned: "This discovery [of conflicts] becomes a turning point in the life of any member of the second generation as he asks, 'Am I of my father's race or am I an American?'" (95). To affirm the latter possibility, of course, meant changing not one's "race" but rather one's culture. Nevertheless, in reconfiguring her difference as cultural rather than racial, Wong mirrored the NAACP's vision of sociology's usefulness in establishing arguments for integration and assimilation, as was concurrently being argued in *Brown*. The State Department thus made use of *Fifth Chinese Daughter* and *Brown* v. *Board of Education* for the same reason: both texts registered the same social science–based solution to the foreign policy problem of white supremacy in the United States.

One cost of this paradigm shift becomes apparent when Wong recounts a reaction to her speech in Malaysia. She was questioned by an "uninvited East Indian," who asked, "From your speech, Miss Wong, do you imply that there is no racial prejudice in the United States?" Wong's answer is informative because it reveals that her value to the State Department was due to her Booker T. Washington–like logic on race prejudice:

> There was a sudden silence. It was the first time she had been asked this publicly. She talked about prejudice where she had found it in employment and housing; but she emphasized that in the United States racial prejudice had never stopped her from getting where or what she wanted, and that the dimensions which her ancestral culture had added to her life offset occasional disadvantages.
>
> "Fear of prejudice and the excuse it offers for personal failure are chronically more damaging to a person of a minority race than to expect the reality of encountering and dealing with prejudice" [82].

This, only months before *Brown*. The East Indian's reply is not offered. The cost of this Boasian turn from racial to cultural difference, then, was the disappearance of race as an enduring social category that might underline continuing oppression and differences of economic and political power. As Lee says of another Cold War orientalist text, "Chop suey ethnicity erases from memory the history of the Chinese in America as a racialized minority" (175); it erases from view any possible analysis of enduring racialized structures of power and prejudice. Wong is laying claim to America, but not in as intellectually complicated a way as her contemporary Ralph Ellison, whose *Invisible Man* also addressed the Cold War crisis in racialized citizenship.

Though this turn from race to ethnicity was a strategically smart move on Wong's part, a second problematic consequence of that move (and of other moves like it) has left a peculiar legacy for Chinese American fiction. The conditions for Wong's status as autoethnographer, and her politics of ethnic assimilation, are retrospectively laid bare through intertextual allusions to *Fifth Chinese Daughter* from a later text, Maxine Hong Kingston's *The Woman Warrior.* Kingston's revisions to specific episodes in Wong's autobiography not only highlight Kingston's rejection of the notion that authorial status confers ethnographic authority but also suggest some of the problematic consequences of Wong's authority and cultural politics.

Several of Kingston's allusions to *Fifth Chinese Daughter* seem to be reminiscent homage rather than revisionist critique: here, one might name the daughters' resistance to what they perceive as their parents' attempt at arranging a marriage (Wong 227–32; Kingston 193–94); the childhood experience of playing baseball at school (Wong 20; Kingston 173); the tale of the parent who spent a night in a haunted room (Wong 52; Kingston 67); the general childhood project of acquiring an American personality through books and learning (Wong 92) and through speech at school (Kingston 180); and the climactic verbal argument with parental authority around the dinner table (Wong 129–30; Kingston 201–4).

At other moments, Kingston's text produces gently ironic echoes when read in conjunction with Wong's. Jade Snow's "straight A's" reflect her Americanized sense of self-determination in the face of resistance, but when Kingston's narrator reports "straight A's," her mother's response, "Let me tell you a true story about a girl who saved her village," produces for the narrator only further confusion about "her" culture, a confusion ("I could not figure out what was my village") that she cannot settle for her readers (Wong 111; Kingston 45). In another episode, Wong reacts with calm condescension to a schoolmate's racial slur of "Chinky, Chinky, no tickee, no washee, no shirtee!" (Wong 68), whereas a customer's "No tickee, no washee, mamasan?" (Kingston 105) produces a more ambivalent reaction of embarrassment and a counterattempt to name ("Noisy Red-Mouth Ghost," the narrator's mother writes on his package). In another telling example, against Wong's careful tourist-guide descriptions of Chinese foodways (we get, for instance, four pages on how to buy and cook rice and, later, a recipe for egg foo young), Kingston offers only an in-your-face catalogue of icky things the narrator's mother has cooked for her family (Wong 57–60, 159; Kingston 90–92). What *Fifth Chinese Daughter* and *The Woman Warrior* share is their narrators' outrage over gender inequalities in traditional Chinese culture; but even if it is Wong's father who, as a Christian, appears to believe "that women should be freed from certain oppressive rules" (Palumbo-Liu 139) and so is already placed as progressive, it is Kingston's book that does not let American culture off the hook, either, for its own patriarchal systems, as Kingston's child narrator imagines that the field of future identities for girls includes only pom-pom girl, cheerleader, and housewife (Kingston 180).

Other intertextual allusions do more to articulate the way Wong claims, and Kingston rejects, the authority of ethnography in their respective texts. Wong's childhood paintings are understood as early experiments in self-expression, an American mode, initially condemned by her father (18), that she eventually embraces through writing and pottery in "the convergence of two narrative strands: the imperative of highly individualized self-expression meets the need for a cultural representative" (Palumbo-Liu 143). Kingston's parallel self-expression, childhood paintings covered in layers of black ink like "a stage curtain . . . the moment before the curtain parted," becomes richly suggestive, perhaps as merely potential rather than actual cultural expression, "so black and full of possibilities" (Kingston 165), or, reflecting the crucially palinodal structure of Kingston's cultural authority,[7] as the impossibility of cultural or self-representation. Both Wong's and Kingston's narrators, as children, speak of their parents' unwillingness to explain culture and its traditions (Wong 3; Kingston 5, 121), but the way their texts work out this cultural ignorance is vastly different. Wong takes it upon herself to discover and represent Chinese culture to her ignorant readership; far from remaining unknowing, she learns at home, trains as a sociologist at school, and reports her fieldwork in the written word. By contrast, Kingston's book again and again undercuts her status as ethnographic authority.

In one parallel instance, Wong's and Kingston's narrators are forced to consult dictionaries as a way of obtaining cultural information. Wong's lesson is carefully framed by her father, who orders her to look up the word "slippers" in an English dictionary so she will learn that "bedroom attire" is not tolerated in the kitchen, where the result of wearing slippers is "chaos" (Wong 83). Kingston's narrator, however, is driven to a Chinese-English dictionary to try to make sense of the Cantonese phrases *Sit Dom Kuei* and *Ho Chi Kuei* because "I don't know any Chinese I can ask without getting myself scolded or teased, so I've been looking in books" (Kingston 88, 204). Kingston's text, in relaying the findings of her research, thematizes and declares outright its own status as radically unauthoritative ethnography:

> So far I have the following translations for *ho* and/or *chi*: "centipede," "grub," "bastard carp," "chirping insect," "ju-jube tree," "pied wagtail," "grain sieve," "casket sacrifice," "water lily," "good frying," "non-eater," "dustpan-and-broom" (but that's a synonym for "wife"). Or perhaps I've romanized the spelling wrong and it is *Hao* Chi Kuei, which could mean they are calling us "Good Foundation Ghosts." The immigrants could be saying that we were born on Gold Mountain and have advantages [204–5].

Here the very plurality of possible meanings breaks down any anthropological project: our field guide—our cultural insider—has admitted her own inability to sort out the possibilities. Our only recourse is to turn, with the narrator, to the Chinese-English dictionary: we must, as Frank Chin has commanded, do our homework ("This Is Not an Autobiography" 125).[8]

The politics of ethnographic representation are underscored best through Kingston's parody of Wong the field observer, done through the narrator's aunt, Moon Orchid. Moon Orchid arrives from Hong Kong to visit her daughter (and perhaps reclaim her wayward bigamist husband), but she becomes an anthropologist in the new world, studying the children, who have "many savage things to say, raised as [they've] been in the wilderness," "raised away from civilization" (133, 134). Kingston adopts the discourse of colonial America on behalf of Moon Orchid, who imagines that the children's behavior and dress must be "like an Indian" (134), thus playfully reenacting anthropology's primal scene, the encounter with the Native. As Moon Orchid does her ethnographic fieldwork, the result is a humorous treatment of cross-cultural misreading, but its serious corollary is the difficulty—even impossibility—of naming and identifying "American" culture as a whole, just as Kingston's narrator seems unable to get to the bottom of "Chinese" culture in order to represent it to her readers. Here, as elsewhere, Kingston refuses the mantle of ethnography, either as outside expert or as inside informant, that Jade Snow Wong assumes.

Unlike Wong, whose college career (1938–42) spanned an era when Parkian sociology was ascendant, Kingston went to college in Berkeley in the 1960s, when African American students were challenging the way that sociology, as they charged, both disciplined and pathologized race and ethnicity. The consequence of this challenge was the creation of programs and departments of black studies and then of ethnic studies. I can't help but hear a generational change between Wong's 1950 autoethnography and Kingston's 1976 antiautoethnography with respect to the way each consumes the discourse of social science. Kingston's confusion about Chinese culture, far from signifying the generation gap between her American self and her Chinese parents, highlights the very problems with the autoethnographic authority assumed by Wong. Thus Kingston's strategies go against the grain of ethnography: she makes it difficult for us to derive ethnographic knowledge from her literary texts. And, indeed, Kingston's 1982 rejoinder to her ethnographic-minded critics—"Why must I represent someone other than myself?" ("Cultural Mis-readings by American Reviewers" 63)—is part of her resistance to representing culture, or to inviting culturalist readings of her books, by contrast with (as Sau-ling Wong has shown in "'Sugar Sisterhood'") Amy Tan. In Kingston's work, it is not just a problem of epistemology and method; it is the ontology of "culture" itself that comes into question.

Fifth Chinese Daughter was received as expert ethnographic testimony, making clear that Wong's strategic use of the paradigm shift from race to ethnicity was to have a lasting generic legacy. Joyce Geary, writing for the *New York Times Book Review,* understood the text to be "not so much the story of [Wong's] life as . . . a story about San Francisco's Chinatown," thus accepting the text's invitation to be read as cultural typology. *Commonweal*'s E. V. R. Wyatt similarly recognized culture, assimilation, and the generation gap to be the themes of *Fifth Chinese Daughter*: "Jade Snow's story is a study of the conflict in the lives of Chinatown's younger generation—a conflict between the weight of Chinese tradition and the freedom of American ways." An anonymous reviewer in the *New Yorker* likewise understood the text to be representative of a newer generation of "Chinese upbringing" achieving a "break with Chinese traditions." *Fifth Chinese Daughter*'s publication thus helped concretize a dynamic of ethnographic reading, a dynamic that, more than fifty years later, continues to inflect debates within the Asian American community about Chinese American writing and the reception of that writing in the larger, predominantly white, Anglo-America.

Certainly much of the discussion within the Chinese American literary community over the last thirty years has been attended by the assumption that white American audiences are reading Chinese American literature in terms of the ethnographic, realist knowledge it can provide. When the original editors of *Aiiieeeee!* sorted writings by Asian Americans of the previous fifty years for inclusion in or exclusion from their anthology, they did so with this assumption in mind. In categories that Frank Chin later developed, Asian American writers were either "real" or "fake" ("Come All"), meaning that, in the face of white America's insistence on reading their work as true representations of their communities, they either did or did not undertake to write true ethnography. Likewise, the editors' condemnation of stereotypes in Asian American writing reflected an assumption that white audiences were reading these works for their value as accurate pictures. This expectation led the editors to issue a kind of call to realism for Asian American letters: if white Americans were going to read ethnographically, went the implicit logic, then Asian American writers should write ethnographically but should do it properly (Douglas 106–12). Other milestones in the legacy of ethnographic reading were the reception of *The Woman Warrior* among Chinese American and white American reviewers (Douglas 117–26) and Kingston's response to the ethnographic demands of her reviewers ("Cultural Mis-readings").

Sau-ling Wong, in her essay on the reception of Kingston's *The Woman Warrior,* argues that the problematic response to Kingston's work within the

Chinese American community actually rests with readers, not with Kingston herself. When Chinese American critics hold Kingston responsible for white American readers' misreadings, "they do so from a set of assumptions about ethnic literature that are grounded in a keen awareness of the sociopolitical context of minority literary creation" ("Autobiography as Guided Chinatown Tour?" 250). That context is described by Sneja Gunew in the following way:

> The critical reception of both women's writing and ethnic minority writing has been haunted by questions of legitimation, founded on an authenticity supposedly based in experience. In other words, minority writing is characterised by offering the authority and authenticity of the marginal experience. Readers find that minorities are "just like us," or so different that they throw the reader's own coherence into relief. That is to say, readers always rediscover themselves [53].

By reading Chinese American fiction ethnographically, contemporary white American readers are rediscovering themselves and their own cultural-psychic coherence—that is, against the supposed cultural confusion experienced by Tan's young Chinese American heroines, they discover their own unproblematic place within American society. Similarly, Jade Snow Wong's white American readers discovered, during a time of crisis in citizenship and race, their own coherence as American citizens in the face of Wong's ambivalent text: Wong's question "Am I of my father's race or am I an American?" could readily be answered by them, "Because of my father's race, I am an American." Indeed, producing the coherence of the white reader could be said to be one of the functions of Wong's ethnographic text. As Yin and Paulson remark of *Fifth Chinese Daughter,* "The reader is constantly aware of the divided consciousness of the narrator in the divided voice of the author and character," which Yin and Paulson attribute to "her bi-cultural identity" (114–15).

Though the issue of legal citizenship for American minorities appears settled, the ethnographic legacy in contemporary minority writing continues to produce the ambivalent effect of inscribing minorities into the national fabric but simultaneously rendering their cultural citizenship status questionable. Through this uncertainty, white cultural citizenship is rejuvenated and made coherent again. In other words, the old technology of white citizenship—pre-Boasian anthropology devoted to the idea of the biological difference of the other, through which whiteness found itself to be supreme—may not have disappeared entirely. Rather, its successors, cultural anthropology and ethnography, have merely transmogrified the old content of racial superiority into a new technology of cultural coherence, whereby the ethnic whiteness of cultural citizenship is again and again thrown into relief and produced as the norm. Literary ethnography based on cultural essentialism has not broken with the past of racial anthropology, since a core function of such writing is to encourage the structure of reading the typical other in order to produce white coherence and centrality.

Though some of the literature we teach has been produced in part through the mediation of these social science disciplines—primarily with Wong, as I have argued, but also with Black Elk, Pardee Lowe, Zora Neale Hurston, and Richard Wright—we need not let the texts stand in the postures they have assumed. Instead, we can teach these texts' debt to the social sciences and their historically dynamic ideas, in terms of their production, reception, and canonization. And, more to the point, as educators we can question the way in which our teaching of such texts either interrogates or merely reproduces the way these works have been read ethnographically by "mainstream" readers. Do we teach Asian American, African American, Chicano, or Native American texts as windows onto these real communities? Does our pedagogy encourage students to expect cultural accuracy in ethnic minority literatures, an accuracy based, as Gunew points out, on the supposed authority of the writer's experience? As we develop readings of texts in class, do fictional characters or situations assume a synecdochic weight of representativeness, wherein "the Asian American Experience" is contained? Are we content to let stand the traditional premises of American realism, which hold that fiction merely mirrors an already existing social reality but plays no role in producing it as intelligible? Do we dwell unproblematically on what appear to be themes of "culture" at the expense of questions of form, including the question of how a text's formal and rhetorical properties deploy logics of cultural difference? If our pedagogy fails to read against the legacy of ethnographic realism, is it not reiterating the coherence of white cultural citizenship? In short, if our students are invited to a Chinese family's house for dinner, should they bring a bottle of wine? We need to understand, in other words, that basing an ethnography of American ethnic minority communities on these literary traditions is deeply problematic, even as we recognize that (for example) the dynamic of reading Chinese American writing as a source of such knowledge has informed literary criticism and debates about this tradition, and, indeed, helped produce the tradition itself.

BIBLIOGRAPHY

Ancheta, Angelo. *Race, Rights, and the Asian American Experience.* New Brunswick: Rutgers University Press, 1998.

Baker, Lee D. *From Savage to Negro: Anthropology and the Construction of Race, 1896–1954.* Berkeley: University of California Press, 1998.

Chin, Frank. "Come All Ye Asian American Writers of the Real and the Fake." *The Big Aiiieeeee! An Anthology of Chinese American and Japanese American Fiction.* Ed. Jeffery Paul Chan et al. New York: Meridian, 1991. 1–92.

———. "This Is Not an Autobiography." *Genre* 18.2 (1985): 109–30.

———, et al. Introduction. *Aiiieeeee! An Anthology of Asian-American Writers.* Ed. Frank Chin et al. New York: Meridian, 1974.

Clifford, James. "Introduction: Partial Truths." *Writing Culture: The Poetics and Politics of Ethnography.* Ed. James Clifford and George E. Marcus. Berkeley: University of California Press, 1986. 1–26.

Douglas, Christopher. *Reciting America: Culture and Cliché in Contemporary U.S. Fiction.* Urbana: University of Illinois Press, 2001.

Dudziak, Mary L. "Desegregation as Cold War Imperative." *Stanford Law Review* 41 (1988): 61–120.

Eschen, Penny M. "Who's the Real Ambassador? Exploding Cold War Racial Ideology." *Cold War Constructions: The Political Culture of United States Imperialism, 1945–1966.* Ed. Christian G. Appy. Amherst: University of Massachusetts Press, 2000. 110–31.

Fabian, Johannes. *Time and the Other: How Anthropology Makes Its Object.* New York: Columbia University Press, 1983.

Gates, Henry Louis, Jr. "The Master's Pieces: On Canon Formation and the African-American Tradition." *South Atlantic Quarterly* 89.1 (1990): 89–111.

———. *The Signifying Monkey: A Theory of African-American Literary Criticism.* New York: Oxford University Press, 1988.

Geary, Joyce. "A Chinese Girl's World." Review of *Fifth Chinese Daughter,* by Jade Snow Wong. *New York Times Book Review* 29 Oct. 1950: 27.

Gunew, Sneja. *Framing Marginality: Multicultural Literary Studies.* Melbourne: Melbourne University Press, 1994.

Hemenway, Robert E. *Zora Neale Hurston: A Literary Biography.* Urbana: University of Illinois Press, 1977.

Hurston, Zora Neale. *Mules and Men.* Bloomington: Indiana University Press, 1963.

———. "Stories of Conflict." Review of *Uncle Tom's Children,* by Richard Wright. *Saturday Review* 2 (1938): 32.

Irons, Peter, ed. *Justice Delayed: The Record of the Japanese American Internment Cases.* Middletown: Wesleyan University Press, 1989.

Kazin, Alfred. *On Native Grounds: An Interpretation of Modern American Literature.* New York: Reynal and Hitchcock, 1942.

Kim, Elaine H. *Asian American Literature: An Introduction to the Writings and Their Social Context.* Philadelphia: Temple University Press, 1982.

Kingston, Maxine Hong. "Cultural Mis-readings by American Reviewers." *Asian and Western Writers in Dialogue: New Cultural Identities.* Ed. Guy Amirthanayagam. London: Macmillan, 1982. 55–65.

———. *The Woman Warrior: Memoirs of a Girlhood among Ghosts.* New York: Knopf, 1976.

Klein, Christina. "Family Ties and Political Obligation: The Discourse of Adoption and the Cold War Commitment to Asia." *Cold War Constructions: The Political Culture of United States Imperialism, 1945–1966.* Ed. Christian G. Appy. Amherst: University of Massachusetts Press, 2000. 35–66.

Kluger, Richard. *Simple Justice: The History of Brown v. Board of Education and Black America's Struggle for Equality.* New York: Knopf, 1976.

Korematsu v. *United States,* 323 US 214 (1944). Petition for Writ of Error Coram Nobis, U.S. District Court for the Northern District of California. 19 Jan. 1983.

Krupat, Arnold. *Ethnocriticism: Ethnography, History, Literature.* Berkeley: University of California Press, 1992.

Lee, Robert G. *Orientals: Asian Americans in Popular Culture.* Philadelphia: Temple University Press, 1999.

Li, David Leiwei. *Imagining the Nation: Asian American Literature and Cultural Consent.* Stanford: Stanford University Press, 1998.

Ling, Jinqi. *Narrating Nationalisms: Ideology and Form in Asian American Literature.* New York: Oxford University Press, 1998.

Lowe, Lisa. *Immigrant Acts: On Asian American Cultural Politics.* Durham: Duke University Press, 1996.

Lowe, Pardee. *Father and Glorious Descendant.* Boston: Little, Brown, 1943.

Michaelson, Scott. *The Limits of Multiculturalism: Integrating the Origins of American Anthropology.* Minneapolis: University of Minnesota Press, 1999.

Myrdal, Gunnar. *An American Dilemma: The Negro Problem and Modern Democracy.* New York: Harper, 1944.

Omi, Michael, and Howard Winant. *Racial Formation in the United States from the 1960s to the 1980s.* New York: Routledge, 1986.

Palumbo-Liu, David. *Asian/American: Historical Crossings of a Racial Frontier.* Stanford: Stanford University Press, 1999.

Review of *Fifth Chinese Daughter,* by Jade Snow Wong. *The New Yorker* 7 Oct. 1950: 134.

Ross, Dorothy. *The Origins of American Social Science.* Cambridge: Cambridge University Press, 1991.

Sollers, Werner. "Of Mules and Mares in a Land of Difference; or, Quadrupeds All?" *American Quarterly* 42.2 (1990): 167–90.

Staub, Michael. "(Re)Collecting the Past: Writing Native American Speech." *American Quarterly* 43 (1991): 425–56.

Tan, Amy. "In the Canon, for All the Wrong Reasons." *Harper's* Dec. 1996: 27–31.

Turner, Frederick Jackson. "The Significance of the Frontier in American History." *An American Primer.* Ed. Daniel J. Boorstin. New York: Meridian, 1985. 544–67.

Wong, Jade Snow. *Fifth Chinese Daughter.* 1950. Seattle: University of Washington Press, 1989.

———. *No Chinese Stranger.* New York: Harper & Row, 1975.

Wong, Sau-ling. "Autobiography as Guided Chinatown Tour? Maxine Hong Kingston's *The Woman Warrior* and the Chinese-American Autobiographical Controversy." *Multicultural Autobiography: American Lives.* Ed. James Robert Payne. Knoxville: University of Tennessee Press, 1992. 248–79.

———. "'Sugar Sisterhood': Situating the Amy Tan Phenomenon." *The Ethnic Canon: Histories, Institutions, and Interventions.* Ed. David Palumbo-Liu. Minneapolis: University of Minnesota Press, 1995. 174–210.

Wright, Richard. "Between Laughter and Tears." Review of *Their Eyes Were Watching God,* by Zora Neale Hurston. *New Masses* 5 Oct. 1937: n.p.

———. *Black Boy (American Hunger).* 1945, 1977. New York: HarperCollins, 1993.

Wyatt, E. V. R. Review of *Fifth Chinese Daughter,* by Jade Snow Wong. *Commonweal* 53.6 (1950): 182.

Yin, Kathleen Loh Swee, and Kristoffer F. Paulson. "The Divided Voice of Chinese American Narration: Jade Snow Wong's *Fifth Chinese Daughter.*" *Asian-American Women Writers.* Ed. Harold Bloom. Philadelphia: Chelsea House, 1997. 114–15.

NOTES

1. The analysis that follows is indebted to studies examining the way U.S. citizenship has been racialized by citizenship law, and to those studies that have extended citizenship questions beyond the important issue of legal status. See, for instance, Li; Lisa Lowe; and Lee.

2. See, for example, Kim 66–72; Ling 140–46; and Palumbo-Liu 138–46.

3. What becomes obvious in this formulation is not only the invention of anthropological space (China the cultural-other over there) but also, just as Johannes Fabian argues, anthropological time, in which the other is understood to have existed in a prior moment: "Anthropology emerged and established itself as an allochronic discourse; it is a science of other men in another Time" (Fabian 143).

4. The white supremacist and theoretical assumptions and methods of modern ethnography have lately been challenged by "postmodern" ethnographers who, writes Clifford,

> see culture as composed of seriously contested codes and representations; they assume that the poetic and the political are inseparable, that science is in, not above, historical and linguistic processes. They assume that academic and literary genres interpenetrate and that the writing of cultural descriptions is prop-

> erly experimental and ethical. Their focus on text making and rhetoric serves to highlight overly transparent modes of authority, and it draws attention to the historical predicament of ethnography, the fact that it is always caught up in the invention, not the representation, of cultures [2].

In distinction, the kind of ethnography I am concerned with in this essay is decidedly the modern kind: that characterized by "an ideology claiming transparency of representation and immediacy of experience" (Clifford 2).

5. See Wright's condemnation of racist clichés and minstrelsy in his review ("Between Laughter and Tears") of Zora Neale Hurston's *Their Eyes Were Watching God* and Hurston's review ("Stories of Conflict") of Wright's *Uncle Tom's Children*, in which she complained of its caricatured Communist portrayal of black oppression in the South.

6. Although anthropology and ethnography emerged in the nineteenth century as disciplines born from natural history and linguistics, and sociology emerged concurrently from political economy and the historical sciences (Ross 85–97), all three evolved in the twentieth century into disciplines that sought to comprehend a cultural or social reality in its totality, with anthropology and ethnography typically addressing the "other" (whether internally, with Natives, or abroad, with other colonized peoples) and sociology mobilized to study domestic populations (especially those segments considered pathological). Although I am not ignoring the differences among these disciplines, what interests me is each one's epistemological authority to *represent* group identity, in addition to the methodologies of description and interpretation whereby such representation is achieved. Moreover, by the 1930s and 1940s there was a productive interchange of ideas among these disciplines with—as is the primary interest here—Boas's critique of biological inequality and some of his research methodologies influencing Chicago sociology.

7. *The Woman Warrior*'s "governing trope is the palinode, or the taking back of what is said" (Sau-ling Wong, "Autobiography as Guided Chinatown Tour?" 195).

8. What these shared episodes constitute, of course, is a possible series of tropes for a Chinese American literary tradition that rests not on biological "race" or essential ethnic-cultural identity but on a formal repetition and revision of the kind that Henry Louis Gates, Jr., has identified as the African American tradition (Gates; "The Master's Pieces"; see also Gates, *The Signifying Monkey*).

ABRAHAM VERGHESE DOCTORS AUTOBIOGRAPHY IN HIS OWN COUNTRY

RAJINI SRIKANTH

Abraham Verghese's first memoir, *My Own Country: A Doctor's Story of a Town and Its People in the Age of AIDS,* was published to high acclaim in 1994. The memoir's popularity can be attributed in significant part to its release at the height of the AIDS crisis. The text's primary foci are the young homosexual men who return "home" to eastern Tennessee to die and the doctor who enables them to reestablish severed links with their families. This essay seeks to examine Verghese's memoir as a work that skillfully negotiates several polarities: the Western autobiographical tradition of individualism and self-regard (as exhibited by Rousseau, Nietzsche, and Benjamin Franklin, for example) versus communal visions of the self (as revealed by Marcus Aurelius, Augustine, and Native American and female African American autobiographers); immigrant and ethnic autobiography versus "universalist" memoir; and outsider versus insider status.

My Own Country, unlike most other autobiographies, does not so much answer the question "Who am I?" as it does the question "Where do I belong?" For the multiply diasporic Verghese—who was born in Ethiopia to parents of Indian origin and brought up in the country of his birth, studied in India, and completed his medical residency in the United States, where he now lives—the latter question takes on primary urgency. He is largely secure in his identity as a doctor. The question "Who am I?" appears not to be at issue here, and there is little evidence of vulnerability in this regard. The most appropriate way to read his autobiography is as an "act of 'settling down' . . . , an act both of discovery and creation that involves, at the same time, the movement of the self *in* the world, recognizing that the 'land makes man,' and the movement of the self *into* the world, recognizing as well that 'man elects his land'" (Gunn 59).

The distinction between memoir and autobiography is tenuous and shifting. Some scholars of first-person life writing characterize autobiography as more self-consciously literary than memoir (Anderson 8–9), and memoir as relating itself "to the external world of the author in history, not to the inner world of self-reflection" (Cox 143). Such a distinction does little justice, however, to those works that display both a strong sense of historical/sociopolitical context and attention to literary craft, as is the case with Verghese's text. Thus my referring to his work sometimes as autobiography and sometimes as memoir reflects the difficulty of placing it within a rigid literary category. What is common to autobiography, memoir, and several other forms of life writing (journals and diaries, for example) is that in these works author, narrator, and protagonist are the same person (Anderson 2).

As a genre, autobiography charts a journey—typically from youth to old age, from ignorance to knowledge, or from naïveté to maturity. Verghese's memoir encloses two types of journey, whose trajectories are somewhat at odds with one another. There is the homosexual men's "inward" journey back into their families (from which they had departed for big cities that were hospitable to homosexual lifestyles), and there is Verghese's "outward" journey. Both journeys are quests for comfort and refuge: for the AIDS patients, the comfort of knowing that, as they reach their deaths, they are among parents, siblings, and kin; for Verghese, the satisfaction of knowing that, through his doctoring of AIDS patients, he has inserted himself not only into the landscape of eastern Tennessee but more widely into the national psyche. For example, *Time* magazine declared Verghese's memoir one of the five best books of 1994, and at the start of the 1997–98 academic year, 3,474 incoming freshmen at Miami University in Oxford, Ohio, were required to read *My Own Country* before coming to campus, in preparation for an address by and discussion with Verghese on the first day of school. William Gracie, the university's director of liberal education, called Verghese's book "stunning" and declared that it "has taught us how to live."[1] High praise, indeed, for a foreign-born doctor, and a clear signal that Verghese had "arrived" precisely where he wanted to be: he was a national celebrity whose wisdom was not limited to his occupational expertise but extended to the universal conditions of life itself. Early in his memoir, he reveals unabashedly:

> I had made up my mind that I wanted a career in academic medicine. If there was glory in medicine, then I was not satisfied with the glory of saving a patient and having the family and a few others know about it. The rewards of private practice—money, autonomy, the big house, the big car, the big boat, the small plane, the bubble reputation in a provincial

> hospital—were not enough for me. . . . The acclaim of the lecture hall, the lead article in the *New England Journal of Medicine,* the invitations to be a keynote speaker at gatherings of my peers—these were the coins I wished to hoard [25].

What Verghese desired, he has achieved. His fame as both doctor and writer is not centered in his ethnicity or his race; in other words, mainstream recognition of his work does not call attention to his "minority" status. Rather, his fame is a result of his having enabled families to rediscover their connections to their estranged kin, and communities to begin to understand the social and economic implications of an illness to which they had considered themselves immune.

Derek Attridge's observation that "creation always takes place in a culture, not just in a mind" (22) seems manifestly obvious, and yet it is something we often forget in our vision of the writer as someone who pursues a solitary craft. Attridge, in his philosophical meditation on the acts of creating and inventing, declares that "an invention always engages closely with cultural practices and systems as it deforms or disjoins them, and so the inventive act must already have a more-than-casual relation to the contingencies that surround it and that will influence its fate" (23). What the inventor exploits or mines "in the cultural field is not just material but gaps in the material, strains and tensions that suggest the pressure of the other, of the hitherto unthought and unthinkable" (23). Verghese's success can be seen within the framework of Attridge's observations. Just as Maxine Hong Kingston's *The Woman Warrior* appeared at a particularly opportune moment, when late 1960s ethnic activism had combined with an increasingly vocal 1970s feminist movement to thrust the book into the consciousness of millions of Americans, so did Verghese's "story of a town and its people in the age of AIDS" come at a time when the nation was confronting perhaps its most challenging medical and ethical crisis of the century.

THE UNIQUE SELF, THE SELF IN COLLECTIVITY

The interplay between individual and community is particularly critical to Verghese's autobiography because of the book's focus both on himself as an individual per se and on himself as a doctor in relation to his patients and to the wider community of Johnson City and its residents. Verghese serves two functions: he enables the gay men and AIDS patients to fold themselves back into their families, if not into the larger community, and he awakens the community of Johnson City to turn its attention to those of its members whom it has long ignored. In both roles, Verghese deploys his individual expertise not as a self-aggrandizing device but as a means to strengthen community.

James Olney and John Sturrock, among numerous other theorists of the autobiographical genre in the Western world, have distinguished, on the one hand, between Augustine's subordination of love-of-self to love-of-God in his *Confessions* (circa 397 A.D.) and, on the other hand, Jean-Jacques Rousseau's complete preoccupation with the individual self in his autobiographical writings, among them *Dialogues* and *Confessions*. "Augustine established a long tradition of narrative confession as something compelled by God and imposed as a duty on every Christian," says Olney (*Memory and Narrative* 22), seeing in Augustine's "self-abasement" and Rousseau's "self-exaltation" the two ancestral impulses of Western autobiography (422). Sturrock calls Augustine's *Confessions* "a document of self, but traditionally employed for the reassurance of a collectivity, and a collectivity moreover which has as its highest moral imperative the belittling of self" (22). Nietzsche, by contrast, in his *Ecce Homo* going further even than Rousseau, presents the self as unique, "an 'entity' writing in order to proclaim his superiority over a population of nonentities" (Sturrock 13).

American autobiographies exhibit both the Augustinian and the Rousseauvian/Nietzschean impulses. The Puritan settlers' early autobiographical narratives of captivity and conversion presented their narrators with a particularly difficult situation: how to demonstrate God's grace within oneself without committing the grievous sins of self-righteousness and pride? Mary Rowlandson's late-seventeenth-century captivity narrative and Jonathan Edwards's eighteenth-century account of his conversion, for example, show their authors subordinating themselves and their efforts to the intervention of God's grace.[2]

The Augustinian bent of early American autobiography soon gives way, however, to the self-congratulatory model of Benjamin Franklin's late-eighteenth-century *Autobiography*, which displays an unabashed regard for one's own importance and one's own skill in negotiating the difficulties of life.[3] Frederick Douglass's 1845 *Narrative of the Life of Frederick Douglass, an American Slave, Written by Himself* echoes, in interesting ways, the same self-confidence and resourcefulness, so much so that William Lloyd Garrison had to vouch for the authenticity of Douglass's slave experience in order to convince his abolitionist audience that a man as seemingly self-assured as

Douglass had actually suffered the horrors of which he wrote.[4] Douglass's indisputable focus on himself as an extraordinary individual and on his unique struggle is the starting point of what has become a central debate in discussions of African American autobiographies: "the relation between the individual and the communal . . . , the relation that the narrated subjects of the autobiographies bear to the community of African Americans with whom they share their oppression, or in other words the extent to which the narratives are or are not individualistic, celebrating individual struggles and individual triumphs" (Barrett, 105–6).

The degree to which the individual self is emphasized over the group, or subordinated to it, is a critical component of the academic debate attending autobiographies by writers of color, or by white writers like Helen Barolini, who identify themselves first through their ethnicity (Italian American, in Barolini's case).[5] Whether or not it is essentialist and reductive to describe the American character as focused chiefly on the individual at the expense of the collective, one cannot deny that in the latter years of the nineteenth century, during the time that the nation was resurrecting itself from the ravages of the Civil War, precisely such an individualistic philosophy shaped the 1887 Dawes Act and its objective of "Americanizing" the Native American. The Indian problem would be resolved, the nation's leaders declared, only when Indians learned to value individual ownership of land. Therefore, tribally held land was partitioned and distributed among individual heads of household in order to make of the Indian a yeoman farmer.[6] History has unequivocally demonstrated that the Dawes Act was a most misguided policy, contributing to the cultural and psychic evisceration of Native Americans.

Brian Swann and Arnold Krupat, in the introduction to their 1987 collection of autobiographical essays by Native American writers, observe that some of their contributors were deeply conflicted about the process of focusing exclusively on the self. One contributor wrote in a covering letter,

> You should realize that focusing so intently on oneself like that and blithering on about your own life and thoughts is very bad form for Indians. . . . I grew up and continue to live among people who penalize you for talking about yourself and going on endlessly about your struggles [xii].

The subject matter of Verghese's book—AIDS—presents, I would argue, a particularly compelling page upon which to rewrite American notions of the proper relationship between the individual and the collective. Not surprisingly, the AIDS Memorial Quilt became the most visible metaphor for the struggle against AIDS. The quilt's weaving together of disparate pieces embodies the hope that mankind will be able to unite its disparities into a meaningful and useful relationship.[7] The HIV-infected men who return to Johnson City enter as isolated individuals. Over the course of Verghese's narrative, they move from their isolated positions within Johnson City to reconnection with their families and their communities. In the same way, Verghese, who begins in the role of a doctor consulting with and treating patients as individuals, finds that he is quickly drawn into the fabric of his patients' families, frequently becoming a surrogate son or brother. It is helpful to consider Verghese's positioning of himself with respect to his patients and their families in the context of the distinction that Krupat makes between a metonymic and a synecdochic sense of self. In his comparison of Native American autobiography with Western autobiographical writings, Krupat labels as metonymic "the individual's sense of herself predominantly in relation to other distinct individuals," a relationship of part to part in which every part is unique and separate, whereas the term "synecdochic" applies to those instances in which "narration of personal history is more nearly marked by the individual's sense of himself in relation to collective or social groupings," or, in other words, to a relationship of part to whole (Krupat 176).

KAIROS: VERGHESE'S RHETORICAL FINESSE

The memoir's title and subtitle contain the competing impulses that run through the entire book. *My Own Country* is a confident declaration of ownership. The subtitle, however, pulls outward from this bold assertion of self to an increasingly widening landscape in which the self of the "my" gradually diminishes in importance—we go from the specificity of "my" to the generality of "a doctor" and then further outward to a town and its people, and, ultimately, to an entire period in which AIDS, not the speaker behind "my," is the principal player. The text of the memoir parallels this trajectory. Verghese combines individualistic brashness and boldness with self-effacement, diffidence, self-doubt, and humility; he combines a healthy pride in himself as a competent, caring doctor with an interrogation of his diminishing presence as a husband and father. But this slow erasure of his role within the family is compensated for by his increasing visibility in the wider community, as he becomes identified as the AIDS doctor who awakens a reluctant community to the reality of the illness.

Verghese's ethos is immediately evident in the opening passages of his memoir. Right away, he sets out to establish his credibility on several fronts: as writer, as doctor, as community insider. With a confident flourish, he zooms in on the character and the moment that will enable him to appeal to his audience's emotions and position himself as the informed voice:

> Summer, 1985. A young man is driving down from New York to visit his parents in Johnson City, Tennessee. I can hear the radio playing. I can picture his parents waiting, his mother cooking his favorite food, his father pacing. I see the young man driving in my mind, despite the years that have passed; I can see him driving home along a route that he knows well and that I have traveled many times [9].

The audience can relate to the young man's action of visiting home and identify with the parents in their eager expectation of their son's arrival. At the same time that he appeals to the audience's empathy, Verghese establishes his credentials to tell the man's story: the repeated "I" both underscores Verghese's imaginative authority and informs the reader that Verghese is supremely qualified to tell this story—"despite the years that have passed," Verghese remembers, and, moreover, he knows the landscape well, having traveled the same road many times.

Then, quickly, almost without warning, the narrative tension intensifies, but Verghese's brief yet skillfully constructed opening lines make it easy for readers to place their trust in him. We are told that "three hundred or so miles from home, he [the young man] begins to feel his chest tighten. He rolls up the windows. Soon, chills shake his body. He turns the heater on full blast; it is hard for him to keep his foot on the accelerator or his hands on the wheel" (9). Verghese continues in this vein, inhabiting the young man's consciousness and his body, seeing with his eyes, breathing through his gradually failing lungs, and feeling his desire for home.

The finely crafted lyricism of the opening passages switches suddenly to the equally authoritative but vastly different prose of emergency room procedures when the same young man arrives at Johnson City Medical Center: the emergency room cast of characters is described "punctur[ing] the radial artery at the wrist to measure blood oxygen levels" (10), "fe[eding] the endotracheal tube alongside the laryngoscope, down the back of the throat, past the epiglottis, and past the vocal cords" (11). Then, just as suddenly, we are presented with the powerful social drama of the young man's parents learning in the medical center of their son's illness, and their gradual realization of his sexual orientation.

So total is Verghese's conquest of the young man's consciousness, and so commanding is his re-creation of the medical and family drama of the emergency room, that he lets slip in, almost as an aside (and a few pages later), that it wasn't until two months *after* the young man died that he, Verghese, actually came to Johnson City. Only then do we realize that Verghese has relied on other people's memories to imagine and inhabit an earlier time and to establish for himself a "participation" in, a witnessing of, the first AIDS case in Johnson City, Tennessee. Yet even this anamnesis of borrowed memory cannot undermine Verghese's narrative credibility. If anything, it shows how deeply embedded within the community he is: events that predate his arrival in the town have become his own memories.

Yet complicating the self-confident and sometimes even self-righteous presentation of himself as "savior" within the community are Verghese's ruminations, which inhibit us from too readily accepting that persona. Verghese frequently reminds us that he is no self-deluding celebrity caught up in his indispensability to Johnson City. At one level, the memoir could be described as charting Verghese's internal journey to becoming more knowledgeable about the human angle of AIDS and about himself as a physician-husband and physician-father; in this trajectory, the work echoes conventional autobiographies' recording of their protagonists' deepening complexity and developing expertise, culminating in, or hinting at, a capstone achievement. But such is not entirely the case with Verghese. There is a counternarrative in his memoir. A growing exhaustion accompanies the emotional intensity of connecting with his patients, a fatigue that is only partly related to his fragile marriage. It is not without irony that he writes of his voluntary departure from the community that he has come to call his own country. Yet, despite the deep guilt he feels at leaving the community, he finds renewed energy. When he crosses into Iowa, he looks up at the sky and declares his connection to the land, humanity, the cosmos itself:

> I look up at the stars. I feel connected: legs to earth, shoulders to sky. I squint my eyes and see the lines that link stars to make constellations, feel their umbra extend down to me, connecting me with this parcel of land that I stand on. Everything is united: my children, the clouds, God, the moon, the mother of my children . . . [347].

Thus, even as he leaves Johnson City, he already begins to see himself as part of a larger, more grandiose landscape. His move to Iowa emulates the nineteenth-century westward journeys of the settlers of the rapidly expanding American republic. It is thus possible to read the memoir's end less as the relinquishing of a recently found home than as the embracing of home on a much larger scale; to see in the move not so much an erasure of himself from the landscape of Johnson City as an insertion of himself into a national (U.S.) history. Thus the "country" of the title is not necessarily just a reference to a little part of Tennessee; it is also a reference to an entire national territory.

AVOIDING THE VOYEURISTIC LURE

Verghese appears to have avoided the charge of voyeurism—of being a straight man and a man of color writing about gay white men.[8] True, some of Verghese's readers may be inclined to view the gay and HIV-positive men in the memoir as "others" or unfamiliar, but in laying bare the intimacies of these men's lives, Verghese "locks" the gaze of his readers and refuses to let them glance away, thereby forcing an attentiveness and concentration that may cause discomfort and pain.

Carlo Rotella reminds us that it is all too easy to fall for the lure of the ethnographic gaze. In the wake of the 1965 Watts riots, for example, majority-culture (white) readers turned to autobiographical and semiautobiographical works by urban writers of color for data about unfamiliar lives in unfamiliar territory. Claude Brown, Eldridge Cleaver, and Piri Thomas, among others, became seen and presented themselves as experts on this section of the United States, previously little known to majority-culture readers. In fact, as Rotella tells us, Brown, who wrote *Manchild in the Promised Land,* a book about his growing up in Harlem, was invited to testify before a U.S. Senate subcommittee examining the "federal role in urban problems." According to Rotella, "Brown and Dunny [Arthur Dunmeyer, Brown's childhood friend] . . . were there . . . to give the senators insight into the minds of violent young men in whom were concentrated a set of social pathologies understood to drive the urban crisis" (271–72).

Verghese's handling of his subject matter, however, does not allow his readers—regardless of their backgrounds—an easy voyeuristic distance from his patients. AIDS, in this book, is an illness "come home"; it has entered deep into the rural community of Johnson City, Tennessee, affecting the lives of mothers and fathers who have never left the region and who can no more say the words "homosexual" and "AIDS" than deal with the reality that their sons' lives are circumscribed by these phenomena. Verghese's assault on his readers—with detailed medical information, with sensitive portrayals of the patients and their families, with probing examinations into his own motivations—permits no simple traveler's survey of this landscape; rather, it extracts a sustained engagement with the complexities of the situation at hand. Both he and the community, writes Verghese, "were in [their] age of innocence" in 1985. He recalls, "I was an AIDS expert with no AIDS in sight, a rookie looking for a challenge. Now [in late 1989], we had over eighty HIV-infected persons in our practice, we were AIDS-seasoned, and all sense of innocence had vanished. Including my own" (318). Joseph Cady identifies two types of writing about AIDS—"immersive" and "counterimmersive." The former he characterizes as thrusting the reader "into a direct imaginative confrontation with the special horrors of AIDS . . . with . . . no relief or buffer provided by the writer"; the counterimmersive kind of AIDS writing "typically focuses on characters who are in various degrees of denial about AIDS themselves, and it customarily treats its readers the way its characters handle their disturbing contact with AIDS, protecting them from too jarring a confrontation with the subject through a variety of distancing devices" (244). Verghese's memoir employs the techniques of both "immersive" and "counterimmersive" AIDS writing. Readers are forced to experience unmediated the horrors of AIDS but, at the same time, are enabled to identify with characters who question, resist, and oppose Verghese's preoccupation with his patients and their disease. The profound alterations that he details, both in himself and in the residents of Johnson City, are what prevent the book from becoming an ethnographic viewing of an unfamiliar region, a sighting of strange and mysterious terrain from a moving vehicle. In fact, Verghese's increasing involvement with his patients and their lives takes place against the backdrop of his own family's conflicted fortunes—the birth of his two sons and his gradually failing marriage.

THE ETHNIC OTHER

Although Verghese has bucked the racial-ethnic trend and not focused primarily on an ethnic community of color, his memoir offers illustrative moments for engaging with the nuances of representation, particularly as they apply to ethnic and racial others. I have written elsewhere ("Ethnic Outsider-ism as the Ultimate Insider-ism") of Verghese's skillful presentation of his outsider status (he was a brown-skinned foreign man in the American South) as an *advantage* in securing the confidence of his AIDS patients (who, Verghese writes, would never have revealed the details of their lives to a member of their own white community, for fear of being judged).

He is at his most sensitive when he portrays the gay men who turn to him for medical and emotional sustenance.

Where Verghese is most problematic is in his presentation of other foreign medical graduates serving in the rural communities of Tennessee. His portrayal of himself as a socially adept foreign doctor (in contrast to other foreign doctors, who are socially inept) brings him dangerously close to aligning himself with the majority culture. For example, his depiction of Dr. Aziz, a colleague, is especially troubling for its implication that to be foreign is to be uncultured. Verghese here assumes the dominant/colonizing perspective and voice:

> Dr. Aziz . . . hailed from a village outside Karachi. Despite going to medical school in the city, he had retained all his country ways. . . . He spoke with a thick guttural accent, . . . putting the burden of figuring out what he was saying onto the nurses. . . . When he ate in the cafeteria, it was with his mouth open and with loud smacking noises. Had he been approachable, someone might have instructed him on what was considered good manners in America. . . . A nurse, stepping into a staff bathroom that Aziz had just emerged from, called after him and to everyone in earshot, "Did you never learn to raise the seat before you pee? Or at least wipe it clean? Were you brought up in a pig sty?" [40–41]

Perhaps Verghese's especially harsh depiction of Aziz can be attributed to his feeling that Aziz's behavior had a direct effect on how he, Verghese, and all other foreigners were perceived and received. But even if one is to be sympathetic to Verghese's rendition of Aziz, one expects from the author a similar critical stance toward the majority culture's tendency to generalize and essentialize. One hopes that, along with Aziz, the majority culture will come in for its fair share of blame. But, unfortunately, such is not the case. Verghese positions himself as the enlightened egalitarian immigrant (replicating, one is perhaps meant to infer, the disdain for class distinctions that Americans are supposed to exhibit) in contrast to Aziz, who "was full of himself, too taken with the fact that he was a doctor" and who "was abhorred by the nurses because of his curt and chauvinistic way of dealing with them." This depiction of Dr. Aziz comes fairly early in the memoir, almost as though, from the outset, Verghese wishes to distance himself from ethnic (South Asian) affiliation and position himself as the enlightened professional. That Aziz is a Pakistani Muslim is also not without significance.[9] Can it be that Verghese, as an immigrant of Indian ancestry and Christian faith, makes

Aziz both an easy target and the means by which he, Verghese, can align himself with the communities that he considers important to his visibility: mainstream readers and Indian Americans, the largest group among the South Asian population in the United States? That the friendship and support of Indian American doctors in the region matters to Verghese is evident in the memoir's relatively nuanced depictions of them. They are not reduced to mere caricatures, as is Dr. Aziz. In fact, Verghese returns repeatedly to Indian-only social gatherings, revealing his comfort with that crowd and enjoying his role as the *enfant terrible* of the community of Indian Americans, the endearing renegade who encourages the children of his staid ethnic friends to take up AIDS medicine, with all its unknowns and frustrations.

Verghese attempts to both acknowledge and distance himself from his foreignness and his otherness. His positioning of himself as an immigrant ethnic doctor of color is not a central component of his assertion of identity. Rather, ethnicity is one tool among many that he uses as the need arises, and it serves different functions in different contexts. When his outsider status helps him, paradoxically, get closer to his AIDS patients, he becomes aware of his ethnic and racial difference from the majority of the residents of Johnson City. But it is a qualified difference that he wishes to project—a difference that invites confidences from his AIDS patients, but not a difference that marks him as undesirable in the eyes of the hospital staff. When it becomes necessary for him to establish links with his patients' families, he downplays the presentation of difference, focusing instead on being a caring "neighbor," a concerned member of the community. When he wishes to occupy the space in which he can momentarily forget about the pressures of being the AIDS doctor, and yet not entirely forget that he is a doctor, he seeks out the company of the other Indian American doctors in the region.

Verghese, it would appear, is an individual who stumbles into his fame as an AIDS doctor. That fame came to him, however, through the literary medium of the memoir, through the narrative and lyrical presentation of himself as an AIDS doctor. Perhaps, therefore, he is currently in that intersecting zone of being both a doctor and a writer and of deriving his fame from both occupations.

THE DESIRE FOR VISIBILITY

Verghese wrote the book in part while studying at the Iowa Writers' Workshop, but in the memoir there is no mention of his having been at one of the most prestigious writing programs in the nation. Recently, he commented that the program didn't teach him about writing per se but did give him the time "'to read, to write, to take [him]self seriously as a writer'" (quoted in Dutt 35). One could conjecture that Verghese's silence regarding his study of the craft of writing stems from his desire to present the autobiography as *lived* rather than *narrated* life, and in so doing to enhance the credibility and authenticity of the individuals and experiences comprising the book. But, as Jerome Bruner categorically asserts, no autobiographical writing can pretend to be unmediated by interpretation:

> An autobiography is not and cannot be a way of simply signifying or referring to a "life as lived." I take the view that there is no such thing as a "life as lived" to be referred to. In this view, a life is created or constructed by the act of autobiography. It is a way of construing experience—and of reconstruing and reconstruing it until our breath or our pen fails. Construal and reconstrual are interpretive. Like all other forms of interpretation, how we construe our lives is subject to our intentions, [to] the interpretive conventions available to us, and to the meanings imposed upon us by the usages of our culture and language [38].

Similarly, as James Olney observes, we cannot forget that, even in looking back at a past self, we look back from a present self, so that even as "memory recalls those earlier states . . . it does so only as a function of present consciousness: we can recall what we were only from the complex perspective of what we are, which means that we may very well be recalling something that we never were at all" ("Some Versions of Memory" 241). Thus "the life-writer who draws on memory does so in full awareness that the temporal position he or she occupies is the present moment of the past and that an excursion into history can begin only with a backward reading from that point" (*Memory and Narrative* 344). In this view, Verghese's time at the Iowa Writers' Workshop would have had an undeniable influence on his recollection and reconstruction of his pre–writers' workshop experiences in Tennessee, the subject matter of *My Own Country.*

The depth and intensity of Verghese's relationship with his patients may help explain the curious omission from his autobiography of any mention of his apprenticeship at the Iowa Writers' Workshop. Could it be that Verghese feels no small guilt for having left Tennessee and then appropriated the lives of his friends there in the writing of his memoir? Could it be that at some level he wishes to deny his role as authorial and *interpretive* voice in the conquests of consciousness that he must make to speak about his patients' medical and family histories? Verghese's refusal to privilege the craft of writing is not dissimilar to Freud's insistence in his 1935 *Autobiographical Study* that all of his observations and findings about human nature were developed not in speculation or abstraction but "in the concrete experience of the consulting room" (Sturrock 18).

Perhaps Verghese sees himself as a doctor first, and then as a writer, in contrast to William Carlos Williams, who saw himself as both and, toward the end of his life, came to see himself primarily as a poet. Williams's practice of medicine nurtured his writing; it was, he said, "my very food and drink, the very thing which made it possible for me to write" (quoted in Bremen 84). Brian Bremen rightly observes that Williams's decision "to practice medicine among the poor immigrants of his home town gave him . . . the opportunity to make an empathic contact with some romantically more 'authentic' member of the human community through an act of diagnosis" (85). It is worth noting that Williams, although part Puerto Rican (on his mother's side), took a keen interest in the urban Polish immigrants of his time and sought a truly American idiomatic language for his poetry in the rhythms of their speech.[10] For Williams, doctoring was subordinate to writing. This preference is clear in his description of his interactions with his patients:

> I lost myself in the very properties of their minds: for the moment at least I actually became *them*, whoever they should be, so that when I detached myself from them at the end of a half-hour of intense concentration over some illness which was affecting them, it was as though I were reawakening from a sleep [Bremen 85].

As Williams saw it, writing constituted his waking life; the doctoring took place at some less than conscious level. It is not surprising, therefore, that the writing gained priority in his conception of himself, and the doctoring became the conduit that sustained his writing.

In Verghese's case, the situation is quite the reverse. Writing enables Verghese to be a better doctor; by sharpening and deepening his imagination, writing prepares him to better understand his patients as people. It is as though writing allows him access to some region beyond the tangible and observable environment of the examining room and the visible symptoms of illness. At a September 1998 reading of his second memoir, *The Tennis Partner,* Verghese explained that each time he meets a fresh batch of students (at the Texas Tech Health Sciences Medical Center, El Paso, where, at the time, he was chief of infectious diseases) he asks them to describe their current patients. Invariably they come up with descriptions that are variants of "white female [or male] 35+ years of age exhibiting symptoms of acute respiratory congestion, temperature 102, lymph nodes swollen. . . . "[11] Before they can continue in this clinical vein, Verghese stops them, he said, and redirects them to talk about their patients by imagining their patients' lives, by envisioning the circumstances and series of encounters that have brought them to the hospital and led to their care. It is this latter type of inquiry and sensibility, this ability *to become* his patient, that Verghese seems to gain from his writing. The medical context is central to Verghese—the stage, if you will, on which he enacts his life. The craft of writing seems to function in much the same way as props or lighting, that is, as an element that is necessary to the enhancement and enrichment of the play but not indispensable to its performance. Whether this attitude toward writing will change remains to be seen. At his reading of *The Tennis Partner,* Verghese revealed that he now spends part of the week exclusively on his writing, so that he is not doctoring full-time. Also open to question is whether this division of his energies, with his currently more formal allocation of time to writing, will lead him to strip away the mystery surrounding Verghese the writer.

Verghese has more than fulfilled his desire for acclaim. He has been the keynote speaker at numerous gatherings of his peers in the medical profession, spoken at the commencements of several medical schools, and had the satisfaction of seeing his memoir become required reading at many schools of medicine across the country.[12] He has also crossed disciplinary boundaries to serve as the invited "expert" at literary seminars, in the company of such mainstream luminaries as Edmund White, Ann Beattie, and Tony Kushner, and has been writer-in-residence at an M.F.A. program whose invited authors have included Joy Harjo, Maxine Hong Kingston, N. Scott Momaday, Sharon Olds, Alice Walker, Sandra Cisneros, James Dickey, and Donald Barthelme. His renown is evident in the medical and literary fields alike, but his impact is not limited to them. He has laid claim to the attention of diverse constituencies and done what few ethnic immigrant writers of color have been able to accomplish: he has crafted a text that neither eclipses nor illuminates ethnicity and race. The very same skill—that is, the skill of maintaining a fine equilibrium between calling attention to and deflecting attention from ethnicity and race—appears again in his recent article in the *New York Times Magazine,* on the need for quarantining individuals suspected of having Severe Acute Respiratory Syndrome (SARS):[13]

> Recently, we in America have sensed our right to privacy eroding, along with our rights to due process. The justification that such loss of liberty directly improves homeland security is not readily apparent, and it seems quite self-serving. But the virus that causes SARS has no political agenda, no jingoist banner to wave. . . . The virus is democratic to the core, affecting rich and poor, doctor and patient, crossing borders with impunity and thus freezing commerce, threatening a global recession. The temporary loss of liberty that might come with a quarantine for SARS, while painful, is a pill that I would find easier to swallow ["Viral Terrors" 15].

This call illustrates the dexterity with which Verghese uses his medical expertise to comment on an urgent nonmedical issue—the suspension of civil liberties—reminding us once again that his advocacy is not limited to the world of health. His guidance is also valuable to the health of our social order.

BIBLIOGRAPHY

Anderson, Linda. *Autobiography.* London and New York: Routledge, 2001.

Attridge, Derek. "Innovation, Literature, Ethics: Relating to the Other." *PMLA* 114.1 (1999): 20–31.

Barolini, Helen. *Chiaroscuro: Essays of Identity.* Madison: University of Wisconsin Press, 1999.

Barrett, Lindon. "Self-Knowledge, Law, and African American Autobiography: Lucy A. Delaney's *From the Darkness Cometh the Light.*" *The Culture of Autobiography: Constructions of Self-Representation.* Ed. Robert Folkenflik. Stanford: Stanford University Press, 1993. 104–24.

Bremen, Brian A. *William Carlos Williams and the Diagnostics of Culture.* New York: Oxford University Press, 1993.

Bruner, Jerome. "The Autobiographical Process." *The Culture of Autobiography: Constructions of Self-Representation.* Ed. Robert Folkenflik. Stanford: Stanford University Press, 1993. 38–56.

Cady, Joseph. "Immersive and Counterimmersive Writing About AIDS: The Achievement of Paul Monette's *Love Alone.*" *Writing About AIDS: Gay Literature, Language, and Analysis.* Ed. Timothy F. Murphy and Suzanne Poirier. New York: Columbia University Press, 1993. 244–64.

Cox, James M. "Recovering Literature's Lost Ground Through Autobiography." *Autobiography: Essays Theoretical and Critical.* Ed. James Olney. Princeton: Princeton University Press, 1980. 123–46.

Dutt, Ela. "The Immigrant Experience and Other Stories." *India Abroad* 12 Mar. 1999: 35.

Edwards, Jonathan. *Jonathan Edwards.* 1739. Ed. Clarence H. Faust and Thomas H. Johnson. New York: Hill and Wang, 1962.

Franklin, Benjamin. *The Autobiography and Other Writings.* Ed. L. Jesse Lemisch. New York: Signet, 1961.

Gunn, Janet Varner. *Autobiography: Toward a Poetics of Experience.* Philadelphia: University of Pennsylvania Press, 1982.

Hurtado, Albert L., and Peter Iverson, eds. *Major Problems in American Indian History: Documents and Essays.* Lexington: D. C. Heath, 1994.

Kadlec, David. "William Carlos Williams, Prohibition, and Immigration." *Mosaic Modernism: Anarchism, Pragmatism, and Culture.* Baltimore: Johns Hopkins University Press, 2000. 122–52.

Klass, Perri. "AIDS in the Heartland." *New York Times Book Review* 28 Aug. 1994: 21.

Krupat, Arnold. "Native American Autobiography and the Synecdochic Self." *American Autobiography: Retrospect and Prospect.* Ed. Paul John Eakin. Madison: University of Wisconsin Press, 1991. 171–94.

Meyer, Melissa L. "Dispossession and the White Earth Anishinaabeg, 1889–1920." *Major Problems in American Indian History: Documents and Essays.* Ed. Albert L. Hurtado and Peter Iverson. Lexington: D. C. Heath, 1994. 391–403.

Olney, James. *Memory and Narrative: The Weave of Life-Writing.* Chicago: University of Chicago Press, 1998.

———. "Some Versions of Memory/Some Versions of *Bios*: The Ontology of Autobiography." *Autobiography: Essays Theoretical and Critical.* Ed. James Olney. Princeton: Princeton University Press, 1980.

Rotella, Carlo. "The Box of Groceries and the Omnibus Tour: *Manchild in the Promised Land.*" October Cities: The Redevelopment of Urban Literature. Berkeley: University of California Press, 1998. 269–93.

Rowlandson, Mary. *The True Story of the Captivity of Mrs. Mary Rowlandson among the Indians and God's Faithfulness to Her in Her Time of Trial.* Tucson: American Eagle Publications, 1990.

Srikanth, Rajini. "Ethnic Outsider-ism as the Ultimate Insider-ism: The Paradox of Verghese's *My Own Country.*" *MELUS,* forthcoming.

———. *The World Next Door: South Asian American Literature and the Idea of America.* Philadelphia: Temple University Press, 2004.

Stepto, Robert. "Narration, Authentication, and Authorial Control in Frederick Douglass' *Narrative* of 1845." *Afro-American Literature: The Reconstruction of Instruction.* Ed. Dexter Fisher and Robert Stepto. New York: Modern Language Association, 1979. 178–91.

Sturrock, John. *The Language of Autobiography: Studies in the First Person Singular.* Cambridge: Cambridge University Press, 1993.

Swann, Brian, and Arnold Krupat. Introduction. *I Tell You Now: Autobiographical Essays by Native American Writers.* Ed. Brian Swann and Arnold Krupat. Lincoln: University of Nebraska Press, 1987.

Verghese, Abraham. *My Own Country: A Doctor's Story of a Town and Its People in the Age of AIDS*. New York: Simon & Schuster, 1994.

———. *The Tennis Partner: A Doctor's Story of Friendship and Loss.* New York: HarperCollins, 1998.

———. "Viral Terrors." *New York Times Magazine* 20 Apr. 2003: 15.

NOTES

1. Reported by Susan Wenner for *The Miami Student Online;* the article is no longer available on the World Wide Web.

2. See Rowlandson, *The True Story of the Captivity of Mrs. Mary Rowlandson*; and Edwards, *Jonathan Edwards.* Rowlandson reminds readers that her courage and fortitude were the work of God. "Before I knew what affliction meant, I was ready sometimes to wish for it," she says, drawing attention to her precaptivity pride; but, she says, she realized after having endured captivity that "the Lord had His time to scourge and chasten me. The portion of some is to have their affliction by drops, now one drop and then another, but the dregs of the cup, the wine of the astonishment, like a sweeping rain that leaveth no food, did the Lord prepare to be my portion" (57). Likewise, Jonathan Edwards writes of his conversion, "I have a much greater sense of my universal, exceeding dependence on God's grace and strength, and mere good pleasure, of late, than I used formerly to have; and have experienced more of an abhorrence of my own righteousness" (71).

3. Benjamin Franklin, *The Autobiography and Other Writings.* Franklin's self-congratulatory tone is unmistakable: "From the poverty and obscurity in which I was born and in which I passed my earliest years, I have raised myself to a state of affluence and some degree of celebrity in the world" (16).

4. See especially Stepto, "Narration, Authentication, and Authorial Control."

5. See Barolini, *Chiaroscuro*: "Not only Italian Americans, but all groups—the Jewish antiheroes and Ellison's Invisible Man and hosts of others—grapple with . . . the quest to discover the connection between a specific identity and being American" (127).

6. For the text of the Dawes Act, see Hurtado and Iverson, 370–72; for an analysis of the impact of government land policies on one particular tribe, see Meyer, "Dispossession and the White Earth Anishinaabeg."

7. The AIDS Memorial Quilt is a mile-long "blanket" made up of more than forty thousand individual panels to commemorate the tens of thousands of people who have died of the disease. It was first displayed in 1987 and has toured more than two thousand cities in the United States. Though most of the names on the quilt are of people who lived in the United States, there are also names of individuals from thirty-nine other countries, including Zambia, Cuba, Russia, and Thailand. In 1989, the AIDS Memorial Quilt was nominated for a Nobel Peace Prize; it is the largest com-

munity art project in the world. See "AIDS Quilt Draws Huge Crowds to Nation's Capital" at http://www.cnn.com/US/9610/12/aids.activism, accessed May 2004.

8. See Srikanth, "Writing What You're Not," chapter 4 of *The World Next Door,* 150–202.

9. The suspicion and hostility between Indians and Pakistanis dates from 1947, when a bloody partition accompanying the end of colonial rule gave birth to the two independent nations of India and Pakistan in the region that had been known as the Indian subcontinent. Verghese's flat Dr. Aziz stands in marked contrast to the Aziz of E. M. Forster's *A Passage to India* (1924). The Aziz of Forster's novel is a nuanced figure, presented as cultured and sensitive, and modeled on Forster's Muslim lover Syed Masood. Through Aziz, a central character in the novel, Forster meditates on the possibility of a union between East and West, colonizer and native. See also *The World Next Door,* 180–81.

10. See David Kadlec, "William Carlos Williams, Prohibition, and Immigration," for a fascinating discussion on the emergence of Williams's innovative poetic formalism in the context of his resistance to the restrictive traditions of Anglo-Saxon literary and social culture.

11. The reading was at the Borders bookstore in Newton, Massachusetts. The words are not exactly those that Verghese used, but what I wish to convey is the strict "medical speak" with which Verghese's students tend to respond to his question.

12. Institutions where Verghese has given commencement addresses or lectures include the Johns Hopkins University School of Medicine (1995), the College of Wooster (1996), and Loyola University Medical School (1998). He has appeared at countless medical conventions as the keynote speaker, and his memoir is being taught in various departments or discussed in book groups at Vanderbilt University, Duke University, the University of Virginia, and Northeastern Ohio Universities College of Medicine, to name a few.

13. SARS, a flulike illness that is sometimes fatal, is believed to be caused by a rare strain of coronavirus. The spring 2003 outbreak of SARS in China, Hong Kong, Singapore, and Toronto claimed several hundred lives before its symptoms were recognized as being more dangerous than those of influenza and adequate measures were taken globally to control transmission of the virus.

CAMBODIAN AMERICAN AUTOBIOGRAPHY

TESTIMONIAL DISCOURSE

TERI SHAFFER YAMADA

> The gravest and most painful testimony of the modern world, the one that possibly involves all other testimonies to which this epoch must answer . . . , is the testimony of the dissolution, the dislocation, or the conflagration of community. — JEAN-LUC NANCY, *The Inoperative Community*

Autobiography is the quintessential American genre, well suited to embody the national representation of rugged and independent individualism for which America is so mythically famous. Immigrants spanning the ethnic spectrum have popularized the genre since the 1700s as they developed the art of personal reflection into a discursive space for the exploration of American ideology and identity. Yet in the 1980s, a shift in autobiographical perspective from the national to the international occurred in the form of Cambodian American autobiography, a new form of testimonial discourse. As Jean-Luc Nancy suggests, one of the most "painful" testimonies of the modern world is the testimony of dislocation and cultural genocide. That is what Cambodian American autobiography signifies, a painful testimony of cultural genocide and dislocation, as it recenters the ideological discourse of American autobiography from a national debate on the parameters of American identity to an international application of American values in the form of global human rights.

My exploration of Cambodian American autobiography, as a new form of testimonial discourse within Asia/America, begins with an excavation of its historical causes and conditions. After mapping its location on the broader terrain of American autobiography, I discuss its morphological development as a unique form of testimony. Finally, I explore how its form and content act synergistically to frame an ideological perspective reflective of a hybrid

Cambodian American identity, unique to the Cambodian diaspora experience.

MAPPING THE SITE OF CAMBODIAN ASIA/AMERICA

> It would be found that one of the most significant properties of the field of cultural production, explaining its extreme dispersion and the conflicts between rival principles of legitimacy, is the extreme permeability of its frontiers and, consequently, the extreme diversity of the "posts" it offers, which defy any unilinear hierarchization. —PIERRE BOURDIEU, *The Field of Cultural Production*

Pierre Bourdieu's concept of "the *field* of cultural production" provides a useful paradigm for mapping Cambodian American autobiography as a subfield onto the broader landscape of Asian America cultural production.[1] This approach requires a panoptic conceptualization of intersecting subfields of literary production: Cambodian American autobiography intersects the field of Asian American autobiography, itself a subset of American autobiography within the broader field of cultural production. What links them is the ideological[2] subtext of the genre of autobiography.

Cambodian American autobiography shares certain ideological features with its American predecessors. The first American autobiography is attributed to Benjamin Franklin (1706–1790), whose self-articulation of dauntless individualism set the tone for future American autobiographers.[3] The heroic subtext of dominant Euro-American autobiography, represented by Franklin, also has a useful ideological dimension.[4] It substantiates the American assimilationist myth of rags-to-riches individualism through the valorization of "great men" who achieved stellar economic or political success by their tenacity and talent. Later immigrant autobiographies have not always been so ideologically celebratory: while some valorize the American dream, others reveal its hypocrisy or nostalgically reminisce about the homeland (Boelhower, *Immigrant Autobiography in the United States*; Payant and Rose, *The Immigrant Experience in North American Literature*). Some Asian American autobiographers, such as Jade Snow Wong and Easurk Emsen Charr, reinforce the assimilation theme; others, such as Carlos Bulosan, Maxine Hong Kingston, and David Mura, reveal the underbelly of American melting-pot hypocrisy.[5]

Unlike predominant models of American autobiography, including minority American autobiographies, Cambodian American autobiography currently remains situated on an "indeterminate site" (Bourdieu 43). The indeterminacy of Cambodian American autobiographers differs from that of other first- and first-and-a-half-generation Southeast Asian American autobiographers, including the Vietnamese, with whom Cambodians are most frequently associated under the rubric "political refugee." Vietnamese refugee autobiography, generically referred to as "refugee literature" by Renny Christopher ("Blue Dragon, White Tiger"), reveals a "survivor" motif reminiscent of Cambodian American autobiography. This may be true for the first-generation Vietnamese American autobiographers, with their sense of nostalgia for the homeland, who frequently explore the tragedy of the Vietnam War and the trauma of relocation.[6] Among autobiographies by the first-and-a-half generation, however, Andrew X. Pham's memoir *Catfish and Mandala: A Two-Wheeled Voyage through the Landscape and Memory of Vietnam,* which won the 1999 Pacific Rim Book Prize, moves beyond this "refugee" category.[7] Pham, a poetically lyrical writer, has produced a cross-genre text that can be described as part bildungsroman, part travel narrative, and part memoir. His success illustrates a development in the morphology and content of autobiography within the genealogy of Vietnamese American authors, a development not yet shared by Cambodian Americans, whose autobiographies remain situated on a liminal interstice of the national/international, narrowly framed around the tragic 1975–79 experience of the Pol Pot era in Cambodia. These autobiographies' indeterminate site on the borderland of the national/international maintains a doubled ideological position.

GENEALOGY OF A CAMBODIAN CHRONOTOPE

> In the literary artistic chronotope, spatial and temporal indicators are fused into one carefully thought-out, concrete whole. Time, as it were, thickens, takes on flesh, becomes artistically visible; likewise, space becomes charged and responsive to the movements of time, plot and history. This intersection of axes and fusion of indicators characterizes the artistic chronotope.
> —MIKHAIL M. BAKHTIN, *The Dialogic Imagination*

> From 1975–1979—through execution, starvation, disease, and forced labor—the Khmer Rouge systematically killed an estimated two million Cambodians, almost a fourth of the country's population. . . . This is a story of survival: my own and my family's. Though these events constitute my experience, my story mirrors that of millions of Cambodians. If you had been living in Cambodia during this period, this would be your story too.
> — LOUNG UNG, *First They Killed My Father*

The impassioned ideological and political subtext of Cambodian American autobiography provides one explanation for why there has been more life writing by or about Cambodians than by or about any other Asian ethnic cohort in the United States during the past several decades: the need to bear witness. Since the 1980s, Cambodians have written more than a dozen autobiographies published in English, at least seven of them authored by Cambodians in America.[8] Perhaps even more striking than these writers' prolific output is the consistently similar temporal-spatial frame—chronotope—that structures their autobiographical narratives: all foreground a "holocaust" experience in Cambodia under the Khmer Rouge.

This distinctive Cambodian autobiographical chronotope is divided into three parts. The first part of this chronotope typically begins with a short portrayal of urban life in Phnom Penh before 1975, as the city steadily devolves into chaos through the violence of civil war. The second part of the chronotope spans the nearly four-year period under the Khmer Rouge regime, which begins with "Year Zero," on April 17, 1975. On that day, Khmer Rouge cadres began to empty Phnom Penh of its inhabitants, implementing a forced march to the countryside; intellectuals as well as government and military officials were specifically targeted and executed along the way. Over the next three years, city people, referred to by the Khmer Rouge as "new people," were progressively starved to death as they were moved relentlessly around the country and forced to work on various labor-intensive projects, such as the building of dams by hand or the clearing of malarial forest land. Children were isolated from their parents and placed in separate communal work teams; husbands were "disappeared" by Angkar ("the Organization"; see Kiernan, *The Pol Pot Regime*; Vickery, "Cultural Survival in Cambodian Language and Literature"). The third part of the chronotope is essentially a coda. It describes the autobiographer's escape and ultimate arrival in the United States after the Vietnamese invasion of Cambodia, in 1979.[9]

The source of this tripartite chronotope appears to be a 1980 *New York Times Magazine* article by Sydney H. Schanberg that was revised and published five years later in book form as *The Death and Life of Dith Pran,* the same title as that of the original article; the 1984 film *The Killing Fields* was based on Schanberg's work. Schanberg's article begins with the fall of Phnom Penh during his assignment as a reporter there, and it describes his despair at being unable to save his close friend, the Cambodian photographer Dith Pran, from the Khmer Rouge. Schanberg traces Pran's torturous experience, his daring escape to a Thai border camp, and his ultimate relocation to the United States, where Schanberg's reportage ends. Although most Cambodians have read neither the original article nor the book, nearly all have seen the film.[10]

In 1987, Haing Ngor, who played the role of Dith Pran in *The Killing Fields,* authored the first autobiography by a Cambodian who had relocated to the United States.[11] His *Haing Ngor: A Cambodian Odyssey* offers a clue to the ideological and political subtext that underpins the serial production of Cambodian American autobiographies as a form of testimonial discourse. Ngor, providing an emotional context for his survival story, begins with a comment on the unthinkable reversal of fortune that he and other Cambodians experienced during the period between 1975 and 1979:

> I am a survivor of the Cambodian holocaust. That's who I am. . . . To keep the Khmer Rouge soldiers from killing me, I had to pretend I was not a doctor. They had already killed most of my family. And my case was typical. By destroying our culture and by enslaving us, the Khmer Rouge changed millions of happy, normal human beings into something more like animals. They turned people like me into cunning, wild thieves [1].

The need for justice serves as the impetus for producing public testimony and signifies a movement beyond the writer's status of victim to the status of plaintiff, as defined by Jean-François Lyotard (8). This evidentiary testimony also provides the concrete basis, or artifact, that an author can utilize in the role of human rights advocate on the terrain of American justice and the prosecution of international crimes against humanity.

THE TRIAL: SYMBOL OF JUSTICE AND CLOSURE

> This holocaust, while well documented in such treatments as the movie *The Killing Fields* and in the autobiography by Haing Ngor, has been almost totally ignored outside of Southeast Asia. If, however, we have learned nothing in the continuing struggle of man's inhumanity to man, we can confidently state that such "lessons" in history will be repeated as long as they are overlooked by the world community. The continuing reliance upon witnesses to such events serves as a constant reminder of the need to bring them to our attention. —SOPHAL LENG STAGG, *Hear Me Now*

Pin Yathay, the first Cambodian to write of his Khmer Rouge experience, escaped while the regime was still in power. After fleeing the country in 1977, Yathay, an educated professional, immediately relocated to France, where he arranged a series of press conferences with Western reporters in an attempt to inform the world about the atrocities occurring in Cambodia. In 1978, by his own account, he spoke in Paris, Brussels, Montreal, Ottawa, and Washington, "demanding Western action against the Khmer Rouge" (236). He was greeted with polite concern and inaction. Yathay's deep despair at this international silence was echoed more than a decade later in Sophal Leng Stagg's *Hear Me Now*.

Pin Yathay's demand for action initiates us into the shared ideological and political dimension of these autobiographies: the audience is international in scope; the topic is violation of human rights; and the historically accurate testimonial discourse becomes symbolically evidentiary in its ability to substantiate the crime. For Cambodians relocated to America, this broad internationalist, human rights perspective required a Janus-faced positioning, one situated on the boundary between national and international. On the national front, this discourse both positioned itself within and addressed the United States, the ideological land of "liberty and justice for all," and from this base it addressed an international audience, in a plea for human rights and global justice. In the case of some autobiographers, this double movement between national and international deployed America's own ideology of justice against itself. It revealed the hypocrisy of America's policy, that of a Machiavellian national security state, which supported Pol Pot as the official representative of Cambodia in the United Nations during the Vietnamese occupation of Cambodia (1979–89). This double movement could also be used to lobby the U.S. Government for redress of its past wrongs; in this case, redress would have been symbolized by American support for a U.N.-sponsored war crimes tribunal.

Haing Ngor illustrates this Janus-faced ideological position. Toward the end of his autobiography, he describes how the Cambodia Documentation Commission (1985–90) tried to arrange for the trial of top Khmer Rouge leaders before an international tribunal.[12] Ngor explains that David Hawk, a former executive director of Amnesty International U.S.A., has been working with a group of Cambodian refugees, legal scholars, and human rights specialists to document human rights violations under Khmer Rouge rule. In Ngor's words, the Cambodia Documentation Commission was "seeking to bring those responsible to justice in the World Court, under the terms of the UN Convention on the Prevention and Punishment of the Crime of Genocide" (464). Once again, Ngor's activist autobiography reveals the resonance between, on the one hand, Cambodian American autobiography as proof of "crimes against humanity" and, on the other, the politics of international human rights. It reveals the need for justice, symbolized by a trial, which officially recognizes that atrocities have been committed and thereby moves toward punishment of the perpetrators and toward closure for the victims.

Cambodia remained under Vietnamese governance until 1989, with democratic elections finally held May 23–28, 1993, under the auspices of the United Nations, through the Asian Human Rights Commission. Pol Pot remained in a Khmer Rouge camp along the Thai border, free of indictment until he was tried, in July 1997, by rival Khmer Rouge forces at their jungle base in Anlong Veng, in a "people's tribunal." On April 15, 1998, Pol Pot died, supposedly of a heart attack. As this volume went to press, other key players in Khmer Rouge crimes against humanity remained at large. Given the historical context, the failure of justice has become a subtext of these autobiographies. Both the need for evidence, to substantiate Khmer Rouge atrocities, and the desire for international justice continued to be major forces propelling the production of Cambodian autobiographies through the 1990s. The link between these two decades of autobiographical productivity, the 1980s and the 1990s, was the growing political power of the Cambodia Documentation Commission and Yale University's Cambodian Genocide Program (CGP).[13]

The Cambodian Documentation Commission would ultimately achieve its mission: the collection of documents in preparation for a war crimes trial. Its efforts were institutionalized by the United States with the 1994 Cambodian Justice Act, which furnished the political recognition and economic basis for the collection of evidence. The CGP was the result of this effort. Its mandate is to help implement "the policy of the United States to support efforts to bring to justice members of the Khmer Rouge for their crimes against humanity committed in Cambodia between April 17, 1975 and January 7, 1979." The CGP's 1995 report states, "Until now, no detailed picture has existed of specific atrocities, victims and perpetrators of the Cambodian genocide. The Cambodian Genocide Program has made major strides in assembling the documentation necessary to prosecute the authors of the Cambodian genocide."[14] An excellent example of the synergy between this historical project and the production of testimonials is Dith Pran's 1997 anthology, *Children of Cambodia's Killing Fields.* Pran, who worked for the CGP during the 1990s, describes the twenty-nine autobiographical vignettes in his anthology as "testimonials," and he says, "I hope some day the world community will help to find justice for the Cambodian people. The top echelon of the Khmer Rouge who are responsible for the Cambodian Genocide should be brought to trial."[15] As this essay was being written, in 2003, the human rights debate continued. In 1997, the U.N. Commission on Human Rights adopted resolution 1997/49, which enables the U.N.'s secretary general to assist the Cambodian government if it requests help in responding to "serious violations of Cambodian and international law." On March 17, 2003, after years of negotiation, some movement toward a tribunal finally occurred when the U.N. announced an agreement that could lead to a trial (Osborne, "Khmer Rouge Trials in Sight?"). Nevertheless, the terms for a fair war crimes tribunal were still being negotiated with Hun Sen, Cambodia's prime minister, as this volume went to press.

In April 2000, as the twenty-fifth anniversary of the Khmer Rouge conquest of Phnom Penh approached, scores of Cambodian testimonials were published in Cambodian and international newspapers and on various Web sites linked to Cambodian issues. On May 20 of that year, a day devoted to remembrance of the Khmer Rouge atrocities, the Documentation Center of Cambodia (DC-Cam), together with the Cambodian Genocide Program, announced an updated release of the Cambodian Genocide Data Bases (CGDB) on the World Wide Web:

> This latest release features new biographical data in addition to major enhancements to the interactive maps of Cambodia's "killing fields." . . . Researchers at the Documentation Center of Cambodia mapped forty new genocide sites in twelve provinces in 1999, bringing the number of sites recorded to a total of 520. . . . The CGDB was first mounted on the Internet in January 1997, and now includes 10,800 biographical records, 3,000 bibliographic records, and over 6,000 photographs and images, as well as information on the 520 mass graves, prisons, and memorials.[16]

In spite of all this activity, and the political lobbying of the U.S. State Department to support a U.N.-sponsored war tribunal, the government of Cambodia has been able to stall the process. Since the terrorist attacks of September 11, 2001, on the World Trade Center and the Pentagon, the international atmosphere has changed, and the domestic and international impetus for justice against the Khmer Rouge has waned.

It seems probable that as long as a war crimes tribunal is postponed and a sense of injustice prevails among so many Cambodians in diaspora, there will be more survivor autobiographies foregrounding the Cambodian holocaust, and that this situation will persist until the remaining senior Khmer Rouge leaders, such as Nuon Chea, are dead. A fair trial of Khmer Rouge officials who committed crimes against humanity would bring some sense of closure to those Cambodians who have become advocates for an international standard of human rights. Nevertheless, the historical factors that have fostered this new type of "American" testimonial autobiography continue to exist in the post-9/11 realm of the "war on terror," which has undermined the momentum behind international human rights discourse.

FROM VICTIM TO PLAINTIFF

> It is in the nature of a victim not to be able to prove that one has been done a wrong. A plaintiff is someone who has incurred damages and who disposes of the means to prove it. One becomes a victim if one loses these means . . . the "perfect crime" does not consist in killing the victim or the witnesses, but rather in obtaining the silence of the witnesses, the deafness of the judges, and the inconsistency (insanity) of the testimony. —JEAN-FRANÇOIS LYOTARD, *The Differend*

> I cannot completely explain my reasons for the need to write about these experiences except as a testimony to those whose lives were lost and who can no longer speak for themselves. —SOPHAL LENG STAGG, *Hear Me Now*

Most Cambodians are no strangers to trauma. They have been doubly inscribed as victims: once in Cambodia under Pol Pot, and once in the United States under the social service bureaucracy (Ong, "Making the Biopolitical Subject"). Autobiographers of the 1980s and the 1990s alike speak to a common Cambodian experience of tremendous suffering, both here and abroad. Many Cambodians have never fully recovered from the multiple-trauma experience of the Pol Pot years. Obsessive reflections, regret, sorrow, and depression are common emotional states. According to one Western psychological perspective, these symptoms persist for the first-generation Cambodian refugee because of traditional cultural restraints on self-expression as a healing modality (Morelli 128). Many older Cambodians feel that it is inappropriate to publicly reveal such deep, painful feelings, or they feel incapable of verbalizing such horror. Words simply fail to communicate the experience. Western "talking" therapy is often ineffective in the case of Cambodians: ironically, symptoms for many Cambodians with post-traumatic stress disorder (PTSD) are sometimes exacerbated by the disclosure of feelings, simply because talking about it causes the experience to be relived. Moreover, the encouragement to "talk" in a depositional sense, so that information can be collected as evidence, is an American/Western legalistic response to a crime. Cambodian autobiographers often reflect both aspects of "talking": an American sensibility, in their use of autobiography as a form of therapeutic self-disclosure, which includes writing as a healing praxis; and political action, in the form of testimonial discourse. This movement from victim to plaintiff—an action signified by the rupture of an imposed silence—informs most Cambodian American autobiographies.

As the writer of an autobiography of witness, a testimonial of atrocity, the author is typically concerned with a truthful rendition of life experience under the Khmer Rouge. Since one function of this testimonial is to be useful as historical evidence in constructing domestic/international public support for a war crimes tribunal, or formal recognition of atrocity in order to prevent its recurrence, historical accuracy takes on more importance than it would in a non-Cambodian autobiography, whose fictive potentiality has been well explored by scholars of the genre (Mansell; Olney, *Metaphors of Self*). As testimonials of Khmer Rouge atrocities, Cambodian autobiographies can be used, symbolically or ideologically, as depositional discourse. Kim DePaul, executive director of the Dith Pran Holocaust Awareness Project, explains the testimonial significance of Pran's *Children of Cambodia's Killing Fields*:

> The testimonies related here bear poignant witness to the slaughter the Khmer Rouge inflicted on the Cambodian people. . . . They speak [of] their bewilderment and pain as Khmer Rouge cadres tore their families apart, subjected them to harsh brainwashing, drove them from their homes to work in forced-labor camps, and executed captives in front of them. Their stories tell of suffering and the loss of innocence, the struggle to survive against all odds, and the ultimate triumph of the human spirit.[17]

These testimonial autobiographies also refute the forced confessions written by prisoners in S-21, a former school turned into a center for interrogation and torture during the Khmer Rouge regime.[18] Thousands of fabricated confessional documents were created at S-21, often linking the victims' life histories to involvement with the American CIA. S-21's archive of evidentiary confessional documents and photographs was discovered during the early 1980s by a number of U.S. Cambodia scholars (Chandler, *Voices from S-21* 1–13). Cornell University then established a documentation project in cooperation with the museum curator at S-21 to photograph and catalogue the archives. David Chandler, who studied the confessions for over a decade, clarifies their historicity: "I hoped initially to use the archive as the basis for a narrative history of opposition to . . . DK [Democratic Kampuchea]. I soon discovered, however, that the truth or falsity of the confessions, along with the innocence or guilt of the people who produced them, could rarely be corroborated" (ix).

False confessions were the prisoners' attempts to free themselves from the various unthinkable tortures devised by the "truthseekers" associated with S-21, as delineated by Vann Nath in *A Cambodian Prison Portrait*. Most Cambodians were forced to lie in order to survive, as Haing Ngor also states in his lament about being turned into a liar for the sake of self-preservation (1). Therefore, the truthfulness of Cambodian autobiography has a double significance. It becomes socially significant as evidentiary proof to be used against the Khmer Rouge in a war crimes trial, and it is personally significant as a means of rehabilitating oneself. Through the autobiographical act, the author moves from the abject, silenced position of victim to the active status of plaintiff.

HYBRID IDENTITY

> The diaspora experience is defined, not by essence or purity, but by the recognition of a necessary heterogeneity and diversity: by a conception of "identity" which lives with and though, not despite, difference, by *hybridity*.
> —STUART HALL, "Cultural Identity and Cinematic Representation"

Cambodians are the only Southeast Asian refugees in America to have experienced a form of cultural genocide before relocation, a circumstance that makes their experience of Americanization even more problematic. Caught in a process of acculturation and assimilation that requires the abandonment of traditional norms, they simultaneously need to reconstruct these norms as the basis for healing the kind of trauma they have endured ("Voice of Experience"). Moreover, many Cambodian refugees, having relocated to the United States, found themselves experiencing the same pattern of abject or binary identity paradox as other Asians in America, making genuine assimilation an illusive prospect (Cheng, *The Melancholy of Race*).

For some Cambodian American autobiographers, the development of a viable and unique hybrid identity, one that balances Americanization with the heritage culture, can be ascertained beneath the veneer of the texts' homogeneity. The horrible sameness of experience in the killing fields and its ubiquitous trauma serve to obfuscate the differences between authors. Chris Higashi's review of Loung Ung's *First They Killed My Father* and of Chanrithy

Him's *When Broken Glass Floats* illustrates the temptation to read these autobiographies as variations on the same theme:

> These survivors hope to help others to heal by giving voice to those who did not survive and those who still suffer but cannot speak for themselves. They honor their parents, family, friends, and Cambodians who lost their lives. They work to alter the world's perceptions of Cambodia based on images of the brutal Khmer Rouge [4].

Indeed, Him's and Ung's autobiographies are superficially very similar: they have identical chronotopes, both were written by first-and-a-half-generation Cambodian Americans, both authors are female, both were young children under the Khmer Rouge, both relocated to the United States and grew up attending U.S. public schools, and both have experienced the recurrent nightmares associated with PTSD.

To some degree, Him and Ung share a form of hybrid identity. Both have made the requisite double movement, rehabilitating and accommodating Cambodianness while developing an American identity. For each, the rehabilitation of traditional culture clearly takes place through the autobiographical act, as each describes both pre– and post–Khmer Rouge Cambodia and the extent of cultural devolution that took place between 1975 and 1979. This rehabilitation symbolizes a psychological movement away from the cultural abjection created by Cambodia's autogenocide. How much appreciation there was for the emotionally courageous nature of this autobiographical act is illustrated by the adulation initially bestowed on Loung Ung after the publication of *First They Killed My Father* (see "Cambodia: Survivor's Story").

Ung and Him have also both developed a socially active form of Americanness, which signifies the move from victim to plaintiff status in the trajectory of their social development. Their similar structuring of their "American identity" as that of politically or socially active subject-citizen suggests one avenue toward constructing a hybrid Cambodian-American identity. In Him's case, a socially active "Americanness" is expressed through her work with other Cambodian refugees with PTSD in Portland, Oregon; through her participation in international conferences on this issue; and through her published autobiography, which decries the atrocities that have caused this trauma, and which seeks justice for the victims. Ung's pattern is somewhat parallel. She has served as a national spokesperson for the Campaign for a Landmine-Free World, a program of the Vietnam Veterans of America Foundation, and has traveled to Cambodia several times in connection with land mine issues. Ung and Him have both constructed an individualized hybrid identity where national meets international.

Irrespective of such similarities, their paths to hybridity have differed, as must their sense of what that hybridity entails as it develops through an ongoing process of cultural negotiation. Bourdieu's concepts of "trajectory," "habitus," and "field" offer us a useful perspective on the conditions that shaped the content and form of Him's and Ung's autobiographies. Bourdieu's concepts entail both a static and a dynamic concept of self and subject position (trajectory) located within specific social relations informed by familial and cultural conditions (habitus) that intersect broader social, economic, and historical conditions (field). It is through these intersecting domains that Loung Ung and Chanrithy Him have developed their distinctive hybrid identities. Their differences of habitus, both in Cambodia and in America—for example, Ung's upper-class social status and cultural identification as "Chinese" Cambodian in Phnom Penh, compared to Him's rural, middle-class status and her identification as "Cambodian"—partially explain their different perspectives on Cambodian culture and the Khmer Rouge. These differences are also illustrated by the morphological uniqueness of their autobiographies, as symbolized by their inclusion of divergent maps of Cambodia.

On a continuum of facticity, Him displays a conscious concern with the historical veracity of her autobiography, which reveals a multifaceted ideological complexity. Her map of Cambodia includes the 1969–79 B-52 "Menu" targets, the sites of America's illegal bombing of Cambodia, along with the route of her family's forced relocations in the countryside after their evacuation from Phnom Penh in 1975. Ung's map contains the different Khmer Rouge zones and the names of the provinces. Him, without overtly criticizing U.S. policy toward Cambodia in her autobiography, does so indirectly through intertextual complexity. Narrating her story in both first person and historically omniscient voices, she also incorporates "historical records" in the form of newspaper quotations at the beginnings of a number of chapters. Chapter 2, "B-cinquante-deux," begins with an excerpt from a 1973 article by *New York Times* correspondent Seymour M. Hersh:

> Washington, July 18—United States B-52 bombers made at least 3,500 secret bombing raids over Cambodia in a 14-month period beginning in March, 1969, Defense Department sources disclosed today. . . . Military sources did confirm, however, that information about the Cambodian raids was directly provided to President Nixon and his top national security advisers, including Henry A. Kissinger (38).[19]

Him successfully establishes for her American readers a visceral connection between "historical fact" and "personal experience." The bombing and subsequent Vietnamese skirmishes destroyed her family's rural life, forcing them to Phnom Penh. Without polemic, she nudges historically amnesiac American readers toward recognition of their government's complicity in an unpleasant history. Through this interweaving of the historical and the personal, Him's autobiography provides a multifaceted ideological positioning, which both covertly applauds and embraces America's "human rights advocacy" while indirectly criticizing the United States' actual policy of illegal bombing and subsequent support of the Khmer Rouge. She exploits the gap between ideology and reality.

In contrast to Ung's *First They Killed My Father,* Him's autobiography also provides a more historically complex and nuanced representation of the Khmer Rouge: some were brutal, others saved her life. Ung—who, again, identifies as "Chinese" Cambodian—associates the Khmer Rouge's brutality with anti-Chinese ethnic cleansing and repeatedly describes the deep hatred they generate in her, an emotion of such intensity that it may well have saved her life: "I stand in my corner with more conviction than ever to kill these soldiers, to avenge the blood that drips from my brother's skull. Someday, I will kill them all. My hatred for them is boundless" (118–19). Ung was five and Him was eight in 1975, which may explain some differences in their recollections and experiences. Both rely on relatives' memories to reconstruct their stories. Ung, through passages in italics, also explores in dreams and fantasy what may have happened to her "disappeared" father and other relatives, reflecting less concern for historical veracity and a more psychological approach to autobiography, which allows for fictive elements.

In *First They Killed My Father,* Ung is more ideologically pro-American (12) than Him is in her own autobiography. There are no B-52 bombing sites on Ung's map of Cambodia (xv), though she does mention the bombing: "The war in Vietnam spread to Cambodia when the United States bombed Cambodia's borders to try to destroy the North Vietnamese bases. The bombings destroyed many villages and killed many people, allowing the Khmer Rouge to gain support from the peasants and farmers" (40). She may also exploit this less critical ideological stance in her role as an anti–land mine advocate in Washington, D.C., or may ideologically represent what Camara Harrell refers to as a "manichean" mind-set, a dualistic worldview, reflective of many minorities in the United States. One other interpretation is that her actual experience of the Khmer Rouge in Cambodia may well have been more uniformly horrible than Him's. Ung's family was forcibly relocated to the most extreme Khmer Rouge area, Sector 6 in the Northwest Zone, where Ung remained from November 1975 to May 1977, whereas Him was relocated to comparatively less severe areas (Chandler, *The Tragedy of Cambodian History* 269).

Ung was ultimately relocated from a Thai border camp, and in 1980, when she was ten years old, her American habitus became Vermont. She grew up there in her town's only Cambodian family. Rejecting anything Cambodian, she became as American as possible and only in college began seriously to explore and reclaim her Cambodianness, all the while suffering from nightmares common to Cambodians affected by PTSD. She explains her different experience of Americanization:

> When Meng [Ung's brother] and I came to America, I did everything I could to not think about them [her relatives who remained in Cambodia]. In my new country, I immersed myself in American culture during the day, but at night the war haunted me with nightmares. . . . As the Ethiopian crisis faded from the screens and Americans' consciousness, I was even more determined to make myself a normal American girl. I played soccer. I joined the cheerleading squad. . . . I cut and curled my hair. I painted my eyes with dark makeup to make them look more round and Western. I'd hoped being Americanized could erase my memories of the war [235–36].

In contrast, a geographical component of Him's habitus in the United States was Portland, Oregon, where Him grew up in a community with other Cambodian refugee children who attended the same public schools. Since Him was culturally sheltered by a small Cambodian enclave, her experience of rejecting her own Cambodianness was comparatively less deep than Ung's:

> It's different in American culture. When I first came, I had that culture shock. . . . But I think you can laugh about it, and be proud of the differences between us. . . . To me, I'm American, Cambodian-American. I don't know what it means . . . there was still Cambodian culture being thrust on me by my elders and aunts and uncles early on in college, and it was really stressful dealing with this living between two cultures ["Cambodia—Pol Pot's Shadow: Chanrithy Him, the Storyteller"].

Him's experience of growing up in a Cambodian enclave may also partially explain the care she takes with the historical veracity of her autobiographical reconstruction; she absorbed the mainstream understanding of the

Cambodian refugee intellectual community represented by Haing Ngor, Dith Pran, and others with respect to the veridical significance of the Cambodian holocaust discourse. Proof of this is publication of her account "When the Owl Cries" in Dith Pran's *Children of Cambodia's Killing Fields* several years before the publication of her own autobiography (147–53). In contrast, the more isolated and Americanized Ung was probably unaware of any intellectual concern over the historical and cultural accuracy of this testimonial genre. Toward the end of her publicity tour, in 2000, Ung was severely criticized by some members of the Cambodian community—specifically, a cohort of first-and-a-half-generation intellectuals—for misrepresenting their experience while being promoted as their spokesperson (Lay, "The Cambodian Tragedy"). Ironically, Ung's attempt to reclaim her Cambodian identity through this process led to mixed reviews by her own generation of Cambodian Americans in the midst of ubiquitous praise from mainstream media and non-Cambodian readers.[20]

Regardless of this significant difference in habitus, both Chanrithy Him and Loung Ung exemplify how the trajectory from passive to active Cambodianness serves as one path toward the construction of a hybrid identity. Both have published autobiographies, a symbolic act of this transition; both have developed an agency that involves a praxis of social change. Nevertheless, their hybridity is not homogeneous; rather, in the words of Stuart Hall, it "lives with and through, not despite[,] difference" in the context of their respective histories and locations (80).

As a subfield of American autobiography, Cambodian American testimonial discourse is situated on a shifting site, at the boundary between national and international within the diasporic borderlands of American cultural production. Its development has been congruent with the cognitive remapping of Asian American studies that has been taking place since the 1990s, which has reinscribed "Asian America" as a transnational, transcultural, or diasporic site.[21]

This indeterminate site of the national/international within transnational Asia/America also reflects a doubled ideological position and hybrid identity for Cambodian American autobiographers. Their trajectory from passive to active agency, symbolized by the autobiographical act, resituates the Cambodian American author from the silenced position of victim to the site of a social justice advocate: the personally and politically significant movement from victim to plaintiff (Lyotard). This shift also mirrors the development of a socially engaged hybrid identity, which, in the case of Haing Ngor, Ly Y, and others, simultaneously supports and subverts America's domestic ideology/hypocrisy of "freedom and justice" while deploying it transnationally to advocate for universal human rights.

One can anticipate new forms of autobiography in years to come as Cambodian Americans of the second generation make their literary mark on the American landscape. One can also anticipate that the trauma of 1975–79 has so deeply structured the Cambodian diaspora experience that its shadow will continue to haunt the literary formations and identities of that generation.

BIBLIOGRAPHY

Ashe, Var Hong. *From Phnom Penh to Paradise: Escape from Cambodia*. London: Hodder and Stoughton, 1988.

Asian Human Rights Commission. "Cambodian People Demand for Peace." Editorial. *Human Rights Solidarity* 3.2 (1993): n.p. http://www.ahrchk.net/hrsolid/mainfile.php/1993vol03no02/2046, accessed Feb. 2004.

Bakhtin, Mikhail M. *The Dialogic Imagination: Four Essays*. Ed. Michael Holquist. Trans. Caryl Emerson and Michael Holquist. Austin: University of Texas Press, 1981.

Bayoumi, Moustafa, and Andrew Rubin, eds. *The Edward Said Reader*. New York: Vintage, 2000.

Becker, Elizabeth. "Pol Pot: Life of a Tyrant." *BBC News, World Edition* 14 Apr. 2000. http://news.bbc.co.uk/1/hi/world/asia-pacific/78988.stm.

Boelhower, William. *Immigrant Autobiography in the United States (Four Versions of the Italian American Self)*. Verona: Essedue Edizioni, 1982.

Bourdieu, Pierre. *The Field of Cultural Production: Essays on Art and Literature*. New York: Columbia University Press, 1993.

Bulosan, Carlos. *America Is in the Heart: A Personal History*. Seattle: University of Washington Press, 1943.

"Cambodia—Pol Pot's Shadow: Chanrithy Him, the Storyteller." *Frontline/World* Oct. 2002. http://www.pbs.org/frontlineworld/stories/cambodia/him_interview.html, accessed Feb. 2004.

"Cambodia: Survivor's Story." *Nightline*. American Broadcasting Corporation. 8 June 2000.

Cargill, Mary, and Jade Quang Huynh, eds. *Voices of Vietnamese Boat People: Nineteen Narratives of Escape and Survival*. New York: McFarland, 2000.

Chandler, David P. *The Tragedy of Cambodian History: Politics, War, and Revolution since 1945*. New Haven: Yale University Press, 1991.

———. *Voices from S-21: Terror and History in Pol Pot's Secret Prison*. Berkeley: University of California Press, 1999.

Charr, Easurk Emsen. *The Golden Mountain: The Autobiography of a Korean Immigrant.* Urbana: University of Illinois Press, 1996.

Cheah, Pheng. "Posit(ion)ing Human Rights in the Current Global Conjuncture." *Transnational Asia Pacific: Gender, Culture, and the Public Sphere.* Ed. Shirley Geok-lin Lim, Larry E. Smith, and Wimal Dissanayake. Urbana: University of Illinois Press, 1999. 11–42.

Cheng, Anne Anlin. *The Melancholy of Race: Psychoanalysis, Assimilation, and Hidden Grief.* Oxford: Oxford University Press, 2001.

Cheung, King-Kok, ed. *An Interethnic Companion to Asian American Literature.* New York: Cambridge University Press, 1997.

Chow, Rey. *Writing Diaspora: Tactics of Intervention in Contemporary Cultural Studies.* Bloomington: Indiana University Press, 1993.

Christopher, Renny. "Blue Dragon, White Tiger: The Bicultural Stance of Vietnamese American Literature." *Reading the Literatures of Asian America.* Ed. Shirley Geok-lin Lim and Amy Ling. Philadelphia: Temple University Press, 1992. 259–70.

Chuh, K. S., ed. *Orientations: Mapping Studies in the Asian Diaspora.* Durham: Duke University Press, 2001.

Criddle, Joan D., and Teeda Butt Mam. *To Destroy You Is No Loss: The Odyssey of a Cambodian Family.* Dixon, CA: East/West Bridge, 1987.

DePaul, Kim. "The Dith Pran Holocaust Awareness Project, Inc.: Spreading the Word of the Cambodian Genocide." Feb. 2000. http://www.dithpran.org, accessed Feb. 2004.

Dirlik, Arif. "Asians on the Rim: Transnational Capital and Local Community in the Making of Contemporary Asian America." *Amerasia Journal* 22.3 (1996): 1–24.

Elliott, Duong Van Mai. *The Sacred Willow: Four Generations in the Life of a Vietnamese Family.* Oxford: Oxford University Press, 1999.

Fiffer, Sharon Sloan. *Imagining America: Paul Thai's Journey from the Killing Fields of Cambodia to Freedom in the U.S.A.* New York: Paragon House, 1991.

Fifield, A. *A Blessing over Ashes: The Remarkable Odyssey of My Unlikely Brother.* New York: Avon, 2000.

Franklin, Benjamin. *Benjamin Franklin: His Life as He Wrote It.* Ed. Esmond Wright. Cambridge: Harvard University Press, 1990.

Freeman, James A. *Hearts of Sorrow: Vietnamese-American Lives.* Stanford: Stanford University Press, 1989.

Geertz, Clifford. *The Interpretation of Cultures.* New York: Basic Books, 1973.

Gerber, Lane. "We Must Hear Each Other's Cry: Lessons from Pol Pot Survivors." *Genocide, War, and Human Survival.* Ed. Charles B. Strozier and Michael Flynn. Lanham, MD: Rowman and Littlefield, 1996. 297–317.

Grossberg, Lawrence. "Identity and Cultural Studies: Is That All There Is?" *Questions of Cultural Identity.* Ed. Stuart Hall and Paul du Gay. London: Sage, 1996. 87–106.

Hall, Stuart. "Cultural Identity and Cinematic Representation." *Framework* 36 (1989): 68–81.

———, and Paul du Gay, eds. *Questions of Cultural Identity.* London: Sage, 1996.

Harrell, Camara Jules P. *Manichean Psychology: Racism and the Minds of People of African Descent.* Washington, DC: Howard University Press, 1999.

Hayslip, Le Ly. *Child of War, Woman of Peace.* New York: Doubleday, 1993.

———. *When Heaven and Earth Changed Places: A Vietnamese Woman's Journey from War to Peace.* New York: Doubleday, 1989.

Higashi, Chris. "Out of the Darkness: Three Young Survivors of Cambodia's Killing Fields Remember." *International Examiner* 27.9 (2000): 4.

Him, Chanrithy. "When the Owl Cries." *Children of Cambodia's Killing Fields: Memoirs by Survivors.* Comp. Dith Pran. Ed. Kim DePaul. New Haven: Yale University Press, 1997. 147–53.

———. *When Broken Glass Floats: Growing Up under the Khmer Rouge.* New York: Norton, 2000.

Hitchens, Christopher. *The Trial of Henry Kissinger.* New York: Verso, 2001.

Hu-DeHart, Evelyn. *Across the Pacific: Asian Americans and Globalization.* Philadelphia: Temple University Press, 1999.

Huynh, Jade Ngoc Quang. *South Wind Changing.* Saint Paul: Graywolf Press, 1994.

Imam, V. *When Elephants Fight: A Memoir.* St. Leonards, Australia: Allen and Unwin, 2000.

Joseph, May. *Nomadic Identities: The Performance of Citizenship.* Public Worlds 5. Minneapolis: University of Minnesota Press, 1999.

Kiernan, Ben. *The Pol Pot Regime: Race, Power, and Genocide in Cambodia under the Khmer Rouge, 1975–79.* New Haven: Yale University Press, 1996.

Lafreniere, Bree, and Daran Kravan. *Music through the Dark: A Tale of Survival in Cambodia.* Honolulu: University of Hawaii Press, 2000.

Lay, Sody. "The Cambodian Tragedy: Its Writer and Representations." *Amerasia Journal* 27.2 (2001): 171–82.

Lee, Jid. *From the Promised Land to Home: Trajectories of Selfhood in Asian-American Women's Autobiography.* Las Colinas, TX: Ide House, 1998.

Lim, Shirley Geok-lin, and Wimal Dissanayake. Introduction. *Transnational Asia Pacific: Gender, Culture, and the Public Sphere.* Ed. Shirley Geok-lin Lim, Larry E. Smith, and Wimal Dissanayake. Urbana: University of Illinois Press, 1999. 1–9.

———. Larry E. Smith, and Wimal Dissanayake, eds. *Transnational Asia Pacific: Gender, Culture, and the Public Sphere.* Urbana: University Illinois Press, 1999.

Lyotard, Jean-François. *The Differend: Phrases in Dispute.* George Van Den Abbeele, trans. Theory and History of Literature 46. Minneapolis: University of Minnesota Press, 1986.

Mansell, Darrel. "Unsettling the Colonel's Hash: 'Fact' in Autobiography." *The American Autobiography: A Collection of Critical Essays.* Ed. Albert E. Stone. Englewood Cliffs, NJ: Prentice-Hall, 1981. 61–79.

Marcus, Laura. *Auto/biographical Discourses: Criticism, Theory, Practice.* Manchester: Manchester University Press, 1994.

May, Someth. *Cambodian Witness: The Autobiography of Someth May.* New York: Random House, 1986.

Minatoya, Linda. *Talking to High Monks in the Snow: An Asian American Odyssey.* New York: HarperCollins, 1992.

Morelli, Paula Toki Tanemura. "Trauma and Healing: The Construction of Meaning among Survivors of the Cambodian Holocaust." Diss. University of Washington, 1996.

Nancy, Jean-Luc. *The Inoperative Community.* Theory and History of Literature 76. Minneapolis: University of Minnesota Press, 1991.

Ngor, Haing. *Haing Ngor: A Cambodian Odyssey.* New York: Macmillan, 1987.

Nguyen, Thi Thu-Lam. *Fallen Leaves: Memoirs of a Vietnamese Woman from 1940–1975.* New Haven: Yale Southeast Asian Studies, 1989.

Olney, James, ed. *Autobiography: Essays Theoretical and Critical.* Princeton: Princeton University Press, 1980.

———. *Metaphors of Self: The Meaning of Autobiography.* Princeton: Princeton University Press, 1972.

Ong, Aihwa. *Flexible Citizenship: The Cultural Logics of Transnationality.* Durham: Duke University Press, 1999.

———. "Making the Biopolitical Subject: Cambodian Immigrants, Refugee Medicine, and Cultural Citizenship in California." *Social Science Medicine* 40.9 (1995): 1243–57.

———. "On the Edge of Empires: Flexible Citizenship among Chinese in Diaspora." *Positions* 1.3 (1993): 744–78.

Ong, Paul, Edna Bonachich, and Lucie Cheng, eds. *The New Asian Immigration in Los Angeles and Global Restructuring.* Philadelphia: Temple University Press, 1994.

Osborne, Milton. "Khmer Rouge Trials in Sight?" *Asian Analysis* Apr. 2003. http://www.aseanfocus.com/asiananalysis/article.cfm?articleID=630, accessed Feb. 2004.

Palumbo-Liu, David. *Asian/American: Historical Crossings of a Racial Frontier.* Stanford: Stanford University Press, 1999.

———. "Modeling the Nation: The Asian/American Split." *Orientations: Mapping Studies in the Asian Diaspora.* Ed. K. S. Chuh. Durham: Duke University Press, 2001. 213–27.

Pascal, Roy. *Design and Truth in Autobiography.* Cambridge: Harvard University Press, 1960.

Payant, Katherine B., and Toby Rose. *The Immigrant Experience in North American Literature: Carving Out a Niche.* Westport: Greenwood, 1999.

Pham, Andrew X. *Catfish and Mandala: A Two-Wheeled Voyage through the Landscape and Memory of Vietnam.* New York: Farrar, Straus & Giroux, 1999.

Pran, Dith, comp. Kim DePaul, ed. *Children of Cambodia's Killing Fields: Memoirs by Survivors.* New Haven: Yale University Press, 1997.

Radhakrishnan, R. *Diasporic Mediations: Between Home and Location.* Minneapolis: University of Minnesota Press, 1996.

Rockmore, Tom, ed. *Lukács Today: Essays in Marxist Philosophy.* Dordrecht: D. Reidel, 1988.
Sasaki, Ruth. *The Loom and Other Stories.* Saint Paul: Graywolf Press, 1991.
Schanberg, Sydney H. *The Death and Life of Dith Pran.* New York: Penguin, 1985.
Sheehy, Gail. *Spirit of Survival.* New York: William Morrow, 1986.
Silove, Derrick, R. Chang, and V. Manicavasagar. "Impact of Recounting Trauma Stories on the Emotional State of Cambodian Refugees." *Psychiatric Services* 46.12 (1985): 1287–88.
Stagg, Sophal Leng. *Hear Me Now: Tragedy in Cambodia.* Tampa: Mancorp, 1996.
Starling, Marion W. *The Slave Narrative: Its Place in American History.* Washington, DC: Howard University Press, 1988.
Stone, Albert E., ed. *The American Autobiography: A Collection of Critical Essays.* Englewood Cliffs, NJ: Prentice-Hall, 1981.
Swain, Jon. *River of Time: A Memoir of Vietnam and Cambodia.* New York: Berkley, 1995.
Szymusiak, Molyda. *The Stones Cry Out: A Cambodian Childhood, 1975–1980.* Trans. Linda Coverdale. 1986. Bloomington: Indiana University Press, 1999.
Thompson, John. B. *Ideology and Modern Culture: Critical Social Theory in the Era of Mass Communication.* Stanford: Stanford University Press, 1990.
Ung, Loung. *First They Killed My Father: A Daughter of Cambodia Remembers.* New York: HarperCollins, 2000.
Vann, Nath. *A Cambodian Prison Portrait: One Year in the Khmer Rouge's S-21.* Thailand: White Lotus, 1998.
Vany, Ma. *Life in Danger: The Story of Ma Vany.* Pittsburgh: Dorrance, 1996.
Vickery, Michael. "Cultural Survival in Cambodian Language and Literature." *Cultural Survival Quarterly* 14.3 (1990): 49–52.
"Voice of Experience: Cambodian Trauma in America." *The Infinite Mind.* Narrated by Fred Goodwin. National Public Radio. WNYC, New York. 5 March 2003.
Yathay, Pin, and John Man. *Stay Alive, My Son.* New York: Free Press, 1987.

NOTES

The term "Cambodian American" is broadly used to refer to any Cambodian living in the United States. Definitions for "autobiography" abound. The definition used in this essay is based largely upon the analyses of James Olney, Albert Stone, Roy Pascal, and Laura Marcus. As James Olney states, "One creates from moment to moment and continuously the reality to which one gives a metaphoric name and shape, and that shape is one's own shape" (*Metaphors of Self* 34).

1. For reasons of space, I must limit this discussion to the field of American literature, although the topic of this essay has international scope.

2. The term "ideology" has a long history of change and a broad semantic field. For this essay, I use Thompson's definition: socially constructed "meaning in the service of power" (7).

3. Franklin establishes the preeminent autobiography of American "Whig history." The beginning of American autobiography is actually captive and slave narratives (Starling, *The Slave Narrative*). Franklin began his autobiography in 1771–72.

4. Not all immigrant autobiographies or ethnic autobiographies are heroic success stories. Some are highly critical of the United States and constitute an oppositional literature; as a result, they tend to be more marginal to mainstream consumption. William Boelhower elucidates several kinds of Italian immigrant autobiographies, including one that fits the heroic type. Ethnic Cambodian autobiographies do not fit into any of Boelhower's categories, nor do they fall under Northrop Frye's two usual forms: apology and confession (see Marcus, *Auto/biographical Discourses*).

5. For a detailed and complex account of the thematic diversity and changes in Asian American women's autobiography, see Jid Lee, *From the Promised Land to Home*.

6. This mode of refugee autobiography is characteristic of Vietnamese American life writings from the 1980s to the present. See Le Ly Hayslip, *Child of War, Woman of Peace* and *When Heaven and Earth Changed Places*; Nguyen Thi Thu-Lam, *Fallen Leaves*; James Freeman, *Hearts of Sorrow*; and Mary Cargill and Jade Quang Huynh, *Voices of Vietnamese Boat People*.

7. Jade Ngoc Quang Huynh's *South Wind Changing* (1994) remains transitional. Duong Van Mai Elliott expands this refugee genre into a historical memoir in *The Sacred Willow*.

8. See Haing Ngor, *Haing Ngor: A Cambodian Odyssey*; Sophal Leng Stagg, *Hear Me Now*; Loung Ung, *First They Killed My Father*; Chanrithy Him, *When Broken Glass Floats*; and Bree Lafreniere and Daran Kravan, *Music through the Dark*.

9. Some authors first escaped to either Great Britain or France and then relocated to the United States.

10. Schanberg's format seems to be a model for several Cambodian autobiographies. Molyda Szymusiak, for instance, mentions *The Killing Fields* in her preface to *The Stones Cry Out*.

11. It is true that Pin Yathay's account preceded Ngor's autobiography, but Yathay had relocated to France, not to the United States.

12. Cambodian refugees, along with specialists in human rights, law, and Cambodia, established the Cambodia Documentation Commission (1985–90). The director of the commission is David R. Hawk of the Columbia University Center for the Study of Human Rights. Their documents are located at http://rmc.library.cornell.edu/EAD/htmldocs/RMM04499.html, "Guide to the Cambodia Documentation Records, 1985–1990," accessed November 2004.

13. The Cambodian Genocide Program is based at the Yale Center for International and Area Studies, Council of Southeast Asia Studies, Yale Law School, Orville H. Schell Jr. Center for International Human Rights. Corresponding with this period of intense documentation work by the CGP is the second period of Cambodian American autobiography. These 1990s autobiographies, whose precedent is Molyda Szymusiak's *The Stones Cry Out*, are predominantly by young women of the first-and-a-half generation. See Stagg, *Hear Me Now*; Ung, *First They Killed My Father*; and Him, *When Broken Glass Floats*. They all employ a tripartite format similar to that used by male autobiographers whose accounts were published in the 1980s. Unlike the male autobiographers, however, the women were children during the Khmer Rouge regime. In contrast, the male autobiographers of the 1980s, such as Haing Ngor, Dith Pran, Someth May (*Cambodian Witness*), and Pin Yathay, were mature professionals when the Khmer Rouge forced them to flee Phnom Penh. Their life experience in traditional Cambodian culture before the rupture is revealed in the depth of their analyses of the Khmer Rouge's impact on traditional Cambodian culture and family structure. The female autobiographies of the 1990s foreground a "traumatic" childhood under the Khmer Rouge, including forced separation from parents, witnessing of torture and death, indoctrination into Khmer Rouge ideology, and, in Ung's case, instruction in how to kill. The 1980s and 1990s autobiographies are linked by their similar testimonial structure, their human rights subtext, and their quest for an international audience.

14. These citations are from the Cambodian Genocide Program's *First Progress Report* (Sept. 15, 1995). The report is available at http://www.gwu.edu/~nsarchiv/CWIHP/BULLETINS/b6–7a23.htm, accessed May 2004.

15. Pran's comments can be found at www.cambodian.com/dithpran/book, accessed Feb. 2004.

16. This information is available at www.dithpran.org/documentcenter.htm, accessed Feb. 2004.

17. DePaul's comments can be found at http://www.cambodian.com/dithpran/book, accessed Feb. 2004.

18. Among other documents, the archives contained more than four thousand typed or handwritten confessions, each from one to several hundred pages in length (Chandler, *Voices from S-21* viiii).

19. For Kissinger's complicity in the illegal bombing of Cambodia, see Christopher Hitchens, *The Trial of Henry Kissinger* 30.

20. The first generation of elders generally praised Ung's memoir, since they seemed to be pleased that a Cambodian American had appeared in the mainstream media. The second generation of Cambodian Americans generally thought Ung was terrific. Having little knowledge of the Cambodian holocaust, since many parents don't discuss the experience with them, and since Cambodian history, with rare exceptions, isn't taught in public schools, they generally embraced Ung's autobiography. The recognition that Ung received in the mainstream media essentially gave the sec-

ond generation permission to discuss this experience among themselves and with their parents. In contrast, a number of meetings with first-and-a-half-generation Cambodian American students that I attended in Long Beach revealed their concern about Ung's representation of Cambodian history and culture. Simply because her memoir had achieved such widespread notice in the media, they were concerned that her "misrepresentations" (as they saw them, on the basis of their own experience) would be taken as the truth by second-generation Cambodian Americans and the American public.

21. For recent scholarship on the Asian American diaspora, see Paul Ong, Edna Bonachich, and Lucie Cheng, *The New Asian Immigration in Los Angeles*; Aihwa Ong, "Making the Biopolitical Subject"; and Evelyn Hu-DeHart, *Across the Pacific*.

TWO HAT SOFTENERS "IN THE TRADE CONFESSION"

JOHN YAU AND KIMIKO HAHN

ZHOU XIAOJING

In his 1993 introduction to *The Open Boat: Poems from Asian America,* Garrett Hongo notes that the prevailing modes of Asian American criticism tend to evaluate a creative work according to opposing categories of the "assimilationist" and the "essentially Asian American" models (xxxv). Hongo's remark calls critical attention to the problems of polarized critical approaches to Asian American literature.[1] Debates on the conditions for a distinct Asian American poetics often focus on the poets' articulation of ethnic identities as a primary condition for reading their poetry within a mutually exclusive binary scheme. Within this scheme, a particular poet's work is read in terms of either a resistant or an "assimilationist" relationship with "mainstream" American culture and literature.[2] But how resistance or assimilation is enacted through form and language in Asian American poetry tends either to be overlooked or to be restricted to a dichotomized relationship between "Asian" and "American" attributes. In her critique of binary readings of Asian American poetry, Sunn Shelley Wong points out the problems inherent in defining "Asian American" in terms of "two discrete poles of a split identity rather than [in terms of] the mutually constitutive aspects of a labile subjectivity" (289). Wong's essay raises provocative questions: What constitutes an Asian American poetics if this poetics does not emerge from an oppositional position? How is this poetics related to mainstream American poetic traditions, and to what effect?

This essay explores these questions through analysis of the poetics of John Yau and Kimiko Hahn with respect to an American lyric mode: confessional poetry. My reading of their poems will focus on the poets' responses to the confessional lyric from the subject position of the raced and gendered "Other." I contend that Yau's and Hahn's respective thematic concerns and formal strategies are shaped not only by their subject positions and their experiences as Asian Americans but also by their negotiations with hegemonic cultural discourses and literary traditions. Their critical engagement with these discourses and traditions generates their themes and shapes their respective poetics, which resist, appropriate, and transform a mainstream American poetic tradition.

These subversive and transformative possibilities of their poetics are obscured, however, by readings that focus on content at the expense of form. For instance, in his thought-provoking essay "Form and Identity in Language Poetry and Asian American Poetry," Timothy Yu reads both types of poetry as responses to and disruptions of the institutionalized American poetic "mainstream" (425). He argues that Asian American poetry, like Language poetry, unveils the "politics" hidden in the so-called naturalness of voice, narrative, and language, a naturalness that characterizes the dominant American lyric mode of the 1970s and 1980s. Yu observes that, whereas Language poets use "radical forms" to critique the politics underlying this naturalizing poetics of the "MFA mainstream" (Shetley 20)—or what Charles Bernstein calls the "official verse culture" (*Content's Dream* 246)—Asian American poets expose "the mainstream voice as a white voice" through "injection of explicitly Asian American themes and voices into poetry" (Yu 425). However, Yu notes that "Language poetry and Asian American poetry, read against each other in their development through the 1970s and 1980s, . . . show the limits of the other's poetic and political project" (424). While Asian American poetry "exposes some of the strains and limits in the political project of Language poetry, particularly around the issues of race and identity," "Language poetry's critique of mainstream poetry may also map the limits of the Asian American poetic project, insofar as it relies upon a commodifiable 'ethnic" individuality" (424). Yu singles out John Yau "as representative of a moment beyond [the] deadlocks in some recent work" (424). By situating the emergence of Asian American poetry against the American poetic establishment, and by aligning this poetry and its political effects with a major established American poetic school—Language poetry—Yu resolutely breaks away from a predominant critical approach that defines Asian American poetics in terms of Asian cultural origins. More important, his critical methodology renders it possible for Asian American poetry to be read outside the double bind of stable ancestral origins and a racialized identity.

Nevertheless, in his attempt to define the characteristics of two complex, diverse, and, to a certain extent, interrelated poetic traditions by identifying the limits in the writings of some poets from both camps, Yu seems to reiterate the dichotomy he sets out to undermine. By emphasizing "Asian American themes and voices" as opposed to the "radical forms" of Language poetry, and by treating these phenomena as distinct vital elements of two separate categories of poetry, Yu may unwittingly be reinforcing the binarism that renders formal experiment and ethnic themes (and voices) mutually exclusive.[3]

Language poets' preoccupation with radical forms, and particularly with the primacy of language in making meaning, aims at foregrounding the politics of writing. The politics and poetics of Language poetry are most clearly articulated in *L=A=N=G=U=A=G=E,* the bimonthly magazine whose first issue appeared in February 1978. Many of the essays from the first three volumes of this magazine, which was published for five years, are collected in *The L=A=N=G=U=A=G=E Book* (1984), edited by Bruce Andrews and Charles Bernstein. In their introduction to that collection, "Repossessing the Word," Bernstein and Andrews state that their project "involved exploring the numerous ways that meanings and values can be (& are) realized—revealed—produced in writing" (ix). For them, writing in a way that challenges language as a transparent vessel of meaning "is inevitably a social and political activity as well as an aesthetic one"; as they assert, "one major preoccupation of *L=A=N=G=U=A=G=E* has therefore been to generate discussion on the relation of writing to politics, particularly to articulate some of the ways that writing can act to critique society" (x). This insistence on the politics of aesthetics, and on the ways that writing can enact social critique through manipulation of language and form, also informs the poetics of John Yau and Kimiko Hahn. But Yau and Hahn, in their poems, refuse to get rid of "ethnic" voices or the speaking subject.

The poems of Yau and Hahn are salient examples of a complex, dynamic, and mutually constitutive relationship between Asian American poetry and mainstream American culture and literary traditions.[4] While Yau resists and parodies the centrality of the "lyric I" in the confessional mode, Hahn makes use of the possibilities of the confessional genre to render the self a part of the political and the historical through autobiographical materials and intertextual interactions.

Confessional poetry in the United States emerged in the late 1950s, and it developed during the 1960s and 1970s as a revolt against the impersonal, symbolic, highly crafted poetics favored by the New Criticism, which had dominated American poetry for several decades. Direct self-exposure and relentless self-exploration, realistic expressions, and idiomatic language, together with recurrent themes of alienation, suffering, and failures in life and relationships, are characteristics of confessional poems. Robert Lowell's *Life Studies* (1959) is generally considered a seminal book, one that marked this transition in American poetry, and M. L. Rosenthal is the critic who first used the label "confessional" in his review of *Life Studies*. Rosenthal writes, "Because of the way Lowell brought his private humiliations, sufferings, and psychological problems into the poems of *Life Studies*, the word 'confessional' seemed appropriate enough" (26). Lowell himself and his family history are at the center of the poems in *Life Studies*. As Robert Phillips observes, "The confessional poets chiefly employ the Self as sole poetic symbol" (7–8). The self and family history are a central area of subject matter that confessional poets interrogate. Phillips argues that American confessional poetry, "written with the Self as primary subject, the Self treated with the utmost frankness and lack of restraint" (4), can be traced through Whitman, Baudelaire, Rilke, and Rousseau, and as far back as Augustine, Catullus, and Sappho.

For Yau, the self in American confessional poetry is a privileged category.[5] In a 1990 interview, Yau said that he disliked "the subjective excesses" of Robert Lowell's poetry, and that he had consciously rebelled against writing "in a language that comes from an 'I,' from an interior subjectivity" (Foster 45, 46). Almost from the beginning of his career as a poet, Yau has been trying to break away from that solipsistic "I"—the "'I' as victim," which he associates with Lowell and Sylvia Plath, as he reveals in a recent conversation: "There seemed to be something wrong with it [that "I"], something privileged" (quoted in Tabios 386). Yau's resistance to the privileged "I" is something that he attributes in part to his being Asian American: his family "spent hours talking about the importance of family versus the individual." Like many other Asian American families, however, Yau's family was "dysfunctional" and "traumatized," its members having been uprooted and dislocated as refugees from China at the end of World War II. "So I didn't believe in the family," Yau says, "but I also didn't believe in the 'I'—particularly the 'I' as victim" (Tabios 386). In a 1994 essay, Yau asserts his position regarding the poet's voice in Western lyric poetry:

> I do not believe in the lyric I—the single modulating voice that names itself and others in an easily consumable narrative—writing in a language that is transparent, a window overlooking a world we all have in common. It is not a world which includes me. . . . I am the Other ("Between the Forest and Its Trees" 40].

While deploring the centrality and authority of the "lyric I," Yau reveals both his sense of alienation from mainstream America and his awareness of how ideologies and subject positions are inscribed in language, form, and voice.

Yau's resistance to the assumptions and authority of the "lyric I" forces him to search for a language and form that will enable him to break away from the confessional mode of solipsistic self-expression. One of Yau's techniques for getting beyond the "lyric I" to generate a poem is the use of narrative and formal constraints as opposed to reliance on the observations or heightened emotional state of the lyric speaker. According to Yau, he learned this technique from Harry Matthews, a member of OULIPO (Ouvroir de Littérature Potentielle, or Workshop of Potential Literature), a group of experimental writers whose writing principle, Yau explains, is based on the fact that "the writer is the rat who constructs the maze from which he must escape" (quoted in Tabios 383). Yau finds that the use of constraints can also force him to break his writing habits and push the limits of established forms, thus leading him to new discoveries (Tabios 383).

Yau's prose poem series "Corpse and Mirror," collected in the volume *Radiant Silhouette,* can serve as an example of his writing according to the OULIPO principle. Drawing on ancient Egyptian burial customs, Yau creates a mythical world in which people's lives and deaths are governed by strict rules and codes of conduct. The opening paragraph of part 1, "Corpse and Mirror I," immediately states the purpose of burial customs: "When one of our citizens dies, his corpse is placed in his chariot. To help him reach his destination, his favorite horses are buried with him." If the dead man's sins "outweigh his acts of kindness," the horses will collapse and the dead man will revive but will remain a corpse, "doomed to wander in the desert, like a vulture without wings." But he will be given another chance on condition that "one of his neighbors dreams about him in the week following his death. In the dream the man must give his exact location beneath the stars" (*Radiant Silhouette* 126–27). In addition, this neighbor must ride out at dawn to the designated spot to see if the man is there. If he is not, the neighbor "must dismount at once and begin praying." If the neighbor fails to carry this chain of actions out exactly as described, the man's wandering corpse will never find his way back to the city (*Radiant Silhouette* 127). Even in death, the deceased will affect the life of a living person, whose actions will in turn determine the fate of the dead. An individual is part of an intricate net of relations and actions.

The connections between the dead and the living in part 2 of the poem also regulate people's lives and determine the eventual form of burial for the dead in another society, where "when one of our citizens dies, his head is cut off and placed inside a mirror-lined box" (*Radiant Silhouette* 128). How the message from this head is understood and carried out by the person who keeps vigil will shape the latter's life. In the mysterious worlds of "Corpse and Mirror," the inexplicable rules and codes of conduct are meaningful and functional because of the communities in which an individual's life and death are intricately connected to those of others and are controlled by forces beyond the grasp of the self. These connections, uncertainties, and inexplicable mysteries displace the transcendental "poet-I," disrupt the autonomy of the self, and undermine the sufficiency of consciousness or reason of the subject in traditional Western lyric poetry.

Yau also explores the possibilities of breaking away from the self-centered "lyric I" by using montage while shifting the pronouns from "I" to "he," to "she," and to "they" in "Variations on Corpse and Mirror." Thus the "I" does not occupy center stage as in confessional poems, appearing only occasionally among numerous other people. Yau's method of montage composition enables him to bring plural, heterogeneous temporal-spatial happenings into the poem, which consists of eighteen segments of discontinuous descriptions and narratives. As a result, the poem presents a world with multiple centers rather than a self-centered world. The apparently random, fragmentary images and moments are in fact carefully arranged in such a way that the reader's attention is constantly directed away from the "I" and toward the surrounding world, and toward other people:

> 14
>
> I left the stadium when the outcome was no longer in doubt. Birds were struggling to form a red necklace above the rooftops. Later, I saw waves leapfrogging in the harbor, stone after stone sliding into place, until a boat tilted precariously among the pyramids of ice.
>
> 15
>
> From his seat he watches, hears himself whisper, fear etching its imprint into the tunnel burrowing through his voice.
>
> 16
>
> Often she turned, and turned away. Slender neck above a white dress. What she remembered most was the moon's cold and bitter wine.

17

> That morning they stood at the bus stop, each wishing the other would mention what had happened to the flowers. . . .
> (*Radiant Silhouette* 137)

Yau's montage composition creates a simultaneity that subverts the expectations set up by the conventional stance of the lyric "I." There is no turning inward of the self. What the lyric "I/eye" sees is not brought into the light of reason for the speaking subject's knowledge, or for revelation of truth; the visible remains opaque, irreducible to the speaker's observation. Moreover, the constant switching of pronouns and the subsequent shifting of perspectives enable Yau to avoid privileging the experience of the "I." In "Variations on Corpse and Mirror," as in Jackson Pollock's abstract expressionist paintings, there is no foreground or background, no central, dominating perspective. At the same time, Yau's descriptions, such as those in sections 15 and 16, cited above, appropriate the nonrepresentational techniques of abstract expressionist paintings, the forms of which do not correspond to any specific shapes that we can recognize or name. Thus, rather than functioning as metaphors or familiar things in themselves, Yau's images—such as "the tunnel burrowing through his voice" and "the moon's cold and bitter wine"—are similar to those in Willem de Kooning's paintings, which, Jonathan Holden notes, "allude so strongly to familiar forms and landscapes, to shapes that never quite materialize" (*The Rhetoric of the Contemporary Lyric* 98).

Holden identifies this allusiveness of abstract expressionist painting with that of John Ashbery's "abstract-expressionist poetry." He contends that Ashbery's poems, through masterful manipulation of syntax, create a "relentless sense of being 'about' something specific, or moving toward some point that, like the end of a rainbow, always just eludes us" (98). Hence he argues that, for Ashbery, "syntax in writing is the equivalent of composition in painting: it has an intrinsic beauty and authority almost wholly independent of any specific context. Thus, in Ashbery's poetry . . . each *sentence* is analogous to a brushstroke . . . recorded in paint on a canvas" (99; emphasis in original). Some of Yau's poems share these qualities of Ashbery's poetry. Like Ashbery, Yau is an art critic; both have incorporated into their poems some of the concepts and techniques associated with avant-garde painting, including collage juxtaposition, montage simultaneity, and what Ashbery calls an "anti-referential sensuousness" (quoted in Stitt 410). Like abstract expressionist paintings, Yau's syntax and images disrupt the naturalness of the supposedly transparent meanings embedded in realism and undermine structuralist assumptions about the stability of meaning produced through language; at the same time, they foreground, paradoxically, the constructedness of meaning and knowledge. Yet Yau refuses to allow his lucid syntax and familiar images to remain forever elusive or isolated from specific social contexts.

In fact, Yau explores semantic indeterminacy and the aural possibilities of language in combination with uncanny surrealistic images, not simply to subvert the authority and transcendence of the "lyric I" but also to undermine representations of Asian Americans in Hollywood films. In accomplishing this task in his poems, he draws on the confessional mode of self-exploration and self-expression to interrogate individual subjectivity in relation to collective identity and racial ideology, as in the series titled "Genghis Chan: Private Eye," collected in *Edificio Sayonara*.[6] As the title of this series indicates, its component poems parody Charlie Chan, the Hollywood–Hawaiian–Chinese American detective who outsmarts everyone but remains subordinate to his white bosses, and who frequently quotes supposedly Chinese sayings as a mark of his ancient wisdom and cultural Otherness. The name "Genghis Chan" simultaneously evokes the historical figure Genghis Khan and the Hollywood "Charlie Chan" productions, suggesting a containment of the threatening "yellow peril" through its transformation into a harmless "model minority" image by way of representational tactics. The allusion to Charlie Chan's profession as a detective—"Private Eye"—also puns on the "lyric I" whose utterance is supposed to be private, overheard by the reader, and whose social transcendence is supposed to be the virtue of lyric poetry.[7] Yau's use of this racially marked name at once evokes and subverts the autonomy of the "lyric I" and situates the speaker's private speech in its social and cultural contexts. In poems VIII and XIV of the "Genghis Chan" series, Yau employs surrealist images to expose Hollywood's construction and reproduction of racialized Asian American identity as a cultural commodity. In the voice of the white actor who played the role of Charlie Chan, the speaker draws the reader's attention to the fictitiousness of his racial image while highlighting the silencing of the Chinese American whose voice is rendered "inaudible" by the white man who is supposed to be imitating it: "I plugged in the new image fertilizer / and complained to my inaudible copy" (*Edificio Sayonara* 73). In poem XIV of this series, Yau plays on the resonances of words and phrases to further suggest a connection between the circulation of racial stereotypes and the commodification of the racialized Other. The seemingly confessional self-exposure by the speaker actually reveals a socially and culturally constructed racial identity:

> My new yellow name
> was ladled over
>
> your installment plan
> Another blue dollar special
>
> bubbling below
> the Avenue of Ovens
>
> (*Edificio Sayonara* 79)

While the speaker's reference to his "new yellow name" implies a new version of Asians' racially marked stereotype, his mispronunciation of the word "labeled" as "ladled" is a subversive mimicry. In keeping with the selling and eating of food evoked by the phrased "ladled over," Yau employs images associated with cheap popular food, like the blue-plate specials served at diners, to mock Charlie Chan's artificial pidgin (supposed to indicate his "foreignness") and expose the popular consumption of the alien Other.

But Genghis Chan, in Yau's poems, is more than a copy of the Hollywood Charlie Chan who satisfies mainstream America's fetish for the assimilated and contained Other; he is part of the unsettling presence of immigrants of color who challenge the claims of American democracy. In "Genghis Chan: Private Eye XIX," Yau displaces several words in Genghis Chan's speech to disrupt the meaning of familiar English phrases and sayings, thus articulating Asian immigrants' resistance to assimilation through language. The speaker's autobiographical reference in the poem at once mimics and departs from the autobiographical "poet-I" in confessional poetry:

> My stamped mother
> used to fling to me
>
> . . .
>
> and I
> her lump of muck
>
> . . .
>
> I could dandle
> on my wasted plea

the chink of meat
we knew that linked us

to the junk
going by

(*Edificio Sayonara* 85–86)

As is typical of confessional poetry, this poem focuses on the family drama in which the poet's relationship with his or her parent(s) is a major subject. But the speaker's disclosure of a "family secret" in Yau's poem actually unveils social problems. The seemingly misplaced words satirize Chinese immigrants' status and reveal racism against them. Yau's wordplay seems to have incorporated some of Language poets' beliefs and ways of using language, which are intended to show that "writing can act to critique society" and that writing must involve the reader in "repossessing" the language "through close attention to, and active participation in, its production" (Bernstein and Andrews x). Yau's linguistic manipulation, and the speaker's insistence on his connection to his "stamped mother" (marked officially and symbolically as immigrant and alien Other) and their connection to "the junk," create a disturbing effect that undermines Charlie Chan's image as the epitome of the assimilated, submissive "model minority."

In his 1996 collection *Forbidden Entries,* Yau adds to his "Genghis Chan: Private Eye" series a group of prose poem monologues in the voice of Peter Lorre, who played the sneaky Japanese Mr. Moto in several Hollywood films. In fact, Yau parodies and reinvents the confessional "I" who in speaking of himself reveals that his identity is produced not simply by Hollywood but also by a racist ideology with no national borders. In "Peter Lorre Improvises Mr. Moto's Monologue," the speaker's self-assertion confronts the politics of representation while revealing and protesting against how his appearance and behavior are manipulated by "hidden" forces:

> I float outside your windows on rainy nights, a blanket of gray mist you can't peel from the glass.
>
> . . .
>
> I begin to twist and bend like tall grass on a spring day. Twitch and quiver on hidden command.
>
> the cobbled alleyways of Berlin. Charcoal city smoldering on the frigid Roman plains. Hovel of bunglers and chumps. Ratty fur,

> bad teeth, cracked hands. . . . Hollywood didn't mold me into what I am, a diminutive silk hurricane approaching America's crafty shores, dapper neon silhouette slipping behind a foil moon, draped bones in a metallic black suit.
>
> (*Forbidden Entries* 77–78)

Yau's employment of surrealistic images enlarges the signifying capacity of his poem. Mr. Moto's reference to his birth, his time travel, and his "ratty fur" and "bad teeth" suggest that racial stereotypes like this one are not a new product; their roots can be traced to colonialism, imperialism, and racism. Despite its comparatively subtle presentation of a disguised racial stereotype, Hollywood's construction of Asian characters such as Mr. Moto is reminiscent of Nazi Germany's portrayals of Jews as rats.

Like Charlie Chan and Mr. Moto, Asian women in Hollywood films reflect the ideology of racial hierarchy. In "Peter Lorre Dreams He Is the Third Reincarnation of a Geisha," Yau exposes the containment of Asians within prescribed boundaries of racial stereotypes, which are always gendered as exotically feminine:

> First I was delicate, a white peony, then I was a shiny delicateness, something to snuffle over and return. . . . I am a reflection, a wall you have smeared with feces and blood.
>
> (*Forbidden Entries* 81)

By blurring Peter Lorre's gender, Yau alludes to the effeminate, racialized images of Asian and Asian American men in Hollywood films. These images construct their identities of race and gender in a heterosexual economy of patriarchy and racial hierarchy. Thus marked and contained, Asian Americans have little choice about who they are allowed to be. As the speaker says in "Peter Lorre Confesses His Desire to Be a Poet," "After I became a citizen, these were my options. Be a giant among shrimps or a dwarf among giants" (*Forbidden Entries* 84). Through the confessional mode of interior monologue in the voice of Mr. Moto, Peter Lorre at once exposes and undermines the representation of Asians and Asian Americans in American popular culture:

> To them, I was nothing more than an ornate doorway through which strangled vowels and stomped consonants spilled their sweat, a geiger counter registering the tremors of those who

> surrounded me. But I knew better. I was pure contempt grinning feebly inside my trade mark.
>
> (*Forbidden Entries* 85)

While asserting recognition of his marginalized and imposed subject position, the speaker of this monologue subverts the construct of his identity by emphasizing its fabricated characteristics of race and gender. The assumptions underlying the confessional monologue of "truth telling," of exposing "secrets" through the speaker's own words, serve to simultaneously reveal and reject commodified Asian and Asian American stereotypes.

The racially marked confessional monologues of Yau's speaker break open the self-enclosure of the conventional "lyric I" whose identity is grounded in self-consciousness. The "I" in Yau's poems, as discussed above, articulates a self similar to that in feminist confessional poetry, which, as Judith Harris argues, "demonstrates, through testimony, an individual relationship to a community" (254). Moreover, the relationship between the raced, gendered self and Asian Americans is a point of departure in Yau's poems about identity construction, poems that raise epistemological questions by exposing the politics of representation. In breaking away from the conventions of using a "transparent language," and its underlying assumption of possessing the "truth" of the world, of the Other, and of the self, particularly of the privileged, authoritative "lyric I," Yau redefines the American confessional lyric. As the speaker in "Genghis Chan: Private Eye XXI" says, "I am a hat softener / in the trade confession" (*Forbidden Entries* 92).

Like Yau, Kimiko Hahn appropriates and transforms the confessional lyric in her search for a poetics capable of dealing with the personal and political dimensions of the self. Her poetics, to a large extent, is shaped by feminist ideology, which breaks down the barriers separating the public and the private spheres. Hahn finds inspiration in the classical literature of Japanese women and in a female language and writing invented by Chinese women, as well as in the critical writings of Edward Said and of such feminist writers as Hélène Cixous, Luce Irigaray, Catherine Clément, and Adrienne Rich (Tabios 24).[8] With her feminist political "awakening," Hahn says, "my own sexuality became a territory for me. . . . This 'territory' also gave me an increasing awareness that women's bodies historically have not always belonged to them" ("Three Voices Together" 10). Discussing the impact of feminism on contemporary American women's novels, Katherine B. Payant contends that "feminism has changed women's writing by opening up and legitimizing new plots and themes " and has enabled writers to explore "many types of female experiences," including the experience of women of color (209). The same is true of the influence of feminism on contemporary American poetry by women, particularly the confessional and autobiographical mode. Rita Felski argues that "generic categories of the confession . . . provide a means to illuminate two key features of feminist literature—its autobiographical function and its construction of narrative" (84). She notes, "Feminist confession thus seeks to affirm a female experience which has often been repressed and rendered invisible by speaking about it, by writing it into existence" (112). This is precisely what Hahn accomplishes in her poems. Moreover, she complicates the female experience by confronting the differences of race and class.

Hahn's thematic concerns and technical strategies demonstrate a feminist poetics that represents the female body as a site of contending ideologies. In many of her poems, Hahn articulates female desire to reposition female subjects. While writing frankly about the body and sexual desire in the confessional mode, Hahn breaks away from European-American feminist confessional models. Her autobiographical poems differ from those by such confessional women poets as Sylvia Plath and Anne Sexton, not only in form but also in content, for her poems about women's sexuality and desire deal with what Traise Yamamoto refers to as "the complexities of embodied subjectivity, which have traditionally been negatively race- and gender-marked" (237).

In her interrogation of the politics of women's bodies and the construction of gender identity, Hahn uses autobiographical materials and fragments from theoretical and literary texts, hence contesting theories with lived experience. For instance, in "Cruising Barthes," Hahn engages in an intertextual dialogue with Roland Barthes's *The Pleasure of the Text* on the symbolic meanings of the body. Most of the seven parts of the poem begin with a citation from Barthes's text, and then the rest of each part is a response to the citation. In each section of the poem introduced by a citation from Barthes, the content of the citation provides the topic and generates the narrative and contemplation. For instance, Part I of the poem begins with Barthes's remarks about reading: "Many readings are perverse, implying a split, a cleavage. Just as the child knows its mother has no penis and simultaneously believes she has one" (quoted in Hahn, *The Unbearable Heart* 33). In juxtaposition to the quotation, Hahn describes personal experience to counter Barthes's Freudian statement about the formation of gender identity:

I cannot recall believing my mother possessed
the same genitalia as father
though I've never seen, in memory, my parents naked.
The first penis I saw must have been a tiny one,
almost as minuscule as a woman's clitoris,
that part of her self my three-year-old calls her penis
ever since she showered with Ted or me
and noticed the reassuring differences
not as anxieties leading to envy
except perhaps for peeing in the park

. . .

So Barthes' metaphor is inexact.
His split, the site of loss and bliss
cannot be illustrated by a dated interpretation

. . .

I do not want a penis, dear Freud, or even mother's breast,
dear Klein. I want to tunnel
away from light to half-light,
from the sounds that articulate our loss finally,
the most primitive irony,
where what *is* simultaneous is not the noun cleavage
but the verb, *cleave*: to split
or to cling. That pleasure.

(*The Unbearable Heart* 33–34)

Private life and sexual experiences in this and Hahn's other poems become evidence that undermines the phallocentric ideology of the sexed body. At the same time, Hahn also rejects Melanie Klein's notion of the mother-daughter relationship in which the mother's breasts are central to the daughter's conflicting feelings of desire, envy, and gratitude.[9] In challenging Barthes's and Klein's theories of the sexed body, both of which are based on the girl's "lack" (of penis or breasts) in the development of her female subjectivity, Hahn articulates pleasure in the power of the word, which counters female jealousy of embodied power as theorized by Barthes and Klein. It seems that Hahn rejects both Barthes's and Klein's theories about the primacy of the body in the formation of sexed and gendered subjects because those theories are detached from their specific social and cultural contexts.

Hahn insists on exploring the formation of female subjectivity within gendered and raced power relationships. In her prose poem "The Hemisphere: Kuchuk Hanem," Hahn makes use of the possibilities of confessional poetry and intertextuality to situate an autobiographical narrative about mother-daughter relationships in historical and cultural contexts beyond national borders. As the title indicates, Edward Said's criticism of Gustave Flaubert's orientalist portrayal of Kuchuk Hanem, an Egyptian dancer and courtesan, in part generates the poem. Like Yau, Hahn employs collage to break away from the conventional mode of Western lyric, in which the "lyric I" is the organizing principle. "The Hemisphere: Kuchuk Hanem" consists of citations from Said's *Orientalism* and Flaubert's *Flaubert in Egypt,* autobiographical fragments of Hahn's persona, Hanem's speeches as imagined by Hahn, and Hahn's commentary on these speeches.

Hahn juxtaposes interrupted autobiographical narratives with fragmentary texts and speeches. This method of composition enables her to situate the mother-daughter relationship at the intersection of sexism, racism, Orientalism, and feminism. She begins the poem with a childhood memory of waking up from a nap, looking for her mother, and finding her mother taking a bath. Then she interrupts this narrative, which includes her seeing her mother's naked body that looks different from her own, with references to Flaubert's writing about Kuchuk Hanem and Egypt, and to Said's critique of it. Through resonances and contrasts of collage, Hahn relates the absence of her mother, who is Japanese, to Orientalist constructs of Asian women, such as Flaubert's writing about his encounter with the "Oriental" Other, in which Kuchuk Hanem's voice has been silenced. Countering Flaubert's power of nationality, wealth, and gender, which "allowed him not only to possess Kuchuk Hanem physically but to speak for her and tell his readers in what way she was typically 'Oriental'" (Said 6), Hahn writes in the voice of Hanem, allowing Hanem to speak for herself and to talk back to Flaubert.

In contrast to Flaubert's essentializing discursive construct of Egypt and the "Orientals," Hanem's speech situates her encounter with the Frenchman in a specific historical moment and geographical location while foregrounding the intersection of race, gender, and class in her identity: "In 1850 a woman with skin the color of sand in the shade of the Sphinx, midday, meant little and of course mine was seen more than veiled and I could earn a living 'dancing'" (*The Unbearable Heart* 46). In the context of colonialism, and from the perspective of a prostitute "with skin the color of sand," Hanem's monologue exposes the moral hypocrisy of the privileged:

> *It's true when all is said and done, I am less a dancer than a whore. . . . That's what I am, a whore and alone. To be despised by the men because who else would let them come as they come but someone with variant morals. . . . I am scorned by the religious. By the courts and by my parents. But I do not fear a man's departure, Know that.*
>
> (*The Unbearable Heart* 47)

Like Genghis Chan's voice and Peter Lorre's monologues in Yau's poems, Hanem's monologue here reveals that her identity is part of a social order and a racial hierarchy. Hanem emphasizes that neither her own image nor Flaubert's is personal; both are implicated in the structures of power. "*My image does not entirely belong to me. And neither does yours, master or slave*" (*The Unbearable Heart* 47). Hahn's employment of the confessional mode of lyric enables her to give voice to Hanem's thoughts and feelings, which are absent from Flaubert's narrative.

In giving voice to Hanem, Hahn allows her to occupy a subject position where agency is possible. Responding to Flaubert's representation of herself and Egypt, Hanem asserts her views of France and French men, and her views subvert Flaubert's Orientalist portrayal of Egypt while undermining the notion that French men's unmarked bodies and privileged sensibility and sexuality are the norm:

> *When he* [Flaubert] *writes about Egypt he will write what he has experienced: the adoration of the historical Cleopatra from boyhood lessons, Kuchuk Hanem—my cunt, my dance—the Nile, the squalor, a man slitting his belly and pulling his intestines in and out then bandaging himself with cotton and oils, people fucking animals which I'm told also happens in France but not in the cities. Because there are no animals.*
>
> (*The Unbearable Heart* 47–48)

These imagined remarks of Hanem transform her from the silent sexual object that she is in Flaubert's text into an articulate subject. Hahn achieves a new subject position for Hanem through intertextual dialogues, which are interactions between subject positions.

The collage composition Hahn employs enables her to contest racialized gender identity and sexuality through juxtaposition of fragmentary speeches by a number of speakers from different subject positions. The following texts, juxtaposed with Hanem's monologues, suggest connections between sexual stereotypes of Asian women in the twentieth century and Orientalist discursive constructs of the Other in the nineteenth century:

> I knew what he wanted. He wanted to fuck me. He guesses I was 16. . . . Why would this Portuguese sailor come over to me and in his broken English point to the tattoo of a geisha as if I would identify with it. And I did a little.
>
> He wanted someone who did not resemble his mother or his friends' sisters or wives. The mistress he had dumped before departure. He wanted license. The kind available not even in one's own imagination—but in geographic departure.
>
> *"The morning we arrived in Egypt . . . we had scarcely set foot on shore when Max, the old lecher, got excited over a negress who was drawing water at a fountain. He is just as excited by the little negro boys. By whom is he not excited? Or, rather, by what?"* [Flaubert, 43]
>
> (*The Unbearable Heart* 48)

Hahn's employment of the confessional mode of direct exposure of the private matches Flaubert's sensational, voyeuristic representation of French men's sexual adventures in the East while suggesting that these white men's sexual desires for the Other are inseparable from the Other's racialized identity. Furthermore, by juxtaposing Hanem's speeches with fragments from Flaubert's book, Hahn also challenges the epistemology of the Western gaze. For instance, Hanem notes in another monologue, "Yet what he witnesses on tour and what I see are experienced differently" (*The Unbearable Heart* 48). Hanem's monologues counter Flaubert's power to possess her body and to speak for her and for Egypt.

Hahn herself, however, raises provocative questions about her own speaking in Hanem's voice and articulating Hanem's sexuality from her own Western feminist position. "Will I fall into the trap of writing from the imperialists' point of view?" she asks. "What would an anti-imperialistic framework look like?" She further questions whether she can speak for any other woman of color: "Can I speak for her? For the Turkish, Nubian, the—brown, black, blacker? (*The Unbearable Heart* 51). Regardless of what Hahn risks, however, in assuming the voice of Kuchuk Hanem, she does not allow her critical awareness of that risk to prevent her from taking it. Even though she imagines that when she eventually pays Hanem a visit, Hanem may not regard her as a friend, Hahn indicates that she and Hanem and other women of color, including her mother, share similar positions in their respective relationships to power.

Hahn suggests a correlation between her mother's silence about herself, on the one hand, and Orientalist, patriarchal discourses, on the other. She juxtaposes her narrative about her mother, tending to her children, with Hanem's speeches and Flaubert's voyeuristic description of Hanem's body as well as with the mother's reading from "Grimm's Fairy Tales where the youngest daughter is always the prettiest and the stepmother murderous" (*The Unbearable Heart* 49). As Hanem is rendered "a continent," "a hemisphere" (49, 51), by Flaubert's writing, the mother's identity is implicated in both Orientalist and patriarchal discourses. The racialization of Hanem's sexed and gendered body, like the naturalization of antagonistic mother-daughter relationships in these discourses, suppresses women's desire, silences women's voices. This suppression and silencing, Hahn suggests, has a direct impact on "the way I wish mother to speak up so I can become a woman" (53), and on Asian women's experience and identity. Just as Hanem has become "a continent," representing "half the globe" (49) in Flaubert's account, Asian women, including Hahn herself, continue to be reduced to sexual objects or stereotypes of the East, as the following fragments and rhetorical question indicate:

> "You know you want it and it's big" . . . "Sit on my face, China" . . .
> "Nice titties" . . . "Do you want me to teach you some
> English?" . . . "Are you from Saigon?"
> What is my stake in this?
>
> (*The Unbearable Heart* 60)

These utterances, like Hanem's imagined speeches and Flaubert's remarks about her, assume particular subject positions, which Hahn juxtaposes, challenges, or subverts in the poem. In this and in her other poems, Hahn explores the possibility of a female aesthetic by turning to women's shared and different experiences and gendered relationships. Like Yau's exploration and articulation of the self, Hahn's treatment of the personal is irreducibly political and ideological.

Hahn's appropriations of the confessional mode of poetry, like Yau's resistance to and parody of it, dismantle the binarism that renders the private and the public, the personal and the political, mutually exclusive. This dichotomy underlies much criticism of the self-indulgence in American confessional poetry. Marjorie Perloff, in her critique of the self-indulgence of Robert Lowell's circle, notes that even though "the self was regularly positioned in a literary or historical field," as in Lowell's and Berryman's poems, "others were endowed with life primarily so as to function in the poet's own drama" (113). Similarly, Paul Breslin argues that the confessional poets' "autobiographical impulse," which privileges the poets' own experience, fails, unfortunately, to fully realize their potential for making "the most valuable contribution" to poetry, that is, "developing a poetic style that could handle particular detail and social nuance" (53). It seems that the poems of Yau and Hahn, which cannot be reduced merely to the personal dramas of the poets, have succeeded in making this valuable contribution to American poetry. In their exploration of raced and gendered identities, they have extended the possibilities of the confessional mode and reinvented poetic forms that are adequate to the lyrical as well as the social and historical dimensions of personal experience.

John Yau's and Kimiko Hahn's poems challenge any binary scheme that reduces the complexity and political implications of Asian American poetics. Their cross-genre appropriations and revisions indicate that an Asian American poetics emerging from the poets' critical engagement with dominant cultures and mainstream poetic traditions, and from the subject positions of the gendered, racialized Other, is a political and aesthetic choice. As Yau says of the question facing every minority American artist, "Should he or she investigate the constantly changing polymorphous conditions affecting identity, tradition, and reality? Or should he or she choose to assimilate into the mainstream art world by focussing on the approved aesthetic issues?" ("Please Wait by the Coatroom" 59). Yau and Hahn enact resistance and subversion through the politics of the aesthetics underlying their formal inventions. Their lyric speakers disrupt the autonomy of the self and undermine the privileged primacy of self-consciousness in defining essential humanity and individuality. In dismantling the foundation for defining subjectivity in terms of autonomous consciousness, Yau's and Hahn's poetry calls into question the prevailing models of subjectivity in conventional Western lyric poetry. These unsettling effects of their work result from a poetics that is irreducible to dichotomized aesthetic and identity categories in which the terms "Asian" and "American" remain stable and mutually exclusive. Their work suggests that a resistant Asian American poetics must resist the containment of ethnic ghettos without losing the subject position of a racial minority.

BIBLIOGRAPHY

Barthes, Roland. *The Pleasure of the Text*. Trans. Richard Miller. New York: Noonday Press, 1989.

Bernstein, Charles. *Content's Dream: Essays 1975–1984*. Los Angeles: Sun & Moon, 1986.

———, and Bruce Andrews. "Repossessing the Word." *The L=A=N=G=U=A=G=E Book*. Ed. Bruce Andrews and Charles Bernstein. Carbondale: Southern Illinois University Press, 1984. ix–xi.

Breslin, Paul. *The Psycho-Political Muse: American Poetry since the Fifties*. Chicago: University of Chicago Press, 1987.

Felski, Rita. *Beyond Feminist Aesthetics: Feminist Literature and Social Change*. Cambridge, MA: Oxford University Press, 1989.

Flaubert, Gustave. *Flaubert in Egypt: A Sensibility on Tour*. Ed. and trans. Francis Steegmuller. New York: Penguin, 1996.

Foster, Edward. "An Interview with John Yau." *Talisman* 5 (1990): 31–50.

Hahn, Kimiko. *Mosquito and Ant*. New York: Norton, 1999.

———. "Three Voices Together: A Collage: Kimiko Hahn, Gale Jackson, Susan Sherman." *We Stand Our Ground: Three Women, Their Vision, Their Poems*. By Kimiko Hahn, Gale Jackson, and Susan Sherman. New York: Ikon, 1988. 9–29.

———. *The Unbearable Heart*. New York: Kaya Production, 1995.

Harris, Judith. "Breaking the Code of Silence: Ideology and Women's Confessional Poetry." *After Confession: Poetry as Autobiography*. Ed. Kate Sontag and David Graham. Saint Paul, MN: Graywolf Press, 2001. 254–68.

Holden, Jonathan. *The Rhetoric of the Contemporary Lyric*. Bloomington: Indiana University Press, 1980.

Hongo, Garrett, ed. Introduction. *The Open Boat: Poems from Asian America*. New York: Anchor, 1993. xvii–xlii.

Klein, Melanie. *Envy and Gratitude and Other Works, 1946–1963*. London: Virago, 1993.

Lowell, Robert. *Life Studies*. New York: Farrar, Straus, & Cudahy, 1959.

Payant, Katherine B. *Becoming and Bonding: Contemporary Feminism and Popular Fiction by American Women Writers*. Westport: Greenwood, 1993.

Perloff, Marjorie. "*Poètes Maudits* of the Genteel Tradition: Lowell and Berryman." *Robert Lowell: Essays on the Poetry*. Ed. Steven Gould Axelrod and Helen Deese. Cambridge: Cambridge University Press, 1986. 99–116.

Phillips, Robert. *The Confessional Poets*. Carbondale: Southern Illinois University Press, 1973.

Rosenthal, M. L. *The New Poets: American and British Poetry Since World War II*. New York: Oxford University Press, 1967.

Said, Edward W. *Orientalism*. New York: Vintage, 1979.

Shetley, Vernon. *After the Death of Poetry: Poet and Audience in Contemporary America*. Durham: Duke University Press, 1993.

Stitt, Peter. "John Ashbery." *Poets at Work: The Paris Review Interviews.* Ed. George Plimpton. New York: Penguin, 1989. 387–412.

Tabios, Eileen. *Black Lightning: Poetry-in-Progress.* New York: Asian American Writers' Workshop, 1998.

Vendler, Helen. *Soul Says: On Recent Poetry.* Cambridge: Belknap Press of Harvard University Press, 1995.

Wang, Dorothy J. "Undercover Asian: John Yau and the Politics of Ethnic Self-Identification." *Asian American Literature in the International Context: Readings on Fiction, Poetry, and Performance.* Ed. Rocío G. Davis and Sämi Ludwig. Münster: LIT Verlag, 2002. 135–55.

Wong, Sau-ling Cynthia, and Stephen H. Sumida, eds. *The Resource Guide to Asian American Literature.* New York: Modern Language Association, 2001.

Wong, Sunn Shelley. "Sizing Up Asian American Poetry." *The Resource Guide to Asian American Literature.* Ed. Sau-ling Cynthia Wong and Stephen H. Sumida. New York: Modern Language Association, 2001. 285–308.

Yamamoto, Traise. *Masking Selves, Making Subjects: Japanese American Women, Identity, and the Body.* Berkeley: University of California Press, 1999.

Yau, John. "Between the Forest and Its Trees: Where We Are Is in a Sentence." *Amerasia Journal* 20.3 (1994): 37–43.

———. *Edificio Sayonara.* Santa Rosa: Black Sparrow Press, 1992.

———. *Forbidden Entries.* Santa Rosa: Black Sparrow Press, 1996.

———. "Please Wait by the Coatroom: Wifredo Lam in the Museum of Modern Art." *Arts Magazine* 63.4 (1988): 59.

———. *Radiant Silhouette: New & Selected Work, 1974–1988.* Santa Rosa: Black Sparrow Press, 1989.

Yu, Timothy. "Form and Identity in Language Poetry and Asian American Poetry." *Contemporary Literature* 41.3 (2000): 422–51.

Zhou, Xiaojing. "Postmodernism and Subversive Parody: John Yau's 'Genghis Chan: Private Eye' Series." *College Literature* 31.1 (2004): 73–102.

NOTES

1. Sunn Shelley Wong, in her essay "Sizing Up Asian American Poetry," discusses extensively the problems embedded in the oppositions between aesthetics and politics, which, she contends, Garrett Hongo sets up rhetorically in his introduction.

2. The term "mainstream" is usually used in Asian American discourses to refer to white America, or to the dominance of European American culture, particularly the institutional preeminence of Anglo-American culture and literature.

3. Many Asian American poets' work resists a single, binary paradigm for defining resistant poetics. John Yau, Catalina Cariaga, and Myung Mi Kim, for instance, have

written language-oriented poems marked by distinct ethnic voices. Poets such as Lawson Fusao Inada and Marilyn Chin experiment with elements of jazz and blues in addition to forms of haiku and Chinese classical poems, respectively; Kimiko Hahn incorporates Japanese and Chinese women's literary forms and aesthetic styles; Arthur Sze combines elements from physics, biology, and Native American and Chinese cultures in developing an ecopoetics; and Mei-Mei Berssenbrugge draws from post-modern visual arts, and from scientific and philosophical writings, in inventing a radical poetics that resists being defined in terms of either a Language poetry or an ethnic identity.

4. For an insightful discussion of John Yau's poetry that resists the label of any particular school of poetry, see Dorothy J. Wang, "Undercover Asian."

5. I explore at length the ambivalence in John Yau's use of the lyric voice in another essay, "Postmodernism and Subversive Parody," in which my reading of Yau's poems from this series is much fuller than what I can offer in this essay.

6. For an extended discussion of Yau's "Genghis Chan" poems and their relation to *film noir,* see Zhou, "Postmodernism and Subversive Parody: John Yau's 'Genghis Chan: Private Eye' Series."

7. See for instance, Helen Vendler, *Soul Says* 6–7.

8. For an incisive discussion of Kimiko Hahn's appropriation of Japanese women's literature and her negotiation with Japanese language and culture in exploring both women's subjectivity and her own biracial identity, see Traise Yamamoto, *Masking Selves, Making Subjects* 236–52. For Hahn's evocation and emulation of Chinese women's writing, see her volume *Mosquito and Ant.*

9. See Melanie Klein, *Envy and Gratitude.*

BEYOND THE LENGTH OF AN AVERAGE PENIS

READING ACROSS TRADITIONS IN THE POETRY OF TIMOTHY LIU

RICHARD SERRANO

> Read all the poets (living and dead) you can so that you can then get in on the great conversation that poetry is, a conversation that exists both in time and in eternity. —TIMOTHY LIU

Because our students live in a world of war and famine televised from every distant corner of the globe, as well as in neighborhoods in which violence has become routine; because they have heard nearly every possible obscenity, sometimes in multiple languages, often from the mouths of their own parents; because plane crashes and stock market crashes unfold simultaneously and instantaneously around them; only poetry, it seems, is still able to shock them. Not any poetry, of course, although Petrarch's sadistic idolization of Laura, the perfectly realized alexandrines of Racine's tormented Phèdre, the ancient Chinese poet Qu Yuan railing against his ruler's evil advisers, never fail to shock me, even if they (at first) leave my students unmoved. But there remains enough that is shocking in contemporary American poetry that I usually begin introductory literature courses with poets fearless of speaking the truths they have come to know, through the language of poetry they have come to master, even if these truths and this mastery remain provisional. For this is what shocks students: speaking aloud what everyone has tacitly agreed to forget, or, at least, what no one would expect to remember in a mere literature course.

Lesbian and gay poets who speak from beyond the closet are doubly shocking, despite our recent flip to a topsy-turvy lit-crit world of celebrating the margins and marginalized. Most American readers still do not expect to confront these voices at all. Several years ago, one colleague tried to have another colleague fired because he taught a poem by Olga Broumas, a San Francisco lesbian poet, which began, "I let them whip and fuck me." This first line was shocking, at least in the context of an English composition course, although I must add that the students were less easily shocked than the colleague. Ironically, the first colleague never seemed to understand that Broumas wrote this poem in the voice of a straight woman—the "them" of the poem is masculine. The first colleague could not bear to hear a lesbian poet break through the silence imposed upon her, although Broumas spoke only after she had masqueraded herself away from the margins and back to the center by taking on a heterosexual identity.

Yet more shocking is the discovery that lesbian and gay poets of color not only speak but sometimes speak *to each other*—and in such a way that the hapless heterosexual or Caucasian reader is little more than an eavesdropper on a conversation that both implicates yet excludes him or her. Here I will examine how the gay Chinese American Timothy Liu engages in a dialogue with his fellow gay poet, the African American Essex Hemphill, by performing an ironic rereading of the canonical nineteenth-century poet and gay icon Walt Whitman. Liu and Hemphill speak to each other and to their respective overlapping and multiple audiences across a shared poetic tradition in which Whitman looms large. Timothy Liu has published four volumes of poetry: *Vox Angelica* (1992), which won the Norma Farber First Book Award; *Burnt Offerings* (1995); *Say Goodnight* (1998); and *Hard Evidence* (2001). Essex Hemphill's volume of collected prose and poetry, *Ceremonies,* was published in 1992. He achieved notoriety in 1991, when the Marlon Riggs film *Tongues Untied,* in which Hemphill's poetry and voice played a major role, aired on PBS. Although Hemphill is no longer living, in order to be grammatically consistent I will refer to him in the present tense throughout this essay.

Teaching the poems of Liu and Hemphill together has proved so fruitful that I nearly always begin introductory literature classes with a poem by one of these two poets and immediately follow it with a poem by the other. Sometimes I throw in Robert Graves's "Down, wanton, down!" or Denise Levertov's "Hypocrite Women" (an odd poem that uses the word "cunts") for further consideration, and to reassure students that not only gay poets or male poets have felt compelled to write about their genitalia. Both Liu and Hemphill, then, are using motifs already apparent in the mainstream of twentieth-century American poetry. Here are the two poems, the first by Essex Hemphill and the second by Timothy Liu:

BLACK MACHISMO

Metaphorically speaking
his black dick is so big
when it stands up erect
it silences
the sound of his voice.
It obscures his view
of the territory, his history,
the cosmology of his identity
is rendered invisible.

When his big black dick
is not erect
it drags behind him,
a heavy, obtuse thing,
his balls and chains
clattering, making
so much noise
I cannot hear him
even if I want to listen.

(*Ceremonies* 130)

THE SIZE OF IT

I knew the length of an average penis
        was five to seven inches, a fact
I learned upstairs in the stacks marked 610
        or HQ, not down in the basement
where I knelt behind a toilet stall, waiting
        for eight-and-a-half inches or more
to fill my mouth with a deeper truth. The heart
        grows smaller, like a cut rose drying
in the sun. Back then I was only fourteen
        with four-and-three-quarters inches
at full erection. I began equating
        Asian with inadequate, unable

to compete with others in the locker room
        after an icy swim (a shriveled
bud between my fingers as I tried to shake
        some semblance of life back into it).
Three times a day, I jacked off faithfully, yet
        nothing would enlarge my future, not
ads for vacuum pumps, nor ancient herbs. Other
        men had to compensate, one billion
Chinese measured against what? Some said my cock
        had a classical shape, and I longed
for the ruins of Greece. Others took it up
        the ass, reassuring in their way,
yet nothing helped me much on my knees at night
        praying one more inch would make me whole.

(*Burnt Offerings* 11)

I do not know for certain that Liu read Hemphill before composing his own poem. Since there is an inevitable lag between the composition of a poem and its appearance between the two covers of a collection, I am not even certain that Liu's poem was written after Hemphill's was published, or even, for that matter, which poem was written first, though I would hazard to guess that Hemphill's is earlier. I am certain, however, that both poets are voracious readers of American poetry. Liu, for example, has read an average of five volumes of poetry a week since his twenty-first birthday, which adds up to thousands of volumes by now (Tabios 71). Regardless of chronology, Timothy Liu and Essex Hemphill speak to each other because they both speak in response to the same body of American poetry. Liu's and Hemphill's poems understand each other because they both speak in the language learned from the poets who precede and surround them. Finally, Liu and Hemphill speak in the same poetic language because, since Hemphill all but invented (or reinvented, if one cares to look back as far as the Harlem Renaissance) gay African American poetry, and since Liu has all but invented gay Asian American poetry, their respective traditions have not diverged sufficiently to render them mutually unintelligible. I do not mean to imply that Hemphill is the first gay African American poet or that Liu is the first gay Asian American poet; in fact, I know that this is not the case. Neither Liu nor Hemphill, however, draws from a poetic tradition specifically Asian American, or specifically African American, or specifically gay, from which to take the raw materials of poetry, to the exclusion of the larger American tradition. Indeed, as noted in the epigraph to this essay, Liu recommends that young poets read all poets, living or dead, in order to take part in the great poetic conversations, timely and timeless.

Both poets frequently allude to other poets and writers, although one might argue that Hemphill's references are racialized, whereas Liu's are not. In *Burnt Offerings,* Liu refers to, among others, Thoreau, Walt Whitman, Dante, Blake, Paul Celan, and *Ecclesiastes,* sources representative of a body of work that Hemphill undoubtedly also knows well. In *Ceremonies,* Hemphill refers to, among others, Aimé Césaire (the Black francophone poet from Martinique), Whitman, James Baldwin, William Carlos Williams, and Lord Alfred Douglas ("I am the love that dare not speak its name"). Hemphill's most obvious and admitted borrowings come from Black writers, gay writers, and American poets. When Liu and Hemphill refer to music or art, their paths further diverge. Hemphill alludes to Marvin Gaye, Liu to Wagner or Hindemith. Hemphill writes about the photographer Robert Mapplethorpe, soundly criticizing him for his objectification of Black men, while Liu turns to Giacometti and Matisse for inspiration. Hemphill would, at first glance, seem to be more deeply implicated in the writers of his race than Liu is in the writers of his. Even when Liu writes poems in *Say Goodnight* such as "Reading Tu Fu" or "Reading Lu Chi," there is little sense that Liu is invoking them because they are Chinese; in fact, the two poems form a trio with "Reading Cavafy," the latter a gay Greek poet writing in Egypt.

This short list of artists and composers suggests that the differences between the two poets in these realms have more to do with class than with race. And, in fact, I would suggest that the convergence of their voices in the two poems above is all the more remarkable if we consider the worlds that separate them. Although both poets often write about sexual transgression and neither shies away from the occasional graphic description—Hemphill's "In america, / I place my ring / on your cock / where it belongs" (170), Liu's "our tongues made holy / by licking each other's asshole clean" (*Burnt Offerings* 13)—it is obvious that the potential punishment for these transgressions is much more likely to be severe for Hemphill's HIV-positive man looking for partners in the bushes of a park in Washington, D.C., than for Liu's student lurking for the same reason in the men's room of a university library.

We should also keep in mind that the two poets came of age at radically different moments in gay American history, Hemphill in the late 1970s and early 1980s, Liu in the 1990s. AIDS is not absent from the world of *Burnt Offerings,* but it exists mostly in the frenzied imaginations of straight people (in "Thoreau," the narrator's stepmother has banished him from the house because she fears catching AIDS). Death can remain a beautiful and evocative abstraction for Liu—"What lies buried under six feet of snow," in "Benediction" (*Burnt Offerings* 68)—but for Hemphill, death, or, more precisely, dying, is too immediate and real to stay at the level of metaphor. "I die twice as fast / as any other American / between eighteen and thirty-five" (124) might be metaphorical in any other American's poetry, but in Hemphill's it is a statement of the obvious, with a metaphorical edge—and, of course, it might leave us to wonder if he is dying twice as fast because he is a Black man or because he is HIV-positive. Hemphill writes, "When I die, / honey chil', / my angels / will be tall / Black drag queens" (81), and he is not imagining some distant event but planning for tomorrow, all the while imagining a world where those at the bottom of the heap (this poem is pre–RuPaul) will for one moment reach the heavens. In Hemphill's poetry, that which metaphor would veil surfaces unbidden, and beyond control. Nevertheless, although the poet's death may be inevitable, it need not go unheralded. The ceremony that acknowledges Hemphill's death is his to craft.

Liu, however, is not unaware of how death has haunted the gay community for the past twenty years. In one of his most beautiful poems, rich with images that would have delighted the influential American poet William Carlos Williams, whose most famous poem is undoubtedly "The Red Wheelbarrow" ("so much depends / upon // a red wheel / barrow . . ."; Williams 224), Liu writes:

WHITE MOTHS

espaliered
to a radiator grille
or hurled
from the glass cave
of a child's mason jar
into the garden spider's web—
a slow dance
of paralytic
stings, death's handiwork

spun out of silk, cradled
by the wind—
and the bodies
warm to touch in the rising

drone of dusk still flutter
among
    the bronzed backs
of men in the park—
        pale wings
fanning a glitter of dust.

(*Burnt Offerings* 42)

Indeed, so much depends on white moths in this poem. The "men in the park," on the other hand, are almost lost amid the fluttering of wings, especially on a first reading. Who are they? What are they doing? Why are they barebacked (and, since bronzed, often barebacked)? We already know that Liu is a gay poet, since he has been marketed as such; and since we have likely found his work in a gay-oriented bookstore, or in the Gay and Lesbian Studies section of Barnes & Noble, we can decode this image as being about sex among men. Since Liu elsewhere in this collection writes about sex in public places, it is not unfair to assume that these men have gathered in search of sexual partners. As Fone points out, the sexual retreat to a bucolic site is a trope of same-sex love dating back at least to Virgil's second Eclogue, "wherein Corydon laments his lost Alexis and invites him to return to his own sacred grove and, like Marlowe's Shepherd, to come live with him and be his love" (136). Both sociological and literary precedent eroticize the poem so that when we reach the image of barebacked men, we can retroactively sexualize the earlier phrase, "and the bodies / warm to touch in the rising," which we might have first assumed pertained to the moths only.

Although so much about this poem depends on the legacy of William Carlos Williams—the central, elaborated image, the short lines and careful attention to line breaks, the poem's immediacy and insistence on its self-sufficiency as a poem—it also seems oddly Chinese to me. This is not completely surprising, and not because Liu is Chinese American but because the imagist poets, such as Williams, who influence Liu were themselves influenced by translations of Chinese poetry. The moths have nothing to do with the men in the park; the moths have everything to do with the men in the park. Both statements are true, although I call this poetics of continuity within discontinuity Chinese not because of some orientalist fantasy of the mystical pseudophilosophical Zen of white moths or cruising parks; no, the disjunction that insists on connection reminds me of some of China's earliest poetry, found in the *Shi Jing*, or *Classic of Poetry*. I do not want to overemphasize this connection, for fear of exoticizing Timothy Liu, but this characteristic reminiscent of a certain kind of Chinese poetry is something we find in Liu and not in Hemphill (and, I might add, in Williams and not in Whitman). Ironically, if I find Chinese elements in Liu's poetry, it is certainly not because he is Chinese American but because he has imbibed the whole of American poetry, including the imagistic residue of Chinese poems long ago translated into English.

The *Classic of Poetry* contains poems dating back as early as 800 B.C.E. and is traditionally believed to have been compiled by Confucius himself. A distinguishing feature of this poetry is its use of a certain kind of image called a *xing*. The earliest extant Confucian commentaries, dating from the Han Dynasty, long after Confucius himself, label as *xing* the images borrowed from nature that are found in the first lines of many of these poems, without ever explaining what a *xing* is. A *xing* may be that which inspires the poem, it may be that which resonates after the poem is finished, or it may be simply a way to start a poem. In any case, these initial images usually have little or no discernible connection to the rest of the poem. Indeed, the commentaries expend a great deal of energy trying to account for the relationship of the *xing* to the poem it begins. The following poem in the *Classic of Poetry* is a good example:

> In the wilds is a dead deer—white grass wraps it
> there is a girl longing for spring—a worthy knight seduces her
> in the forest is a small tree—in the wilds is a dead deer
> white grass wraps it—there is a girl like jade
> slowly and very slowly
> do not move my sash
> do not make the dog bark.
>
> ("Mao #23" Chang 111–14)

The above translation is mine, although Ezra Pound's translations of these Chinese poems are probably the most famous (no doubt Liu has read them). How do we begin to interpret this poem? What does the dead deer wrapped in white grass have to do with the girl like jade, which in traditional Chinese poetry is white and represents purity? That both the girl and the dead deer are white encourages us to draw some sort of analogy between them. The fourth line seems to further emphasize this connection by juxtaposing the two images of whiteness. In an interpretation that always strikes my students as wild, the Han commentator Zheng Xuan explains the context of the poem: "Because of the feelings of a chaste girl, who wants to cause others to use white grass to wrap up the deer meat that has been divided by the hunters in the fields, they come with propriety / bearing gifts" (my translation).

I prefer, in an essay about contemporary gay American poetry, not to debate the merits of commentaries written by men dead nearly two millennia except to point out that this interpretation does some hermeneutic violence to a poem that in turn seems to imply the danger of violence to the girl—she is, after all, juxtaposed with a dead deer. The point of the Confucian explanation of the poem, however, is that the startling images of the dead deer wrapped in white grass and the girl pure as jade exist in the same world. Whatever the metaphorical implications of either the deer or the girl, we cannot make sense of the poem by merely replacing one with the other. The dead deer does not make the jade girl go away, and vice versa. The ambiguity of the connection between dead deer and jade girl and our tentative attempts to make sense of it force us to think of both images in more complex ways and encourage us to imagine an emotional context for the poem, just as it encouraged Confucian commentators to imagine its historical (and therefore moral) context.

The relationship between the moths and men in "White Moths" also remains ambiguous enough that we cannot replace one with the other. The men with bronzed backs are not simply human equivalents of the moths that have met their deaths, splatting against the radiator grille of an oncoming car or hurled into a spider's web by a malicious child. Nevertheless, having read what happens to the moths, it is difficult for us to forget them when we unexpectedly encounter the men in the park. As in the Chinese commentaries to "In the wilds is a dead deer . . . ," the natural image is part of the world of the human image. Like the men, the moths appear in the park at dusk. Since we know almost nothing about the men and a great deal about the moths, we extrapolate from the moth world in order to make sense of the human world. What would be the equivalent of the radiator grille in the lives of these men? What would be the equivalent of the spider's web? Liu omits details about the men in the park that would permit us to begin allegorizing the poem. Instead he uses the image of the white moths to unsettle our understanding of what we might otherwise perceive (according to our attitude toward anonymous sex among men in parks) as merely a good time, a sign of immoral behavior, or an instance of boys being boys. Even those readers who come to the poem without a moral agenda cannot read joy or untarnished pleasure into the gathering, because the white moths get in the way.

Nevertheless, and regardless of the moths and the discomfort they inject into the poem, the male body remains beautiful, is still an object of devotion, in "White Moths." This celebration of the male body is shared by Essex Hemphill and no doubt explains the attraction of both poets to the poetry of Walt Whitman. Whitman was the first great gay American poet, although neither he nor any of his contemporaries would have understood him as such, since when he was writing *Leaves of Grass,* in the 1850s, the word "homosexual" had not yet been invented. Whitman did himself recognize, however, that he was the first to write about "manly friendship" (Fone 20). And while Whitman could never have written about sex in the park or in a bathroom stall, even if he had been inclined to seek partners in such places, more than one gay male reader has seen his own desire reflected in such lines as "The march of firemen in their own costumes, the / play of masculine muscle through clean-setting trousers / and waist-straps, / . . . / Swim with the swimmers, wrestle with wrestlers, march in line with the firemen, and pause, listen, / and count" (293). Although Whitman also describes women in his poems, since they, too, are among the "leaves of grass" he wishes to count and account for, only the men are nearly always described in terms of physical beauty.

Liu's bronze-backed men in the park could come straight out of *Leaves of Grass,* although Whitman would see them as a group brought together by a common profession or task and further linked by a common humanity. Liu ironizes Whitman by giving his group common cause of a different nature, thereby suggesting that Whitman's men also had other cause to assemble, whether or not Whitman would or could write of it explicitly. As we have already seen, Liu reworks the beauty of this Whitmanesque situation by disturbing it with the image of the white moths. Liu uses a poetic strategy reminiscent of that found in a certain type of classical Chinese poetry in order to distance himself from Whitman's poetics and ideology. Hemphill's most obvious reference to Whitman, which he points out in his notes, is also ironizing, but he does not distance himself with this irony. Instead he personalizes Whitman's text.

In the second poem of *Ceremonies,* Hemphill cites two lines from "Burial," the penultimate poem of *Leaves of Grass*: "Do you think I could walk pleasantly / and well-suited toward annihilation?" (6) It is important that Hemphill sees fit to cite what is nearly the last poem of Whitman's collection in the first poem of his own *Ceremonies*. Whitman has the luxury of pushing "Burial" to the end of his celebration of life; and, indeed, to reinsert Whitman's lines into their original context is to reestablish their optimism:

> Do you suspect death? If I were to suspect death, I
> should die now,
> Do you think I could walk pleasantly and well-suited
> toward annihilation?
>
> Pleasantly and well-suited I walk,
> Whither I walk I cannot define, but I know it is good,
> The whole universe indicates that it is good,
> The past and the present indicate that it is good.
>
> (447)

By taking Whitman's lines out of context and inserting them into his own poem, Hemphill changes their meaning. Reminding us of his dialogue on death with Liu, Hemphill makes concrete the rhetorical, poetico-spiritual question of Whitman. For Hemphill not only suspects death, he sees it and lives just this side of it, always and everywhere. Whitman can attend a burial and witness it as yet a further celebration of life. The universe, past, present together assure Whitman that wherever he is going, wherever life or death, life and death, life with death take him, is good. Whereas Whitman's question doubts annihilation, refuses to suspect that death (here presumably spiritual rather than physical, since Whitman has witnessed burial as a ceremony marking physical death) is coming, Hemphill casts doubt on the manner by which he goes to death.

Ceremonies is not a pleasant walk toward death but is more like kicking and screaming interspersed with wry moments meant to put death off, to protest death, to pull a fast one on the early death demanded of the poet. Hemphill refuses to accept that he is "well-suited" to die, here shifting the meaning of Whitman's hyphenated "well-suited" to "suitable" from its original "well-dressed," as if to suggest that the most obvious reasons for his dying, that he is both Black and gay, are not so suitable after all. Hemphill's poetry, however, is not always relentlessly grim, since he precedes his citation of Whitman with "Why is some destruction so beautiful?" (6) So many of Hemphill's poems are about the destruction caused by intimacies among men either aborted or gone wrong. The pull of Whitman's songs of community even one hundred thirty years after their publication is evident in the anger with which Hemphill chronicles, in "The Edge," the beauty of the desperate impossibility of realizing this community in the world he knows: "Behind a wall of mirrors / I tell my skeleton of youth / I am beautiful. / I will endure" (162).

Liu, too, ironizes Whitman by recontextualizing his poetry. In "Reading Whitman in a Toilet Stall," Liu gives us two citations, providing equal time to a few lines of Whitman and to a few lines of graffiti on a wall separating two stalls in a public restroom. This poem merits citation in full:

READING WHITMAN IN A TOILET STALL

A security-man who stood, arms crossed, outside
the men's room (making sure that no one lingered)
met my eyes with the same dispassionate gaze as
a woman inside, kneeling to clean the toilets.

The faintly buzzing flicker of fluorescent light
Erased the contours of a place where strangers
Openly parade their sex. Efficient, silent,
all ammonia and rubber gloves, she was in and

out of there in minutes, taking no notice
of the pocket Whitman that I leafed my way through
before the others arrived. *In paths untrodden, /*
In the growth by margins of pondwaters, / Escaped

from the light that exhibits itself—how those words
came flooding back to me while men began to take
their seats, glory holes the size of silver dollars
in the farthest stall where no adolescent went

unnoticed. O daguerreotyped Walt, your collar
unbuttoned, hat lopsided, hand on hip, your sex
never evading our view! How we are confined
by steel partitions, dates and initials carved

into the latest coat of paint, an old car key
the implement of our secret desires. *Wanted:*
uncut men with lots of cheese. No fats. No femmes.
Under twenty a real plus. How each of us must

learn to decipher the erotic hieroglyphs
of our age, prayers on squares of one-ply paper
flushed daily down the john where women have knelt
in silence, where men with folded arms stand guard

while we go about our task, our tongues made holy
by licking each other's asshole clean, shock of sperm
warm in our mouths, white against the clothes we wear
as we walk out of our secrets into the world.

(*Burnt Offerings* 12–13)

It is obvious that Liu is meditating on more than just the cited snippet from the first of Whitman's "Calamus" poems. I quote at greater length the poem Liu cites in order to better explain its meaning in its original context:

In paths untrodden,
In the growth by margins of pondwaters,
Escaped from the light that exhibits itself
Here, by myself, away from the clank of the world,
Tallying and talked to here by tongues aromatic,
No longer abashed—for in this secluded spot I can respond as I would not dare elsewhere,
Strong upon me the life that does not exhibit itself, yet contains all the rest,
Resolved to sing no songs to-day but those of manly attachment . . .
I proceed, for all who are, or who have been, young men,
To tell the secret of my nights and days,
To celebrate the need of comrades.

(Whitman 341–42)

Obviously, Liu's relationship to Whitman is so complex that I will need to unpack my explanation of it slowly.

Whitman, of course, never really did tell his readers the secret of his nights and days, at least not publicly. Liu's poem seems to be in part about the legacy of this secret never made explicit. Liu's narrator—in this poem I want to think of him as a somewhat naïve version of the poet, a younger version struggling to make sense of the world through poetry, a character who becomes the poet by the end of the poem—enters the men's room in search of the sort of masculine camaraderie he has read about in Whitman. Hemphill does something similar with a reference to James Baldwin's *Giovanni's Room* in "Heavy Breathing": "I am looking / for Giovanni's room / in this bathhouse. / I know he's here" (12). David, the protagonist of Baldwin's novel, did not find Giovanni by looking for him anywhere, let alone in a bathhouse. Both Liu and Hemphill make a point of contrasting the tawdry mechanics of lived gay life in the 1980s and 1990s with the idealized or sentimental depictions of "camaraderie" and love found in iconic gay authors.

In Liu's "Reading Whitman in a Toilet Stall," the conversing tongues of Whitman's poem give way to tongues too busy with other tasks to bother with talk. And "task" is precisely the word Liu chooses. The men licking each other's assholes are as efficient as the cleaning woman. Liu emphasizes the odd similarity of their tasks with the suggestion of religious ritual in both the woman's kneeling and the purification stemming from anonymous analingus. Whereas Hemphill explores the beauty of destruction, Liu shows us the beauty of obstruction. The security guard and the cleaning woman, as well as the metal walls dividing one man from the next, recognize and ritualize the desire that brings them together. This *is* a holy place, as holy as any Whitmanesque site of congregation.

Like Whitman away from the clank of the world, the narrator takes this moment of solitude to celebrate the needs of his anonymous comrades. Yet the closest the narrator comes to establishing a feeling of community is in the exchange of "dispassionate" gazes with the security guard and the cleaning woman. For what sort of community is implied by the graffiti that the poet italicizes in the same way he italicizes Whitman's verse? A very restricted one defined by multiple exclusions. The comrade expressing his desire in graffiti excludes the overweight, the effeminate, all but near-adolescents, the circumcised, and the uncircumcised who wash their genitalia frequently enough to avoid generating "cheese." In his brilliant book on the transformation of gay culture, Daniel Harris explains how such discrimination (as reflected in personal ads) fractures a gay community only recently formed. Harris notes, however, that technological advances privileging shared patterns of consumption, which have permitted scattered and isolated gay individuals to form such a community, really serve only to make homosexuals ideal shoppers (see Harris, *The Rise and Fall of Gay Culture,* especially 40–63). Liu's narrator in a bathroom stall is a long way from the untrodden paths and manly attachments of Whitman.

When I last spoke about gay and lesbian writers in a public forum, I was asked if there were such a thing as a gay culture, if there were truly such a thing as a gay community. I am certainly not going to claim, in this age of globalization and transnationality, that there exists a discrete and autonomous gay or lesbian culture. Nevertheless, I think we can see how elements of American culture and literature are distorted as they make their way through the matrix of multiple, interlocking identities that seems to be part of nearly anyone's life in this country today. There is no "gay culture," but there are several recognizably gay sensibilities that interact both with each other and with other sorts of identity, based on race or ethnicity, language, profession, class, education, and targeted marketing, as well as with the culture at large. There is no "gay community," especially with the threat of AIDS to American gay men (a threat perceived by some as receding), but instead there are individuals whose shared sexual orientation, and the reaction it inspires from less progressive elements in this country (a reaction that sometimes even takes the form of torture and murder, as it did for Matthew Shepard in Wyoming), may cause them to recognize at times that they have certain rights and responsibilities in common. I have insisted throughout this essay that Liu and Hemphill share an American poetic heritage, but I want to return to the two poems with which we began, in order to show how each poet reacts to and manipulates this heritage through a matrix of increasingly restricted identities, one that excludes them from "mainstream" culture and eventually separates them from each other.

Why do both Hemphill and Liu write about racially determined penis length? A walk through a Chelsea bar reveals pecs, thighs, and biceps of cartoonish dimension. This obsession with projecting an image of hypermasculinity, the flip side of the drag queen sashaying through a room in her lipstick and pumps, cannot be blamed entirely on Whitman, but certainly his eroticization of the male laborer's body is one of its distant sources. In "Black Machismo" and "The Size of It," Hemphill and Liu explore what happens when the gay American obsession with the most superficial manifestations of masculinity is tangled up with racism borrowed from the nation at large and amplified. Both poets realize that the penises of Black and Asian men are measured against the "norm" of Caucasian penises. The erotics of racial difference must be played out to whatever lengths necessary. The gazes of the security guard and the cleaning woman in Liu's "Reading Whitman in a Toilet Stall" have nothing on the appraising and excluding gaze of the white gay man as directed at the Black gay man and the Asian gay man. Richard Fung's seminal article "Looking for My Penis: The Eroticized Asian in Gay Video Porn" explains the economy of racialized gay erotica (although, as he points out, racialized gay erotica predates the advent of video porn). If the Caucasian man is to be just right, then the Black man's penis must be as abnormally large as the Asian man's is abnormally small.

Such stereotypes inflict damage beyond the gay video–viewing community. Hemphill explains how Robert Mapplethorpe, a cause célèbre in the gay white community in the 1980s, exploits Black men and aestheticizes stereotypes of the Black male body:

> Mapplethorpe's "Man in a Polyester Suit" . . . presents a Black man without a head, wearing a business suit, his trousers unzipped, and his fat, long penis dangling down. . . . What is insulting and endangering to Black men is Mapplethorpe's *conscious* determination that the faces, the heads, and by extension, the minds and experiences of some of his Black subjects are not as important as close-up shots of their cocks ["Does Your Mama Know about Me?" 38–39].

In other words, Mapplethorpe's photographs of Black men reinforce the notion that their sole value to the gay (white) community comes in the form of a big black dick. As with all the other poems my students read with me, I begin our discussion of Hemphill's poem by asking for a volunteer to read it aloud. So deeply ingrained is this myth about the enormity of the Black man's member—and so clever is Hemphill in breaking the line so that he all but forces the reader to trip over this myth—that all my students who have ever read this poem aloud, regardless of their gender, ethnicity, or age, got the second line wrong, reading "big black dick" for "black dick is so big." Even students who, one might assume, have never seen a black dick apparently cannot think of "black" and "dick" without throwing in a gratuitous "big." Such is the rush to reach the expected "big" that they bump it up to the head of the sentence. I always insist that they reread the line until they get it right. For some, it takes three attempts before what seems to be the obligatory adjectival immensity is omitted.

Hemphill is very careful not to accept the stereotype on anything but a metaphorical level, for it is not the enormousness of any particular Black man's member that is at stake, nor is it a question of whether or not a team of anthropologists can determine that the average black penis is larger or smaller than the average penis in any other racial group. This metaphorical big black dick both blinds and silences the Black man. Hemphill recognizes that this objectification is directed at other groups of people as well, sometimes by Black men themselves; the objectified are not free from the need to objectify others. In "Heavy Breathing," for example, Hemphill criticizes straight Black men who act "as if all females / between eight and eighty / are simply pussies with legs" (6). He also criticizes gay Black men who enter pathological relationships with white men, as in "The Tomb of Sorrow": "When you told me / your first lover, / a white man, / wanted you to spit, / shit, piss on, / fist-fuck and / and throw him down stairs, / alarms should have / blared forth / like hordes / of screaming queens" (86).

"Black Machismo" insists that the metaphorical big black dick has two functions. In connection with the first, the Black man sees only his own erect dick, forgetting everything else about himself: where he is, where he comes from, who he is. The second function comes when his dick is no longer erect and therefore no longer attracts even single-minded attention from others. Even someone who wants to listen cannot hear what the Black man has to say because of the background noise generated by his metaphorical big black dick. We can see, then, why Hemphill would be so outraged by Mapplethorpe's photos. They render concrete, even daringly artsy, the myth of the big black dick, making it more believable, if not always more palatable, to his viewers.

Liu's poem takes up where Hemphill's leaves off; if black dicks are freakishly large and white dicks just right, then Asian dicks must be uselessly small. There must be some odd comfort in this gay sexual economy, unless, of course, your ethnicity places you on the freakish fringes of the community. The details of Liu's poem emphasize the pathological absurdity of determining adequacy from penis length. Just one more inch would make the narrator whole. The precision of length he ascribes to his penis implies that he has carefully measured it. His anxiety has caused him to look up standard penis measurements in the library. His partners reassure him, either by letting him play the insertive role or by linking him with the ancient Greeks, a people who, like Whitman, have achieved iconic status within gay American consciousness. Unfortunately for the well-being of Liu's narrator, the ancient Greek constructions of homosexuality have little to do with those in America today. We can perhaps thank Whitman for that, since he never indicates any appreciation of sex between men and boys. He always preferred his men strapping and sweaty, as far as we know. Associating the narrator's penis with forms that are classical—and he understands that the reference is not to classical China, since no one suggests that he has a Chang An cock or a Taoist willie—necessarily deracializes him. The classicizing partner renders him acceptable by making him an honorary gay white man with an honorary classically Western penis.

Liu's narrator begins to equate "Asian" with "inadequate," as if the quarter-inch by which he falls short of that vaunted five-to-seven-inch average is due to his racial heritage. Then he projects his own racialized inadequacy onto "one billion / Chinese measured against what?" Against whom? I would like to suggest that the inadequacy of Liu's Asian man and the invisibility/silence of Hemphill's Black man are both measured against the hyper-adequacy and loquacious omnipresence of Whitman and the sort of masculinity celebrated in *Leaves of Grass*. In a section of the book titled "Chants Democratic," Whitman exults:

> America always!
> Always me joined with you, whoever you are!
>
> (159)

That joining becomes problematic if you are an Asian with a dick of a mere four and three-quarters inches or a Black man with your big black dick disappointingly detumescent, dragging behind you and dragging you down. In all fairness to Whitman, he also sang:

> Let every one answer! Let those who sleep be waked!
> Let none evade—not you, any more than others!

This call both Liu and Hemphill answer, speaking to each other over Whitman's gatherings of beautiful male bodies.

BIBLIOGRAPHY

Chang, Zhenguo, ed. *Shi Sanjia Yi Jishu*. Beijing: Zhonghua Shuju Chuban, 1987.

Fone, Byrne R. S. *Masculine Landscapes: Walt Whitman and the Homoerotic Text*. Carbondale: Southern Illinois University Press, 1992.

Fung, Richard. "Looking for My Penis: The Eroticized Asian in Gay Video Porn." *Asian American Sexualities: Dimensions of the Gay and Lesbian Experience*. Ed. Russell Leong. New York: Routledge, 1996. 181–98.

Harris, Daniel. *The Rise and Fall of Gay Culture*. New York: Hyperion, 1997.

Hemphill, Essex. *Ceremonies: Prose and Poetry*. New York: Plume, 1992.

Levertov, Denise. *Poems 1960–1967*. New York: New Directions, 1983.

Liu, Timothy. *Burnt Offerings*. Port Townsend, WA: Copper Canyon Press, 1995.

———. *Hard Evidence.* Jersey City, NJ: Talisman House, 2001.

———. *Say Goodnight.* Port Townsend, WA: Copper Canyon Press, 1998.

———. *Vox Angelica: Poems.* Cambridge: Alice James Books, 1992.

Tabios, Eileen. *Black Lightning: Poetry-in-Progress.* New York: Asian American Writers' Workshop, 1998.

Whitman, Walt. *Leaves of Grass.* Ithaca: Cornell University Press, 1961.

Williams, William Carlos. *The Collected Poems of William Carlos Williams: 1909–1939.* New York: New Directions, 1986.

DECOLONIZING THE BILDUNGSROMAN

NARRATIVES OF WAR AND WOMANHOOD IN NORA OKJA KELLER'S *COMFORT WOMAN*

SAMINA NAJMI

> After whole generations, inside and outside of Germany, have believed for a hundred years that the Bildungsroman is the characteristic German form, shall it be removed from German literary history entirely and applied instead to altogether foreign phenomena? — JEFFREY SAMMONS ("The Bildungsroman for Nonspecialists")

> The writing of the "decolonizing novel" takes place necessarily by way of a detour into the excavation of "history." — LISA LOWE (*Immigrant Acts: On Asian American Cultural Politics*)

Nora Okja Keller's *Comfort Woman*, published a generation after Maxine Hong Kingston's *The Woman Warrior*, is both recognizably descended from Kingston's narrative of formation and representative of a new direction in Asian American women's fiction. Specifically, the turn of the twenty-first century has seen an efflorescence of novels by Asian American women that demonstrate a determination to confront not only personal histories but a collective "Asian" past, as experienced in the first half of the twentieth century. Set at least partially in a geographically specific, ancestral Asia, these contemporary American novels relate female coming-of-age stories against the backdrop of a violent political history of invasion and colonization, or of civil war as it erupts in the aftermath of colonization. They thus refigure the female subject's formation in relation to nationhood, and because they do so within the historical context of colonialism, they move the gendered, raced subject beyond the U.S. nation space, rendering tangential the theme of assimilation, which has formed the focus of critics of Asian American bildungsromane, notably Lisa Lowe and Patricia Chu. In the process, these novels intervene in, and transform, both the traditional bildungsroman and the war narrative—genres of the novel that have been overwhelmingly andocentric and Eurocentric in emphasis. *Comfort Woman* represents a potent example of such generic subversions by contemporary Asian American women. In relating the bildung (education and self-realization) of a Korean girl during the Japanese invasion of her homeland, and the coming of age of her Korean American daughter in Hawaii, this dual narrative raises poignant questions for the critic regarding the connections among identity, ideology, and genre. My argument begins by examining the critical terrain of the bildungsroman and the war narrative, in order to demonstrate how Keller's novel fuses the two genres, simultaneously gendering and "Asianizing" them, to interrupt dominant feminist and nationalist discourses.

Our political investment in the bildungsroman has received due critical attention in recent years.[1] In *Immigrant Acts*, Lisa Lowe specifically identifies the ideological function of the bildungsroman:

> The novel of formation has a special status among the works selected for a canon, for it elicits the reader's identification with the bildung narrative of ethical formation, itself a narrative of the individual's relinquishing of particularity and difference through identification with an idealized "national" form of subjectivity [Lowe 98].

Building on Lowe's definition, Patricia Chu adds that Asian American literature reinscribes the differences thus erased in the conventional bildungsroman, by authoring "an alternative version of the genre, one in which authorship signifies not only the capacity to speak but the belief that speech—or literary representation—is also a claiming of political and social agency" (Chu 3). Lowe's and Chu's analyses shed light on why the bildungsroman represents such a contested site in literary criticism, igniting territorial battles based on gender, race, and nationality. They suggest that political and social visibility, and indeed nationhood itself, are at stake in the writing of the genre.

No surprise, then, that scholars of the genre seem to converge on only one point: that "bildungsroman" is an elusive literary term. Some, like Jeffrey Sammons, have in fact declared it a defunct or even "phantom" genre of the novel. The term "bildungsroman" originated in Germany, was first used by

Karl von Morgenstern in 1819, and was made popular by Wilhelm Dilthey at the turn of the twentieth century. Quickly absorbed into the nationalistic climate of the times, the bildungsroman was claimed as a uniquely German genre, representing Germany's particular contribution to the novel as epitomized in Goethe's 1795 *Wilhelm Meisters Lehrjahre*.[2] Thus the bildungsroman has a long history of engagement, and even identification, with nationhood. In turn, nationhood itself becomes gender-specific: Dilthey defined the bildungsroman in phallocentric terms, as the story of a young man "who enters into life in a blissful state of ignorance, seeks related souls, experiences friendship and love, struggles with the hard realities of the world and thus armed with a variety of experiences, matures, finds himself and his mission in the world."[3] A century later, Jerome Buckley's *Season of Youth*—the first comprehensive study of the English bildungsroman—did not define the genre so much as describe it, again as male-centered: a sensitive youth growing up in a provincial town finds his "free imagination" constrained by family and society; his schooling having been limited and frustrating, he leaves home to experience the world in a big city; here his "real education" begins, including career and sexual encounters, which require him to "reappraise his values" and eventually come to terms with "the modern world" (17). Like Dilthey, Buckley casts female subjects as incidental to the principal interest of the narrative; they serve as factors in the bildung of a normative male protagonist, with whom all readers must identify. Buckley discusses, among other bildungsromane, Charles Dickens's *David Copperfield*, George Eliot's *Middlemarch*, Samuel Butler's *The Way of All Flesh*, D. H. Lawrence's *Sons and Lovers*, James Joyce's *A Portrait of the Artist as a Young Man*, and W. Somerset Maugham's *Of Human Bondage*. Discussions of the American bildungsroman, following Buckley's lead but relocating the genre across the Atlantic, have centered traditionally on texts by and about white men, such as Mark Twain's *Huckleberry Finn* (if only to call it an antibildungsroman), and works by Henry James, F. Scott Fitzgerald, Ernest Hemingway, J. D. Salinger, and so on.

Since the last quarter of the twentieth century, such andocentric definitions of the bildungsroman have been found wanting by feminist critics, some arguing for greater inclusiveness, others dismissing the genre altogether as unsuited to the concerns of most women. The success of feminist criticism in redefining the genre can be measured by the purist anxiety evident in the collection of essays *Reflection and Action*, edited by James Hardin. Far from finding Buckley's definition too constraining, as most feminists do, Hardin and other contributors to the volume consider him too vague in his application of the term. Admitting the difficulty of defining the bildungsroman—"the genre and the theory about it is simply too problematic and dynamic" (xxvi)—the collection nevertheless aims to circumscribe the use of the term once and for all (x). For instance, the editor dismisses feminist revisions of fairy tales and lesbian coming-out tales as "strain[ing] the link with the Bildungsroman to the breaking point" (xviii). Indeed, Hardin's otherwise useful introduction is fraught with peevish comments about other scholars' alleged ignorance of the linguistic, historical, and cultural specificity of the bildungsroman, and about their use of the term "in a careless, cavalier, or simply naive or confused way" (x).[4] Although Hardin apparently concedes that "no one these days would characterize the Bildungsroman as an exclusively German genre" (xxiii; emphasis in original), his collection does exactly that. Sixteen of the seventeen essays focus exclusively on German male bildungsromane. While I find the scholarship of *Reflection and Action* useful, I am most struck by its insistence on confining the bildungsroman to a certain time and place, and by its refusal to acknowledge that terms and genres do indeed cross national, linguistic, temporal, and cultural lines, becoming fruitfully hybridized in the process. But this 1990s white male anxiety about genre purity, buttressed by claims to superior "insider" knowledge—claims at once anxious and arrogant—comes as no surprise in light of recent appropriations of the bildungsroman by feminists and by writers and scholars of color.

A brief overview of feminist scholarship on the bildungsroman will make manifest both the extent of its intervention in male-dominated discourse and its abiding Eurocentricism. The editors of *The Voyage In*, the influential, primarily white feminist, collection published in 1983, prefer to use the term "fictions of female development," arguing that "even the broadest definitions of the Bildungsroman presuppose a range of social options available only to men" (7), but other feminist critics identify a uniquely female version of the genre. For instance, Esther Labovitz's study of twentieth-century female bildungsromane cuts across international lines to include novels by English, French, South African, and German women, all of them white. She argues that the female bildungsroman—an integral element of which she identifies as the heroine's quest for self-knowledge and self-development—was made possible "only when Bildung became a reality for women" (7). According to Labovitz, the appearance of the female bildungsroman challenged the traditional male genre by "shatter[ing] the mold of the quiescent, unpolitical bourgeois German ideology" and creating the rebellious heroine (246). Labovitz sees female bildungsromane as contrasting with male equivalents in their emphasis on sexual equality and on a wide array of social movements rather than on simple class mobility. These characteristics, among others, fashion the bildungsroman into a genre that Labovitz declares to be "representative of women's culture" (257).

Useful as Labovitz's discussion certainly is, its glaring omission of a racial qualifier symptomizes most white feminist writings on the bildungsroman since feminism's Second Wave. In studies such as Labovitz's there is no acknowledgment of the role of whiteness in the bildung of white women or of the many options that whiteness makes available to them, options that women of color cannot take for granted and that shape the white female bildungsroman in a different way. In 1983, the same year that saw the publication of *The Voyage In*, Bonnie Hoover Braendlin argued not only for gender inclusiveness but also for a more racially nuanced definition of the bildungsroman. She suggests that while white male authors may seek "to destroy the Bildungsroman through parody because the genre no longer confirms their concepts of identity," members of racially and sexually marginalized groups are "revitalizing the genre out of a sense of urgency that outweighs cynicism" (86). Braendlin defines this generic transformation in the following terms:

> The Bildungsroman of these disenfranchised Americans expresses their struggle for individuation and a part in the American dream, which society simultaneously proffers and denies to them. This new Bildungsroman asserts an identity defined by the outsiders themselves or by their own cultures, not by the patriarchal Anglo-American power structure: it evinces a revaluation, a transvaluation, of traditional Bildung by new standards and perspectives [75].

Further, bildungsromane by and about women of color necessarily differ from those by white women and by men of color. Sondra O'Neale distinguishes the black female bildungsroman from bildungsromane by Ralph Ellison, Richard Wright, and James Baldwin, finding the latter closer to the Western tradition of the genre as defined by Buckley and others. Aside from identifying an absence of initiation scenes in black female bildungsromane, such as the "battle royal" in Ellison's *Invisible Man*, O'Neale argues that

> when using Bildungsroman themes these [black] women writers did not even choose the adolescent years as appropriate frameworks for Black feminine rites of passage; nor as novelists do they concentrate on youth-

> ful recognition of racial rejection by the dominant white society. Rather, they collectively depict the Black woman's internal struggle to unravel the immense complexities of racial identity, gender definitions (in context of Black and not white experience), and awakening of sexual being—in short to discover, direct, and recreate the self in the midst of hostile racial, sexual and other societal repression—to produce a literature not confined to "usual" Bildung development at set chronological ages [25].

O'Neale's comment applies also to bildungsromane by other women of color. Among the characteristics that these bildungsromane share are a greater emphasis on communal identity, defined by ethnic background, by a community of women, and by working-class concerns; use of the "talk story" as a vehicle of bildung; and the theme of art as a means of arrival at self-awareness. (This last element overlaps with the more specific genre of the kunstlerroman.) Some familiar examples include Paule Marshall's *Brown Girl, Brownstones,* Kingston's *The Woman Warrior,* Alice Walker's *The Color Purple,* and Sandra Cisneros's *The House on Mango Street.* As these examples suggest, many contemporary female bildungsromane by women of color share the autobiographical element of the traditional genre, often emphasizing mother-daughter relationships. But they dismiss or invert other characteristics of traditional bildung stories. For instance, Pin-Chia Feng, in her excellent study, shows how it is not only harder for the protagonists of these stories to sever themselves from their pasts in general but also how, in narratives by women of color, the conventional liberating move from country to city (as Buckley describes it) becomes urban entrapment in ghettos and barrios. Similarly, as Feng points out, the theme of finding a vocation "does not always work for minority people either, since their job options are considerably limited" (7). Feng also argues that epiphanies in the Western Christian tradition do not apply, since women writers of color "have different concepts of spirituality, such as [those that involve] spirits or ghosts coexisting constantly with the living" (13). Neither O'Neale nor Feng sees patterns of initiation and awakening in these bildung narratives, for when "the fog of delusion"—in Buckley's terms—lifts, women of color find themselves still contending with mainstream America's sexual and racial biases, frequently accompanied by class oppression.

Among the characteristics Feng sees as unique to bildungsromane by women of color, the most relevant to my discussion of Asian American literature is the "politics of rememory" or "counter-memory." (Toni Morrison uses the word "rememory" in *Beloved.*) Feng identifies the politics of rememory as a means of insisting upon "textual 'recognition'" of a history that mainstream America would rather forget. Resisting and protesting this collective amnesia, women writers of color employ a politics of rememory, "exposing the marks of repression and oppression on their characters" (20; emphasis in original). Important aspects of this rememory are the talk story, "the renewed search for the missing [or apparently unknowable] mother, which inevitably brings back the repressed memory of racial oppression," and a coming to terms with the "ghosts" of the past, who often have a physical presence in the narrative (21–23). In all cases, the protagonist's personal bildung also articulates the political agenda of her racial group. As such, these bildung stories are necessarily tentative; rather than arriving at some conclusive harmony with society at large, they are, to borrow Feng's term, process-oriented, "demonstrat[ing] that instead of a unified identity, an ethnic woman is engaging in an endless negotiation of her contradictory multiplicity" (41). Hence also the writers' preference for circular narratives, fragments, and flashbacks rather than for traditional linearity. All of these traits manifest themselves in Kingston's groundbreaking *The Woman Warrior* and can be traced in subsequent narratives by Asian American women, particularly in Keller's *Comfort Woman.*

While *The Woman Warrior* remains a crucial frame of reference for Asian American female bildungsromane, the 1990s saw developments that distinguish these works, formally, from Kingston's narrative as well as from works by other women writers of color, developments that at once claim, subvert, and revolutionize the genre. Contemporary Asian American women writers' single most striking innovation in narrative form consists of their synthesis of the bildungsroman with another traditionally male genre: the war narrative. Traditionally, war has been defined as male territory, considered as exclusively male a sphere as birthing has been considered a female one. Indeed, critics have made explicit comparisons between war and birthing, including theories of war as menstruation envy (Marcus 141). Historically, women's relationship to war has been an important political issue; especially until World War I, men argued for superior civil rights, such as the right to vote, on the basis of the fact that they, and not women, participated in war. Feminists rebutted them with "the fact of women's crucial contributions to culture and civilization, even going so far as to say . . . that the risks women ran in giving birth, providing 'the primal munition of war,' greatly outweighed the risks men took on the battlefield" (Mumford 168). Certainly, "home front" and "battlefront" have traditionally been constructed as binary opposites, the defense of women and children being used consistently as the excuse for war. In the words of one group of feminists, "a culturally produced activity that is as rigidly defined by sex differentiation and as committed to sexual exclusion as is war points to a crucial site where meanings about gender are being produced, reproduced, and circulated back into society."[5]

As these words indicate, feminists have challenged conventional constructs of war. In her World War II essay "Thoughts on Peace in an Air Raid," Virginia Woolf argues that the links between war and male glory, and between childbirth and female glory, need to be broken. In *A Room of One's Own*, she goes so far as to claim that women's exclusion from war results in their marginalization in the literary sphere, for it keeps them from producing works as artistically self-assured as *War and Peace*. Feminist intervention in traditional war discourse has been particularly pronounced since the 1980s. Some feminists identify the "Homeric ideal of the warrior-hero . . . as the basis for community structures founded on dominance [and] violence" (Mumford 176). Others have exploded the oversimple binarism of warlike men and peaceful women, reminding us that Mars and Venus are, after all, mythic bedfellows (Cooper et al. 10). Contemporary feminist critics have shown that at least since the nuclear attack on Hiroshima, and in the postcolonial era, the lines between home front and battlefront have blurred, as have the lines between civilian and soldier, peacetime and wartime. Today, not only do women have more visible roles in war, they are also writing themselves into it. As Cooper et al. put it, women are challenging "two culturally repressed activities for women's arms—war and writing" (14).

This is territory that Asian American women writers, above all, are claiming. Yet most feminist analyses of women's war narratives have focused on the West, specifically on the American Civil War and the two world wars as experienced in Europe, and have included discussions of works by Willa Cather, Edith Wharton, Virginia Woolf, Katherine Anne Porter, and so on.[6] Such analyses, based on the historically specific situation of white women, argue that the greatest handicap facing most women writers of war narratives has been their inability, except as ambulance drivers and nurses, to claim personal experience of war. Further, not only was it a breach of propriety for women to write explicitly about the male anatomy, it was also an act of political transgression to presume to comment on the exclusively male suffering of the battlefield (Higonnet, "Not So Quiet in No-Woman's Land"). Nevertheless, as Miriam Cooke's discussions of Arab—or West Asian—women's fiction show, Asia provides a different context for women's war narratives. Neat divisions between national wars and civil wars, or between wars fought "out there" versus on home ground, no longer apply. For instance, in "Civil Wars and Sexual Territories," Margaret Higonnet argues that nationalist wars tend to repress feminist movements, whereas civil wars "by contrast may occasion explicit political choices for women [because] once a change in government can be conceived, sexual politics can also become an overt political issue" (80). This may be true in white women's experience, especially during World War I, but for most contemporary women writers of Asian descent, nationalist wars have been anticolonial wars fought "at home" against white Western powers or other Asian powers, such as the Japanese. Again, in the case of Japanese Americans, who were interned in camps during World War II, the self-division normally associated with civil war becomes externally imposed by racist "American" agendas.[7] In short, while mainstream feminist critics have revised the war story in important ways, exposing its deeply gendered basis, they cannot be said to speak for all women.

In acts of rememory spanning as many as sixty years, Asian American women writers are rewriting the war narrative to revise not only what men—white and Asian—but also what most white women have said about it. If white women's war literature "runs the gamut from patriotic propaganda to pacifist protest" (Marcus 132), Asian American women's writings resist these polarities in a unique synthesis of the two, which informs both the form and the content of their works. In doing so, they intervene not only in mainstream feminist discourse but also in nationalist discourses, for theirs are "decolonizing novels," in Lowe's sense of the term. Lowe invokes Frantz Fanon's definition of decolonization as set forth in *The Wretched of the Earth:* "a process of thorough social transformation that disorganizes the stratified social hierarchy beyond the nationalist party's capture of the state from the colonizer" (quoted in Lowe 107). She goes on to say:

> Decolonization, in Fanon's sense, does not prematurely signify the end of colonialism but refers to the multifaceted, ongoing project of resistance struggles that can persist for decades in the midst of neocolonial exploitation [107].

Following Fanon, Lowe's discussion links "bourgeois nationalism" with colonial domination, proposing "decolonization as a third alternative to colonialism and nationalism." In this sense, "the project of decolonization is carried forth in the 'postcolonial' site but may equally be deployed by immigrant and diasporic populations" (108); thus the particular applicability of the word "decolonization" to Asian American literature.

Lowe's definition of the decolonizing novel applies not only to Keller's *Comfort Woman* but also to other contemporary narratives, and it is significant that many of them are by women of Asian ethnicities that have been inadequately represented in Asian American literature. For instance, the Pakistani American writer Bapsi Sidhwa's finely crafted novel *Cracking India* revisits the site of the British-authored partition of India that resulted in the formation of Pakistan, an event accompanied by sectarian bloodshed. The story is told from the perspective of an eight-year-old girl who journeys toward adolescence as Pakistan comes into being, her sexual forays forming an innocently comic yet disturbing parallel to women's sexual exploitation on both sides of the war. Like Sidhwa's novel, Cecilia Manguerra Brainard's *When the Rainbow Goddess Wept* abridges the traditional narrative span of bildung to the preadolescent years, recounting the 1940s Japanese invasion of the Philippines from the perspective of eight-year-old Yvonne. Brainard's novel represents the Japanese invasion on a continuum with the Spanish and American colonizations of the Philippines, weaving the historical narrative of a newly independent nation with that of Yvonne's own newly acquired sense of Pilipina womanhood (as symbolized in Philippine liberation's coinciding with Yvonne's first menstruation). A still more recent novel, Lan Cao's *Monkey Bridge,* published in the same year as *Comfort Woman,* shares much with Keller's narrative. It relates the dual bildungsroman of a Vietnamese mother, Thanh, and a daughter who comes of age in the United States, representing sexual oppression as "a very old war" (49) and linking woman's menstrual and virginal blood both to familial bonds and to blood spilled on the battlefield. As in *Comfort Woman,* part of war's violence as experienced by women lies in denying them the right/rite to ceremonize the body of a beloved woman in death, while the violence of naming victimizes them as it colonizes their land. In a passage from *Monkey Bridge,* encapsulating what I see as a thematic and formal fusion of genres, Thanh interprets her husband's "love" as military violence:

> Gorgeous gestures backed by a thousand years of tradition may not be much different from wars and other acts more stark and obvious in their capacity for violence. Victory bestows upon the victors certain privileges. Vietnam became Cochin Chine, Annam, and Tonkin. . . . Saigon, of course, is now called by its new name, Ho Chi Minh City. That was my transformation, both by name and by deed, only mine had been shrouded in love [186–87].

Here, naming becomes a violent objectification of women and a reconstruction of their gendered identities in marriage, just as it signals the violent colonization of nations. Thus contemporary Asian American women's fiction fuses the two traditionally male/Western literary genres of bildungsroman and war narrative to articulate a stance against both sexual and racial-colonial domination. In the process, the narratives redefine nationalism as love of land and of one's countrywomen. What Miriam Cooke says of the Palestinian writer Sahar Khalifa's protagonists applies also to these women writers of South Asian, East Asian, and Southeast Asian descent: "Each holds on to the struggle as double-edged, against an external enemy of their land and an internal enemy of their freedom" (*Women and the War Story* 200), recognizing that one kind of freedom is not possible without the other.[8]

Cooke's description of Khalifa's protagonists as struggling against both external and internal enemies applies also to Soon Hyo/Akiko, the principal character in Keller's *Comfort Woman*. The novel is a double bildungsroman—not in the conventional sense of having male and female protagonists, as in Cather's *My Ántonia*, but in the sense that it relates the dual bildung of mother and daughter, as does Lan Cao's *Monkey Bridge*. This dual narrative structure is in fact common in contemporary novels by Asian American women, not only suggesting, as most women writers of color do, that an individual is defined by her context but also emphasizing that the most crucial of these contexts is the relationship between mother and daughter. In an Asian American context, this emphasis on mother-daughter relationships may also be seen as a rewriting of the immigrant romance, to borrow Patricia Chu's phrase about Amy Tan's novels. In such mother-daughter romances, as Chu argues, the Asian American daughters represent America for their mothers, whereas the mothers are represented variously as "mythic, essentialized forces of nature; as witnesses and victims of a backward, oppressive, ahistorical culture; as feminist tricksters and critics of American Orientalism; and as the empowering sources for Asian American feminist consciousness" (22). As this representational range indicates, the mother-daughter romance in Asian American novels is fraught with contradictions. More generally, works by Nancy Chodorow and others have illuminated the fact that if, as Freud believed, the process of arriving at a sense of one's own selfhood depends on separation from the mother, then it is obviously a far more complex process for daughters, who identify with their female parents, than for sons. In *Comfort Woman*, as in *The Woman Warrior*, the process is further complicated by different geographical contexts. In Keller's novel, geography becomes as crucial a context for the bildung of mother and daughter as are history and gender, and all these contexts are themselves contained within the framing narrative of war, which shapes the bildung of both protagonists over two generations.

Unlike most popular World War II texts, *Comfort Woman* shifts the focus from Europe to Asia, from the war as it affected men to its impact on Asian women—specifically, impoverished young women from Korean villages. The novel's chief protagonist, Soon Hyo—known through most of the novel by her Japanese name, Akiko—is born in Sulsulham, the fourth and youngest daughter of the family, and, orphaned at the age of twelve, is sold by her eldest sister to the Japanese soldiers occupying the country. Taken to a "comfort camp," she is auctioned off to the highest bidder before she has even had her first period and is thereafter used as a "free for all" sex slave of the Japanese soldiers. Soon Hyo escapes the camp after an enforced abortion, but her trust is betrayed again by an old woman who "sells" her to Christian missionaries in Pyongyang. With nowhere to go when the missionaries leave Korea, Soon Hyo marries a much older American missionary, Rick Bradley, whose lust for the now fourteen-year-old girl masks itself as concern for her soul's salvation. Soon Hyo has to leave Korea and travel to America with her husband. Much later, Bradley dies a few years after their daughter Beccah's birth, and Soon Hyo, intending to return to Korea with her daughter, gets only as far as Hawaii before lack of money compels her to give up the journey. Unlike the bildung of Soon Hyo, whose narrative begins in Korea, Beccah's bildung occurs in the context of contemporary Hawaii. The single most important frame of reference for her bildung is her relationship with her mother, whose "trances" spirit Soon Hyo away into another world for days at a time and force Beccah herself to assume the maternal role.

While a mother's influence on her daughter's growth forms an important part of most bildungsromane by women of color, *Comfort Woman* asserts that the reverse is equally true: a woman's identity may be defined as much by her daughter as by her mother. Indeed, Soon Hyo's bildung is inseparable from Beccah's, the one impossible without the other. Beccah arrives twenty years after Soon Hyo's "death" at the comfort camp, rekindling her mother's life and, when Soon Hyo dies, retrieving for her what she lost at the camp. From the beginning, the link between the bodies of mother and daughter is erotically evoked, and women's bodies in general are represented as being connected not only to one another but to the land that gave them birth. Women groom each other in death as in life. They comb one another's hair even in the comfort camp, their sisterhood represented by the mythical Seven Stars. It is a ritual spanning generations: the grandmother of Soon

Hyo clips her teenage daughter's nails in a ritual of mourning for her as she stages her daughter's death in order to save her life. (As a young girl, Soon Hyo's mother demonstrated against the Japanese occupation of Korea, and this had put her life in danger.) When death really does take Soon Hyo's mother, her head is resting in twelve-year-old Soon Hyo's lap, her temples massaged by her youngest daughter's fingers. The sensuous connection of Soon Hyo to her own daughter, who arrives twenty years after the abortion Soon Hyo endures in the comfort camp, finds tangible expression in the bit of umbilical cord that Soon Hyo keeps—"this one piece of flesh that was both me and my daughter" (97).

The connection between mother and daughter forms only part of their bildung, however. Keller's novel suggests that a woman arrives at a sense of self not only in relation to other women but also in relation to the earth that roots her. When Soon Hyo is pregnant with Beccah, she drinks tea made with dirt from the garden, nourishing her daughter with the earth so she may never feel lost. "After her birth, I rubbed that same earth across my nipples and touched it to my daughter's lips, so that, with her first suck, with her first taste of the dirt and the salt and the milk that is me, she would know that I am, and will always be, her home" (113). Similarly, when Beccah begins to menstruate, Soon Hyo ceremonizes Beccah's initiation into womanhood by insisting that she dip her bloodied finger into the river. Asking her to listen to the river's song, Soon Hyo tells her daughter: "Now you share the river's body. . . . Its blood is your blood, and when you are ready to let your spirit fly, it will always follow the water back to its source" (191). As these two passages indicate, the novel defines "home" as a sense of being anchored in both a community of women—here, one's mother specifically—and in the land. And a sense of home thus defined is what gives a woman her identity.

It is here that the bildungsroman fuses with the war narrative, feminizing both genres and redefining nationalism as love of land and love of other Korean women. Just as Soon Hyo's mother had died a symbolic death, as a consequence of her protest against the Japanese occupation of 1919, so does Soon Hyo experience the later Japanese invasion of Korea as an invasion of her self, literalized in the invasion of her body by countless soldiers. Korea itself is represented as a feminized body with head, feet, and navel—a body later cut callously in two (105), and one with the abused bodies of thousands of Korean women forced into Japanese recreation camps. The unity of Korean land and Korean woman finds poignant expression in a comfort woman called Akiko 40, who one night breaks all the rules against silence, yelling at the Japanese soldiers "to stop their invasion of her country and her body.

Even as they mounted her, she shouted: I am Korea, I am a woman, I am alive. I am seventeen, I had a family just like you do, I am a daughter, I am a sister" (20). Reclaiming her Korean name and ancestry, the woman chants her mother's recipes, recasting patriotism as generational and cultural continuity among women. Indeed, "patriotism" seems a misnomer here, since her love for Korea is more properly called "matriotism"—love for a maternalized Korea that defines her own identity as a woman. The next morning Akiko 40 is killed, skewered from vagina to mouth as a brutal warning to the rest of the women. Although Soon Hyo is denied the right to groom Akiko's body in death, she inherits her legacy, literally being given her clothes and her name, whereupon she becomes Akiko 41. After Soon Hyo has left the camp, Akiko 40's spirit visits her as Induk, the Birth Grandmother, whose face sometimes appears as the faces of Soon Hyo's mother, grandmother, and other maternal ancestors. The same Induk, as both Woman and Korea, appears to Beccah the night she begins to menstruate, first as a vision of her mother and then as Beccah herself.

Comfort Woman thus blurs the lines conventionally drawn between a masculinized, militant nationalism and a feminized, apolitical pacifism. To the women in the novel, love of the land is love of themselves and of other women—a passion erotically evoked in the spiritual lovemaking between Induk/Akiko 40 and Soon Hyo (145). The generic fusion of bildungsroman and war narrative here asserts that military aggression, colonization, and sexual oppression are various faces of the same negative force, interlocking with and overlapping one another. In the stories that Soon Hyo tells Beccah, this force is represented by Saja the Death Messenger. As "soldier of death," Saja symbolizes military aggression and annihilation; as a handsome young man, "alluring and virile" (46), he also represents the threat of male sexual aggression. Thus he manifests himself as the Japanese soldiers in the comfort camps, "each one of them Saja, Death's Demon Soldier" (195), as well as the power that demands the sacrifice of Beccah's young body and that must be fooled with other offerings instead (45). Not coincidentally, Saja's identity merges in Soon Hyo's and Beccah's minds with the identity of the missionary who married the orphan Soon Hyo. And Soon Hyo, in helpless agony during her trances, calls out to both, leading Beccah to imagine that "Saja looked like my father, the handsomest man I could imagine" (46). For Soon Hyo sees the Christian mission itself both as an aggressive religion whose God "listens to men" (127) and as one that colonizes Korea in ways less obvious than the Japanese invasion. Representing the mission house in images reminiscent of the camp, Soon Hyo refers to her "stall" there, and to resignedly "giving her body" to the missionary women, who insist on bathing, dressing, and feeding it (63). Specifically, she recognizes the same lust in Rick Bradley's eyes that she saw in the Japanese soldiers who used her body, and when he slaps the pulpit during his sermon, she recalls the sound of women's naked buttocks being slapped by the troops. Later, when he lectures in the United States on "spreading the light," he makes his wife stand beside him in Korean dress as a living success story, his co-optation of her body paralleled by his apparent triumph over her soul.

Language figures prominently in this invasion and colonization of a woman's body and spirit; hence Soon Hyo's distrust of it. Aside from the linguistic chauvinism of the Japanese, who claim that the Koreans' "gift for languages" proves that they were meant to be dominated, Soon Hyo resents her husband's attempts to teach their baby the four languages he knows. To her, language as men understand it is about dominance, the power to name. Just as her mother never hears her name again once she becomes a wife, Soon Hyo suffers the violence of imposed names like "Akiko" and "Mary," assigned by those with power over her—the Japanese army and the Christian missionaries. Even in a romantically consensual relationship like that between Beccah and her first boyfriend, Max, the latter's naming of her physical characteristics results in Beccah's sense of self-alienation and disintegration: "Each time he pointed to something about me, it was as if it fell away from me, foreign and unrecognizable. . . . By the end of the third week of Max's attention, I was in pieces, waiting for him to make me whole again" (132). In *Articulating Silences,* King-Kok Cheung has argued persuasively against Western feminists' privileging of speech over silence, seeing in it a form of cultural chauvinism. But while it is true that Keller's novel often casts silence as self-preservation (as in the camps), the novel ultimately resists binary constructions of speech and silence. Instead, *Comfort Woman* redefines language, distinguishing it from speech. Soon Hyo, whose name means "the true voice, the pure tongue," communicates with her daughter in "language I know is true" (21)—that is, body language, song, and story. She touches her baby in a conscious attempt to counterbalance her husband's linguistic aggressiveness:

> And each night, I touch each part of her body, waiting until I see recognition in her eyes. I wait until I see that she knows that all of what I touch is her and hers to name in her own mind, before language dissects her into pieces that can be swallowed and digested by others not herself [22].

Body language, song, and story—Soon Hyo interprets these as a feminine language, connecting her both to her daughter and to her mother, in the same way that body language permits the comfort women to communicate and care for one another in the guise of silence. And as the women's bodies merge with Korea's, so do their songs and stories bind their identity as women to Korea. Love of womanhood—including love of oneself and of other women—becomes indistinguishable from love of Korea.

The river song, a recurring motif in the novel, represents this love of land and womanhood, first and foremost in its association with the Yalu. This is the river in whose care Soon Hyo and her mother left their dead or unformed babies, and in whose waters Soon Hyo cleanses her own body after her escape from the Japanese comfort camp, when Induk first comes to her. Second, the river song represents the fusion of this dual love, of land and of womanhood, in its significance as a lullaby, celebrating the continuity of love between generations of mothers and daughters. In Soon Hyo's words, "It's a song full of tears, but one my mother sang for her country and for herself. A song she gave to me and one that I will give to my daughter" (71). It is also the song that cracks her ears open after a period of deafness and muteness in the mission house; what she alone hears in the hymn triggers the rememory that saves her:

> And in that song I heard things that I had almost forgotten: the enduring whisper of women who continued to pass messages under the ears of the soldiers; a defiant Induk bellowing the Korean national anthem even after the soldiers had knocked her teeth out; . . . the lullabies my mother hummed as she put her daughters to sleep; the song the river sings when she finds her freedom in the ocean [71].

Recasting baptism as immersion in a feminized Korean river, Soon Hyo feels "the need to dissolve into her [the river's] body" (103). She opens her eyes and mouth "to taste her," this river that is at once a maternalized Korea and a mother's womb, but is yanked away by the missionary who intends to make her his child bride and take her away from Korea, to the United States. Before she leaves, Soon Hyo savors and swallows the Korean earth, "metallic as blood," literalizing the unity of Korea's body and her own, and ensuring that no matter where the missionary might take her, "my country would always be part of me" (104). It is only after her husband's death that Soon Hyo finally makes a home for herself and her daughter—an entirely feminized space—in a house in Manoa by the river, another Yalu, where both can hear the river song together.

Keller's evocative conclusion synchronizes the bildung of mother and daughter, in a moment that the novel represents as death, on the one hand, and as life retrieved, on the other. The major threads of the novel come together here: the unity of land and womanhood, and—in a single act of rememory—the reclamation of both from forces of aggression, including the colonizing violence of language. Beccah, immediately after Soon Hyo's death, discovers the truth about her mother's life, including Akiko's real name as well as her own—"Bek-hap," the pure one. She now transcribes the words Soon Hyo had tape-recorded in her lifetime, writing them on a bedsheet. Her mother's words address all the women Soon Hyo loved and lost in life: her mother and her grandmother, her sisters, Akiko 40/Induk, "so that you will remember. So that I will remember. So that those who come after me will know. . . . So many true names unknown, dead in the heart. So many bodies left unprepared, lost in the river" (192). Later, as Beccah prepares her mother's body for its final journey, she wraps it in strips of this same sheet, a mother's words in her daughter's script. Touching every part of her mother's naked body with fingers dipped in the waters of the river, Beccah reenacts her mother's tenderness toward her as a baby and at the same time retraces the path of the Japanese soldiers' violence, but with the sanctity of a daughter's love. As she reappropriates her mother's body for her, she also gives her mother back her true name—the name to which Soon Hyo felt she had lost the right. Brushing her mother's hair and clipping her nails in death, Beccah also reclaims these rites/rights for Akiko 40's skewered body and, symbolically, for all women so violated and erased. Again, in Beccah's song of rememory, the women are one with Korea: "Mugunghwa for courage and independence, Omoni. And for Korea. I remember. I remember" (208). And as she scatters her mother's ashes into the same river that initiated her into womanhood, she touches them to her lips: "Your body in mine . . . so you will always be with me, even when your spirit finds its way home. To Korea. To Sulsulham. And across the river of heaven to the Seven Sisters" (212). Beccah thus assists her mother's spirit "home," her mother's spirit now anchored in the integrity of her own body, in her daughter, in a community of women, and in the river that is both mother's womb and Korea.

If Soon Hyo's bildung finds completion in this moment, so too does Beccah's, for she arrives at self-knowledge through her act of rememory, that is, by "remembering" her own and her mother's true name, her maternal ancestors, and Korea. But Beccah's bildung also entails the rewriting of other scripts. Not only does her mother's death free Beccah from an exploitative sexual relationship with her married boss, Sanford, it also releases her father's hold over her. Having grown up idealizing him as the handsome prince who would one day rescue her and her mother, Beccah instead reencounters him in her imagination, a caricature, embodied in the Bible-spouting vagrant known as the Manoa Walker. Although at first his eyes and voice make her call him "Daddy," her womanhood resists his patriarchal, Christianizing, colonizing power so utterly that "blue fire crackled between us, and the Walker fell back as if he had been shot" (168). Instead of waiting for her father to rescue her and her mother, Beccah herself becomes the rescuer when she performs the funeral rites for Soon Hyo. As a little girl, she had asked how she could help her mother find what she had lost; as a woman, she retrieves that loss in her act of rememory. Reliving one of Soon Hyo's stories, Beccah becomes Princess Pari who, recognizing her mother by her singing of the river song, retrieves her from Saja's gates of hell.

Rememory and retrieval notwithstanding, Beccah's bildung also entails a reevaluation of her mother as strong rather than weak and childlike. Not only does she wonder how Soon Hyo survived the comfort camp as she herself could not have, she also learns from her mother's friend, Reno, that Soon Hyo's spirituality coexisted with a sound business sense. Thus exploding the binarism of spiritual and material, Soon Hyo's mediations with the supernatural world on behalf of others had been translated into concrete cash, profiting both herself and Reno, as her business manager. Anticipating and beating the Japanese real-estate boom in Hawaii, Soon Hyo had paid cash for the house in Manoa—the home by the river, her legacy to her daughter. That Reno communicates this important information about Soon Hyo to her daughter befits the conclusion of a novel that so consistently stresses women's community. For all its lyrical evocations of sisterhood, however, *Comfort Woman* preempts any naïvely sentimental view of women's relationships with one other. Recall that Soon Hyo is sold twice, both times by women, one of them the eldest sister on whom she had relied for protection as a twelve-year-old orphan. For Soon Hyo and Beccah alike, then, the bildung process includes a recognition of both the ideal and the imperfect reality. Just as Soon Hyo "remembers" and names her sister in forgiveness, Beccah comes to a better understanding of her mother's relationship with Reno. Having always assumed that Reno was exploiting Soon Hyo financially, Beccah learns not only that her mother was nobody's fool but also that the two women understood each other's strengths and weaknesses and profited mutually from that understanding. The concluding chapter suggests that Reno, the worldly character who has provided the reader with comic relief, not only represents a valuable, if imperfect, sisterhood but also functions as Soon Hyo's alter ego. Soon Hyo, lying in her casket, looks enough like Reno that the undertaker assumes they are sisters, and when Reno smooths Beccah's hair, her fingers remind Beccah of her mother's. Appropriately, Reno gives Soon Hyo another funeral, this one "for her other self, dah one she showed to people" as "one performah" (206). Even more appropriately, and humorously, those who attend the standing-room-only funeral do not realize that they are honoring an empty casket—a secret only Beccah and Reno share.

Finally, Beccah's coming of age is represented by a revision in the script of her dreams. In her recurring childhood nightmare, she sees herself drowning, somebody's hands clutching her feet. Immediately after Soon Hyo's death, the hands become those of her mother, who seeks to be rescued but only drowns them both; in fact, Beccah awakes to find herself "sinking" toward Sanford on the waterbed. Once Beccah has reclaimed her mother in death, however, freeing her spirit in the ritual of rememory, the dream recasts itself, not as annihilation but as liberation. Yielding to her mother instead of resisting her, Beccah discovers that she is swimming not through ocean but through sky, "dizzy with the freedom of light and air." All the novel's major motifs and themes come together in its final image: Beccah swimming high into the sky, a "river of light" connecting her to the earth, where she sleeps, "coiled tight around a small seed planted by my mother, waiting to be born" (213).

To the extent that *Comfort Woman* intervenes critically in traditional novels of formation, it is a bildungsroman in Morgenstern's original sense of the word: a narrative that not only relates the bildung of its protagonist but also facilitates the bildung of the reader. Keller's novel does so in both form and content, drawing attention to an untold and unheard story that demands a new mode of telling. Fusing two traditionally male genres, bildungsroman and war narrative, it transforms both in the process, at once gendering, colorizing, and Asianizing them. While the novel molds the two genres to accommodate the needs of womanhood, it also challenges mainstream feminist perspectives on war and coming of age. And though Keller shares the concerns of other women writers of color, *Comfort Woman* typifies the themes and narrative strategies of contemporary Asian American women's fiction, specifically. Moving away from a narrow focus on the assimilation of the subject into the U.S. nation state, Keller's novel resituates its protagonists in the context of Asian colonial history. In narrating war as bildung and bildung as war, *Comfort Woman* redefines freedom, a word that has served as America's fiercest nationalist battle cry, justifying its aggression toward Asian nations from the Philippines to Iraq. Keller genders freedom as a woman's sense of rootedness in a community of women, especially as defined by mother and daughter, and she Asianizes freedom as a woman's identification with a colonized ancestral land. Her novel thus remolds masculinist constructs of nationalism as power-driven and militaristic, recasting nationalism as love of a feminized homeland. Transforming the genres of both bildungsroman and war narrative, *Comfort Woman* exemplifies contemporary Asian American women writers' transformative interventions in dominant feminist and nationalist discourses.

BIBLIOGRAPHY

Abel, Elizabeth, et al., eds. *The Voyage In*. Hanover: University Press of New England, 1983.

Braendlin, Bonnie Hoover. "*Bildung* in Ethnic Women Writers." *Denver Quarterly* 17.4 (1983): 75–87.

Brainard, Cecilia Manguerra. *When the Rainbow Goddess Wept*. New York: Plume, 1994.

Buckley, Jerome. *Season of Youth: The Bildungsroman from Dickens to Golding*. Cambridge: Harvard University Press, 1974.

Cao, Lan. *Monkey Bridge*. New York: Penguin, 1997.

Cheung, King-Kok. *Articulate Silences: Hisaye Yamamoto, Maxine Hong Kingston, Joy Kogawa*. Ithaca: Cornell University Press, 1993.

Chu, Patricia P. *Assimilating Asians: Gendered Strategies of Authorship in Asian America*. Durham: Duke University Press, 2000.

Cooke, Miriam. *Women and the War Story*. Berkeley: University of California Press, 1996.

———, and Roshni Rustomji-Kerns. *Blood into Ink: South Asian and Middle Eastern Women Write War*. Boulder: Westview Press, 1994.

———, and Angela Woollacott, eds. *Gendering War Talk*. Princeton: Princeton University Press, 1993.

Cooper, Helen, et al., eds. *Arms and the Woman*. Chapel Hill: University of North Carolina Press, 1989.

Feng, Pin-Chia. *The Female Bildungsroman by Toni Morrison and Maxine Hong Kingston*. New York: Peter Lang, 1997.

Fraiman, Susan. *Unbecoming Women: British Women Writers and the Novel of Development*. New York: Columbia University Press, 1993.

Goethe, Johann Wolfgang von. *Wilhelm Meisters Lehrjahre.* 1795. Berlin: Aufbau-Verlag, 1970.
Hardin, James, ed. *Reflection and Action: Essays on the Bildungsroman.* Columbia: University of South Carolina Press, 1991.
Higonnet, Margaret. "Civil Wars and Sexual Territories." *Arms and the Woman.* Ed. Helen Cooper et al. Chapel Hill: University of North Carolina Press, 1989. 80–97.
———. "Not So Quiet in No-Woman's Land." *Gendering War Talk.* Ed. Miriam Cooke and Angela Woollacott. Princeton: Princeton University Press, 1993. 205–26.
———, et al., eds. *Behind the Lines: Gender and the Two World Wars.* New Haven: Yale University Press, 1987.
Keller, Nora Okja. *Comfort Woman.* New York: Penguin, 1997.
Kingston, Maxine Hong. *The Woman Warrior.* 1975. New York: Vintage, 1989.
Labovitz, Esther. *The Myth of the Heroine: The Female Bildungsroman in the Twentieth Century.* New York: Peter Lang, 1988.
Lowe, Lisa. *Immigrant Acts: On Asian American Cultural Politics.* Durham: Duke University Press, 1996.
Marcus, Jane. "Corpus/Corps/Corpse: Writing the Body in/at War." *Arms and the Woman.* Ed. Helen Cooper et al. Chapel Hill: University of North Carolina Press, 1989. 124–67.
Morrison, Toni. *Beloved.* 1987. New York: Plume, 1988.
Mumford, Laura. "May Sinclair's *The Tree of Heaven:* The Vortex of Feminism, the Community of War." *Arms and the Woman.* Ed. Helen Cooper et al. Chapel Hill: University of North Carolina Press, 1989. 168–83.
O'Neale, Sondra. "Race, Sex, and Self: Aspects of Bildung in Select Novels by Black American Women Novelists." *MELUS* 9.4 (1982): 25–37.
Okada, John. *No-No Boy.* 1957. Seattle: University of Washington Press, 1976.
Sammons, Jeffrey. "The Bildungsroman for Nonspecialists." *Reflection and Action: Essays on the Bildungsroman.* Ed. James Hardin. Columbia: University of South Carolina Press, 1991.
Sidhwa, Bapsi. *Cracking India.* Minneapolis: Milkweed, 1991.
Woolf, Virginia. *A Room of One's Own.* 1929. San Diego: Harcourt Brace Jovanovich, 1957.
———. "Thoughts on Peace in an Air Raid." *Death of the Moth and Other Essays.* 1942. New York: Harcourt Brace Jovanovich, 1974.
Yamada, Mitsuye. *Camp Notes and Other Writings.* New Brunswick: Rutgers University Press, 1998.

NOTES

1. See Zhou's introduction to this volume.
2. See Susan Fraiman on the "continual fetishizing of *Wilhelm Meister* as originary text" (*Unbecoming Women* 9–10) in discussions of the bildungsroman.

3. Quoted in James Hardin, *Reflection and Action*; Hardin's translation.

4. Hardin also declares that "American literary criticism in general lacks knowledge of the great tradition in the Bildungsroman, and is imprecise," while feminist criticism "suffers from a restricted vision of the genre" (*Reflection and Action* xxii).

5. Lynda Boose et al., proposal for a Dartmouth College institute on gender and war, 1990; quoted in Miriam Cooke and Angela Woollacott, *Gendering War Talk* ix.

6. See, for instance, Higonnet et al., *Behind the Lines*; Cooper et al., *Arms and the Woman*. Both are important, groundbreaking collections but are limited in scope to Euro-America. Works of broader scope include Cooke and Woollacott, *Gendering War Talk*; Cooke, *Women and the War Story*; and Cooke and Roshni Rustomji-Kerns, *Blood into Ink*, a collection of poetry and fiction focusing on anticolonial wars in Asia and postcolonial strife in the Middle East and South Asia.

7. Such self-division, unique to the Japanese American experience, finds expression in the works of John Okada and Mitsuye Yamada, for instance. It may be argued that the 442nd (Japanese American) regiment—the most decorated of all U.S. regiments during World War II—sought to heal this split through potentially self-eliminating acts of courage against the enemies of Allied forces.

8. Since 9/11, memoirs by women of Afghan, Iraqi, and Iranian descent echo similar sentiments.

SHORT STORY CYCLE AND HAWAI'I BILDUNGSROMAN

WRITING SELF, PLACE, AND FAMILY IN LOIS-ANN YAMANAKA'S *WILD MEAT AND THE BULLY BURGERS*

ROCÍO G. DAVIS

Recent developments in Asian American literature stress the imperative to reevaluate and expand the theoretical boundaries that define it, to comprehend increasingly multilayered strategies of meaning. Renewed critical concerns oblige us to read these texts "as theoretically informed and informing rather than as transparently referential human documents over which we place a grid of sophisticated Euro-American theory in order to extract meaning" (Goellnicht 340). Only when Asian American literature liberates its sources of meaning from hegemonic impositions and begins to subvert traditional signifying strategies can it begin to reconfigure cultural interpretation. A specific example of this revisionary strategy lies in the recurrence, in Asian American fiction, of the short story cycle—a form until now most clearly defined within the Euro-American literary tradition, one that many ethnic writers have adapted for the articulation of the processes of subjectivity formation. Amy Tan's *The Joy Luck Club,* Sigrid Nunez's *A Feather on the Breath of God,* Wang Ping's *American Visa,* and Sylvia Watanabe's *Talking to the Dead,* among other works, emblematize how Asian American writers appropriate the specifics of this narrative genre to negotiate the dynamics of meaning. This essay will explore how the Hawai'i writer Lois-Ann Yamanaka subverts a traditional American literary form in order to formulate a renewed manner of presenting local realities, perspectives, and styles.[1] Her *Wild Meat and the Bully Burgers* expands the range of the short story cycle by presenting a coming-of-age narrative that foregrounds a culture-specific portrait of self, place, and family, developing identities and fostering imaginative communities. This design also responds to a new impetus evident in writers from Hawai'i, who, as Stephen Sumida argues, attend to "processes of creating new national narratives out of their old and their recent indigenous, colonial, and current postcolonial histories and languages" ("Postcolonialism" 274). The particular characteristics of literature from Hawai'i make such a strategy critical on both contextual and textual levels of narrative. These negotiations are realized, first, through narrative structure, as the dynamics of the short story cycle make it appropriate for the enactment of cultural productions that incorporate immigrant legacies while adapting to the literary forms as defined by the culture in which these works are created. Second, Yamanaka's narrative of education further links her production with Euro-American practice while expanding ways of informing the representation of subjectivity. Thus her short story cycle incorporates, revises, and challenges the European paradigm of the bildungsroman, to offer extended perspectives on the transcultural subject and the possibilities of Asian American writing.[2] It is important to note that as Yamanaka incorporates the thematic paradigms of the bildungsroman into a new generic configuration—discrete stories rather than a chronologically developed long narrative—she performs an act of writerly agency to expand the traditional scripts of coming-of-age chronicles.

To engage Asian American narratives effectively, we must move beyond an analytical model of merely reading the surface of texts for potential meanings, and attend to the cultural and generic codes addressed by their authors to unravel what the texts execute within the context of larger questions about cultural and political mobilization. Genre definition and choice direct the act of writing as well as readers' reception of the ideological issues and concerns embedded in the narrative. As Fredric Jameson explains, "Genres are essentially literary *institutions,* or social contracts between a writer and a specific public, whose function is to specify the proper use of a particular cultural artifact" (106; emphasis in original). This affirmation implies that a reconstruction of the bildungsroman as a short story cycle is necessarily inflected by the relationship between creative writing and immigrant or ethnic configurations of subjectivity and national affiliation. Consequently, the choice of genre, and the manipulation of generic dispositions, signifies on the level of discourse. Writers are sensitive to how differences in cultural contexts and paradigms create specific responses, which remove established genres to destabilize ideology and conventional strategies for producing meaning in order to enact distinct sociocultural situations. Readers who encounter these revisionary texts are thus obliged to reexamine their expectations and critical perspectives.

Literary texts are emblematic of the structures that generate or manipulate meanings at specific historical moments as they offer a larger critique of culture and ideology. In this case, we witness the manner in which the inscription of the experiences of particular children bears on or illustrates the development of contemporary societies. Texts that privilege the child character bear a special burden in negotiating the representations of the palimpsestic societies within which they are set. The manner in which the child's self is constituted, therefore, stresses the child's subjectivity, as determined by social formations, language, and political or personal contingencies. The engagement with childhood and the contingencies of history, ethnicity, family, and social class are highlighted by the status of Yamanaka's text as a bildungsroman, the classic narrative of formation. To deploy this narrative genre in the context of ethnic writing is highly meaningful, because, as Lisa Lowe explains, it "elicits the reader's identification with the bildung narrative of ethnical formation, itself a narrative of the individual's relinquishing of particularity and difference through identification with an idealized 'national' form of subjectivity" (98), only to subvert it. The traditional bildungsroman functions as a program for identification with the accepted social order and value system as it chronicles the protagonist's assimilation of his or her society's values. The ethnic bildungsroman departs dramatically from the traditional pattern, to engage the individual's process of awareness of particularity and difference, and the choice of identifying with or rejecting the models society offers. Yamanaka's text manifests this singular approach: rather than merely appropriating accepted societal perspectives, her protagonist explores the nature and predicament of the child on the cusp of change.[3] This position postulates an identity that is self-defined rather than one that merely follows a prescribed pattern and conforms to a pre-established mold; it makes reevaluation as important as learning. As such, the text can also be read as a strategic intervention in psychological or literary constructions of ethnicity, gender, and culture. The process of selfhood in connection with this Asian American child's evolving subjectivity is the covert theme of the text, which stresses the process of becoming, a program that cannot be divorced from the act of representation and the politics of identity and self-formation.

Asian American bildungsromane encode interrogations of the nuances and possibilities of language, immigrant histories, chronotopic positioning, the importance of family, and concepts of nationhood. As part of the challenge to traditional narrative, they project an interdependent dynamic relation that acquires significance as they are marshaled in the representation of highly individual processes of subjectivity and affiliation. These narratives become highly multilayered, particularly when they also challenge traditional narrative structuring, as in the short story cycle by Yamanaka, in Wayson Choy's *The Jade Peony,* and in Shyam Selvadurai's *Funny Boy,* among other works. Because of the displacement of ethnic subjects in American inscriptions of history, Asian American writers who deploy new versions of the bildungsroman are expanding the possibilities of an established genre to limn particular forms of belonging and knowledge. As Asian American writers aesthetically negotiate what Paul Smith has called "positions of subjectivity" (xxxv), these bildung become experimental and revisionary narratives that challenge textual authority and prescriptive paradigms.

Inscribing the process typical of the bildungsroman through a cycle allows the text to signify in multiple ways. A cycle may be defined as "a set of stories linked to each other in such a way as to maintain a balance between the individuality of each of the stories and the necessities of the larger unit . . . [so] that the reader's successive experience in various levels of the pattern of the whole significantly modifies his experience of each of its component parts" (Ingram 15, 19). The term "short story cycle" implies a structural scheme for the working out of an idea, characters, or themes, even a circular disposition in which the constituent narratives are simultaneously independent and interdependent. The challenge of each cycle is twofold: the collection must assert the individuality and independence of each of the component parts while creating a necessary interdependence that emphasizes the wholeness and essential unity of the work. Consistency of theme and an evolution from one story to the next are among the classic requirements of the form, with recurrence and development as the integrated movements that effect final cohesion (Ingram 20). Cycles figure prominently in twentieth-century American literature: Sherwood Anderson's *Winesburg, Ohio,* Ernest Hemingway's *In Our Time,* and Raymond Carver's *Cathedral,* among other texts, have constituted and popularized the form within the mainstream canon.[4] One of the most salient features of the story cycle is its attempt to emulate the act of storytelling, the effort of a speaker to establish solidarity with an implied audience by recounting a series of tales linked by their content or by the conditions in which they are related. Moreover, the narrative structure of short story cycles mirrors the episodic and unchronological method of oral narration. Most cycles do not have a linear plot, emerging rather as portraits of persons or communities pieced together from the diverse elements offered in the individual stories. The fundamental structure of a cycle lies in the interaction of the elements in the independent stories as connective patterns on all levels draw these together into a totality strengthened by varying types of internal cohesion: a title, the development of a central character, the delineation of a community, or an explicit theme. Moreover, the genre intensifies the normally participatory act of reading by insisting that we "fill in the blanks" as we go along, the discovery of connections becoming the reader's task.

Yamanaka, by appropriating and transforming this narrative genre as established and defined by mainstream writers and critics, challenges, like other Asian American writers, the hegemonic prescriptions of dominant Euro-American literary traditions. A text such as *Wild Meat and the Bully Burgers* challenges hegemonic discourse on several levels, as the author exploits the advantages of the established structure and theme to present her coming-of-age-in- Hawai'i tale, blending cultural traditions and codes as she innovates literary representation. Because the inscription of ethnic identity stresses process rather than static dispositions, the act of amalgamation required for the understanding of the short story cycle is analogous to that needed for the comprehension of the protagonist's developing ethnic identity. Donald Goellnicht suggests that, rather than think in binary terms of inside/outside, we should perhaps perceive hybrid positions as "a web of multiply intersecting and shifting strands in which the precise location of the subject is extremely difficult to map [because] subject positions are not the result of essential determinants but are culturally produced (in relation to other positions) and socially learned, a complex and continuous process" (340). The shifting borders of identity, characteristic of a bildungsroman and of the discrete episodes typical of Asian American negotiations with subjectivity, find their structural expression in the stories that make up a cycle. Patricia Chu suggests that, as a creative intervention in the American literary scene, "mastering the [bildungsroman's] rich and subtle range for representing individual experience would provide a way [for Asian American writers] both to establish a character's or narrator's complex interiority and to demonstrate one's mastery of American culture" (16). The ethnic subject, forced to sift constantly through the assorted influences that mold it, seeks connection by trying to organize the diversity it perceives in the world.

Asian American short story cycles may be viewed as formal and contextual manifestations of the pluralistic culture in which they are created and nourished, combining the traditional manner of narrating with contemporary literary devices and themes.[5] Yamanaka's cycle, one among other texts by Asian American writers from Hawai'i, a body of writing that includes Sylvia Watanabe's *Talking to the Dead,* Garrett Hongo's *Volcano: A Memoir of Hawai'i,* and Darrell Lum's *Pass On, No Pass Back,* presents the complex cultural world of those islands. To renegotiate Asian American literatures of Hawai'i, Yamanaka enacts the bildungsroman through a short story cycle about a childhood in Hawai'i, expanding the range of intercultural narrative by blending a local childhood idyll with the Western tradition. This choice also links Yamanaka's narrative to those of other women writers of color, such as Sandra Cisneros, Esmeralda Santiago, Alice Walker, and Jamaica Kincaid, whose nontraditional bildungsromane rearticulate the conventional form, highlighting the specificities of women's quest for self-defined identities in the sociocultural context of the United States. As Maria Karafilis notes, ethnic women who appropriate and modify the traditional genre "not only speak to the options, futures, and responsibilities of their young narrators, but they also comment on dominant Euro-American society by revising or even rejecting some of its values and certain aspects of its literary traditions" (64). Patricia Chu argues, notably, that Asian American writers, who often have to struggle for agency and positionality in American society, "have made the struggle for authorship, and for the founding of a new literary tradition, central tropes for the more fundamental tasks of claiming and constructing Asian American subjectivity" (6). It is interesting that other Asian American writers, among them Maxine Hong Kingston and Amy Tan, also manipulate the cycle form to tell coming-of-age stories, subverting the generic paradigm of the bildungsroman. As Bonnie Hoover Braendlin points out in connection with the ethnic bildungsroman in America, this renewed form "asserts an identity defined by the outsiders themselves or by their own cultures, not by the patriarchal Anglo-American power structure; it evinces a revaluation, a transvaluation, of traditional *Bildung* by new standards and perspectives" (75).

Nevertheless, the current revival of interest on the part of ethnic writers in the bildungsroman does not imply a return to an obsolete or unfashionable literary genre; rather, it may be argued that Yamanaka, like other ethnic writers, appropriates the space provided by the generic model as a site of critical juncture to expand representational possibilities. Further, appropriating the story cycle—characterized by the spaces between stories as much as by the connections among them—to enact this purpose illustrates Homi K. Bhabha's concept of the "in-between" as a "terrain for elaborating strategies of selfhood—singular or communal—that initiate new signs of identity" (1). Rather than serving as simply a new alternative designation, however, Bhabha's "terrain" is the space, "unrepresentable in itself," in which racial self-articulation is disconnected from "primordial unity or fixity" (37). By performing the intersection of the story cycle and bildungsroman, Yamanaka limns the processual character of ethnic identity as she highlights the gaps in her protagonist's itinerary of self-awareness and representation.

To enact the development of a necessarily multiple self, Yamanaka's presentation of the bildungsroman through a story cycle, which signifies as it articulates, connects the variable and shifting influences and meanings of this representation within the context of Hawai'i. Yamanaka's intertextual exercise, therefore, involves the appropriation and revision of two generic models: the short story cycle as it exists in Euro-American theory and practice, and the bildungsroman. Yet her literary production, by its deliberate subversion of traditional characteristics of the form, challenges any potentially limiting view of the subject and style of contemporary bildungsroman. Yamanaka presents, notably, a fragmented circular narrative pattern instead of lineal development, and she foregrounds the experiences of a Japanese American girl in Hawai'i, further complicating cultural representation and strategies of meaning. By privileging the communal as well as the individual, she stresses the role of family and community in the protagonist's journey of self. The episodic or fragmented nature of the narrative mimics the child's own process of recollection and struggle for understanding. The cycle also becomes a highly appropriate manner of conveying the child's initial sense of a disjunction between her romantic plots of belonging and the sociocultural reality that surrounds her. At the end, the mode of the genre also effectively enacts her approach toward connection and transition. In connection with the structural development, Yamanaka develops two themes traditional to literature from Hawai'i as essential aspects of the protagonist's understanding of her place in her complex world: the fundamental values of *aloha 'aina* (love of the land) and *'ohana* (family). These cultural values are closely linked to the experience of Asian immigrants to Hawai'i, whose original home cultures also emphasize family and deep appreciation for the land (Sumida, *And the View from the Shore* 109).

All the stories in *Wild Meat and the Bully Burgers* are narrated by Lovey Nariyoshi, a precocious and engaging child who lives between an imaginative world, peopled by Donny Osmond, Barbies, and Charlie's Angels, and the real world of the Japanese American community in Hawai'i, with its distinctive socioeconomic circumstances. She is the central unifying element of the cycle. The use of a child as the center of consciousness links this text to traditional Western literature, which has often turned to the child archetype as a powerful means of defining the responses of a country's artistic minds to its evolving sociocultural climate.[6] The relationships linking memory, fantasy, imagination, and current mood tend to be an explicit concern of those embarking on the writing of childhood, as these are the prime elements of the portrayal of the ethnic subject in question. Yamanaka's delineation of her protagonist conforms to and expands this idea as the reader follows Lovey's complex revelation of thought and experience. Her manner of comprehending her subjectivity—the cultural context of Hawai'i and her experience of growing up immersed in 1970s pop culture—informs narrative art itself. The element of interest here is not so much the child character per se as a state of awareness, a point of beginning, for which childhood is the most obvious analogy. The voice of the child becomes crucial to two fundamental concerns of the presentation of the ethnic subject: how the self is constituted, and how meaning itself is established.

Lovey's voice immerses the reader in the colors, flowers, and fragrances of her paradisaical home: "I felt the color blue," she rhapsodizes, "*the sky through the band-room window, Punalu'u near the reef where the water turned aqua*" (59; italics in the original). "From Hilo town as we leave in the morning," she says, "I see the *purplemountainmajesty*—Mauna Kea. I know exactly what the song means every time I see the mountain in the middle of my island" (198). The land simultaneously symbolizes both grandeur and destruction; and, in an eruption of Mauna Ulu, Lovey's father loses his sight trying to put the goats who were "burning and melting away" (263) out of their misery. But she will learn most movingly from her father's stories about the true meaning of love for the land and the significance of home. When her father tells her about his own father's death, he privileges the role of the land, in its physical constituents, for a definition of home. His father had carried with him from Japan a package that contained soil, which he had kept under his bed for decades; as he lay dying, he asked his wife to bury him with that soil: "That was his way of going home," Lovey's father says (174). He then assigns his daughter the task of bringing him home in the same way after his death, by burying him with some soil of Haupu Mountain: "Just pour um on me," he says, "and I be home" (180).

Though pastoral elements abound in Lovey's descriptions of her land, she conveys layers of metaphorical and symbolic meaning through her pragmatic vision of the less beautiful aspects of the same realities. *Wild*

Meat and the Bully Burgers illustrates Sumida's classification of the complex Hawaiian pastoral, which tacitly recognizes the imaginative and sentimental power of images of the land but often satirizes and even parodies simplistic claims about earthly paradises come true, frequently giving a major role to "intercultural encounters and interactions in the Hawai'i setting, where differences between cultures, perspectives, and values are considered important" (*And the View from the Shore* 5–6). Lovey never allows the reader to be completely immersed in the idyll, at any level. Potentially exoticizing accounts of animals, for instance, are undercut by such comments as "sheep stew stinks" (78) and "field poison the sugar company uses to kill cane rats makes the owls brain dead, dizzy, and dazed by the time they die" (172); or, in a description of plucking a peacock that has emerald-green feathers, "the body cold but defrosting, smelling a little bad already" (165). Tales of pet animals end in tragic awareness: she witnesses one pet rabbit's tenderness with her young, and she sees another devouring her offspring; Lovey and her sister Calhoon take their pet goat to the zoo, where Nanny is immediately assaulted by the billies in the cage, and the girls eat "wild meat" that their father has hunted and hamburgers made from their pet calf Bully. In the story titled "Dead Animals Spoil the Scenery," Lovey describes, among other things, a dead mouse in a cabinet under the Lei Stand, "X's for eyes and bleeding from its mouth and ears" (151). The world of ghosts, which Calhoon sees, also lurks in the forest and in darkened bedrooms. Birds that have been killed take the form of ladies that come in the night, and the story "Calhoon Never Lies" relates the haunting that arises from Lovey's reckless killing of the Japanese blue pheasant that Calhoon had promised to show her.

In the context of the land, appreciation for family acquires renewed significance. The most vivid illustration of the importance of family, as Lovey perceives it, comes across through the image of the quilt that her grandmother makes from the family's discarded clothes. The quilt includes the following items:

> Aunty Bing's last year's May Day muumuu. Mother's shortie muumuu for Uncle Steven's New Year mochi-pounding party. Grandma's favorite lavender aloha print dress. Calhoon's and my matching County Fair clothes from three years ago with matching bikini bottoms.
>
> And whenever we get a new grandma-made quilt, we lay it down on the floor to see who's there. The more we know, the more we fight for the blanket [196].

The descriptions of the pieces of cloth that make up the quilt serve as a cartography for family identity and history, mapping the diverse family members, their stories and idiosyncrasies, and their place in the constitution of the group. The grandmother's role in the family as caregiver expands to include that of preserver of tradition through the quilt that she makes, and that her granddaughters fight to appropriate. Again, as a symbolic element within a bildungsroman, this image underscores the centrality of family formation and interfamilial relationships, particularly in the manner in which these relationships contribute to the development of the individual, female, self.

Other recurrent images that characterize Lovey and her surroundings derive from 1970s pop culture. The protagonist's consciousness, made of scenes from TV serials and images of teen idols, of popular music and toys, provides the prism through which she approaches and comprehends the world. In the first story, titled "Happy Endings," she explains how she has wished to be like Shirley Temple, "with perfect blond ringlets and pink cheeks and pouty lips, bright eyes and a happy ending every Sunday and crying 'cause of being happy" (3). Her disastrous first perm reminds her of the protagonist of *Get Christie Love*—"fizzy and borinki"—rather than of Shirley Temple (53). She plays with Barbie, Ken, and the entire Mattel clan, converting these toys into the center of her imaginative world. The influence of this culture fosters an innovative angle of vision through the amalgamation of the celluloid world with the immature understanding and unusual perception of a child. By orienting the imaginative background of the narrative to her own worldview, Lovey privileges popular culture as a way of approaching and understanding daily reality. This prism is complicated if we note the absence of people of color in American popular culture. The predominance of white persons as models or norms for beauty, for instance, further complicates Lovey's negotiation of her ethnic identity.

Yamanaka's cycle presents a composite portrait of its child narrator, her family and her world, her ambitions and insecurities, her struggles and her victories. Lovey, a third-generation Japanese American in Hawai'i, must deal with the complex social and cultural structure that governs relationships on her island, in its manifestations at school and in her neighborhood. The author's choice of this theme, apart from presenting her with the opportunity to revitalize the bildungsroman, illustrates Sumida's points regarding the use of the childhood story by writers concerned with staking a claim to Hawai'i's cultural history (*And the View from the Shore* 108). It is important that Lovey's narrating voice communicates the nuances of the experience of Hawai'i through the use of pidgin. This language of self-determination identifies the speaker's class and, more important, challenges imposed colonial standards (Sumida, "Postcolonialism" 280). Gail Y. Okawa also believes that in the context of Hawai'i's social, linguistic, and literary history, the use of pidgin reflects a "growing resistance to the dominant society's stereotypes of and colonial attitudes towards Hawaii's multiethnic people, culture and language" and represents "an autoethnographic reclamation of that culture and language by those who 'own' it" (179). The use of pidgin is, as Sumida explains, "local identity in one of its many forms, whether in daily life or in the poem, and therefore in its treatments of otherwise widespread themes" ("Postcolonialism" 280). The literary use of pidgin—strongly associated with childhood in Hawai'i—acquires heightened significance in a narrative that aims to present the creation of identity. As Lauren Belfer points out, "Language becomes a metaphor for the story itself. . . . [Lovey] searches for an identity that will encompass her family's myths of samurai Japan and the skewed America of Barbie and 'Bewitched'" (11). In the text, Yamanaka uses pidgin and its critical implications as a specific signifier that illustrates "the dual nature of *Bildung:* introspective self-analysis and social interchange" on different levels (Braendlin 81). The language that characterizes Lovey also stipulates her place in her world, establishing her social position. The singularity of her voice springs precisely from the struggle to make sense of the conflicting forces that shape her existence in her place: ethnicity and familial history, popular culture, and current demands of society. Viet Thanh Nguyen points out that the issue of local culture and the concept of community are fundamental to Yamanaka's narrative, writing driven by a "dynamic of inclusion and exclusion" (164); as such, her text explores and perhaps materializes "the messiness of diversity and heterogeneity, represented in this case through Hawai'i's local culture, where panethnicity can break down into interethnic strife" (157–58). Moreover, Yamanaka's focus on local community locates the text more firmly within the classification of a Hawai'i bildungsroman, as it privileges culture—specific manners of expression and local condition.

For Lovey, who describes herself as "kind of short and fat" (89) and is fascinated by the appealing white culture that excludes her, pidgin represents all she does not want to be: "I don't tell anyone, not even Jerry, how ashamed I am of pidgin English. Ashamed of my mother and father, the food we eat, chicken luau with can spinach and tripe stew" (9). Her complex stems from her perception of racial, cultural, and economic inferiority. She dreams of being a haole, a white American like those she sees on TV, but she despairs about the only way she knows how to speak. When her teacher tries to teach Lovey and her classmates proper English, Lovey laments that she cannot talk the way he wants her to unless she is pretending to speak "haole": "But the sound, the sound from my mouth, if I let it rip right out of the lips, my words will always come out like home" (13). Home is a reality Lovey alternately embraces and rejects, a Japanese-American-in-Hawai'i world where the child wants desperately to have a "white" name like Vicky or Jenny, and not to have to suffer the condescension of mainland cousins who pointedly ask why Lovey and her family speak so strangely (28–29). She perceives the entire system of social classification in her world, how ethnicities are ranked on a (shifting) scale of popularity and admiration. "In our school," she explains, "if part Hawaiian goes with pure Jap, that's the ultimate. Everybody wants a hapa [mixed-race] girlfriend or boyfriend. Everybody wants a part Hawaiian person" (217). At this point in history, on the basis of specific moments of evolving identity and cultural politics, some ethnicities become more acceptable than others in the world Lovey wants to belong in. For Lovey, comprehending this structure implies struggling vainly to enter it. Her immersion in her imaginative world, and her chafing under the strictures of the real one, cause the narrative tone to shift constantly between optimism and despair. But the marginal position she places herself in is balanced by her resilience, her ability to derive pleasure from the things of ordinary life.

Braendlin argues that "although women often select the subjective lyric to express strong personal feelings, the objectivity of the bildungsroman offers female authors distancing devices, such as irony and retrospective point of view, which convey the complexity of the female quest for selfhood" (77). Lovey, engaged in a process of physical and psychological growth, finds herself constantly in transition and struggles against her awareness of liminality. The self-assurance of the girls at school, even that of her own sister, contrasts sharply with her constant efforts to be someone else in order to belong. She unconsciously seeks obliteration, preferring to be transformed into someone beautiful and popular. Her family perceives her desperation: her sister asks her why she wants to be something she isn't (72), and her father reprimands her: "You always make like we something we not, I tell you. When you going open your eyes and learn, hah? You ain't rich, you ain't haole, and you ain't strong inside. You just one little girl" (260). In order to stake a claim to selfhood, Lovey must learn to accept the multiple registers that define her place in Hawai'i. The different stories enact discrete episodes in her process of gaining cultural and personal maturity and permit entry into her private world of imagination and longings. In "Rhapsody" and "Crazy Like a Dream," she indulges, respectively, in musical fantasies and dreams about being pregnant and having a neighbor's baby call her Aunty Lovey. "What Love Is" describes her relationship with Jerry, a misfit in his own right. She concludes the story with this explanation: "I'll tell you what love is. Jerry and me in the Kress store. We bought matching T-shirts to wear to school. . . . We walk to the bus stop wearing each other's rubber slippers" (88). "Lessons," composed of numbered instructions on avoiding the anger of Jerry's older brother, juxtaposes cruelty with childhood innocence, whereas "Bitter Tastes Sweet" ends with her betrayal of Jerry, and his revenge. Other stories narrate childhood crushes and misguided devotion. She admires Crystal Kawasaki for her perfect, self-assured beauty; she also falls under the spell of a teacher, a religious fanatic who traumatizes her into seeing ghosts. "Rags" tells of her anguish at her first menstruation, and in "Water Black and Bright" and "Wrong Words," she witnesses the downfall of her idol, Crystal. In "The Last Dance Is Always a Slow Dance," she spends most of a party waiting for Jenks, with whom she is in love, to dance the last dance with her. These discrete accounts are linked by the experience of change, the awareness of her otherness and of the establishment of relationships, and the definition of the dynamically shifting margins of her identity.

In the highly metaphorical "Lovey's Homemade Singer Sewing Class Patchwork Denim Hiphuggers," she alternates hunting stories with her account of how she learned to sew, and she describes the process of making leather from animal hide. She helps her father make a vest out of the hide, learning how a garment carries meaning and strength, and she imaginatively constructs a vest of her own, assembled from the hides of the different animals she has cared for or watched (the calf they refused to eat; their goat, Nanny; their pet rabbits). "And no one—no one can name them but me" (203). Thus, in an almost transcendental gesture, and as an act of affirmation and acceptance, Lovey chooses to appropriate for her vest all the animals that have played a part in her life. Fashioning the vest from her experiences shows her awareness of the things of the past as constituent parts of herself, necessary in order for her to face the demands of the present. On a more domestic level, the hiphuggers that she and Calhoon sew unite scraps from her family members, creating, more than denim jeans, a testimony to her determination: "Grandma, Mother, Calhoon, Father and me at that moment in the patchwork denim bell-bottom hiphuggers whose scraps nobody in the room could name but me" (204). Her ability to name the animals in her vest and identify the scraps on the jeans signals her ability to appropriate her experience, an exercise in agency. Through these two metaphors, she pulls the diverse elements of her experience together—love of the land and of her family—alleviating somewhat her struggle with language and artistic expression. Her consciousness of the process of self-formation is underlined by the significance she attributes to the naming of the parts of the whole. She understands and accepts her position in her land and within her family. The act of sewing, like the act of storytelling, becomes a means of empowerment for the child, signaling the moment she takes control of her world. This signals a crucial movement within the bildungsroman, as the possibility of individual transcendence and self-awareness overcomes earlier limitations. Ultimately, this suggests the possibility of achieving a coherent, individual subjectivity through the revised bildungsroman. It is important to observe that these images serve as contextual metaphors for the dynamics of the cycle itself. Just as the significant pieces of animal hide and denim swatches unite to create Lovey's vest and hiphuggers, the different stories and fragmented episodes of her life bind together to make a whole greater than the sum of its parts. In the telling of her stories, as in the sewing of the garments she will wear proudly, Lovey finds her means of liberation from the shackles of her Barbie world's illusions. Her potentially fragmented, alienated personality achieves a sense of cohesion and expression in the creative wholeness of the short story cycle, which embraces the diversity and the paradoxes of her childhood experiences, conferring connection and a sense of harmony.

Lovey's bildungsroman thus becomes a journey of self-awareness, characterized by her gradual acceptance of her place within her family and her land. Her true epiphany comes in the last story, "The Burning," the denouement of many of her secret fears and the revelation of her hidden strength and possibilities. When her father tragically loses his sight, she will come to terms with the meaning of family. Her father's oldest brother comes to visit and, in conversations with Lovey, opens up to her a world of possibilities: "Never you mind if you're limited because you're a girl—reach for the stars, the future is yours" (265). She also begins to understand the link between land and family, the reasons why her father is so attached to the place of his boyhood, as well as what she can do for him. Lovey then goes to Haupu Mountain to bring for her father, in a Ziploc bag, dirt and stones from his original home. When she brings them to him, she says, "You said you gonna see heaven on earth, remember? And be home again. You going know you home" (275). Her present to her father signals her affirmation of belonging to a land, a history, a people, and the determination to preserve that tradition. At the conclusion of this story, Lovey finally achieves her wish, enunciated in the very first story: to have a happy ending, "real happy, so someone watching can cry too" (3). By bringing her father home, she completes the cycle for herself as well. Because the structure of the cycle echoes the progression of the subject, the final story confirms the appropriateness of the cycle for Lovey's bildungsroman. As Nguyen points out, at the conclusion of the text the protagonist overcomes diverse forms of alienation and, more important, "what is redeemed by the conclusion is not only the protagonist but also her local culture, which is both her home and her source of adolescent angst and perceived cultural inferiority" (161). Where the child once saw only a claustrophobic place, life is now represented in the form of widening spaces, with boundaries to be explored and the passage to adolescence to be mapped out.

Wild Meat and the Bully Burgers, a short story cycle that engages ethnic self-definition, blends the established Euro-American genre with the bildungsroman of a child of Hawai'i, to simultaneously articulate and signify. Lois-Ann Yamanaka turns to family, community, and ethnicity, and to the subversion of traditional genres and themes of literature, to interrogate and revitalize sources of personal identity and creative expression. The manner in which she uses the cycle to inscribe the formation of self-awareness becomes a metaphor for the complexity of ethnic lives and the articulation of the increasingly complex Asian American subjectivity. Her appropriation of the bildungsroman in order to reinvent the Hawaiian pastoral attests to the flexibility of the bildungsroman and the intertextual process evident in contemporary Asian American fiction. Alluding to and appropriating literary traditions of the past, Yamanaka does not support a rejection of those forms; rather, she encourages the transformation of those terrains into fertile ground for the renewed complexity of contemporary Asian American representations of self, place, and community. As Chu points out, texts such as these become "strategic interventions in American literary constructions of race, ethnicity, and gender. Such an approach underscores the agency of Asian Americans as authors as well as the importance of authorship as the vehicle and trope for agency in this literature. With this in mind, I argue that the literary genre of the bildungsroman is a central site for Asian American re-visions of American subject formation" (11). The subsequent narrative becomes a multilayered dynamic of cultural production that forges an organic link between forms of narrative and revisionary perspectives on subjectivity, multiplying the strategies of meaning in Asian American narratives as well as the forms of reading them.

BIBLIOGRAPHY

Anderson, Sherwood. *Winesburg, Ohio*. 1919. New York: Bantam, 1995.

Belfer, Lauren. Review of *Wild Meat and the Bully Burgers*, by Lois-Ann Yamanaka. *New York Times Book Review* 31 Dec. 1995: 11.

Bhabha, Homi K. *The Location of Culture*. London and New York: Routledge, 1994.

Braendlin, Bonnie Hoover. "*Bildung* in Ethnic Women Writers." *Denver Quarterly* 17.4 (1983): 75–87.

Carver, Raymond. *Cathedral*. 1983. New York: Vintage, 1989.

Choy, Wayson. *The Jade Peony*. 1995. New York: Picador, 1997.

Chu, Patricia P. *Assimilating Asians: Gendered Strategies of Authorship in Asian America*. Durham: Duke University Press, 2000.

Coveney, Peter. *The Image of Childhood*. Rev. ed. London: Penguin, 1967.

Davis, Rocío G. *Transcultural Reinventions: Asian American and Asian Canadian Short story Cycles*. Toronto: TSAR, 2001.

Dunn, Maggie, and Ann Morris. *The Composite Novel: The Short Story Cycle in Transition*. New York: Twayne, 1995.

Goellnicht, Donald C. "Blurring Boundaries: Asian American Literature as Theory." *An Interethnic Companion to Asian American Literature*. Ed. King-Kok Cheung. New York: Cambridge University Press, 1997. 338–65.

Hemingway, Ernest. *In Our Time*. 1925. New York: Scribner, 1996.

Hongo, Garrett. *Volcano: A Memoir of Hawai'i*. New York: Vintage Departures, 1995.

Ingram, Forrest L. *Representative Short Story Cycles of the Twentieth Century: Studies in a Literary Genre*. The Hague: Mouton, 1971.

Jameson, Fredric. *The Political Unconscious: Narrative as a Socially Symbolic Act*. Ithaca: Cornell University Press, 1981.

Karafilis, Maria. "Crossing the Borders of Genre: Revisions of the *Bildungsroman* in Sandra Cisneros's *The House on Mango Street* and Jamaica Kinkcaid's *Annie John*." *MMLA: Journal of the Midwest Modern Language Association* 31.2 (1998): 63–78.

Kennedy, J. Gerald. *Modern American Short Story Sequences: Composite Fictions and Fictive Communities*. New York: Cambridge University Press, 1995.

———. "Towards a Poetics of the Short Story Cycle." *Journal of the Short Story in English* 11 (1988): 9–24.

Lowe, Lisa. *Immigrant Acts: On Asian American Cultural Politics*. Durham: Duke University Press, 1996.

Lum, Darrell. *Pass On, No Pass Back*. Honolulu: Bamboo Ridge Press, 1990.

Lundén, Rolf. *The United Stories of America: Studies in the Short Story Composite*. Amsterdam and Atlanta: Rodopi, 1999.

Luscher, Robert M. "The Short Story Sequence: An Open Book." *Short Story Theory at a Crossroads*. Ed. Susan Lohafer and Jo Ellyn Clarey. Baton Rouge: Louisiana State University Press, 1989. 148–67.

Lynch, Gerald. *The One and the Many: English-Canadian Short Story Cycles.* Toronto: University of Toronto Press, 2001.
Mann, Susan Garland. *The Short Story Cycle: A Genre Companion and Reference Guide.* New York: Greenwood, 1989.
Nguyen, Viet Thanh. *Race and Resistance: Literature and Politics in Asian America.* New York: Oxford University Press, 2002.
Nunez, Sigrid. *A Feather on the Breath of God.* New York: HarperCollins, 1995.
Okawa, Gail Y. "Resistance and Reclamation: Hawaii 'Pidgin English' and Autoethnography in the Short Stories of Darrell H. Y. Lum." *Ethnicity and the American Short Story.* Ed. Julie Brown. New York: Garland, 1997. 177–96.
Selvadurai, Shyam. *Funny Boy.* Toronto: McClelland & Stewart, 1994.
Smith, Paul. *Discerning the Subject.* Minneapolis: University of Minnesota Press, 1988.
Sumida, Stephen H. *And the View from the Shore: Literary Traditions of Hawai'i.* Seattle: University of Washington Press, 1991.
———. "Postcolonialism, Nationalism, and the Emergence of Asian/Pacific Literatures." *An Interethnic Companion to Asian American Literature.* Ed. King-Kok Cheung. New York: Cambridge University Press, 1997. 274–88.
Tan, Amy. *The Joy Luck Club.* New York: Ivy Books, 1989.
Wang, Ping. *American Visa.* Minneapolis: Coffee House Press, 1994.
Watanabe, Sylvia. *Talking to the Dead.* London: Women's Press, 1994.
Yamanaka, Lois-Ann. *Blu's Hanging.* New York: Avon, 1997.
———. *Heads by Harry.* New York: Farrar, Straus & Giroux, 1999.
———. *Name Me Nobody.* New York: Hyperion, 2000.
———. *Wild Meat and the Bully Burgers.* San Diego: Harcourt Brace and Company, 1997.

NOTES

1. Stephen Sumida has analyzed the controversy attached to the expression "Hawaiian writer" when it is used to refer to immigrants rather than to native people. In his study on the literary traditions of Hawai'i, he reserves "the word 'Hawaiian' to identify native Hawaiian (i.e., Polynesian) people and culture. For a non-Polynesian, [he] refer[s] to a 'Hawai'i' person" (*And the View from the Shore* xxiii). I will follow the criteria he establishes and use "Hawai'i writer" when discussing Yamanaka and other Asian American writers from Hawai'i. With regard to the nuances of the term "local," Brenda Lee Kwon defines it as a label that "can be used to refer to anyone of Asian, Hawaiian, or other Pacific Island descent, and usually designates those who have been in Hawai'i for more than one generation, although more politicized definitions call for a lineage that can be traced back to the plantation labor experience" (quoted in Nguyen 158). The term is not without its controversy, as Nguyen explores in some detail (158–60).

2. Nguyen points out the complex position of Yamanaka's work in the context

of what constitutes Asian American literature: "Many Asian American intellectuals have considered Yamanaka's work to be part of Asian American literature, since the Association for Asian American Studies has recognized her work with its annual book awards, but many critics and writers of Hawaii's 'local' literature insist that Hawaii's local culture, from which Yamanaka's work originates, is quite distinct [from] Asian American culture, due to the particular historical conditions that have shaped cultural formation" (157). While attentive to the differences between Asian American literature on the mainland and in Hawai'i, for the purposes of this paper I will read her cycle in the context of Asian American literature.

3. Yamanaka's later novels, *Blu's Hanging* and *Heads by Harry*, as well as her children's novel, *Name Me Nobody*, are also bildungsromane that privilege local identity and nonstandard uses of English, in addition to issues of race, class, and gender, and engage complex forms of socialization in their negotiation of the process of maturation.

4. For deeper analyses of theories and development of the short story cycle in North America, in both mainstream and ethnic literature, see Forrest Ingram, *Representative Short Story Cycles*; J. Gerald Kennedy, *Modern American Short Story Sequences*; Susan Garland Mann, *The Short Story Cycle*; Robert Luscher, "The Short Story Sequence: An Open Book"; Maggie Dunn and Ann Morris, *The Composite Novel*; Rolf Lundén, *The United Stories of America*; and Gerald Lynch, *The One and the Many*.

5. My *Transcultural Reinventions* offers a detailed examination of the theoretical paradigms and creative practice of the short story cycle in Asian North American writing.

6. Peter Coveney's seminal *The Image of Childhood* emphasizes the advantages of the child as a literary theme in texts that center on the consequences of cultural transfer in the modern world: "One can see the possibilities of identification between the artist and the consciousness of the child whose difficulty and chief source of pain often lie in adjustment and accommodation to environment. In childhood [lies] the perfect image of insecurity and isolation, of fear and bewilderment, of vulnerability and potential violation" (31–32).

RECASTING THE SPY, REWRITING THE STORY

THE POLITICS OF GENRE IN *NATIVE SPEAKER* BY CHANG-RAE LEE

TINA Y. CHEN

> I am an invisible man. No, I am not a spook like those who haunted Edgar Allan Poe; nor am I one of your Hollywood-movie ectoplasms. I am a man of substance, of flesh and bone, fiber and liquids—and I might even be said to possess a mind. I am invisible, understand, simply because people refuse to see me. — RALPH ELLISON *(Invisible Man)*

Henry Park is an invisible man. Like the nameless protagonist of Ralph Ellison's 1952 novel, he suffers from the refusal of others to see him. However, unlike Ellison's character, however, his invisibility is both a matter of the refusal of others to see him and the logical effect of his occupation. In Chang-rae Lee's 1995 novel *Native Speaker,* Henry Park *is* a spook, haunting those against whom he is paid to spy. That Lee's protagonist is a spy is no coincidence: Henry's vanishing acts, a professional opportunity to enact the spy's "multiple roles," are a logical extension of his personal history as a Korean American struggling to negotiate the divide that separates how others perceive him from how he sees himself. *Native Speaker* weaves an intricate web of intrigue in order to examine the multiple forces that create Henry as a spy who gets caught up in the messy tangle of his many deceptions. Lee writes about a spy, yet the novel is not a typical spy novel. Henry's stories—lyrical, cryptic, introspective—do not conform to the conventions of the spy story. The disjunction between the teller and his tale marks Lee's deliberate reworking of the genre of the spy story, altering it to accommodate the exigencies of a spy whose racially determined invisibility signals not license but a debilitating erasure of self and power. Although Henry's spying is a metaphor for his uneasy position as a Korean American struggling to figure out his place in American society, spying in *Native Speaker* moves beyond metaphor and provides Lee with an opportunity to criticize formally the generic conventions that make the telling of Henry's story such a difficult thing. By rewriting the generic conventions of the spy story, Lee designates Henry as a postmodern operative whose troubles with language and performance lead him to question the roles he has been given to play and the ways in which he has been encouraged to speak.

Native Speaker explores its preoccupations—with the conventions of genre and of narrative, with racial invisibility and disappearing acts, with linguistic fluency and rhetorical style—on levels both formal and thematic. Henry's exploration of what it means to be a spy and a storyteller not only represents the self-examination of a man who is afraid he has lost his identity; it is also the chronicle of immigrant success and failure, and of the price exacted by the immigrant practice of "gently and not so gently exploit[ing one's] own" (50). The tensions that structure Henry's story make the telling of it a difficult thing. His lyricism and eloquence falter into strange silences, broken narratives, cryptic phrases. Such problems with how to fashion narrative symbolize the multiple anxieties that Henry experiences: as a Korean American whose American birth does not preclude his grappling with linguistic fluency and a cultural legacy of silence; as a man who woos his speech therapist wife without truly fathoming the mysteries of how to make himself heard and understood; and as a spy whose professional success is predicated on his ability to impersonate someone else, to speak a story not his own.

Henry is a problematic storyteller. There are questions that others—his boss, his wife, his colleagues, and his friends—have about his reliability. Even more important, Henry himself cannot always distinguish his facts from his own narrative impulses: his confusion about which stories to tell and how to tell them is the result of his multiple betrayals, each one contributing to the unraveling of both narrative and identity. A good father, a dutiful son, a loving husband, a trustworthy friend, and an accomplished spy: he is, at times, all of these things as well as none of them. Lost behind the masks and impostures he affects as part of his job, he discovers that his consummate ability to cast for others "the perfect picture of a face" (12) carries with it a heavy price: the dissolution of self-coherence. Working as an undercover "ethnic operative" for Glimmer and Co., an intelligence firm specializing in the accumulation and exchange of information, Henry eventually confronts "the magnificent and horrifying level of [his own] virtuosity" (150) in all areas of his life. That confrontation, provoked by the death of his son, his wife's subsequent decision to leave him, and his interactions with councilman John Kwang, forces Henry to deal with the extent to which his identity is the result of his own performative choices as well as of the role his American education has taught him to play.

Ultimately, Henry discovers that he is both victim and perpetrator of the crimes he commits. Before he can own up to the ways in which his many betrayals have led to a self-betrayal, Henry must wrestle with the histories that shape him: the conditioning that teaches him that his "truest place in the culture" (118) is as a spy; the practice of imposture that problematizes the authenticity he craves; and the difficult mastery of linguistic fluency. His engagement with these dilemmas implicates him in a romantic notion of identity as the final mask that will not fall away even as they mark him as a cultural informant whose acts of "serial identity" (30) foreground the impossibility of ever fully removing the masks he wears. As Henry discerns the paradoxical truth, that the masks he wears prevent him from speaking even as they are the very things that enable him to articulate a semblance of self, readers of *Native Speaker* discover that Lee's novel itself operates behind the mask of the spy story in order to expose the limitations of form in narrating Henry's story . . . but also to acknowledge the important role conventions play in dictating the stories by which we know ourselves and others.

RECASTING THE SPY, REWRITING THE STORY

Henry is a spy, but his story is not a "spy story" in the conventional sense. Although the spy novelist Eric Ambler claimed that the only ingredient one needs to create a spy story is a protagonist who happens to be a spy, critical discussions of the genre detail the importance of a number of conventions in the construction and consumption of the spy story. As is the case with all other formula fiction, the spy story relies on a set of well-defined narrative formulas for its shape and meaning. Roth argues that, unlike the conventions of "literature," which "are regarded as scaffolding," conventions in spy and detective fiction are "the crucial relays of meaning and pleasure" (10). These generic conventions extend beyond subject matter to include the style and structure of the narrative, the social positioning of the protagonist, the ways in which the plot unfolds, and the functions of conspiracy, suspense, and resolution. With "its own methods of plot construction, characteristic techniques of presentation, and a code of ethical values peculiar to itself" (Murch 11), spy fiction exists as a form whose meaning and pleasure derive from a relatively strict adherence to the formulas with which it is associated, and which its readers both expect and demand.[1]

In writing the story of Henry Park, Lee rearticulates the standard concerns of the spy story—a fascination with the trope of undetectability; an exploration of the license and voyeuristic thrills that characterize the "fantasy of invisibility"; the double plot of detection; and the presentation of the spy as a storyteller, the story itself a paradigm for the processes of reading and writing—to accommodate the inflections of race on the spy's invisibility as well as to expose the failure of the conventions to narrate the story of such a spy. *Native Speaker* begins its rewriting of genre by examining the spy's authorial agency and revealing the ways in which recasting the spy necessitates rewriting the spy story. Henry's Korean background proves valuable to his boss, Dennis Hoagland, who constantly

> bemoaned the fact that Americans generally made the worst spies. Mostly he meant whites. Even with methodical training they were inclined to run off at the mouth, make unnecessary displays of themselves, unconsciously slip in the tiniest flourish that could scare off a nervous contact. . . . They felt this subcutaneous aching to let everyone know they were a spook [160].

Henry's lack of flamboyance, the quality that makes him an excellent mole, is also, ironically, what makes him an unconventional spy hero. However unrealistic, one of the genre's primary conventions involves the nature of the protagonist as hero and the representation of his mission as dangerous and exciting. Ian Fleming's James Bond, whose espionage practice is characterized almost entirely by the "unnecessary displays" that Hoagland despises, is perhaps the best-known example of such an agent. While it would seem that 007's excessive displays make him a bad spy because they are so at odds with the secret agent's injunction to be unnoticed, what makes James Bond a bad spy in reality is precisely what makes him a popular fictional character. Citing the "non-mimetic" nature of the spy thriller as its most distinguishing characteristic, Merry argues that the literary representation of espionage activity almost never "corresponds to the known and ascertainable facts about real-life spy networks and intelligence operations" (1). Somerset Maugham adds that "the work of an agent in the Intelligence department is on the whole monotonous. A lot of it is uncommonly useless. The material it offers for stories is scrappy and pointless; the author has himself to make it coherent, dramatic, and probable" (cited in Merry 47).

Glimmer and Co. specializes in the accumulation of information, and the methods Henry uses to obtain his intelligence are decidedly unromantic. The set pieces of the popular spy story are curiously absent: there are no flagrant disguises, no hairsbreadth escapes, no specialized technologies in use. Henry employs only a computer, which he uses to record indiscriminate literary snapshots of his subjects. He represents himself as detached from his literary production, fulfilling his charge "to be a clean writer, of the most reasonable eye, and present the subject in question like some sentient machine of transcription" (189). In essence, he is commissioned to provide *nothing but* the "scrappy and pointless" material of which Maugham speaks, cautioned not to give his reports too much shape or "drama" (189). Henry's efforts to remove himself from his narratives emblematize as well as perpetuate his lack of agency as an Asian American spy. In order to find voice and expression, Henry must move away from his position as a "clean writer" and acknowledge his own investments in the stories he writes.

Henry demonstrates an extended knowledge of his reader's generic expectations from the very beginning of his own story. In fact, he begins the narrative with a warning that our expectations—expectations that have been shaped by the nature of the genre and the conventions inherent in it—will not be met.[2] Cautioning us that he and his fellow operatives "weren't the kind of figures you naturally thought of or maybe even hoped existed" (15), Henry goes on to refute, quickly and concisely, all the popular conventions structuring the spy story:

> We pledged allegiance to no government. We weren't ourselves political creatures. We weren't patriots. Even less, heroes. We systematically overassessed risk, made it a bad word. Guns spooked us. Jack kept a pistol in his desk but it didn't work. We knew nothing of weaponry, torture, psychological warfare, extortion, electronics, supercomputers, explosives. Never anything like that [15].

By thus casting himself as an antiheroic protagonist, Henry rewrites one of the basic rules of the spy story. Such a rewriting is rendered necessary by virtue of his compromised social positioning as a "virtual" American. Although the spy is always marked by his status as an outsider, the transformation of what Palmer identifies as the spy hero's "insider-outsider" status into a condition that more closely resembles the "total outsider" positioning usually associated with the villain of the genre allows Lee to figure Henry as a highly ironic and self-conscious narrator.

Since irony involves a "signaling of difference at the very heart of similarity" (Hutcheon, *A Poetics of Postmodernism* 26), the reader's familiarity with a genre's forms and conventions leads to "conventions [being] paradoxically functional in the disintegration of . . . genre" (Tani 43).[3] Henry ironizes the conventions of the genre throughout *Native Speaker* by highlighting the readerly expectations created by the spy story. He parodies the improvisational adventure associated with spy work, noting that while a "camera . . . installed behind the mirror[ed door]" at Glimmer and Co. was monitored by the office secretary via video screen, "no one had ever shown up unexpectedly" (26). He mocks Hoagland's office rituals, critiquing the "thespian formality" that governs their meetings even though the meetings to drop off information between agents are "always routine and uneventful" (295). Hoagland's operational strategies, which include a distrust of the mails, a penchant for sending unknown couriers who "display an edge, some suspicion" (295), and a special fondness for using his own name as a code phrase during transactions, are parodic reenactments of popular ideas regarding the practice of the secret agent. Given the lack of danger characterizing the work performed by Glimmer and Co., the scenarios mimic, in an excessive and theatrical fashion, the conventions of the genre.

Nevertheless, even as Henry pushes his readers to acknowledge the expectations they bring to his story by parodying the established representational practices governing the genre, he also admits to the allure of conventional representation. Hutcheon, expounding on Hayden White's identification of irony's "transideological nature," asserts that "irony can and does function tactically in the service of a wide range of political positions, legitimating or undercutting a wide variety of interests" (*Irony's Edge* 10). The ambivalence of positionality made possible by the ironic mode characterizes Henry's wry notice of his own attraction to the very conventions he ironizes. While watching a "new technothriller" replete with "laser-guided weapons, gunboats" and "muscular agents" (227), he embellishes one of Hoagland's stories and imagines his friend and fellow operative Jack Kalantzakos "in Cyprus, both knees broken, blood gluing his teeth, taking aim and shooting his young captor in the eye while lying on the ground" (227, 228). Although Henry professes a distaste for the movie, his fantasies about Jack's past exploits, triggered by watching the film, mark his own susceptibility to the romance of conventional representation. His mocking awareness of the invincibility of the film's hero is in turn parodied by the gymnastics of his own imagination, forcing him to concede that "in our fictions, a lucky shot saves your life" (228).

DISAPPEARING ACTS

Henry is at pains to distance himself from the spy hero. The unheroic nature of his daily work and his inability to divorce his personal problems from his professional obligations make him an unlikely candidate for such a role. Nevertheless, his own participation in the construction of "*our* fictions" reveals a fascination with the exploits and abilities of such a figure. According to Cawelti and Rosenberg, the secret agent protagonist is an immensely popular mythical hero (2); such popularity stems not only from the spy's role as facilitator of the reader's secret desires and fears but also from the power afforded by a "fantasy of invisibility":

> The spy is invisible in a number of senses: he is the secret observer who, himself unseen, watches through a peephole or, in our modern technological age, through a telescope or some electronic device; he is invisible in the sense that his commission as a spy frees him from responsibility and gives him license to do things he could not ordinarily do without serious consequences. . . . These aspects of invisibility—voyeurism, self-concealment, and license—clearly have a powerful attraction quite apart from the purpose that they are intended to serve [13].

The invisibility of the spy hero delineated by Cawelti and Rosenberg results in a license that may allow him to kill and otherwise transgress the boundaries of social policy that constrain the rest of society. Henry feels destined to engage in spying because he considers his marginal position in American culture as one that easily translates into the spy's marginalized status as "secret observer." The qualities that make Henry a good spy are the result of his successful racialization; his history as "the obedient, soft-spoken son" in his family, and as the invisible Asian Other in American society, prepares him to move unseen when he wishes.

Despite his ability to perform the disappearing acts required of a spy, Henry discovers that the spy's empowering positionality is confounded when the invisibility of the spy coincides with the in/visibilities of race. Cawelti and Rosenberg's characterization of the "fantasy of invisibility" as liberating is a characterization that figures invisibility as a mode of awareness and control, a position of power from which the spy is able to manipulate and observe others. This emphasis on the powerful aspects of invisibility is further developed by Phelan in her study of the ideology of the invisible, where she argues for a reconsideration of the political emphasis on visibility and the corresponding implication that invisibility is characterized by impotence. Contending that visibility is, as often as not, a trap that "summons surveillance and the law . . . [and] provokes voyeurism, fetishism, the colonialist/imperial appetite for possession" (6), Phelan emphasizes the liberating possibilities of invisibility by encouraging an exploration of being "unmarked, unspoken, and unseen" (7).

Although Phelan identifies a number of critically important insights regarding the imbrications between the "given to be seen" and the careful blindnesses that demarcate it, her discussion of the unmarked fails to take into account the fissures that problematize any easy correspondence between that which we cannot see and that which is unmarked. Despite the potential of "the unmarked [to] summon the other eye to see what the mark is blind to—what the given to be seen fails to show, what the other cannot offer" (Phelan 32), being invisible is not necessarily the same as being unmarked. As Lee's novel makes clear, it is indeed possible to be invisible and yet still bear the marks of that erasure. Such a condition is one of in/visibility, where the hypervisibility of race is the precondition for the ways in which one is mis-seen or unseen. For all of Henry's performative forays into the realm of invisibility, his enactment of the "active disappearance" that constitutes Phelan's unmarking leaves an imprint that cannot simply be shrugged off: "My years with [Hoagland] and the rest of them, even good Jack, had somehow colored me funny, marked me" (19).

The marks that Henry cannot shrug off are the direct result of the complicated in/visibility he bears. He discovers that his in/visibility is not privileged in the ways argued by Cawelti and Rosenberg and by Phelan. Unlike the performers of whom Phelan writes, Henry cannot simply "give up the mark." His marks, contoured on his face and lodged in his overcareful speech, cannot be voluntarily relinquished. Henry, burdened by his "difficult face" (300), operates in a visual economy where being visible is the precondition for his in/visibility. While the power of the spy is predicated on an aptitude for exploiting his invisibility, the license granted to the spy occupying the position of "the secret observer who [is] himself unseen" (Cawelti and Rosenberg 13) eludes Henry, whose position is more akin to that of the voyeur at the keyhole who is himself confronted by *"le regard"* or "an awareness of himself-as-spectacle" (Silverman 164). According to Silverman, "The voyeur's apprehension of his own specularity . . . leads to the discovery . . . that he 'exists for the Other'" (165). Henry's position as a minority subject compels his awareness of the ways in which his professional voyeurism shadows how he himself is observed and defined. The power of the gaze has been understood as coextensive with the power to limit and define. Palumbo-Liu argues that the gaze grants "the dominant Other . . . one power inaccessible to the minority Self—it can withhold . . . possibilities [of self-definition] and foist upon the minority Self a set of predetermined and necessarily limited sites of representation" (76).

Henry's entry into espionage is certainly the result of the limitations that he feels have been imposed on him, a matter of exploiting one of Palumbo-Liu's "predetermined . . . sites of representation" to which Henry feels constrained:

> I had always thought that I could be anyone, perhaps several anyones at once. But Dennis Hoagland and his private firm had conveniently appeared at the right time, offering the perfect vocation for the person I was, someone who could reside in his one place and take half-steps out whenever he wished. For that I felt indebted to him for my life . . . for I thought I had finally found my truest place in the culture [118].

His talents as a spy depend on the cultural negotiations he learns as a Korean American. Marked as a foreigner although he is American by birth, Henry is familiar with "that secret living" demanded from those who are not seen as "native"; it is significant as well that he sees his entry into Glimmer and Co. as one granting that experience "a bizarre sanction" (163). Working as a spy, Henry feels the useful conjoining of his life experience with his professional interests. His outsider status and the alienation that delimit his cultural position as an "American" are precisely the qualities that his spymaster values.

A history of self-effacement prepares Henry for his performances as a spy. Hoagland requires the impossible: self-effacement so complete that the spy becomes nothing but a camera's eye, recording without the subjectivity of interpretation. In his work for Glimmer and Co., Henry must dissect his subjects and present them for analysis, neat packages of information from which strategic decisions might be made. He specializes in sterile deconstructions—a fact that is reflected in his reports, which are "exemplary" (137). Henry seeks to pinpoint the essence of a man's identity by stripping his own prose of interpretive nuances:

> In the commentary, I won't employ anything that even smacks of theme or moral. I will know nothing of the crafts of argument or narrative or drama. Nothing of beauty or art. And I am to stay on the uncomplicated task of rendering a man's life and ambition and leave to the unseen experts the arcana of human interpretation. The palmistry, the scriptology, the rest of their esoterica. The deep science [189].

Although Henry represents his task as "uncomplicated" and purports to be good at it, he must eventually acknowledge that it is not so easy—in fact, impossible—to transcribe without narrative or interpretation. To help him maintain, as much as possible, his pose as "a clean writer" and prevent the possibility of his own biases and judgments getting in the way of performing the role of "the most reasonable eye," his superiors never divulge to him the reasons behind his missions. Rather than requiring him to look for particular details, Henry's undercover assignments involve his recording everything and leaving "the arcana of human interpretation" to others. It is notable that those to whom such a task falls, the "unseen experts," are those whom even Henry cannot perceive; they are elusive by virtue of the fact that their invisibility renders them immune to the scrutinizing gaze they train on their subjects as well as on those they employ.

Native Speaker, acknowledging the psychological damages of in/visibility, is a meditation on fractured identity, the loss of internal coherence, and the longing for a wholeness that is ever deferred, ever impossible to attain. Ultimately, Henry recognizes that his impostures and false acts as a spy have come to mark him personally: he is a man whose very identity is in question. The list that Henry's wife, Lelia, leaves for him at the beginning of the novel, "visions of [him] in the whitest raw light" (1), is meant as a compass by which he might realize how far away he has drifted from her and from the person she wishes him to be. Lelia's careful compilation reveals nothing concrete, however, mapping only the shadowy outline of a man whose (pre)occupation with serial identity renders him no longer able to distinguish between "real" and "fake" performances—even when those performances are of his own staging. Without the ability to figure out what makes each act of impersonation a false act founded on a "true ontological bearing," Henry feels cut off from the identities he would claim as his own. Ultimately, Henry learns "to look at [his] life not just from a singular mode but through the crucible of a larger narrative" (192), and in so doing he learns to appreciate the nuances that trouble his original notions of truth and authenticity: "Is this what I have left? . . . That I no longer can simply flash a light inside a character, paint a figure like Kwang with a momentary language, but that I know the greater truths [that] reside in our necessary fictions spanning human event and time?"

DETECTING THE ASIAN AMERICAN AGENT

Like Henry, Lee acknowledges in his work with genre the ways in which "greater truths" are concealed in his "necessary fictions." The necessary fictions with which Lee engages in *Native Speaker* are manifold. As a careful reading reveals, Lee's novel is written both with and against a variety of disparate textual and representational legacies: the thematization of racial invisibility offered by the African American literary tradition; minority and women writers' ongoing literary revisions of the generic conventions of spy and detective fiction; and the development and reassessment of the Asian/American[4] as a figure of stealth and subterfuge.

As Hong has noted, "with echoes of Ralph Ellison, Chang-rae Lee's extraordinary debut speaks for another kind of invisible man: the Asian immigrant in America" (236). While Ellison's protagonist is clearly not a spy in the vocational sense, he shares with Henry a thematic preoccupation with the problems and possibilities of racial in/visibility. Even so, the figure of the racial minority as spy emerges (or should I say lurks?) in Ellison's text as surely, if not in the same ways structurally, as it does in *Native Speaker.* The narrator of *Invisible Man* discovers in a conversation with his grandfather—an ex-slave who was "the meekest of men" and who "never made any trouble"—that the acquiescent exterior his grandfather presents to the world conceals a keen understanding: "Our life is a war and I have been a traitor all my born days, a spy in the enemy's country" (Ellison, *Invisible Man* 17). Clearly, the protagonist's grandfather, despite—or rather *because of*—the "tranquillized mask of subordination" (Accardo and Portelli 78) that he dons, is able to perform the dangerous role of "spy in the enemy's country," an operation dependent on the ability "to overcome 'em with yesses, undermin 'em with grins, agree 'em to death and destruction, let 'em swoller you till they vomit or bust wide open" (Ellison, *Invisible Man* 17).

In many ways, the kind of double performance proposed in *Invisible Man* is precisely what Henry is asked to undertake on behalf of Glimmer and Co., and what he struggles to learn how to enact for himself. Lee's metafictional double performance with regard to genre significantly echoes the practice of his protagonist, and it constitutes a textual contribution to the work of a number of ethnic American, women, and gay and lesbian writers who are also seeking to revise the spoken and unspoken conventions dictating the form and meaning of contemporary spy and detective fiction. For Cawelti, popular fiction acts as a kind of "social or cultural ritual" ("The Concept of Formula" 734) that proffers different groups an opportunity to participate in synthesizing divergent values, (re)affirming shared understandings, and exploring new social values or relations; thus the "creation of representative detective [and spy] heroes has become an important social ritual for minority groups who would claim a meaningful place in the larger social context" (Cawelti, "Canonization, Modern Literature, and the Detective Story" 8).[5] Hutcheon, theorizing that "perhaps the most potent mode of subversion is that which can speak directly to a 'conventional' reader" (*A Poetics of Postmodernism* 202), echoes the efficacy of such an engagement with popular form on the part of minority writers who seek to subvert the very forms they utilize. The particularities of how individual minority and women writers have chosen to revise the genre vary, but it would be relatively safe to state that such writers' incorporation of "new" content into the "old" forms of spy story or detective fiction often results not only in the questioning of these forms but also in innovations in the conventions by which formula fiction derives its meaning. As Ellison affirms, "protest [in art] . . . does not necessarily take the form of speaking for a political or social program. It might appear in a novel as a *technical assault against the styles which have gone before*" (*Shadow and Act* 137; emphasis mine).

Like many other minority writers, Lee revises a number of the conventions of the spy novel to accommodate his Korean American protagonist, but the figure of the Asian spy is itself a cultural convention. For example, the internment of Japanese Americans during World War II was justified by the suspicion that Japanese Americans were secretly working as "spies, saboteurs, and fifth columnists" for the Japanese government (Daniels 200).[6] Asians, stereotyped as sneaky and inscrutable, have proved particularly compelling in combination with clandestinity.

In casting Henry as a professional spy who succeeds by exploiting his own community, Lee presents a provocative thematization of racial in/visibility. The use of espionage as a formal and thematic trope not only highlights the myriad ways in which Asian American bodies have been represented as in/visible but provides an opportunity for Lee to redress the popular stereotypes of Asian secret agents created by Anglo-American writers. (In)famous sleuths like Charlie Chan, created by Earl Derr Biggers in 1925, and Mr. Moto, the Japanese secret agent that John P. Marquand introduced in the *Saturday Evening Post* in 1935, captured the public imagination with their powers of detection. These two characters are generally considered a response to the figure of Dr. Fu Manchu, whose very name became synonymous with Asian secrecy, cunning, and threat.[7] Roth traces one of the spy thriller's defining characteristics, "a conspiracy of deception or evil" (226), to Sax Rohmer's yellow peril romances about the Devil Doctor. The "racist ambivalence" that writers like Lee are addressing when they rework the figure of the Asian spy is identified by Cawelti and Rosenberg as the primary ingredient of the heroic spy story, where "a fascination with alien cultures coexists with an overt fear and condemnation of these cultures" (44).

While a number of contemporary Asian American artists have participated in the project of revising and redeploying the stereotypes of Asian secrecy and cunning through their use of the figure of the Asian/American spy or detective, Lee's particular contributions in this area can be demonstrated through a brief comparison of his work with David Henry Hwang's award-winning 1989 Broadway play *M. Butterfly* and with Leonard Chang's 2001 *Over the Shoulder: A Novel of Intrigue.*[8] As a discussion of these texts will demonstrate, Lee participates in an ongoing conversation with other Asian American writers that explores the nature of Asian/American hypervisibility and challenges the representational forms of popular culture through the secret agent protagonist. *M. Butterfly* joins *Native Speaker* in examining images of Asian invisibility, inscrutability, and stealth by recasting Song Liling as an agent whose spying activities are both problematized and contingent on his racial identity. Like Lee, Hwang suggests that the stereotype about and practice of Asian subterfuge is emblematized by the figure of the Asian/American spy. Song Liling's flamboyance as a secret agent—his gender masquerade in many ways an "open secret" in the play; his ability to impersonate a female Chinese opera singer contingent not only on his skill in deception but on the willingness of his partner, René Gallimard, to believe in the fantasy of the submissive Asian woman that he exploits—runs counter to Henry's "silent guise," but both Lee and Hwang insist on the dangerous possibilities of the impersonation of espionage work turning into a debilitating imposture of self. Because Hwang's play attempts to deconstruct the stereotype of the submissive Asian woman, particularly as it was represented in Puccini's opera *Madama Butterfly*, Song's spying does predominantly act as a metaphor through which issues of desire, secrecy, and racial in/visibility can be explored.

In *Over the Shoulder*, many of the same concerns illuminated by *Native Speaker* are taken up and reworked yet again. The two texts seem remarkably similar on the surface: both feature Korean American male protagonists who are trained to capitalize on their Asian backgrounds in order to do their jobs as secret and not so secret agents; both men face difficult family issues; both authors have been praised for the ways in which they have explored issues of racial assimilation by developing the uncanny conflation of their protagonists' occupations and preoccupations; and both novels have been characterized as "literary" revisions of popular forms. *Native Speaker*, which preceded *Over the Shoulder* by six years, differs from Chang's novel in both the nature and effect of its revision of genre. Chang makes his revision of genre much more visible than Lee does: applauded for the ways in which he has produced "an absorbing blend of literary novel and crime thriller" (Zaleski 57), Chang ensures that despite the distinctive characteristics of his protagonist Allen Choice—whose "dis-ease" with life (50) manifests itself in a philosophy of *"removement*, the state of being removed from everything" (89)—he also includes all the generic conventions (of plot, pacing, technical execution) that conventional readers of thrillers would expect. In contrast, Lee is more reluctant than Chang to gratify his readers' conventional expectations even as he is also more subtle about the ways in which he actively (re)writes generic conventions so that their absence must still be acknowledged as critically important to his novel's meaning.

Lee accomplishes his nuanced subversion of the spy story's conventions by capitalizing on the ways in which the genre's inherent fascination with the effects and functions of invisibility paradoxically reinforces as well as opposes the perspectives that minority detectives and secret agents bring to the story. One reviewer of *Native Speaker* applauds the ways in which "the spy's sense of doubleness is doubled by the immigrant's sense of doubleness" (Klinkenborg 77). This redoubling exposes unspoken assumptions about the ways in which race, power, and privilege structure the spy story, often to the point where the story is transformed into a new form whose ironic connection to the old signifies less a reworking of genre than a radical departure from it.[9] This departure may confuse and frustrate readers who misrecognize the new form or simply regard it as a bad attempt to write according to the conventions of the genre. For example, Pavey's sole criticism of the text stems from just such a misrecognition: "But was it necessary to add in the spy story as well, fun though it is? Henry is so much more like a writer than a spy; perhaps he could just have been one" (32).

Suggesting that maybe Henry "could just have been" a writer is to miss the implications of Lee's work with genre. As I've argued, Henry's spying is not just a metaphor for his cultural dividedness as a Korean American but is also an opportunity to examine the complicated negotiation with genre and the conventions of narrative in which both Henry Park and Chang-rae Lee engage. Clearly, the adaptation of the form of the spy story to take into account the exigencies of racial in/visibility is fueled by a skepticism about the genre that finds expression in a number of ways. Henry's wry acknowledgment of the narrative expectations of genre exists alongside a recognition of his own investments in some of the very conventions he decries. Similarly, Lee manifests a complex relationship to the genre: he is drawn to the ways it illuminates the in/visibility of his protagonist even as he writes against the genre to reflect Henry's ontological dilemmas. As such, *Native Speaker*'s ironic treatment of the conventions of the spy story, its subversion of the rules of the genre, renders it a kind of postmodern spy story and Henry himself, a man constantly deconstructing the rules by which he plays the game, a kind of postmodern operative. It is significant that whereas Henry may be seen as a postmodern operative, and *Native Speaker* may be read as one version of the postmodern spy story, Lee refuses to abide by either set of conventions. The text refuses the clarity of division and categorical distinction, demonstrating a keen awareness of the conventions of both the traditional and the postmodern spy story even as it experiments with the assumptions by which conventions work to delimit the genre. In essence, both Henry as a subject and *Native Speaker* as a text share an ambivalent relationship with the conventions of narrative that embodies the not so secret nature of impersonation as a performance of divided allegiance to both authenticity and mimicry.

Tani suggests that the reworking of genre often renders conventions "deceitful clues planted by the writer to rouse the attention of the reader before disappointing his expectations" (42–43). *Native Speaker* does not attempt to deceive the reader about the ways in which it reworks genre. Rather, the novel emphasizes the limitations of the spy story's narrative conventions in order to expose Henry as an agent who struggles to write himself into the picture. Through his use and deployment of narrative conventions, Lee demonstrates an interest in authorial agency and the difficulties that attend the kinds of stories Henry wishes to tell about himself, his father, and John Kwang. By not just using Henry's spying as a metaphor for his cultural dilemmas as a Korean American, but by engaging with the ways in which the genre of the spy story affects the ways in which Henry's acts of (self-) impersonation can be narrated and understood, Lee illuminates the complex entanglements of voice, desire, and performance that motivate any attempt to articulate minority subject formation. In this way, Lee suggests that Henry's discovery must also be our own: the constraints of convention that limit our ways of reading are also integral to our understanding of the powerful fictions by which we live.

BIBLIOGRAPHY

Accardo, Annalucia, and Alessandro Portelli. "A Spy in the Enemy's Country: Domestic Slaves as Internal Foes." *The Black Columbiad: Defining Moments in African American Literature and Culture.* Ed. Werner Sollors and Maria Diedrich. Cambridge: Harvard University Press, 1994. 77–87.

Cawelti, John G. *Adventure, Mystery, and Romance.* Chicago: University of Chicago Press, 1975.

———. "Canonization, Modern Literature, and the Detective Story." *Theory and Practice of Classic Detective Fiction.* Ed. Jerome H. Delamater and Ruth Prigozy. Westport: Greenwood, 1997. 5–20.

———. "The Concept of Formula in the Study of Popular Literature." *Popular Fiction: An Anthology.* Ed. Gary Hoppenstand. New York: Longman, 1998. 730–36.

———, and Bruce A. Rosenberg. *The Spy Story.* Chicago: University of Chicago Press, 1987.

Chang, Leonard. *Over the Shoulder: A Novel of Intrigue.* New York: Ecco Press, 2001.

Chen, Tina. "Dissecting the Devil Doctor: Stereotype and Sensationalism in Sax Rohmer's Fu Manchu." *Re/Collecting Early Asian America.* Ed. Josephine Lee, Imogene Lim, and Yuko Matsukawa. Philadelphia: Temple University Press, 2002. 218–37.

Daniels, Roger. *Asian America: Chinese and Japanese in the United States Since 1850.* Seattle: University of Washington Press, 1988.

Derrida, Jacques. "Living On: Border Lines." *A Derrida Reader: Between the Blinds.* Ed. Peggy Kamuf. New York: Columbia University Press, 1991. 254–68.

Ellison, Ralph. *Invisible Man.* 1952. New York: Vintage, 1990.

———. *Shadow and Act.* New York: Random House, 1964.

Gosselin, Adrienne Johnson, ed. *Multicultural Detective Fiction: Murder from the "Other" Side.* New York: Garland, 1999.

Green, Martin. *Seven Types of Adventure Tale: An Etiology of a Major Genre.* University Park: The Pennsylvania State UP, 1991.

Hagedorn, Jessica. Introduction. *Charlie Chan Is Dead: An Anthology of Contemporary Asian American Fiction.* New York: Penguin, 1993. xxi–xxx.

Hong, Catherine. "In Brief—*Native Speaker* by Chang-rae Lee." *Vogue* Apr. 1995: 236.
Hutcheon, Linda. *Irony's Edge: The Theory and Politics of Irony*. London: Routledge, 1994.
———. *A Poetics of Postmodernism: History, Theory, Fiction*. New York: Routledge, 1988.
Hwang, David Henry. *M. Butterfly*. New York: Plume, 1989.
Klein, Kathleen Gregory, ed. *Diversity and Detective Fiction*. Bowling Green, OH: Bowling Green State University Popular Press, 1999.
Klinkenborg, Verlyn. Review of *Native Speaker*, by Chang-rae Lee. *New Yorker* July 10, 1995: 76–77.
Lee, Chang-rae. *Native Speaker*. New York: Riverhead, 1995.
Merry, Bruce. *Anatomy of the Spy Thriller*. Montreal: McGill-Queen's University Press, 1977.
Murch, Alma Elizabeth. *The Development of the Detective Novel*. Westport: Greenwood, 1958.
Palmer, Jerry. *Thrillers: Genesis and Structure of a Popular Genre*. London: Edward Arnold, 1978.
Palumbo-Liu, David. "The Minority Self as Other: Problematics of Representation in Asian-American Literature." *Cultural Critique* 28 (1994): 75–102.
Pavey, Ruth. Review of *Native Speaker*, by Chang-rae Lee. *New Statesman & Society* 8 (1995): 32.
Phelan, Peggy. *Unmarked: The Politics of Performance*. London: Routledge, 1993.
Roth, Marty. *Fair and Foul Play: Reading Genre in Classic Detective Fiction*. Athens: University of Georgia Press, 1995.
Shiomi, R. A. *Yellow Fever*. Toronto: Playwrights Canada, 1984.
Silverman, Kaja. *The Threshold of the Visible World*. New York: Routledge, 1996.
Smith, Myron J., Jr., and Terry White. *Cloak and Dagger Fiction: An Annotated Guide to Spy Thrillers*. Westport: Greenwood, 1995.
Soitos, Stephen. *The Blues Detective: A Study of African American Detective Fiction*. Amherst: University of Massachusetts Press, 1996.
Symons, Julian. *Mortal Consequences*. New York: Viking, 1985.
Takaki, Ronald. *Strangers from a Different Shore: A History of Asian Americans*. New York: Penguin, 1989.
Tani, Stefano. *The Doomed Detective: The Contribution of the Detective Novel to Postmodern American and Italian Fiction*. Carbondale: Southern Illinois University Press, 1984.
Todorov, Tzvetan. *The Fantastic: A Structural Approach to a Literary Genre*. Ithaca: Cornell University Press, 1975.
Zaleski, Jeff. Review of *Native Speaker*, by Chang-rae Lee. *Publisher's Weekly* Dec. 18, 2000: 57.

NOTES

This essay is adapted from my article "Impersonation and Other Disappearing Acts in *Native Speaker* by Chang-rae Lee," originally published in *Modern Fiction Studies* 48.3 (2002): 637–67.

1. For discussions of the various formulas associated with spy and detective fiction, see Cawelti and Rosenberg; Cawelti, *Adventure, Mystery, and Romance*; and Symons. Although many critics insist on reading spy fiction as a subcategory of detective fiction, Green categorizes "espionage and private eye fiction, insofar as they send their protagonists traveling," as "adventure tales" (157–58).

2. According to some critics (and fans) the danger of not meeting readers' expectations by subverting the conventions of the formula story is that it can result in some devastating outcomes. With regard to detective fiction, Todorov suggests that it "has its norm; to 'develop' [generic conventions] is also to disappoint them: to 'improve upon' detective fiction is to write 'literature,' not detective fiction. The whodunit par excellence is not the one which transgresses the rules of the genre, but the one which conforms to them" (43). Similarly, another critic offers the following advice to writers who might be tempted to write "literature" instead of a spy story: "Mistakes to avoid—making the hero an anti-hero, killing off your hero, letting the hero figure out which door hides the tiger too early in the tale, letting the bad guys win. Now you can do any one or all of these things, but if you do you no longer have a spy thriller: you have written a serious novel that can be sold only to intellectuals, a small, miserable, nitpicking, poverty-stricken audience that you will starve to death trying to please" (Stephen Coonts, cited in Smith and White 655).

3. Derrida also gestures to the paradoxical function of the self-reflexivity necessary to the process that Tani describes and that *Native Speaker* enacts: "What are we doing when, to practice a 'genre,' we quote a genre, represent it, stage it, expose its *generic law,* analyze it practically? Are we still practicing the genre? Does the 'work' still belong to the genre it re-cites? But inversely, how could we make a genre work without referring to it [quasi]quotationally, indicating at some point, 'See, this is a work of such-and-such a genre'? Such an indication does not belong to the genre and makes the statement of belonging an ironical exercise. It interrupts the very belonging of which it is a necessary condition" (259).

4. Here and in subsequent passages, a distinction is made between the terms "Asian/American" and "Asian American."

5. In this article, Cawelti lists a number of writers who have created protagonists who reflect the concerns of a number of minority groups. For excellent essays on the work of specific minority and women writers who are reworking the conventions of the detective story, see Gosselin; Klein. See Soitos for a study on the ways in which African Americans have utilized "African American detective tropes on both classical and hardboiled detective conventions to create a new type of detective fiction" (3).

6. No Japanese Americans were ever convicted of espionage, but the condemna-

tion of the entire Japanese American community on the basis of such fears was a material effect of the "yellow peril" mentality that had been influencing American responses to Asian immigration since the nineteenth century. For a discussion of the fears of and accusations against the Japanese that led to internment, see Takaki 379–405. Ironically, Japanese Americans who did work in intelligence were operating on behalf of the U.S. government and, according to Daniels, "the feats of the Japanese American intelligence specialists [have] received almost no public notice" (247).

7. Both Cawelti and Roth trace the lineage of the spy story to Rohmer's Dr. Fu Manchu. For a detailed discussion of the cultural resonance of Dr. Fu Manchu, see Chen, "Dissecting the Devil Doctor."

8. In addition to the work of Lee, Hwang, and Chang, R. A. Shiomi, in *Yellow Fever,* has written a parodic and humorous revision of the conventional hard-boiled detective story, and Wayne Wang's 1982 film *Chan Is Missing* depicts a highly ironic sleuthing expedition that turns up no solutions. See also Hagedorn.

9. Tani argues that "every innovation in the detective story genre has occurred in reaction to the current that had long been the dominant one and that later seemed closed to variation" (36). Drawing on the observations of the Russian formalist critic Jurij Tynjanov, who identifies the series of stages whereby any literary practice undergoes "automatization" and revision, Tani posits that the "anti-detective novel and its frustrating nonsolution (or parodic solution)" will eventually "be exhausted [and] ready to be replaced by some opposite constructive principle" (37).

TELLING TWICE-TOLD TALES ALL OVER AGAIN

LITERARY AND HISTORICAL SUBVERSION IN BHARATI MUKHERJEE'S *THE HOLDER OF THE WORLD*

PALLAVI RASTOGI

It is difficult, if not impossible, to map the works of Bharati Mukherjee onto any schema of literary ontology. Although her fiction, not to mention much of her nonfiction, seems to follow in almost organic progression, it eludes a broader taxonomy of classification simply, yet not only, because the author herself is so resistant to the making and maintaining of categories. While most of Mukherjee's fiction reveals an aversion to ethnic categorization, her 1993 novel *The Holder of the World* also deconstructs the categories of literature, history, and literary history. In this essay I argue that Mukherjee destabilizes literary and historical categories through the trope of subversion and in the process also questions the homogenizing impulses of mainstream American culture.

My analysis of *The Holder of the World* engages with Mukherjee criticism in general and takes issue with the divisive polarities—either effusively laudatory or sharply critical—that have shaped academic discourse on her writing. Mukherjee has often been criticized for her less than nuanced celebration of the diasporic state: novel after novel confirms Mukherjee as an enthusiastic proponent of the United States' wonderful ability to synthesize its diverse population into a harmonious—as well as simultaneously multicultural—whole. My project here is not to recuperate Bharati Mukherjee as a writer but to focus on how a single novel in her oeuvre stands out as an embodiment of the vast possibilities of cultural exchange. Instead of advocating absorption into a greater American identity, *The Holder of the World* presents a nonassimilationist approach to diasporic contact. Keeping in mind some of the problems that regularly surface in Mukherjee's writing, I argue that *The Holder of the World* marks a shift in the assimilationist stance advocated in such earlier novels as *Jasmine, The Tiger's Daughter,* and *Wife* and instead searches for a dialectic of intercultural negotiation through which mainstream American society is dramatically altered as much as it alters its own immigrant population.

The Holder of the World has often been described as a rewriting of Nathaniel Hawthorne's 1850 novel *The Scarlet Letter,* although its aspirations are much more ambitious: Mukherjee seeks to establish a connection between the United States and India that goes back more than four hundred years. I read Mukherjee's novel as providing a prehistory of *The Scarlet Letter* rather than a revision of its themes. Mukherjee transports Hannah Easton, the woman who would become Hawthorne's Hester, to seventeenth-century India, where she discards her Puritan repressions and enters into a lusty affair with an Indian king. The affair ends, thanks to the plundering rampages of the Mughal emperor Aurangzeb. Hannah returns to Salem carrying a child, appropriately named Pearl Singh.

At one of its many levels, then, the novel is a whimsically unpredictable retelling of the antecedents of *The Scarlet Letter,* as Mukherjee claims that Hawthorne deliberately kept hidden the real origins of Hester Prynne, Puritan adulteress. The novel moves across complex chronological and cultural zones: Puritan New England, medieval India, the contemporary United States, and modern India. These fluid narrative spaces allow Mukherjee to reveal the connections made possible by leaps of the imagination and, at a more personal level, to link herself and her writing across cultures, eras, and ideologies. The novel's message of cultural symbiosis is transmitted powerfully through the trope of literary and historical subversion.

Mukherjee subverts Western literary lineage both structurally and thematically: in the first instance, by crafting a nonlinear narrative that completely overturns canonical Western notions of cohesiveness and order; in the second instance, by excavating the historical origins of Hawthorne's story. Mukherjee develops new thematic modes in her writing with the publication of this novel, concerned as it is with ideas of cultural and geographical exchange rather than with the themes of dislocation, alienation, and necessary assimilation that recur in such novels as *The Tiger's Daughter, Wife,* and *Jasmine.* If immigrant writing can actually be celebratory, this situation gestures toward a new problematic, to which I will return later in this essay.

In *Bharati Mukherjee,* Fakrul Alam relates that Mukherjee began writing the novel after she came across

> a seventeenth-century miniature painting in a 1989 pre-auction viewing in New York. According to Mukherjee, what she saw in the painting, "a blonde-Caucasian woman in ornate Mughal court dress[,] holding a lotus bloom[,] was the original stimulus for the novel." [This] led Mukherjee to look at the recorded history of colonial New England, the East India company and Mughal India. Evidently, Mukherjee found in the process enough evidence to produce a book that suggests that there could have been connections made between America and India in earlier centuries—connections that can inspire connections between cultures in our time [130].

The Holder of the World is a literary meditation on this painting. Mukherjee uses the many cultures in and around the painting to emphasize the Indian presence not only in the present but also in the past and the future of the United States. The painting—and, later, the novel—metonymically suggest the eternalness of this presence in American life. After all, it depicts "a blonde-Caucasian woman in ornate Mughal court dress." That the auction is in New York City, considered by many to be the hub of the world, emphasizes the current reality of this presence in the contemporary United States.

The novel's longing for links between cultures, what Mukherjee calls "a hunger for connectedness" (*Holder* 11), can be discredited as an impulse toward assimilation. Nevertheless, Mukherjee's articulation, in *The Holder of the World,* of the process through which an intertemporal link between cultures is established can be translated as a yearning for cultural cross-pollination. Beigh Masters, the novel's contemporary white woman narrator, is an asset collector searching for the Emperor's Tear, which, according to legend, is the most pristine diamond in the world. Beigh's quest for this diamond leads her to discover Hannah Easton, a Puritan woman known as the Salem Bibi, who was transported across history and cultures to become the mistress of an Indian king, later to return to Salem and become Hawthorne's Hester Prynne, as described earlier. But Beigh's search for the pristine diamond is also a metaphor for a deeper search: the search for connections not only between Hannah and herself but also between the American and the Indian. By fusing Indian themes within the originally Euro-American form of the novel, Mukherjee attempts to negotiate the chasm of cultural division. Mukherjee further complicates our ideas of "Indian themes" and "Euro-American forms," however, by freely mixing into her narrative such creative modalities as oral narrative, previously considered "Oriental," and such all-American themes as the making of the American nation and the nature of American national identity.

To subvert cultural hegemony, *The Holder of the World* conceives of an elaborate analogy of similarity via difference. Hannah Easton and Beigh Masters are separated by chronology and culture, but their similarities are marked through an assertion of connection across chronology and culture. It is thus necessary for Mukherjee to set the novel across many "time zones" so that she can constantly emphasize the connections between historical periods and cultures and the peoples in those periods and cultures. That Beigh can actually "transcend time" (Iyer 34) and so make time hybrid seems to be a statement on the porousness of time and culture, concepts usually considered linear and unitary. It is significant that Beigh can travel through time only by means of the scientific know-how of her Indian lover. Such forceful eruptions in the narrative reaffirm the presence of the Indian in the American, for it is people like Venn (a work-absorbed scientist at MIT) who make the United States the technologically advanced nation that it is. Venn, then, is a tribute to the scientific contributions of the Indian American community to the United States. This is important in the context of the assertion of similarity via difference. Just as Mukherjee, through the presence of Venn, celebrates the contributions of Indians to the contemporary United States, she will also acknowledge, through the tropological presence of Pearl Singh—so separated from Venn by time and culture—the importance of Indians in the making of the American past, therefore putting forward the provocative thesis that Indians have always been contributory figures in the United States.

In an interview with Beverley Byers-Pevitts, Mukherjee says, "I wanted virtual reality because many of the new immigrants are involved in that kind of technology, and I wanted people to experience history rather than have pallets of history, tombs of history, limp data laid on them" (197). This notion of history—as a constantly modified experiential instance of the lived life—excavates the forgotten voices of the marginalized in the making of the United States. Even though Mukherjee recuperates history from the margins, her rewriting of history, using the discursive patterns of the dominant culture—by identifying her texts as American and refusing a hyphenated designation—has earned Mukherjee her share of detractors who see this as subservience to the insistent call of hegemony. Commenting on a remark by Jasmine in the eponymous novel, Walter Gobel says:

> In murdering the past, however, there is the danger of blackening the image of the mother country, in dreaming within a hegemonic culture the danger of affirming its ideology—here specifically: of freedom, possibility, adaptability and continued renewal [116].

Indisputably, *The Holder of the World* is a dreamy meditation within and through the images of the dominant culture. The novel clearly identifies itself as an American text, and for that political destination to be attained, the "mother country" is not necessarily "blackened" so much as its description is secured by an uncomfortably orientalist flavor. Here is Beigh describing a painting called *The Apocalypse*:

> Beautiful Salem Bibi stands on the cannon-breached rampart of a Hindu fort. Under a sky on fire, villages smolder on purple hillocks. Banners of green crescent moons flutter from a thousand tents beyond the forest, where tethered horses graze among the bloated carcasses of fallen mounts. Leopards and tigers prowl the outer ring of high grass; the scene is rich in crow-and-buzzard, hyena-and-jackal, *in every way the opposite of fertile Marblehead* [*Holder* 17; emphasis added].

An uncharitable reading of Mukherjee would mark this as a limitation in her creative range.[1] More baldly put: Mukherjee's array of representation is limited to the two extremities of stock Western imagery, either through the lens of extreme chaos, as in *The Tiger's Daughter*, or through excessive orientalism, as in *The Holder of the World*. While it is tempting to fling finger-wagging accusations of "orientalism" against Mukherjee, we should also consider why she creates these polarities. *The Holder of the World* is written to confirm the mutual hybridization of cultures ostensibly unconnected and disparate. In claiming that the India of *The Apocalypse* is "in every way the opposite of fertile Marblehead," Mukherjee also makes the far bolder claim in the course of the novel that "arid India" and "fertile Marblehead" are not really all that different.[2]

It takes an undergraduate thesis to bring to Beigh "a belief that with sufficient passion and intelligence we can deconstruct the barriers of time and geography. Maybe that led, circuitously, to Venn. And to the Salem Bibi and the tangled lines of India and New England" (*Holder* 11). The use of the word "tangled"—evoking, among other images, a shared colonial history—is significant. Mukherjee creates this reflection of East and West by a strategy of reverse orientalism. Here, Beigh is viewing a Mughal painting by an Indian artist who imagines the Salem Bibi at her point of origin:

> In the first of the series, she stands ankle-deep in a cove, a gold-haired, pale-bodied child-woman against a backdrop of New England evoked with *wild, sensual* color. The cove is covered with cold-weather, color-changing

> maples and oaks whose leaves shimmer in a *monsoon's juicy green luxuriance.* . . . Crouched behind her in the tiny triangle of gravelly shore visible between her muscled legs, black-robed women with haggard faces tug loose edible tufts of samphire and sea-grasses. I was right—they were fascinated by us. The artist cannot contain the wonders, fish and bird life burst over the border [*Holder* 15–16; emphasis added].

Clearly it is New England that is being exoticized and orientalized here by its association with fecundity, ripeness, and excess. Beigh's authorial comment is even more significant: "I was right—they were fascinated by us." Here the Indian painter fixes his gaze on the Occidental and reproduces the moment of contact in a flamboyantly orientalist gesture. While reverse orientalism as a strategy may be problematic, it nevertheless underlines the similarities that different cultures may share. It also subverts the tired depiction of the Western world as stable, rational, and controlled. The question that the novel wants us to ask is: How does the Mughal painter, who has never crossed the borders of India, know how to paint New England?

This conundrum is reasserted through a suggestion of parallax in the young Hannah's art. Hannah is not only a beautiful seamstress—she is, after all, reproduced as Hawthorne's Hester—but also a creative artist. One particular piece of tapestry becomes, in the young Hannah's hands, a "pure vision":

> A twelve-year-old Puritan who had never been out of Massachusetts imagined an ocean, palm trees, thatched cottages, and black-skinned men casting nests and colorfully garbed bare-breasted women mending them; native barks, and on the horizon, high-masted schooners. Colonial gentlemen in breeches and ruffled lace, buckled hats and long black coats pacing the shore. In the distance, through bright-green foliage, a ghostly white building—it could even be the Taj Mahal rising [*Holder* 44].

Hannah can visualize the Other and give it imaginative life through her needlework. Orientalist rhetoric sought to define the Other as the binary opposite of the Western norm, but here the Mughal painter and Hannah share similar modes of visual perception. This returns us to the dominant theme in the novel: the interconnectivity of India and the United States, which plays itself out on the body of the Indo-American text. Hannah's tapestry, the Mughal paintings, the novel itself, stand as eloquent testimony to the redemptive nature of art in substantiating the endurance of a presence that refuses to be effaced by centuries of white Western dominance.

The process of "un-Othering" also challenges the ideas of home, origin, and nationality. While Mukherjee affirms her American identity, she also acknowledges a debt of gratitude to her origins. In representing the "new American" and "in examining the new identity, she says she wants to explore the consciousness of those who are not of one ethnic group or another, but of many different ethnicities" (Byers-Pevitts 189). Whatever Mukherjee's intent may be, the effect of the novel promises us something else: the "new" hybrid American straddling multiple ethnicities was always present, even in the America traditionally thought of as the most monoethnic, as in Puritan New England, where the name "Puritan" itself conveys the idea of a certain self-contained purity.

In this novel, Hannah, the white Puritan woman, is allegorized as the figure of immigrant difference. After Jadav Singh, her Indian lover, is killed in battle, Hannah returns to Salem as a figure of radical otherness, bringing back with her a child from an interracial union, thus quietly yet firmly lodging the Indian within the American. Nalini Iyer marks this as a moment of historical rewriting:

> Black Pearl [as the residents of Salem call the child] is Indo-American; her very existence signifies the merging of cultures. Hawthorne's Pearl is white, and in creating Black Pearl, *The Holder of the World* forcibly inserts immigrant culture and history into the American canon [42].

It is Pearl rather than Mother-of-Pearl who becomes an agent of cultural change. Half-American, half-Indian, she nevertheless is entitled to an American identity, as her "adulteress" mother is not. It is significant that Pearl is born in a liminal space in "1701 somewhere in the South Atlantic on the long voyage home" (*Holder* 284) and links the Indian and the American by her very liminality. Black Pearl is the representative of the new hybrid American who gives to race and hybridity the importance denied them by a society relentlessly masquerading as white and pure. But, as the novel claims, this new hybrid American is really not "new" at all but can be traced back as an active agent in the originary myth of nation building: "Pearl Singh . . . saw in her old age the birth of this country, an event she had spent a life-time advocating and suffering for" (*Holder* 284). Thus Mukherjee asserts both the presence and the agency given to the Indian American in the creation of canonical American history and the making of the American nation. But the American identity and the American nation to which Pearl Singh stakes a claim is never—and was never—a white Christian identity or nation.

Instead, the idea of Americanness is fractured into bits and pieces, with no one, not even Puritan Americans, able to lay claim to it in any holistic way. The figure of Pearl Singh as second-generation diasporic brings to light the international mooring of the homogeneous cultural terrain of Puritan Salem. Mukherjee thus destabilizes the impenetrable borders of the American nation-state, pushes open the boundaries of American citizenship, and subverts the teleology of American history.

The imagination then enables this rewriting of quintessential Americana, for it is textual action that reconfigures the linearity of a hegemonic mythology. Fakrul Alam comments:

> *The Holder of the World* is written to show [that] what makes a historical novel come alive is the writer's imagination. . . . Mukherjee is[,] in fact, emphasizing the role the creative imagination plays in transforming what would otherwise be seen as silence or slow time into events and characters full of life [131].

The imagination becomes the agent of subversion through which Mukherjee makes a giant leap for "immigrantkind" into the historical antecedents of the United States. By writing Indian history into an American life narrative, Mukherjee firmly establishes the reality of this presence in American life and letters. Moreover, as the novel progresses, Beigh learns to question her research methodologies and supplement them with a rare imaginative transcendence. While Venn is seeking to synthesize time into a giant reality, where each moment of history can be made easily available by the mere push of a button, Beigh learns to "trust the psychological integrity" of that which is being researched (*Holder* 232).[3] The object—in particular, the objectified—has an integrity of its own that is often erased by the process of time. The writer/researcher/reader brings back to life, through acts of the imagination, that which has been previously silenced or pushed to the margins of history: here, the presence of India and Indians in the making of the early United States.

The Holder of the World, however, does much more than reproduce the American past in a hybrid image. While the process of rewriting is significant, Mukherjee also turns a few quotidian concepts upside down and inside out. This process of turning the structuring schematics of everyday life topsy-turvy is common in Mukherjee's fiction. Gobel, commenting on Mukherjee's short story "The World According to Hsu," says, "The concept of being home is transferred here into a shared homelessness with a heteroglot community situated on an island of the mind" (116). These ideas insinuate themselves into *The Holder of the World,* but what is most significant in the later work is Mukherjee's rewriting of her earlier ideas of hybridity and belonging. In her earlier writing, she indicates that it was hybridity that engendered cultural angst within immigrants, both in their homelands and in the places to which they had migrated.[4] In *The Holder of the World,* Mukherjee does away with the exclusivity (only immigrants are hybrid) implied by the category "immigrant." Hybridity is a sustained process that emerges from intercultural contact and alters all it encompasses. Beigh thus becomes hybrid, in spite of being a white woman, not only through her love affair with Venn but also through her meditation on and interchange with the Salem Bibi and with contemporary and medieval India. While it is true that Mukherjee advocates a certain kind of universal hybridity, her position is much more complex than the cheap cop-out that such a reading would imply. Mukherjee does not so much carve out an assimilationist space for immigrants as explode the concept of hegemony by assigning the qualities of hybridity to all: here, specifically through subverting notions of race, ethnicity, citizenship, history, nation building, and, on a more abstract level, those of time and space. Thus Hannah Easton and Beigh Masters become allegorized as immigrants because each belongs to a world other than that of her present physical reality. The immigrant, too, lives in these myriad regions, belonging and yet not belonging to this multiplicity. The novel is an expression of Mukherjee's ironic sympathy for those who straddle many realities, many worlds. "Home," then, becomes a loaded term unable to attach itself to any fixed point for anyone who inhabits the world of this novel. Gobel's "shared homelessness" is not confined to those who belong to ethnically marginal communities.

Mukherjee's relationship with "home," in the literal sense of the word, is also somewhat vexed. Maya Manju Sharma sees Mukherjee as displaced even within India (20). Here, it is important to affirm the heterogeneity of the polyglot community that is India. Given the frightening trend toward right-wing Hindu nationalism today, it is easy to see why anyone might feel ill at ease in a country where everyone, at some level, is in a minority. Mukherjee's Bengali-speaking background places her at a distant periphery in a nation controlled linguistically by the Hindi-speaking north. For Mukherjee, then, consciously accepting the identity of immigrant means positioning herself away from the secondary status accorded to her community in India and finding in the United States a space she can call home. Thus to commit herself to the idea of America is

> not necessarily to pledge allegiance to the forces of racism and imperialism worldwide. . . . [In] accepting the role of immigrant, she has not redefined herself as an American. Rather she has consented to be part of that long procession of peoples who have over the years redefined America [Sharma 20].

Sharma, interestingly, gives Mukherjee the very same agency in the making of the United States that Mukherjee gives to Black Pearl. In *The Holder of the World,* Mukherjee reminds us that the United States itself is a nation of immigrants, that it was always already a hybrid space. By giving American-as-apple-pie characters like Beigh access to hybridity, the novel demonstrates the vitality of cultural exchange, which alters both dominant and peripheral cultures in significant ways. Moreover, as the historical subversion enacted by the novel daringly suggests, the United States has fundamentally impure antecedents, which have made all future generations multiethnic rather than merely monoethnic.

Mukherjee also excavates the experience of women—silent and expressive—across time and culture: indigenous Indian or immigrant women, the Yale-educated white woman or the illiterate Puritan turned mistress of Hindu Rajah. Here, the feminine principle not only is given space in which to articulate and be articulated but also creates that space itself: the novel, Hannah's embroidery, Pearl's advocacy of an American nation, and Beigh's research also stand in for and double as the presence of the female immigrant. This is not to say that there is a universal female or immigrant experience that Mukherjee articulates, or that Mukherjee conflates femininity and the immigrant experience. If there is any conclusion that this novel points to, it is that feminine and immigrant space are not as different from the dominant culture as they are made out to be. Over time, the feminine and immigrant populations have asserted themselves, fracturing in the process the will to power of the hegemonic masculine white order. The dominant culture is also not an unyielding monolith; rather, it is a pliant entity susceptible to being changed as much as it seeks to change. In interacting with the Other, the dominant culture is also fractured, a consequence of intercultural contact that then makes us question the veracity of such categories as "dominant" and "peripheral." Mukherjee's novel attests to this universal multiplicity assigned to both center and periphery. It is significant that the novel's opening words are "I live in three time zones, *not* Eastern, Central and Pacific. I mean the past, the present and the future" (*Holder* 5; emphasis added). This announcement instantly undercuts, as a structuring presence in the novel, the paramount importance of the United States and its methods of living life, and it establishes the importance of multiplicity and of the innate ability to see into, indeed be in, many worlds. Succumbing to the drive toward hybridity and cultural exchange has to be a participatory exercise, not only for the Indian immigrant but also for white women (and white men), the so-called original Americans.

Now, to link the ideas of hybridity, enunciated above, to this essay's organizing trope of subversion, I will return to the structuring modality of the novel, a modality through which Mukherjee makes the great Western literary tradition into a hothouse hybrid. That this novel is very preoccupied with the literary canon is indisputable. While the novel is thematically attentive to the prehistory of Hawthorne's *The Scarlet Letter,* the structure is adapted from one particular ode of John Keats: his "Ode on a Grecian Urn." The four parts of the novel are opened by epigraphs that form an orderly yet randomly selected sequence in Keats's poem. The first section of the novel is heralded by lines from the first stanza of Keats's ode. I want to draw attention to the second line of that epigraph: "Thou foster-child of Silence and slow Time." At one level, Mukherjee uses Keats to insert herself into the tradition that she has been denied by canonical literature. At another level, she makes the contents of the verse relate yet not relate to her text. Iyer likens the use of Keats's ode to Hannah's needlework—"they are both static and dynamic in their tale-telling" (36)—but she does not further her exploration of Mukherjee's very deliberate use of Keats's ode. In "Ode on a Grecian Urn," Keats acknowledges the presence of ancient Greece, both in his own creative fashioning and in that of the English literary tradition in general. By using couplets from this poem to open the four parts of her novel, Mukherjee makes an analogy that acknowledges the debt owed by American literature to the Indian presence. Mukherjee's novel is classified as an American novel, but the narrative tension can come into being only if the importance of India is conceded in the making of the United States. The connection that Mukherjee challenges us to make is on a broader, more macroscopic level: the United States must acknowledge its debt to the Indian presence in its midst. Moreover, it is to her own benefit that Mukherjee uses the standard implication, in the Western tradition, of opening each chapter with an epigraph from another, canonized writer. In literary tradition, this method of using epigraphs establishes the connectivity of the literary method: the later writer places himself or herself in the tradition of the earlier writer, thus subtly seeking his or her own canonization.[5] While Mukherjee's writings reflect a similar anxiety of influence, her use of Keats's poetry also leads to an intricate literary subversion, which she achieves by making the text mean things other than what the epigraph leads us to suppose. Here, then, Mukherjee deploys the method of the dominant tradition—use of the epigraph in the tradition of Western literature—but also that tradition's subversion, making sure that the meaning of the epigraph is not always true to the epigraph itself. Thus, in the first epigraph, the "foster-child of silence" is not only Hannah, whose life history has not yet been unearthed, but also the Indian presence in American history. The other three epigraphs make similar subversive sense. Mukherjee's implied comment is that medieval/modern India and Indians play a role in American consciousness similar to that played by classical Greece in the English consciousness. Thus one cannot deny, or perhaps even determine, the impact of the "Other" in our collective and individual making. This explains why Mukherjee needs to have a white narrator who, in seeking to unearth her origins, discovers the interconnectivity of people, time, and places. As the movement of Keats's ode makes the poem itself into the Grecian urn, so too does Mukherjee's novel fashion itself—the Indo-American creative text—as the "holder of the world."

Mukherjee's reworking of the origins of *The Scarlet Letter* is also a significant emissary in the hybridizing of the Western literary canon. On the one hand, Nalini Iyer claims that Mukherjee fashions for herself a canonical American literary identity and "is refusing a hyphenated existence as an Indo-American writer" (42). On the other hand, Fakrul Alam says that Mukherjee, in writing this novel, "attempts to place herself in the American tradition of prose narrative while affirming her origins in the Indian artistic traditions" (x). This statement would imply a contradiction of Iyer's earlier thesis: that Mukherjee is refusing the hyphen, which attaches itself to any writer different from the norm. I would argue, however, that Mukherjee does insert herself into American prose conventions and does emphasize her immigrant status while asserting her obligation to Indian cultural mores, but she also alleges her similarity to the norm via her difference. In other words, in the United States, the hyphen is the norm. We are all doomed or privileged to bear the hyphen, and it is this difference, this hyphen, that makes one "truly" American. The hyphen, then, becomes the scarlet letter, the red badge that marks us all. Mukherjee may explicitly deny herself the hyphen, but the novel resolutely attaches a hyphen to all it encounters.

Furthermore, Iyer's reading—which claims that Mukherjee, by inserting herself into the American canon, insists on an accommodation of the migrant voice into that canon—neglects to take into account that, with this rewriting of Hawthorne, Mukherjee also questions the whole notion of canons, their viability, and their historical veracity: "Who can blame Nathaniel Hawthorne for shying away from the real story of the brave Salem mother and her illegitimate daughter?" Beigh asks, tongue firmly in cheek (*Holder* 284). By proving Hawthorne's account to be potentially false or erroneous, Mukherjee asks us not to trust received information but to breathe life into "false facts," with the necessary privileging of the imagination. The novel is only an infinitesimal tampering with Hawthorne, which never really rewrites the narrative action of *The Scarlet Letter*; yet, in playing around with the historical antecedents of the novel, Mukherjee claims that it is she, not Hawthorne, who has access to the "real" story of Hester Prynne.

All this is not to say that there is not a deep unease about "whiteness" and the "white male tradition" in this novel. Perhaps no other Mukherjee novel has ever been so self-consciously written into a masculine convention. The novel continuously references Hawthorne: the lecherous Indian factor is called Prynne; Hannah's best friend is called Hester; Hannah herself is called Precious as Pearl, and her daughter, Hawthorne's Pearl, is called Black Pearl. This referencing of *The Scarlet Letter* works in a complex way, at two levels. At one level is the anxiety of Hawthorne's influence, which fills this novel with palpable disquiet. Hawthorne never really leaves the novel, and the fact that Mukherjee is compelled to keep creating Hawthornian characters in her text is an indication of this anxiety. At the other level, however, this playing around with Hawthorne is also of vital importance to Mukherjee's central purpose in the novel, which is to establish the interconnectivity of time, place, and people. Again, the name Prynne, which we usually associate with Hester Prynne in Puritan New England, is "translated" into a male factor in India. In Mukherjee's novel, the name Hester is given first to Hannah's best friend and then to Hannah's Indian handmaiden, Bhagmati. A reproduction of history makes it possible to move identities around and among people and places and thereby to question the original assigning of identities. In each of us there is already something of the Other, perhaps of many others. By making canons, we freeze people and places into inflexible artifacts. This is why Mukherjee's use of Keats's ode, which wistfully looks back at a culture now long gone yet frozen in time, becomes so subversive.

The anxiety of Hawthorne's influence also functions as a commentary on the marked absence of a significant white male presence in the novel.

Instead, the novel is crowded with minor white male characters and constant references, thematic and structural, to major white male literary writers: Keats, Hawthorne, and Thomas Pynchon, to name only three.[6] What is the novel trying to say through these silences, gaps, and omissions? Do they generate a problematic in a novel that draws so heavily on the white male tradition yet negates the white man's presence in the actuality of the novel? Does Mukherjee's marking of the absence of the white man foreclose the white man from this hybridization, this hyphenation that Mukherjee celebrates with such vitality and exuberance? The novel brings to the surface the heterogeneity behind the linear teleology of criticism and historiography, thereby implicating the white masculine method of hermeneutics in the silencing of those without power. But the novel implicitly bestows its white male constituency with access to hybridity by arguing that the American nation was always already a diverse entity whose claims to hybridity were hidden but never erased by the imperatives of hegemony.

I will now return to the idea of a possible problematic inherent in the description of Mukherjee as a writer who celebrates the immigrant experience. Because I have pointedly designated *The Holder of the World* as a novel that enshrines individual agency and deconstructs categories, it is important that I also consider Mukherjee's place not only within the broader category of Indo-American fiction but also, and more specifically, in the context of the label that she (who hates all labels) has given herself: that of "immigrant writer." Mukherjee has consciously rejected the term "expatriate" and instead has adopted the identity of the immigrant, an immigrant of the Ellis Island variety (Iyer 29–31; Sharma 18–19). The terms "expatriate" and "immigrant" convey two very different images: the former implies a political and cultural rejection of the point of origin, whereas origin is clearly marked in the cultural affiliations associated with the latter. Mukherjee is self-consciously an immigrant writer who, in *The Holder of the World,* at least, deliberately commemorates the immigrant experience, in the process challenging standard replications of migration and diaspora as being characterized by debilitating doom and gloom. While some critics, such as Jasbir Jain (quoted in Sharma, "The Inner World of Bharati Mukherjee" 10), see immigrant status as always tied to a negative depiction of the home country, others, such as Walter Gobel, see it as a possible negation of one's individual identity: "Perhaps you can have your identity and lose it while exploring and renegotiating a border territory" (118). Gobel refers to the Indian identity as the superfluous identity, the implication being that Mukherjee discards that which marks her as Indian. Nowhere in *The Holder of the World* does this appear to happen, however. In fact, the novel tacitly acknowledges that identity is complex, variable, and created out of a number of interconnected worlds. While this is explicit in *The Holder of the World,* even in Mukherjee's other novels identity formation seems to be a key structuring thematic. Mukherjee, replying to the considerable criticism leveled at her for her supposedly assimilationist stance, says:

> The complexion of America has already changed. Let's admit it, let's deal with it instead of pretending that the White Anglo model still holds for everybody. Each of us, mainstream or minority, is having to change. It's a two-way metamorphosis [quoted in Nelson, *Writers of the Indian Diaspora* 241].

Although this statement predates *The Holder of the World,* its resonances in the novel are startling. More than anything, *The Holder of the World* is an effort to make the "mainstream" an amalgam of "minorstreams," forcing us to think of what these concepts imply, if indeed they imply anything at all.

By placing Hannah Easton's Eastern sojourn (the aural resonance of the name is all too apt) at the center of her narrative, Mukherjee emphasizes the presence of India in the making of the United States, a making that is literary, cultural, and historical. *The Holder of the World* argues that the United States needs to acknowledge its debt of gratitude to those who have shaped it and will continue to shape it. In order for this acknowledgment to be made, first the forgotten voices of these communities need to be excavated, and then American history and culture need to be reconfigured, with the enduring impact of these groups kept in mind. As the novel's subtext seems to indicate, American history would have been vastly different if Hannah Easton had not gone to India and then returned to the West, carrying the East in her belly.

BIBLIOGRAPHY

Alam, Fakrul. *Bharati Mukherjee.* New York: Twayne, 1996.

Byers-Pevitts, Beverley. "An Interview with Bharati Mukherjee." *Speaking of the Short Story: Interviews with Contemporary Writers.* Ed. Farhat Iftekharuddin, Mary Rohrberger, and Maurice Lee. Jackson: University of Mississippi Press, 1997. 189–98.

Gobel, Walter. "Bharati Mukherjee: Expatriation, Americanality, and Literary Form." *Fusion of Cultures?* Ed. Peter O. Stummer and Christopher Balme. Amsterdam and Atlanta: Rodopi, 1996. 111–18.

Hawthorne, Nathaniel. *The Scarlet Letter.* 1850. Orchard Park, NY: Broadview Press, 1995.
Iyer, Nalini. "American/Indian: Metaphors of the Self in Bharati Mukherjee's *The Holder of the World.*" *Ariel: A Review of International English Literature* 27.4 (1996): 29–44.
Mukherjee, Bharati. *The Holder of the World.* New York: Knopf, 1993.
———. *Jasmine.* New York: Grove Weidenfeld, 1989.
———. *The Tiger's Daughter.* Boston: Houghton Mifflin, 1972.
———. *Wife.* Boston: Houghton Mifflin, 1975.
Nelson, Emmanuel S., ed. *Bharati Mukherjee: Critical Perspectives.* New York: Garland, 1993.
———, ed. *Writers of the Indian Diaspora: A Bio-bibliographical Critical Source Book.* Westport: Greenwood, 1993.
Rajan, Gita. "Bharati Mukherjee." *Writers of the Indian Diaspora: A Bio-bibliographical Critical Source Book.* Ed. Emmanuel S. Nelson. Westport: Greenwood, 1993. 235–42.
———. "Fissuring Time, Suturing Space: Reading Bharati Mukherjee's *The Holder of the World.*" *Generations: Academic Feminists in Dialogue.* Ed. Devoney Looser and E. Ann Kaplan. Minneapolis: University of Minnesota Press, 1997. 288–308.
Sharma, Maya Manju. "The Inner World of Bharati Mukherjee: From Expatriate to Immigrant." *Bharati Mukherjee: Critical Perspectives.* Ed. Emmanuel S. Nelson. New York: Garland, 1993. 3–22.

NOTES

1. Jasbir Jain (quoted in Sharma, "The Inner World of Bharati Mukherjee" 10) observes that in *The Tiger's Daughter* and *Wife,* "the attempt to understand India is clouded by the desire to interpret for foreigners, to judge India by their standards and value systems."

2. Interestingly, we do not know to which "fertile Marblehead" Mukherjee is referring. On the one hand, it could be the Marblehead of Beigh's world, which houses the painting titled *The Apocalypse.* On the other hand, it could refer to the Marblehead of Hannah Easton. This ambiguity is meant to further Mukherjee's point about the interconnectivity of cultures.

3. "I have come to trust the psychological integrity of oral narratives," says Beigh (*Holder* 232). For Beigh, this trust of psychological integrity is not limited to the oral, although it becomes significant in the context of immersing India in America, since India's narrative fiction is so steeped in the oral/aural.

4. For example, consider *Jasmine, Wife,* and *The Tiger's Daughter.*

5. Walter Scott's *Ivanhoe* (1791) and George Eliot's *Middlemarch* (1874) are examples that come to mind.

6. In another tongue-in-cheek reference, Beigh comments, "If Thomas Pynchon, perhaps one of the descendants of her failed suitor, had not already written *V.*, I would call her a V" (*Holder* 60). In that this novel is about rewriting a male text and generating a debate about who has authority over history and interpretation, this comment becomes ironically significant.

NOTES ON CONTRIBUTORS

TINA Y. CHEN is assistant professor of English at Vanderbilt University, where she teaches courses on Asian American literature and culture, contemporary multiethnic American literature, twentieth-century American drama, and diversity in higher education. Her publications have appeared in *Modern Fiction Studies, Contemporary Literature, American Literary History, Jouvert: A Journal of Postcolonial Studies, MELUS,* and *[Hitting] Critical Mass: A Journal of Asian American Cultural Criticism,* among other journals. Her work in progress includes an investigation into impersonation as a trope in Asian American representation as well as research on pedagogy and ethics in the teaching of multiethnic literatures.

FLOYD CHEUNG is assistant professor of English and of American Studies at Smith College. He is the editor of a new edition of H. T. Tsiang's 1937 novel *And China Has Hands* (Ironweed Press, 2003) as well as a coeditor of and contributor to *Recovered Legacies: Authority and Identity in Early Asian American Literature* (Temple University Press, forthcoming). He has published in *a/b: Auto/Biography Studies, Jouvert: A Journal of Postcolonial Studies, TDR: The Journal of Performance Studies,* and elsewhere. His work in progress is a book-length study of Asian American autobiographical writing.

ROCÍO G. DAVIS is associate professor of American and postcolonial literatures at the University of Navarra (Spain). She is the author of *Transcultural Reinventions: Asian American and Asian Canadian Short-Story Cycles* (TSAR, 2003). She is also the coeditor (with Rosalia Baena) of *Small Worlds: Transcultural Visions of Childhood* (Ediciones Universidad de Navarra, 2001) and (with Sami Ludwig) of *Asian American Literature in the International Context: Readings in Fiction, Poetry, and Performance* (Lit Verlag, 2002). Her work in progress is a book-length study of Asian American autobiographies of childhood.

CHRISTOPHER DOUGLAS is assistant professor of English at the University of Victoria (British Columbia). He is the author of *Reciting America: Culture and Cliché in Contemporary U.S. Fiction* (University of Illinois Press, 2001), and his articles have appeared in *Critique* and *Postmodern Culture.* With support from the National Endowment for the Humanities, he is completing his second book project, a "prehistory" of literary multiculturalism.

DOMINIKA FERENS teaches American literature at the University of Wroclaw (Poland), where in 1999 she cofounded the Interdisciplinary Gender Studies Group. Her research interests include Asian American literature, the intersections of literature and ethnography, late nineteenth-century popular fiction, and travel narratives. She is the author of *Edith & Winnifred Eaton: Chinatown Missions and Japanese Romances* (University of Illinois Press, 2002) and has published the proceedings of several conferences in Poland on queer studies.

SAMINA NAJMI teaches Asian American literature, gender studies, and cultural studies at Babson College. She edited and wrote the introduction to the reissue of Onoto Watanna/Winnifred Eaton's 1903 novel *The Heart of Hyacinth* (University of Washington Press, 2000) and is the coeditor (with Rajini Srikanth) of *White Women in Racialized Spaces: Imaginative Transformation and Ethical Action in Literature* (State University of New York Press, 2002). She is currently working on a book-length study of war narratives in bildungsromane by contemporary Asian American women.

PALLAVI RASTOGI is assistant professor of English at Louisiana State University, where she teaches colonial, postcolonial, and diasporic literature. Her research interests center on South Asian diaspora studies. She has published essays on landscape in V. S. Naipaul's travel narratives and on the memoirs and letters of Cornelia Sorabji, India's first woman lawyer.

RICHARD SERRANO is associate professor of French and comparative literature at Rutgers University and the author of *Neither a Borrower: Forging Traditions in French, Chinese and Arabic Poetry* (Legenda/European Humanities Research Center, Oxford University, 2002). His research centers on the transformation of information as it is transmitted from one culture to the next. His work in progress includes an English translation of Rachid

Boudjedra's *Ma'rakat az-zuqaq* and research on the Koran in connection with poetry.

DAVID SHIH is assistant professor of English at the University of Wisconsin–Eau Claire, where he teaches Asian American literature, American literature, autobiography, and creative writing. He contributed an article on Louis Chu to *A Resource Guide to Asian American Literature* (Modern Language Association, 2001). He is currently editing an anthology of early Asian American autobiographical writing and coediting an anthology of early American literature about Asians and Asian Americans.

RAJINI SRIKANTH is associate professor of English and of Asian American Studies at the University of Massachusetts, Boston. She is the author of *The World Next Door: South Asian American Literature and the Idea of America* (Temple University Press, 2004). She also coedited *Contours of the Heart: South Asians Map North America* (Temple University Press 1996) with Sunaina Maira and Sucheta Mazumdar; *A Part, Yet Apart: South Asians in Asian America* (Temple University Press, 1998) with Lavina Dhingra Shankar; *Bold Words: A Century of Asian American Writing* (Rutgers University Press, 2001) with Esther Yae Iwanaga; and *White Women in Racialized Spaces: Imaginative Transformation and Ethical Action in Literature* (State University of New York Press, 2002) with Samina Najmi.

TERI SHAFFER YAMADA is associate professor in the Department of Comparative World Literature and Classics at California State University, Long Beach. She is the editor of *Virtual Lotus: Modern Fiction of Southeast Asia* (University of Michigan Press, 2002) and a contributor to *Southeast Asian Studies in the United States* (Center for Southeast Asian Studies Publications, Arizona State University, 2003). She has written numerous articles on modern Cambodian literature and the diaspora and is currently editing a collection of essays on the literary history of modern Southeast Asian fiction, with a focus on the short story. She serves as senior advisor to the Phnom Penh–based Nou Hach Literary Project for the promotion of modern Cambodian literature.

ZHOU XIAOJING is associate professor of English at University of the Pacific. She is the author of *Elizabeth Bishop: Rebel in Shades and Shadows* (Peter Lang, 1999). Her publications have appeared in *College Literature, Chicago*

Review, JAAS: Journal of Asian American Studies, Jouvert: A Journal of Postcolonial Studies, MELUS, and *TSLL: Texas Studies in Literature and Language.* She has also published essays on Asian Pacific American poetry in *Ecopoetry: A Critical Introduction* (University of Utah Press, 2002) and *Asian American Literature in the International Context: Readings on Fiction, Poetry and Performance* (Lit Verlag, 2002). Her book, *The Ethics and Poetics of Alterity: Asian American Poetry,* is forthcoming from University of Iowa Press.

INDEX

Library of Congress
Cataloging-in-Publication Data

Form and transformation in Asian American literature / edited by Zhou Xiaojing and Samina Najmi.
p. cm.—(The Scott and Laurie Oki series in Asian American studies)
Includes bibliographical references and index.
ISBN 0-295-98504-6
1. American literature—Asian American authors—History and criticism.
2. Asian Americans—Intellectual life.
3. Asian Americans in literature.
PS153.A84 F67 2005
810.9'895—dc22
2004027906